NEW ECONOMIC POLICY AND RURAL DEVELOPMENT

NEW ECONOMIC POLICY AND RURAL DEVELOPMENT

M. Soundarapandian

SERIALS PUBLICATIONS
NEW DELHI

First Published - 2006

ISBN : 81-8387-006-6

Published by

SERIALS PUBLICATIONS
4830/24, Prahlad Street, Ansari Road
Darya Ganj, New Delhi-110002 (India)
Phone : 23245225. Fax : 91-11-23272135
E-mail: serials@satyam.net.in

CONTENTS

PREFACE

The New Economic Policy (NEP) has been implemented in India since 1990-91. For the past fourteen years, there are some macro economic policy measures like liberalisation, privatisation and globalisation (LPG) which have the positive and negative impact on the Indian economy. Agriculture and small scale industries are the backbone of the rural India. In order to analyse the impact of New Economic Policy on the Indian economy, a National Level Seminar was organized in our Gandhigram Rural Institute with the assistance of Indian Council of Social Science Research, New Delhi.

A few selected papers are edited as a Book entitled "New Economic Policy and Rural Development". The book has been published in two volumes. The volume I highlighted the critical evaluation of the New Economic Policy, impact of the economic reforms on agriculture and industrial sectors. The role of New Economic Policy in the promotion of the rural sectors especially in the service sector are given in the volume-II. The books will be much useful to the academicians, researchers and policy makers for the effective implementation of New Economic Policy in India.

I am very thankful to Dr. G. Pankajam, Vice Chancellor and Dr. N. Thillainayagam, Professor and Head, Department of Rural Industries and Management, Gandhigram Rural Institute, Gandhigram, for their encouragement for the publication of the book. It gives pleasure in thanking my wife Mrs. S. Indhumathi and my children S. Diwakaran and S. Vidya for their support in completing the work. Finally, we thank the Serials Publications, New Delhi for accepting to publish the book in time.

(M. Soundarapandian)

LIST OF CONTRIBUTORS

Dr. V. Gopalakrishan, Reader and Head, Department of Commerce, Aditanar College of Arts and Science, Tiruchendur, Tamil Nadu.

M. Thaaris Albin, Department of Economics, St. Xavier's College, Palayamkottai-627002.

Bharathi Albin, former RBI Doctoral Fellow at the Madras Institute of Development Studies, Adyar, Chennai.

P. Rajendran, Reader, Research Centre, Department of Commerce, V.H.N.S.N. College, Virudhunagar.

Dr. P.N.P. Mohamed Sahaputheen, Reader and Head, Department of Economics, Jamal Mohamed College, Trichy-20.

A. Hidhayathulla, Lecture in Economics, Jamal Mohamed College, Trichy-20.

Dr. S.R. Choodambigai, Reader in Economics, Avinashilingam University, Coimbatore-43.

Dr. K. Dhanasekaran, Reader in Economics, Gobi Arts and Science College, Gobi Chettipalayam, Erode (Dt).

Dr. (Mrs.) B. Shyamala, Prof. & Head, P.G. Department of Economics, Fatima College, Madurai-18.

Dr. B. Vanitha, Reader in Economics,.PSG College of Arts and Science, Coimbatore-14.

Dr. B. Rajasekaran, Reader & Head, Department of Management Studies, Manonmaniam Sundaranar University, Tirunelveli.

G. Magesh Kuttalam, Lecturer, Department of Management Studies, Manonmaniam Sundaranar University, Tirunelveli.

Dr. Punithavathy Pandian, "Professor, Department of Commerce, Madurai Kamaraj University, Madurai-21.

S. Thanasundari, Selection Grade Lecturer, Department of Commerce, V.V. Vanniaperumal College for Women, Virudhunagar.

Mr. K. Karunaharan, Research Scholar, Department of Economics, Bharathidasan University, Trichy.

Dr. C. Thangamuthu, Professor of Economics, Department of Economics, Bharathidasan University, Trichy-24.

Dr. T. Sethivel, Reader in Agriculture, Faculty of Agriculture & Animal Husbandry, Gandhigram.

M. Arumugam, Ph.D. Scholar, Faculty of Agriculture & Animal Husbandry, Gandhigram.

Dr. M. Soundarapandian, Reader in Rural Industries and Management, Gandhigram Rural Institute (Deemed University), Gandhigram-624 302.

Dr. T.T. Ranganathan, Dean, Faculty of Agriculture and Animal Husbandry, Gandhigram Rural Institute, Gandhigram.

Dr. K. Pazhani, Reader in Economics, T.D.M.N.S. College, T. Kallikulam-627113.

Dr. S. Radhakrishnan, Department of Rural Industries and Management, Gandhigram Rural Institute, Gandhigram.

Dr. K. Balasubramani, Instructor, Department of Rural Industries and Management, Gandhigram Rural Institute, Gandhigram.

Dr. R. Serangarajan, Reader, Department of Rural Industries and Management, Gandhigram Rural Institute, Gandhigram.

P. Muruganandan, Research Scholar, Department of Rural Industries and Management, Gandhigram Rural Institute, Gandhigram.

Dr. N. Meenakshisundaram, Reader in Rural Industries and Management, Gandhigram University, Gandhigram.

Dr. E. Anand, Department of Rural Industries and Management, Gandhigram Rural Institute, Gandhigram.

H. Samvel Thanaraj, Lecturer, Department of Management Studies, The American College, Madurai.

R. Ramkumar Prabu, The American College, Madurai.

Dr. K. Nageswara Rao, Department of Economics, Sri Krishnadevaraya University, Anantapur-515003.

Dr. V.S. Ganesamurthy, Reader in Economics, Sri Vasavi College, Erode.

V. Nachimuthu, Lecturer in Economics, Sri Vasavi College, Erode.

Dr. (Mrs.) T.V. Anandi, Selection Grade Lecturer in Economics, Fatima College, Madurai-18.

Dr. P. Sundara Pandian, Reader in Commerce, V.H.N.S.N. College, Virdhunagar.

J. Kamatchi Eswaran, Research Scholar, V.H.N.S.N. College, Virudhunagar.

Dr. Samwel Kakuko Lopoyetum, Senior Post Doctoral Research Fellow, Department of Cooperation, Gandhigram Rural University, Gandhigram.

Dr. I. Sundar, Lecturer in Economics, Directorate of Distance Education, Annamalai University.

Dr. S. Michael John Peter, Reader in Economics, Arul Anadar College, Karumathur-625514.

V. Saravanan, Research Scholar, Department of Economics, Arul Anadar College, Karumathur-625514.

Dr. (Mrs.) V. Rajam, Reader in Economics, Avinashilingam University, Coimbatore.

Dr. S. Ramalinga Choodambigai, Reader in Economics, Avinashilingam University, Coimbatore.

Dr. M. Sangararadje, Department of Economics, Tagore Government Arts College, Pondicherry.

Dr. K. Ramachandran, Director, Academic Staff College, Pondicherry University, Pondicherry.

G. Senthilkumar, Research Scholar, Bharathiar University, Coimbatore.

A. Balasubramanian, Research Scholar, Bharathiar University, Coimbatore.

Dr. P. Arumugam, Professor in Economics, Bharathiar University, Coimbatore.

Dr. Muaaz Hussein Mohamed, Scholar, Future Studies, Madurai Kamaraj University, Madurai.

Dr. S.P. Kanaga Anbuselvam, Reader in Economics (DDE), Madurai Kamaraj University, Madurai.

N. Murugan, Department of Management Studies, PSNA CET, Dindigul.

K. Amutha, Department of Management Studies, PSNA CET, Dindigul.

Dr. Punithavathy Pandian, Professor, Department of Commerce, Madurai Kamaraj University, Madurai-21.

R. Eswaran, Research Scholar, Department of Commerce, Madurai Kamaraj University, Madurai-21.

1

NEW ECONOMIC POLICY: SOME EMERGING CONCERNS

V. Gopalakrishnan

Introduction

The Indian economy was never under such severe strain as it was during 1990–91. The Gulf War and the uncertain political situation at the Centre brought about a considerable derating of India's credit worthiness in world finance markets. In June 1991, India faced an economic crisis of unprecedental dimensions. The foreign exchange reserves reached an all time low at Rs. 2,600 crores, which was barely sufficient for two weeks imports and the International commercial banks refused to extend new credits. There were large outflows from the NRI deposits as the NRIs were losing confidence in our economy. Inflation, which had begun to accelerate in 1990-91, reached a double-digit peak level of 16.7 percent in August 1990. All these factors necessitated our country to make default on her external payments obligations for the first time.

All these disconcerting features of the economic situations gave a serious threat to the economic development of the country. It was indeed the call of such economic situations that necessitated some major and far-reaching stabilization and structural reforms in our economic regime to overcome this crisis. Therefore, government moved swiftly to the task of pulling the economy back from the brink of disaster on the path of rapid and sustainable growth. Measures undertaken for this purpose had aimed at restoring international confidence, bringing inflation well under control and ensuring viability in the balance of payments. Further, adequate steps were taken in the form of structural reforms for strengthening the growth capability of the economy.

What Is New Economic Policy?

The Government announced a package of structural reforms, as this alone will enable us to achieve our basic goals of growth, self-reliance, modernization, equity, and raising the living standards of the poor people in our country. The structural reforms and new policies have been termed as "New Economic Policy". The former Finance Minister Dr. Manmohan Singh observed, "India has the talent and the genius to be the next economic miracle but it will not happen by itself. It requires all of us to dedicate ourselves to new ways of thought and action and make a success of new economic policies".

These policies had been designed to meet the precarious financial position of the country and as a crisis management technique. The NEP proclaims liberalization, privatization and ultimately globalization of the Indian economy as the only viable alternative left open to it "for making it a competitive, vibrant, dynamic, modern democratic economy".

The New Economic Policy is an amalgam of several policy statements and measures such as devaluation, industrial policy, commerce and trade policy, banking policy, budgetary policy, etc. Though there are various aspects of NEP, the issue of globalization is an important one. Globalization, as the name suggests, means making the Indian economy responsive to the developments taking place in the global level and also move towards the direction of India trying to play a greater role in the world economic development.

The economic reforms that were set in motion brought spectacular changes in the arena of economic policy. Gradually,

Indian economy has been throwing the Yoke of controlled regime and switching over to globalization based on international market system.

The process of economic reforms in the Indian economy has completed more than twelve years of implementation. The economy today has attained a completely different profile compared to June 1991. It is the right time to appraise the achievements and shortcomings of the new economic policy to understand as to whether the country is moving in the right direction. Though there are indications of some positive gains from the new economic policy, it is also equally true that the benefits of economic reforms have not been evenly distributed. Our Prime Minister, Mr. Atal Behari Vajpayee, in his Independence Day address had expressed his doubts and concerns about the effects of economic reforms. Most of his speech was devoted to the actual and perceived problems associated with the economic reforms. He conceded that the benefits of economic reforms had not been evenly distributed. He further observed that inequalities have increased and we shall have to make necessary modifications in the policy to remove imbalances and social inequalities.

Emerging Concerns

This part of the paper attempts to highlight some of the emerging concerns in our country due to the implementation of the New Economic Policy measures since July 1991.

Growth of the Economy

Reforms are means to achieve the ultimate goal of expediting the process of economic development of the country and the well being of its people. As per the 1998 World Bank Report on India, "Reform is not needed for its own sake but for the sake of India's poor and in the interest of having them both contribute to the growth process and benefit from it."

The growth rate of GDP is deemed to be a summary of the performance of the economy. The rate of growth of GDP since

1950 has been a little over 4 percent. During 1980s the growth rate was above 5 percent and accelerated to 6 percent during 1990s. The Eighth Plan (1992-97) achieved a growth rate of 6.5 percent. Accordingly, the growth rate for Ninth Plan was fixed at 7 percent. The first year of the Ninth Plan (1997-98) showed a GDP growth rate of 4.8 percent only, with agricultural sector showing a negative growth rate. The average annual rate of growth during the Ninth Plan was only 5.4 percent. This indicates that there are fluctuations in the growth rate, i.e., growth is not steady in the post reform period. This trend clearly shows that the reform processes have not actually accelerated the growth of our economy as expected.

Agricultural Sector Reforms

An important objective of Globalization, through the Dunkel Draft is to overhaul the agricultural sector of the developing countries. The Agreement on Agriculture has been drafted to favour agriculture in developing countries. But in actual practice, its implementation has seriously affected agriculture in developing countries. According to the agreement, developed countries agreed to reduce the subsidies by 20 percent over six years and developing countries by 13 percent over ten years. However, developed countries under Green Box and Blue Box subsidies continue to support agriculture. Green Box subsidies include amounts spent on government services such as research, disease control, infrastructure and food security while Blue Box subsidies include certain direct payments made to farmers.

As a result of the above, agricultural imports from developed countries are available at a much lower market price than in the domestic economy. Earlier, Indian agricultural prices were lower than international prices. But as a result of heavy subsidization of agricultural exports of developed countries, the situation is fast changing. Since international agricultural prices have become lower than Indian agricultural prices, Indian farmers have been put to a serious disadvantage. The growing phenomenon of farmers' unrest in several states because of the distress of farmers specializing in agricultural commodities and their exports has become a severe human problem. The Punjab farmers are groaning for want of remunerative prices, despite the fact that Punjab exports heavily Basmati Rice and Wheat products. There have been cases of suicides by farmers in several states due to increasing debt burden. The threat of foreigners ruining the prospects of Indian farmers is looming large.

Impact of Multinationals in India

Before the introduction of the NEP of liberalization, privatization and globalization, India has been cherishing prosperity without alienation of its basic premises of its self-reliance, swadeshism and socialism. But today, the process of colonialism through the mighty and prosperous multinational corporations has started to dominate our economy. MNCs tend to invest in the low priority and high profit sectors of our country, ignoring the national priorities. They drain the foreign exchange resources of developing countries rapidly.

A good part of the packed food, beverages and baby food; substantial proportion of the items of daily use such as soap, face powder, cosmetics, cream and lotion; most of the consumer durables like television, stereo, video and other such electronic items; a major part of the office equipments like computers, printers, cellular phones; many of the transport vehicles such as cars, trucks and motor bikes; a significant proportion of the heavy machineries and equipments; and a major share of the basic raw-materials in the large scale industries are now under the control of multinational corporations; which operate through joint ventures or as fully owned subsidiaries. Many more companies are waiting to venture into Indian markets with a view to exploit the urban middle class consumers.

Many Indian Industries involved in producing chemicals and fertilizers, electronic and electrical goods, automobiles, machines and so on are facing the brunt of increasing foreign competition. In fact, the leaders of Indian industries met the

Prime Minister Mr. Atal Behari Vajpayee and had made a passionate plea for protecting the Indian industries from foreign competition by providing adequate concessions. Thus, the impression of secularly interfaced global integration of the Indian economy has become a myth.

Effects of TRIPS on the Indian Economy

The UR agreement of "Trade Related Aspects of Intellectual Property Rights" (TRIPS) will have disastrous effects on our economy, especially in two areas viz; pharmaceuticals and agriculture. Both these areas affect the well being of the people. Under TRIPS, patents are available for any invention whether product or process in all fields of industrial technologies. Patent protection will be extended to micro-organisms, non-biological and micro-biological processes and plant varieties. This implies that the entire industrial and agricultural sectors and to an extent bio-technology sector will be covered under the patent provision.

Under the Indian Patents Act of 1970, patentability of inventions relating to substances intended for use as food, drug or medicine or substances produced by chemical processes is limited to the methods or processes of manufacture only. This means that one can make and market a product similar to the patented product through a different process or method than the patented one. But a dangerous provision has been introduced in the UR Agreement requiring both product and process patents whereby products imported or locally produced will be covered under patent protection without any discrimination. This implies that the patent regime not only tries to establish manufacturing monopoly but it also intends to establish import monopoly. This will affect the drug prices seriously.

At present, in India, the drug prices are very low. Indian pharmaceuticals and drug industries have progressed rapidly and are able to provide life saving drugs very cheaply. Under the new patent regime, heavy payments have to be made to patent holders and consequently, it is feared that this would result in the prices of drugs going up by 5 to 10 times. Such a policy has dangerous implications for the health of our people.

India's ancient use of Haldi (Turmeric) was sought to be patented under the American Law in 1995. Fortunately, it was challenged by India and the US patent office acknowledged its mistake and cancelled the patent on "Haldi". An American company has been granted a patent right for Neem as a pesticide. Basmati rice, which is a universal variety in India, has been patented as Kasmati and Texmati. There is a danger with regard to Tulsi (Basil) plant. These are a few cases of biopiracy of India's herbal wealth and to prevent huge losses. India will have to undertake huge documentation about the use of its herbal wealth.

Rising of Imports

WTO has urged India to lower import duties, remove control on consumer goods imports, and reduce quantitative restrictions, etc. Under the Uruguay Round Agreement, India offered to reduce tariffs and the tariffs have been reduced year after year and at present the maximum rate is 25 percent (2003-04 Budget). As the protection offered by import duties gradually disappeared, Indian industry is facing increasing competition from foreign goods. Confederation of Indian Industry (CII), the apex body, expressed its disapproval against duty-free status of capital goods sector. As a result, CII has pointed out that indigenous capital goods industry on a conservative estimate lost orders worth Rs. 5,000 crores from foreign countries. Instead of ensuring level playing field, indigenous industry has to pay excise, sales tax, octroi, turn over tax while imported goods are allowed duty-free access to our market. Not only the entire manufacturing industry is faced with a crisis, even machine tools industry, gensets and boiler producers are put at a serious disadvantage. Consequently, imports of finished products are displacing indigenously produced products. As a result, many industrial units are being closed and cheap imports have become an important cause of recession in Indian industry.

Further, globalisers advocated the acceptance of the new strategy on the plea that India will get access to foreign markets more effectively. When we analyze this claim it is shocking to note that during 2000-01, when exports grew to a level of 9.8 percent of GDP, while imports jumped up to a level of 13 percent of GDP. As a consequence, trade deficit during 1996-97 to 2000-01 has ranged between 3.1 and 4.0 percent of GDP. This underlines the hard reality that foreigners have been able to penetrate into the Indian market much more effectively than Indians being able to get hold of the foreign markets.

Market Failure

The main aim of the private sector is to minimize the cost and to maximize the profit in a global market. It also supports the creation of a consumption culture influenced by the media under the present technologically advanced situations and not necessarily in tune with the needs of a developing economy.

The crucial key to economic development rests on the reinvestment of the available economic surplus. Under privatization, there is no guarantee that profits will be used for useful investment. The profit makers may use the surplus to accumulate personal wealth without protecting public interest. As a result, a poor country will remain poor. Further, if public interests are not protected, it is very difficult for a country like India to achieve a sustainable economic development.

Rising Unemployment

The policies towards reducing labour absorption in public sector as part of the globalization strategy is likely to lead to adverse effects on employment situation in India. In a developing country like India, unemployment has assumed serious proportions even at the beginning of the process of economic development. The backlog of unemployed persons has increased owing to rapid growth of population and slow growth of job opportunities, and a significant proportion of the population has remained underemployed or disguisedly unemployed. In such a situation, the policy of liberalization and privatization with emphasis of foreign collaboration, which generally means use of capital-intensive technology, has caused further deterioration in employment opportunities.

The employment growth in the economy declined significantly. During the period 1983-94, the annual growth rate of employment was 2.04 percent, but it came down to 0.98 percent during 1994-2000. As a result, the unemployment rate went up from 6.03 percent in 1993-94 to 7.32 percent in 1999-2000. The creation of jobs in the public sector fell from 13.74 lakh during the five years preceding the reform to 4.05 lakh in the five years succeeding the reform. During the past five years, there has been little or no growth in employment opportunities. The impact of slow pace of employment growth in the organized sector, particularly in the public sector is more severe in the case of educated youth belonging to socially weaker sections of the society.

The absence of employment for all the job seekers has led to disastrous consequences in that more and more of those who cannot find regular jobs are forced to enter the informal sector. Many of those employed in informal sector activities work only for a part of the day, part of the week in odd jobs with low wages. Millions enter as casual labour and work for long hours engaged in all kinds of activities with inadequate wages.

Exit Policy

The World Bank conditionality pertaining to structural reforms stipulates liberalization of labour market including the exit policy. Exit policy refers to the policy regarding the retrenchment of manpower resulting from restructuring of industrial units or the workers becoming unemployed by the closer of sick units. It is a part and parcel of the structural adjustment programme. Along with liberalization, delicensing and deregulation and full freedom to monopoly industrial houses and transnational in the matter of investment, the private sector has been demanding a matching freedom, which is the "right to exit", or retrenchment. A popular method adopted to retrench the manpower is the voluntary retirement scheme (VRS). The exit policy substantially reduces the bargaining power of the workers. Employees are forced to choose between unemployment and a lower wage rate.

Adverse Social Consequences

The structural adjustment of India ignores the problem of upgradation of this vast mass of humanity and focuses only on a small part of the population, which is keen to attain very high standard of living. The rich people are very happy with the variety of goods and services available to them even at cheaper prices. For everything now too many choices are available; new goods and services are available in the market; all the markets are now more open; and everybody feels as if greater freedom and autonomy have been granted. But on the other hand, the prices of essentials like water, land, food, fuel, etc. continue to go up and away from the reach of the poor mass ultimately adversely affecting the poor.

Under pressure from IMF and the World Bank, to reduce government budget deficits, many developing countries like India have made deep cuts in social spending. The reform measures of reduction and reorientation of social expenditure have a direct and strong adverse effect on the standard of living of the working classes and the poor sections.

The new policies are profoundly anti-poor. They entail substantial cuts, in spending on minimum needs and employment programmes, poverty alleviation schemes, and health budgets. The standard of health, nutrition, sanitation, housing and other amenities like availability of clean potable water are abysmal for the low segment of the population. The far reaching economic policy changes represent clearly a retreat from the goal set by the freedom struggle of building a prosperous, humane, secular, sovereign, democratic society that pursues growth with equity.

Commercialisation of Education

Now a days, due to policy reforms, a new type of educational institutions has come into existence, namely self-financing educational institutions. Hundreds of unaided/self-financing educational schools and colleges as well as polytechnics and industrial training institutes have come into existence primarily based on profit motive rather than service to the society. Bureaucrats, capitalists, businessmen, politicians, communal associations, religious heads, profiteers and other such individuals, who rarely cherish the idea to serve the society, have promoted these institutions. The growth of these institutions has led to the commercialization of education. Most of these institutions are in lack of infrastructural facilities and qualified teachers. While they collect huge amount of capitation fees and as tuition fees, the salary paid to the teachers is very low compared to those employed in government and aided educational institutions. These teachers are not only denied proper salary but also security of service and other benefits. As a result, a kind of informal system of employment has emerged in the field of education paving the way for exploitation of the educated youth and the society.

Double Standards of Developed Countries in case of Child Labour

When imports from developing countries affect the interests of US, a number of environmental and human rights issues were raised with the objective of imposing a ban on the import of Indian carpets, chemicals, handicrafts, ready made garments on the plea that in their manufacture, child labour was involved. The US banned imports of several products from India on the plea of child labour. But Mr. B.R. Sabade has blown up this tactics of US. He has stated "Many American companies have shifted their factories to remote areas in Mexico, Indonesia and some other countries. Children are employed in these factories in large numbers and they have to work for more than 12 hours. Recently, a study conducted by Rugar University has revealed that 2,90,200 child workers are sweating in shopping malls, factories and farms in the US". With such double standards, the US unethically uses the child labour stick to punish India.

Impact on Environment and Ecology

Developing countries like India are affected by the relocation of polluting industries from the developed to the developing ones. Similarly, several products which are banned in the developed nations are marketed in the under developed world. The dumping of nuclear and hazardous wastes in developing industries and the shifting of polluting industries impose heavy social costs on them. The exploitation of the natural resources of the developing countries to satisfy the global demand also often causes ecological problems. Industries set up by MNCs have affected our environment. Water plants by Coke and Pepsi are draining our water resources.

Conclusion

The globalization, liberalization and privatization programmes under the structural reform process and expenditure cut measures under stabilization process have imposed many economic and social problems. Domestic savings and investment have been adversely affected resulting in stagnation or low growth of the economy. Unemployment and disparity in income levels are increasing. Interest rates are falling while prices of essential goods are shooting up. India faces environmental and ecological problems including depletion of waterbed levels. Trade gap is widening. Research and development especially in agriculture and pharmaceutical sectors encounter serious problems. Therefore the on going economic reform process should be suitably modified. The adverse social and economic consequences warrant us to give a human face to the reform process under the New Economic Policy.

REFERENCES

Ruddar Datt and Sundharam, K.P.M.; "Indian Economy", S. Chand & Company Ltd; New Delhi, 2002.

Agrawal, A.N., "Indian Economy" Wishwa Prakashan, New Delhi, 2002.

Francis Cherunilam, "Global Economy and Business Environment", Himalaya Publishing House, Mumbai, 2001.

Francis Cherunilam, "Business Environment", Himalaya Publishing House, Mumbai, 2003.

Siddheswar Prasad and Jagdish Prasad, "New Economic Policy-Reforms and Development", Mittal Publications, New Delhi, 1993.

Raj Kapila and Uma Kapila, "Understanding India's Economic Reforms", Volumes 1 to 6, Academic Foundation, Delhi, 1995-1996.

Padmanabhan, K.; " A Decade of Trade Liberalization in India", Indian Institute of Public Administration, Tirupattur, 2001.

Victon Louis Anthuran, M.; "New Economic Policy-Its Implications", *Peninsular Economist,* Volume IV, No. 2, 1991-92.

Mumtaj Begum, S.; "The role of the State-A Redefinition", *Peninsular Economist,* Volume XIV, No. 1, 2001-2002.

Ajit Kumar Singh, "Social Consequences of New Economic Policies", *Economic and Political Weekly,* Volume XXVIII, No. 7, February 13, 1993.

Murukadas, C.; "Impact of Liberalization on Employment in India", A Decade of Trade Liberalization in India, Indian Institute of Public Administration, Tirupattur, 2001.

Nagesh Kumar, "Economic Reforms and their Macro-Economic Impact", *Economic and Political Weekly,* Volume XXXV, No. 10, March 4-10, 2000.

Mukta, S. Adi, "India Under WTO", *Southern Economist,* Volume 42, No. 4, June 15, 2003.

2

IMPACT OF ECONOMIC REFORMS IN INDIA: AN EVALUATION

Thaarcis Albin & Bharathi Albin

Introduction

The development experience of any country, or region within a country, would reveal the strategies adopted by them. Economic strategies of all kinds have their theoretical base either in the market driven mechanism or market intervention mechanism (otherwise known as the Govt. regulated mechanism). The development literature in economics is richly blessed with highly qualitative arguments, based on both theoretical and empirical aspects, for favouring and opposing both the mechanisms. Indian economy and its development experiences are not an exception to this as it has the experiences of both mechanisms by now. The present exercise on Impact of Economic Reforms in India: An Evaluation' is an attempt to understand the growth behaviour and response of the economy in its macro perspective against the reform measures implemented in the country-say since the mid eighties in general and the nineties in particular. Nevertheless exercise of this nature would necessarily involve a brief review and reflection on those policies practiced by the government prior to the nineties, as it would form a good background/history to understand what necessitated for the implementation of the new reform measures and it is given in section–I.

SECTION – I

Reviews of the Policy Measures (1948 to 2002)

1. After the independence the first industrial policy was formulated by India in April 1948. Based on the strategic importance the 1948 policy classified the Indian industries into four major categories as (a) industries exclusively reserved for the Central Govt. (b) industries that can be undertaken only by the state (c) industries that need to be controlled and regulated by the Central Govt. and (d) industries reserved for the private sectors and individuals –so that both the government and private sectors can simultaneously indulge in the promotion/progress of industries.

2. The industrial policy regulation of 1956 classified the industries into three broad categories as Schedule A, B and C. Seventeen industries were brought under 'A' and became the responsibility of the state to look after. Schedule B had twelve industries and were made subject to the ownership of the state but the privates were also allowed to play a supplementary role. Industries not covered under schedule A and B were reserved for the private sector but kept under state regulation. These apart, the need for foreign capital, encouragement to the small scale and village industries and reduction in the regional industrial disparities were also aimed at by the 1956 industrial policy.

3. In December 1977 the Janata Government announced a set of policy measures, which insisted more on the promotion of Small-scale sector. 'District Industrial Centres' (DIC) were also set up to serve the same objective. The role of large-scale public sector units was confined to the removal of the supply bottlenecks. Any expansion activities of the existing units were made possible only after obtaining a license. Moreover this is also the period in which the 'inward looking policy'

(otherwise known as the policy of import substitution) was viewed as a major growth strategy under the regulated regime until the seventies. However, it did not escape a severe criticism from the quadrangle of the pro liberal thinkers as they could easily hold responsible the 'inward looking strategy' along with the 'licensing raj' for preventing the growth and expansion of the large enterprises in many ways along with many other arguments listed below. The increase in savings and investment rates experienced over the years that was eaten away by the increased incremental capital-output ratios (ICOR) (see table A1, in the appendix). The then existed administrative complexities that emphasized more on the 'regulation' than the 'development' itself. Rigid labour laws coupled with too much of protections in the name of 'infant industry' arguments weakening the competitive spirit of the Indian industries unlike in the case of Taiwan, South Korea and Brazil and the experience of industrial deceleration that occurred in India from the mid sixties through the mid seventies did only strengthen their criticism further than otherwise (Nayyar, 1994). This compelled the government to look for 'export-led' strategy as an alternative measure and this in turn resulted in the reorientation of the industrial policy announcement of the eighties that saw a reduction in the domestic barriers to entry and expansion.

4. In addition, this is also the period marked with wide spread problem of growing current account imbalances, increasing external debt, unfavorable terms of trade, rising government budget deficits and inflation in almost all the less developing countries of the world. As pointed out earlier, India too was found wrestling almost with the same set of problems and left with rather no option but to yield to the Western Philosophy of Privatization, which began and successfully practiced in Britain during the regime of Margaret Thatcher (De Walle, 1989, p. 601). Such international climate should also be treated as yet

another compelling force behind the industrial policy announcement of the Indian government in 1980 that gave importance to regularize the existing capacity installed over and above the licensed capacity. The liberalized licensing approach was also adopted towards the large industries permitting them to expand their licensed capacity automatically. The raising of MRTP's asset limits from Rs. 20 to Rs. 100 crores, the introduction of 'Broad-Banding', and periodical announcement of tax holidays ensured more flexibility to the manufactures and helped them to adjust their product-mix. The eighties' policies, thus, seams to have provided a new dimension towards the philosophy of 'liberalization', which is, also referred as the philosophy of 'market friendliness'.

5. What began in the eighties as policy measures got intensified since July 1991 when Manmohan took over the finance ministry as, once again, there was no other choice but obey to the pressure to implement privatization policies through the conditions attached to structural and sectoral adjustment loans made by the World Bank and supported by some bilateral donors (Christiansen, 1989, p. 597). For example, simultaneous execution of (a) a fiscal adjustment measure to stabilize the macro-economic situation on the one hand and (b) structural adjustment programme to reform the industry and trade on the other. It involved subsidy cuts in fertilizer and export front; abolition of MRTP act; linking of imports to the exports through the introduction of 'Exim Scrips' that are tradable; partial convertibility of Indian rupee on the current account; devaluation of Indian currency against the international exchange market; inclusion of more commodities under the OGL list etc. along with reduction in the interest rates and tax holidays for investments in certain industrially backward areas are a few to cite. A positive industrial growth response witnessed since the mid seventies through the eighties along with a renewed impetus experienced during the nineties, at the macro

level also, has been seen by many as a reward to the economic reform measures introduced ever since the eighties and nineties in particular. Any policy announcement came since then could only maintain the same direction along with a higher momentum with the promise of 'no going back'. This is increasingly resulted in the privatization of public sector units even as a means to finance the fiscal and revenue deficits of the government (The Hindu, Oct., 2002, p. 10) and an increasingly sudden withdrawal of the government from its participation in the economic activities in particular. This is very much apparent since the eighth plan period 1992-97 (see table A2, in the appendix).

A quick recollection on polices, as mentioned above, thus assumes greater significance in briefing the history of the country's perspectives on development matters. Having seen this as a background, how the economy in India reacted is a matter of concern towards which we turn to section-II.

SECTION – II

Though India is considered to be one among the industrialized countries of the fast changing world today, it was not the case in the beginning. A positive turning point in the economic development of country, in the true sense, came only from the eighties though there are people who could sight dates even prior to it. A close observation, since the inception of the Indian planning until this date would disclose an important feature that how structural transformation within every sector of the country enables the economy to build up resistance to withstand the economic fluctuations of different kinds caused by factors that are both national and international in nature. For instance, apart from the achievements in terms of green revolution, white revolution and blue revolution in the primary segment on the one side and on the other it also reveals how certain industries, within the secondary and tertiary sectors, by overtaking the others, assumed its prominence in the latter stage are a few to mention. Different policy measures adopted at various points of time with the view to promote the modern sector both at national and international level shall be attributed to the so called success stories of the development efforts of the Indian economy despite some failures. It is in this context the new economic policy measures practiced in India over since 1991 would assume greater significance, both at center and state, as they are considered to be a complete turn away from the earlier policies practiced until then and it is already detailed in section-I.

To carryout the analysis further aiming to unearth the 'impact of economic reforms in India' we have confined ourselves to seven selected variables such as the sectoral contribution, number of factories, number of workers/ employments, output, capital formation, gross domestic saving and trade balance.

Sectoral Contribution

A quick glance at the data, given in table 1, on the sectoral contribution of the country reveal a fact that how Indian economy is experiencing a transformation of the production-structure of a backward economy to that of a developing economy. Though it is a welcome sign, all these are achieved only at slow pace as it took more than fifty years to see the sectoral contributions in its present status. The primary sector still occupying for more than 25 percent of the country's GDP and a low share of the secondary sector that has not even crossed the mark of 30 to 40 percent of the GDP are indeed a major cause of concern as they are far below the standard when compared with many developed economies. What prevented the secondary sector from increasing its share in the country's GDP is generally attributed, by the critics, to the then regulated as it created an un-favourable industrial climate. However, we find it very difficult to buy this argument as no improvement is registered by the sector even during the so-called reform period. The only consolation, as of now is the performance of the tertiary sector as it is able to increase its share in the country's GDP at a desirable and faster rate. Throughout the 1990s its share in the GDP is consistently found to be above 40 percent and the average value is calculated to be around 45 percent per annum for the years 1990-91 to 2001-02. For more detail refer figure 1. In the absolute term, even this is considered to be below the marks attained by some of the developed countries. Nevertheless, as mentioned earlier, the current trend observed for this sector indeed remains as consolation. If the regulated regime characterized by many controls such as license, monopoly restrictive trade practices (MRTPs), foreign exchange regulation act (FERA), quotas, high tariff wall etc. is what held responsible for the poor performance of the Indian economy, the common man's expectation is that the economy must be bouncing back completely on the reverse direction once these so-called controls are abolished. Since the mid eighties the government began the process of doing away with all the possible government controls, with a higher momentum, to ensure a 'level playing field' for the industries and a 'market friendly atmosphere' for the whole economy since the beginning of the 1990s. However the results are yet to fulfill the common man's expectations.

Table 1: Sectoral Contribution of Different Sectors in the Indian GDP (values in percent)

Sectors	*1950-51*	*1970-71*	*1990-91*	*1995-96*	*2001-02*
Primary	59.20	48.12	34.93	30.59	26.10
Secondary	13.29	19.91	24.49	25.47	24.44
Tertiary	27.51	31.97	40.58	43.94	49.46
Total	100	100	100	100	100

Source: Govt. of India, Economic Survey, 2002-03 (1993-94=100).

Number of Factories

Though there is a positive trend observed in the growth rate of the number of factories since the mid eighties, the same trend could not continue or display a consistency. Rather it

Figure 1: Share of Tertiary Sector in GDP at Factor Cost (1993-94=100).

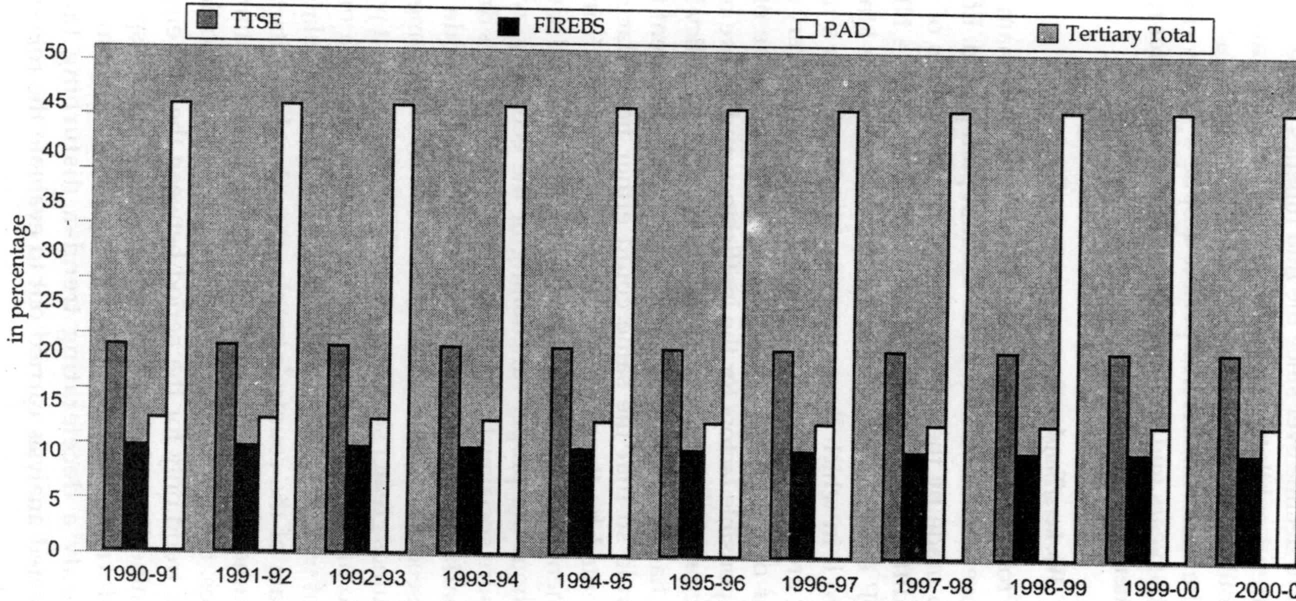

Source: Calculated from the Government of India, Economic Survey, 2002-03.

Note: TTSC = Trade, Transport, Storage and Communication. FIREBS = Financing, Insurance, Real Estates and Business Services. PAD = Public Administration and Defense and other services.

registered to decline ever since the mid nineties. Moreover the positive trend exhibited between the mid eighties and mid nineties could not even math those high growth points achieved prior to the economic reform period despite a steady decline between the years mid seventies and mid eighties. Refer figure 2 for further details.

Number of Workers/Employment

The Problem of unemployment continues to remain as a major cause of concern ever since the first plan period. Efforts were also made by the government at various points of time through different policy measures, both specific (like NREP, JRY, IRDP etc.) and general in nature to find some kind of solution to it in which the government itself acted as a major player by providing employment opportunities. The very such behaviour of the government itself latter became one of the major responsible factors for the inefficiency and failure of the public sector units. Strong recommendations at the policy level therefore had to be sought to withdraw the government from its lead role so that the same could either be replaced or supplemented by the private sectors. This major shift in the development strategy of the government indeed raised several doubts about the proper functioning of the economy, which could ensure social justice as private sectors are always driven by the 'market signal' in which the 'rent seeking' attitude is an inherent seed. It is in this context; the issue on employment in India assumes greater significance and any attempt on it would help us to unearth the reality on this matter. The data on the number of workers is used as a proxy measure to calculate the growth rate of the country's employment level and its trend and the same is given in figure 3. As in the case of the number of factories, the analysis on the number of workers also depict a positive trend only for the period between the mid eighties and mid nineties and almost in all the other years, irrespective of the reform processes, the employment growth in India reveals only a decelerating trend–a disturbing fact. A disaggregated analysis carried out to evaluate the role of the

Figure 2 : Growth Rate of Number of Factories in India

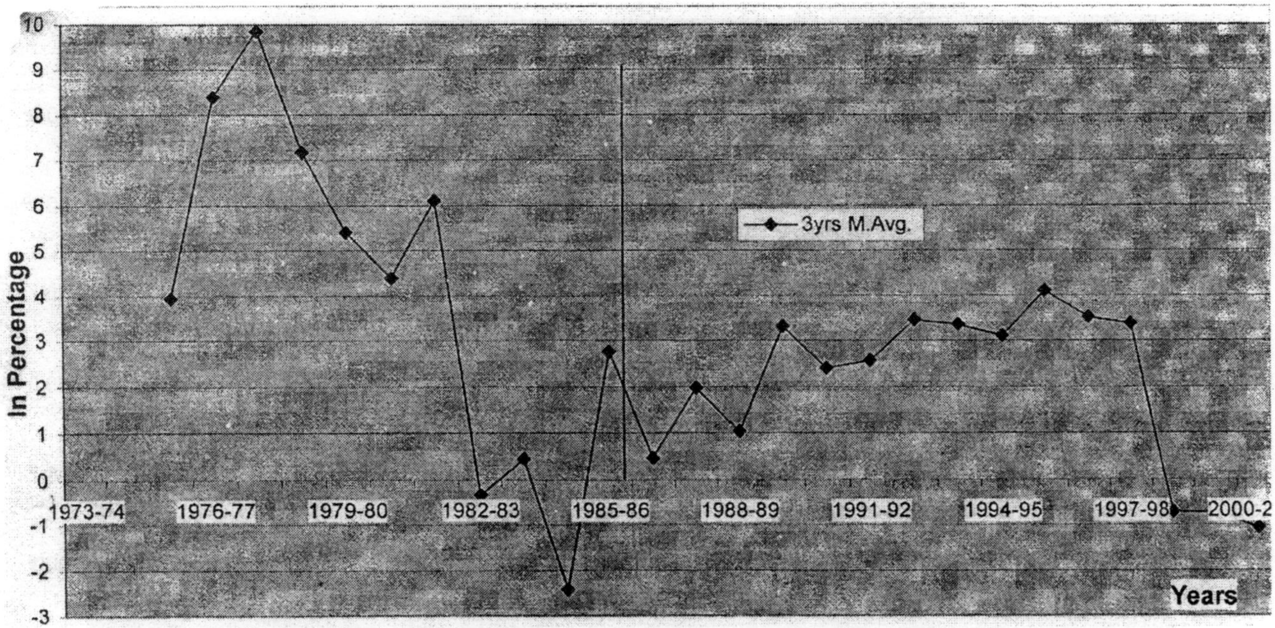

Source: Calculated from the Annual Survey of Industries, various issues.

Figure 3 : Growth Rate of Number of Workers in India

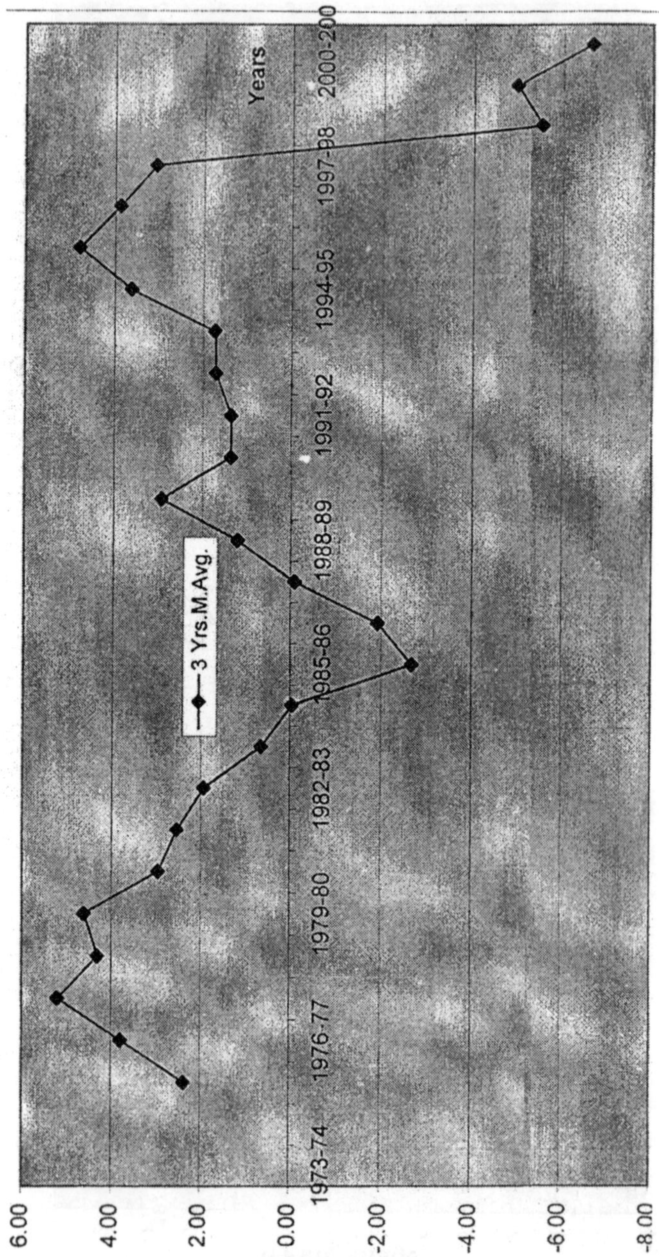

Source: Annual Survey of Industry, various issues.

private sector at this juncture also exposes a failure of the private sector, as against the ordinary expectation. Despite a very favourable climate created for the private sector to play a lead role particularly during the 1990s 'a no increase' observed in the share of employment in the private sector (see table 2) could only reconfirm and further strengthen our earlier doubts on the reliability of the supplementary role that could be expected out of the rent seeking market agents. However, a marginal decline in the share of employment in the public sector is also simultaneously noticed and this could be attributed to the post reform effect of the 1990s as the government is asked to withdraw from its economic activities at the maximum.

Table 2: Share of Employment in the Private and Public Sectors in India (in percent)

Year	*Private Sector*	*Public sector*	*Total*
1981	32.32	67.68	100
1989	28.78	71.22	100
1990	28.78	71.22	100
1991	28.72	71.28	100
1992	29.00	71.00	100
1993	28.89	71.11	100
1994	28.97	71.03	100
1995	29.28	70.72	100
1996	30.46	69.54	100
1997	30.75	69.25	100
1998	31.06	68.94	100
1999	30.94	69.06	100
2000	30.92	69.08	100

Source: Government of India, Economic Survey 2002-03.

Output

Industrial output is an important variable in explaining and evaluating the economic performance. More so is the 'used-based' analysis on the growth rate of industrial output, as it has the potential not only to reveal the general trend in the industrial growth behavior but also the very structural composition of the industries per se. When the same exercise is carried out for India we could identify a major structural transformation taking place in the Indian economy as industries with higher weight losing their prominence to those with lesser weight during the nineties.

The changing weight of the industries observed between the two different base years (1980-81=100 and 1993-94=100) itself is a sufficient testimony to this fact. Capital goods and Consumer durables are the fine example to cite as the weight of the former declined from 16.4 to mere 9.3 while the latter increased its weight by almost 100 percent (see table 3). These apart, a closer scrutiny on the growth rates of the used-based industries also portrays almost a similar feature as the growth

Table 3: Growth Rate of Industrial Production by used-based classification (1993-94=100)

Year	*Basic Goods*	*Capital Goods*	*Inter-mediate*	*Consumer Goods (A+B)*	*(A) Durables*	*(B) Non Durables*
Weight	35.5 (39.4)	9.3 (16.4)	26.5 (20.5)	28.7 (23.6)	5.4 (2.6)	23.3 (21.0)
1981-82	10.9	6.7	3.7	13.8	10.9	14.1
1990-91	3.8	17.4	6.1	10.4	14.4	9.4
1994-95	9.6	9.2	8.3	12.1	16.2	11.2
1995-96	10.8	5.3	19.4	12.8	25.8	9.8
1996-97	3.0	11.5	8.1	6.2	4.6	6.6
1997-98	6.9	5.8	8.0	5.5	7.8	4.8
1998-99	1.6	12.6	6.1	2.2	5.6	1.2
1999-00	5.5	6.9	8.8	5.7	14.1	3.2
2000-01	3.9	1.8	4.7	8.0	14.5	5.8
2001-02	2.6	-3.4	1.5	6.0	11.5	4.1

Source: GOI, Economic Survey 2002-03 & A.N. Agarwal (2003): 'Indian Economy', p. 374.

Note: The weights in brackets relate to the Index of Industrial Production (IIP) with the base 1980-81=100. For others the base is 1993-94=100.

rate of the consumer durable sector displayed a better performance than the capital and basic goods sectors. In our view this is a newly emerging trend of the nineties in which the industrial growth is being led by the consumer durable sector. Nevertheless a similar symptom had been noticed for India ever since the beginning of the country's market friendly approach. As a trend we may not be able to support it fully as it calls for a direct trade off between the present and future consumptions. A provision for the latter would be of a better choice as it alone can ensure for a better gross fixed capital formation, which is a basic necessity for the growth of any less developing country like India in nature. See table 3, for further observations on this matter.

Capital Formation

The importance of capital formation and its role in the making of an economy does not require any new or extra explanation. India's keen interest in building up of a very strong base for capital formation ever since the inception of the Mahalanobis model, thus, can well be appreciated. Almost as a single agent the special role of the public sector in materializing this task during the pre-reform period can be well recognized beyond anybody's doubt. However, there were some shortcomings in meeting the targets set during certain plan periods. These apart, some more mistakes in creating excess inventories largely on the part of the government-food stock for instance (see table A3 in the Appendix)-also became a kind of 'the last straw'. From where it also became very easy for those who believed in the western philosophy, as wanted by the international funding agencies, to strongly advice the government to withdraw from its development activities of the economy so that a direct invitation to the market agents are made very easy in replacing the former since the nineties at a rapid pace. Whether this strategicaly shifts could resolve those problems related to the issues of capital formation traced by the critics for the pre-reform period is indeed a matter of real concern. The statistics collected and presented by the

Table 4: Gross Fixed Capital Formation as percentage of GDP at Current Prices.

Years	*Pub. Sect.*	*Pvt. Sect.*	*Total*
1990-91	9.00	13.90	22.90
1991-92	9.20	12.90	22.00
1992-93	8.20	14.20	22.40
1993-94	8.00	13.40	21.40
1994-95	8.80	13.20	21.90
1995-96	7.70	16.70	24.40
1996-97	6.90	15.90	22.80
1997-98	6.40	15.30	21.70
1998-99	6.50	15.10	21.50
1999-00	6.40	15.20	21.60
2000-01	6.80	15.10	21.90

Source: Government of India, Economic Survey, 2002-03 and CSO.

government on this matter are given in tables 4 and 5. Going by the absolute data presented in these tables 4 and 5 obviously give us a very glowing and positive picture of the private sector's successful story of the supplementary role in building up of the country's capital formation. Unfortunately the reliability of these data is being challenged by a very recent study as it could identity a problem of overestimation of gross fixed capital formation in private corporate sector and recommends for a moderation (Dennis Raja Kumar, 2003). If the findings of this study is true, once again the public sector along with the household sector remain as the major contributing factor of the country's capital formation and not the private sector as portrayed in the table 4 and 5. These apart, be it GDFCF or GDCF as a percentage of the GDP, throughout the period of our analysis, remained far below 30 percent and a matter of serious concern for India as low level of capital formation tends to remain as a great tumbling block in preventing the economy from growing. This is true particularly when the country is aiming for a Gap growth rate for more than 7 percent per annum (the targeted GDP growth rate of 7.93 percent per annum for the 10th, plan needs to be recollected here).

Table 5: Gross Domestic Capital Formation as percentage of GDP at Current Prices

Years	*Pub. Sect.*	*Pvt. Sect.*	*Total*
1990-91	9.30	14.70	24.10
1991-92	8.80	13.10	21.90
1992-93	8.50	15.20	23.80
1993-94	8.20	13.00	21.30
1994-95	8.70	14.70	23.40
1995-96	7.70	18.90	26.50
1996-97	7.00	14.70	21.80
1997-98	6.60	16.00	22.60
1998-99	6.60	14.80	21.40
1999-00	7.10	16.10	23.30
2000-01	7.10	15.80	22.90

Source: Government of India, Economic Survey, 2002-03 and CSO.

Gross Domestic Savings

The country's aggregate saving ratio as a percentage of GDP throughout the reform period remained below 25 Percent. The contribution of corporate sectors is far below the expectation and it is more true in the case of private sector as it has failed to emerge as a major player despite a very favourable industrial climate cater to their need is being created. Nevertheless, irrespective of the reform it is once again the household sector that continues to act as the major factor in keeping up the country's saving ratio (see table 6). Having a high saving potential in the household sector and a simultaneous failure of it for not getting reflected in the reduction of poverty level in India tempts us to treat the high and increasing share of gross domestic saving of the household sector in GDP as a proxy measure to indicate the increasing skewed income distribution in India during the reform period also.

Principal Imports and Trade Balance

The import commodity basket of India is mainly constituted by eight different categories and they, on an average, continue to occupy for more than 70 percent of the country's total import

Table 6: Gross Domestic Savings as percentage of GDP at Current Market Prices

Years	*H. Hold*	*Pvt. Sect.*	*Pub. Sect.*	*Total*
1990-91	19.30	2.70	1.10	23.10
1991-92	17.00	3.10	2.00	22.00
1992-93	17.50	2.70	1.60	21.80
1993-94	18.40	3.50	0.60	22.50
1994-95	19.70	3.50	1.70	24.80
1995-96	18.20	4.90	2.00	25.10
1996-97	17.00	4.50	1.70	23.20
1997-98	17.60	4.20	1.30	23.10
1998-99	8.90	3.70	-1.00	21.70
1999-00	20.30	3.70	-0.90	23.20
2000-01	20.90	4.20	-1.70	23.40

Source: Government of India, Economic Survey, 2002-03.

bill for several years irrespective of various policy measures followed in the years between 1960-61 and 2000-01. See table 7. However, a decline in share of the capital goods, iron and steel, fertilizer and transport equipments shall be attributed to the country's gaining self-sufficiencies in these areas–for which the foundations already laid during the pre-1980s and 1990s' policies (i.e., the import substituting regime) did play a crucial role and hence the credit can not be fully given to the nineties' policy. Moreover, there are studies, which hold the 1990s' economic policies responsible for the country's newly increasing dependence on the technological front (Nagaraj, 2003, pp. 1708 & 09) and this is just the opposite of what had been practiced until then. A country like India aiming at more self-reliance, therefore, cannot afford to continue with the policies of the present nature. These apart, the trade balance which always remained or kept within the control by the government under the regulated regime of market intervention mechanism' never remained the same after the introduction of the 'market driven mechanism' except for the period 1991-92 to 1994-95. It is clearly exhibited in the figure 4. Given the fact that India has a better foreign exchange reserve at present, in our view, the widening gap between the export and import is a

Table 7: Principal Imports of India (values in million US $, in percent)

Years	*Petroleum Oil & Lubricants*	*Edible Oil*	*Fertilizer & its Manufacturing*	*Pearl, Precious & Semi P.Stones worked or un-*	*Iron and Steel*	*Capital Goods*	*Non-electrical machinery apparatus & appliances including M. tool*	*Transport Equipment*	*Total of columns 2 to 9*	*Other*	*Import of India*
1	2	3	4	5	6	7	8	9	10	11	12
1960-61	6.16	0.34	1.15	0.08	10.96	31.75	18.10	6.42	74.97	25.03	100
1970-71	8.33	1.43	6.15	1.53	8.97	24.70	15.77	4.07	70.95	29.05	100
1980-81	41.94	5.40	6.52	3.32	6.79	15.22	8.68	3.76	91.64	8.36	100
1990-91	25.04	0.76	4.09	8.65	4.89	24.23	9.82	3.87	81.34	18.66	100
1995-96	20.52	1.84	4.59	5.74	3.94	23.06	11.72	3.01	74.42	25.58	100
1997-98	19.68	1.79	2.46	8.06	3.43	18.17	9.75	2.53	65.87	34.13	100
1998-99	15.09	4.26	2.38	8.87	2.51	18.11	8.00	1.88	61.11	38.89	100
1999-00	25.39	3.74	2.58	10.94	1.78	12.02	8.04	2.29	66.79	33.21	100
2000-01q	30.97	2.64	1.31	9.97	1.55	10.95	7.33	1.89	66.20	33.80	100

Source : Government of India, Economic Survey 2002-03.

Figure 4: Export, Import and Trade Balance of India (values in million US $)

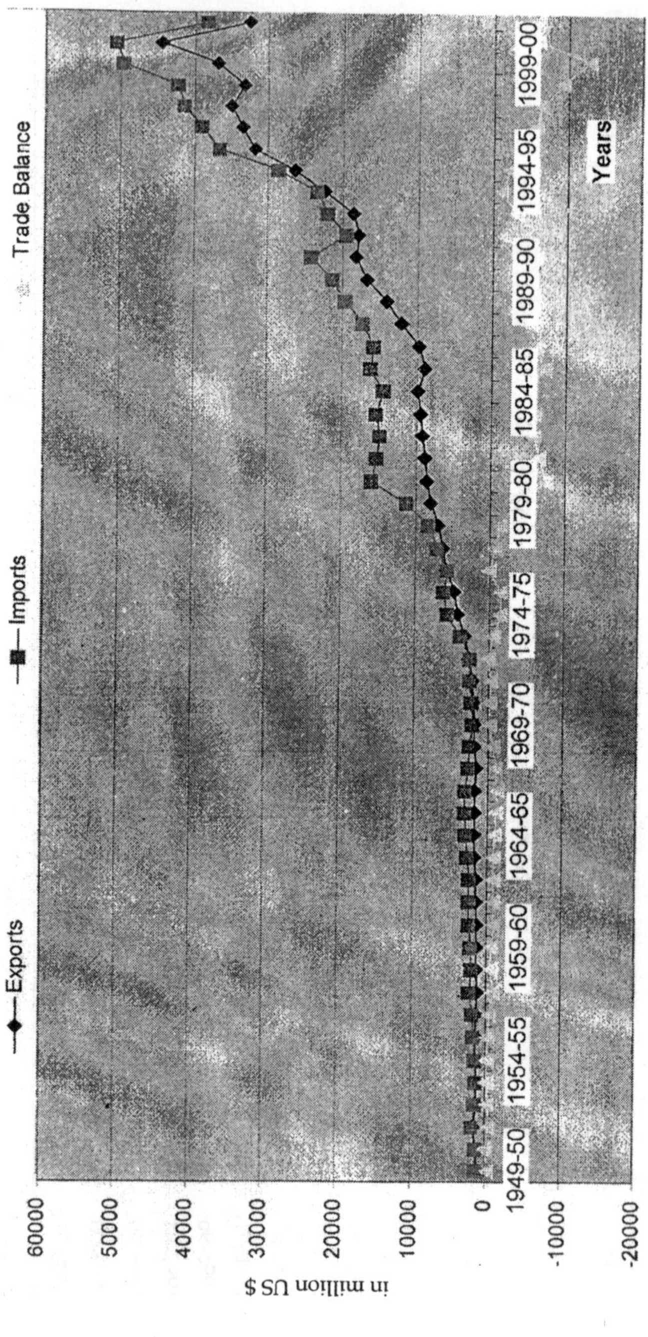

Source: Government of India, Economic Survey 2002-03.

newly invited trouble capable of causing all possible damages in the country's balance of trade, which would have been very well avoided.

SECTION – III

Summary and Findings

The attempt to evaluate the impact of economic reforms in India since the mid eighties in general and the nineties in particular, under the background of the earlier policy regimes, limiting our self to some selected variables of sectoral contribution, number of factories, number of workers/ employments, output, capital formation, gross domestic saving and trade balance made us to place on record the following findings along with a summary.

With the primary sector still occupying for more than 25 percent of the country's GDP, and the secondary sector struggling to cross the level of 30 percent-only with the exception of tertiary sector, (however below 50 percent), even after the introduction of the economic reform packages for more than two decades the worries are still continuing as they yet to undergo a great transformation at a faster rate. The growth rate of number of factories that began with a very positive note during the early nineties disappeared in half way through. Irrespective of the reform processes, the growth rate of number of workers/employment in India displayed a decelerating trend throughout the period of analysis, except for the years between 1985 and 1995, and hence no negative remarks could be attributed to the regulated regime as nothing positive could also be attributed to the pro-market regime by us. Nevertheless, the absence of any positive impact in terms of the variables such as the number of factories and employment even after the creation of a congenial atmosphere, yielding to the industrial lobbies, is indeed a matter of grave concern. The 'used based' analysis on the industrial output for the reform period portrayed the emerging trend of industrial growth led by the consumer durables calling for an open choice between the present and future consumption–posing a possible threat to the foundation of the capital formation on which the very issue on the country's growth lies. The serious doubt raised on the reliability of the data based on which the share of gross fixed capital formation (GFCF) of the private sector of the country's GDP is calculated, is indeed a real challenge and hence the success story of the role of the private sector as presented by the data source is yet to be proved. When this issue is clubbed along with the gross domestic saving (GDS) of the country as a percentage of the GDP, the role of the private sector is once again nowhere near to the traditional household sector. Which is yet another setback on the performance of the economy in terms GFCF and GDS during the reform period. The analysis on the country's export, import and trade balance exposed the growing gap between the export and import ever since the mid seventies, except for a small period between 1991-92 to 1994-95, which was not the case prior to it. These, observations, therefore, safely permits us to say a fact that the nineties economic reforms could bring nothing more than what India had been otherwise enjoying prior to the pro-market regime.

Thus we could once again reiterate a fact that the purpose of introducing controls was to end decision-making by discretion. Instead what we have is a state that is open to lobbies by those who have wealth and power. Thus it is increasingly becoming obvious from our current exercise, which attempted to evaluate the impact of the Indian economic reform, that the economy cannot be made efficient just by the rules of the market alone.

APPENDIX

Table A1: Incremental Capital Output Ratio in India (at market prices)

Year	*ICOR*
1951-52 to1964-65	3.92
1965-66 to 1975-76	5.66
1976-77 to 1991-92	4.48
1992-93 to 1995-96	4.00
1997-98 to 2001-02	4.53
2002-03 to 2006-07 (10th Plan expectation)	3.58

Source: Ruddar Datt and K.P.M. Sundaram, (2002), 'Indian Economy', p. 325 and A.N. Agarwal, (2003), 'Indian Economy', p. 708.

Table A2: Public Sector Investment in Different Plan Periods (in percent)

Plan periods		*Percent Share of Pub. Sect. in the Total Investment in Organized Industry and Minerals.*
First Plan	(1951-56)	16
Second Plan	(1956-61)	47
Third Plan	(1961-66)	51
Fourth Plan	(1969-74)	58
Fifth Plan	(1974-79)	62
Sixth Plan	(1980-85)	40
Seventh Plan	(1985-90)	40
Eigth Plan	(1992-97)	33.3
Ninth Plan	(1997-02)	14.3

Source: Mid-term appraisal of five-year plans, various issues.

Table A3: Central Food Grains Stock (in million tones)

Year	*Minimum Norm*	*Actual Stock*
1994	15.4	22.0
1995	15.4	30.3
1996	15.4	28.5
1997	15.4	20.0
1998	15.4	18.3
1999	16.8	24.4
2000	16.8	31.4
2001	16.8	45.7

Source: S. Swaminathan (2001), The Hindu, March 01, p. BS. 01.

REFERENCES

Agarwal, A.N., (2003), *'Indian Economy: Problems of Development & Planning'*, Wishwa Prakashan, New Delhi.

Albin, T., (1992), 'Diffusion of Computer Numerically Controlled Machine Tools in India', *M.Phil Dissertation,* submitted to the Jawaharlal Nehru University, New Delhi at the Centre for Development Studies, *Unpublished.*

Albin, T., (1994), 'New Trends in Indian Industries, Book Review', *Madras Development Seminar Series Bulletin,* Madras Institute of Development Studies, Chennai, August.

Albin, T., (1995), 'Indian Industrial Growth : Some Explanations for its Performance', *Hind Econ.,* S.T. Hindu College, Nagercoil, April.

Ahluwalia, I.J., (1992), Trade Policy and Industrialization in India', Annual Lecture Delivered at the *Exim Bank,* Bombay, March 05.

Christiansen, R.E., (1989), 'Editor's Introduction', *World Development,* Pergamon Press, New York, Vol. 17, (5), May.

Datt, Ruddar and K.P.M. Sundaram, (2002), *'Indian Economy'*, S. Chand & Company Ltd., New Delhi.

De Walle N. V., (1989), 'Privatization in Developing Countries; Review of the Issues', *World Development,* Pergamon Press, New York, Vol. 17 (5), May.

GOI (2002-03), *'Economic Survey'*, Ministry of Finance, Government of India.

Jayanth, V., (1993), States and Fiscal Reforms', *The Hindu,* October 16, p. 10.

Kurien, C.T. and J. James, (1979), *'Economic Changes in Tamilnadu 1960-1970-A Regionally and Functionally Disaggregated Analysis'*, Allied Publishers Pvt. Ltd., Mumbai.

MIDS, (1988), *'Tamil Nadu Economy: Performance and Issues'*, Oxford and IBH Publishing Co. Pvt. Ltd., New Delhi.

Nagaraj, R., (1989), 'Growth in manufacturing output since 1980 : Some Preliminary Findings', *Economic and Political Weekly,* July 1.

Nagaraj, R., (1993), Foreign Direct Investment in India in the 1990s Trends and Issues', *Economic and Political Weekly,* Vol. XXXVIII (17), April 12, May 2, pp. 1701-1712.

Nayyar, D., (ed.) (1994) , '*Industrial Growth and Stagnation : The Debate in India*', Sameeksha Trust, Oxford University Press, Mumbai.

Rajakumar, Dennis J., (2003), 'How Real Are Estimates of Corporate Investments?, *Economic and Political Weekly,* Vol. XXXVIII, (22), May 31, pp. 2155-2158.

Swaminathan, S., (2001), '*Economic Survey and the Unfinished Reforms Agenda*', The Hindu, March 01, p. BS. 01.

3

NEW ECONOMIC POLICIES— A CRITICAL EVALUATION

P. Rajendran

Introduction

During the 20th century, developed market economies experienced two major economic crises, which forced them to evolve new economic structures to overcome these crises. During 1930s, developed market economic experienced their first major crisis of the last century, known as the Great Depression. Economists diagnosed that this crisis had emerged due to the lack of aggregate demand to meet the growing potential of the supply side. This crisis necessitated the restructuring of the market economies according to the Keynesian prescriptions. The most important component of Keynesian prescription was that market fails to arrive at equilibrium with full employment; therefore, Government should intervene for maintaining full-employment by managing aggregate demand to realize the full potential of supply side. The result was the creation of elaborate institutional and legislative structure to regulate different markets. The emergence of this crisis justified the prediction of Marx that the market economies have a tendency to experience instability caused by their inherent characteristics, and its outcome justified the strength of the market economies identified by Schumpeter, (128, p. 361). It is because market economies were able to avoid the occurrence of significant reversionary tendencies after restructuring their economies along Keynesian lines for quite some time.

After 1980s, developed market economies experienced yet another major crisis with a unique combination of twin macro economics evils i.e., inflation and unemployment, occurring simultaneously. These two macro economic problems have developed such a symbiotic existence that if one tried to solve the other evil become more acute. This crisis was described as stagflation. This time economists identified that the main reason for the occurrence of this crisis was the lack of response of the supply side to market conditions. They argued that the lack of response of supply side was due to the fact that it was kept hostage by the institutions and regulations that these economies evolved to overcome the great depression. The removal of supply side constraints amounts to the removal of government intervention. Therefore, policy makers suggests for the restructuring of these economies in such a way that it removed government failure by removing all institutional and regulatory constraints to achieve supply side flexibility.

In 1990s almost all Asian countries in general and South East Asian countries in particular failed to balance their economic position in an ideal manner. India too experienced economic crisis especially in the external sector during that period. The devaluation of the rupee under the advice of the IMF and World Bank and Indian experts, brought in a new set of exchange parities for the rupee. Thereafter the rupee continued to depreciate and the dollar was a clean winner in the race

The present paper focuses its attention on the possibilities of getting success in stabilizing the Indian rupee value in the international market. Developed market saved from two crises by applying Keynesian prescriptions. India also applied structural adjustment programme to save the crisis of 1991 on the line of Keynesian prescription. Whether India should adopt competitive or win-win strategy in its economic fundamentals of new economic policies to strengthen the economy is answered.

The American dollar is priced at Rs. 45.17 today (Oct. 21, 2003) against Rs. 49.08 on the same day a year ago. This drop of 7.76 percent in the rupee price of the dollar has been hailed as a great achievement in the Indian press. It is legitimate to ask the question: has the tide turned in favor of the Indian rupee and against the American dollar.

Let us go back to the history of the rupee-dollar relationship during the past five decades.

In 1947, when India became independence the exchange rate of the rupee with respect to the US dollar was Rs. 3.318 while the corresponding rate with the pound sterling was Rs. 13.33. In 1949, the Common Wealth Currencies, other than that of Pakistan, were devalued with respect to the U.S. dollar. The parity then became Rs. 4.762 per dollar. Till the fateful first week of June 1966, this rate continued.

The devaluation of the rupee by 36.5 percent on June 6, 1966 under the advice of the IMF and Indian Experts like Dr. Jagdish Bhagwathi, brought in a new set of exchange parties for the rupee. The dollar was valued at Rs. 7.676, and the pound at about Rs. 21. From December 1, 1967 till end-March 1968, the pound was valued at Rs. 18, because of the devaluation of the pound on November 18, 1967. The rupee more or less continued at Rs. 7.6 per dollar till 1972, when it became Rs. 8.08 per dollar. In 1979, it appreciated to Rs. 7.9 per dollar. But it came down to Rs. 9.1 in 1981, thereafter it kept falling and reached a level of Rs. 18.07 in 1990.

In end July 1991, it slid down further to Rs. 25.83. In 1993, it was Rs. 31.38 and in 1995 it moved down further to Rs. 35.18. In 1998 it slid down further to Rs. 42.62. Currently it is ruling at around Rs. 45.17. The equivalence with the Pound Sterling hovered between Rs. 17 and 18 till 1979–80. Therefore, barring 1980-81, it moved upto around Rs. 15 till 1985–86 when it dipped to Rs. 18.25. After this, it kept falling and reached a level of Rs. 34.05 in 1990–91 and to Rs. 45 in 1991–92. The Rupee-Pound rate now hovers at Rs. 76.20.

Thus the rupee continued to depreciate year after year and the dollar was a clean winner in this race. Nearly after a decade of depreciating against the dollar–under the new economic system, Indian rupee is showing signs of appreciation since the past one year.

The attention needs to be focused on the relationship between the two currencies in the recent past. What has happened in the Indian economy or the US economy to alter this long-established relationship?

The terrorist attacks on September 11, 2001 in New York and Washington, and the war with Iraq have folted the American economy in no small measure. Consequently, the U.S. trading partners such as the European countries, Japan and India have made gains, whereas the Euro scored over the dollar by more than 25 percent, the pound by nearly 13 percent and the yen by about 9 percent, the Indian rupee gained by about 7 percent only. Surely, the American economy suffered a blow and this imparted weakness to the dollar. These figures illustrate that the dollar depreciated heavily against the currencies of Europe and Japan and only by a low level in the case of India.

Though this appreciation is the result of economic and related aspects, it was least expected that rupee could ever appreciate for such a long period of time. On the other side, rupee has been continuing its trend of depreciating vis-à-vis other major currencies like Euro and Yen. At the same time, Dollar is depreciating against Euro and Yen. This clearly indicates that the rupee's appreciation comes at the backdrop of global economic outlook. While a host of other factors are helping the rupee to appreciate, the debatable issue is whether these factors can sustain the momentum.

One of the factors that is acting strongly in favour of rupee is the economic outlook. The prolonged slowdown is taking its toll on the US economy and the Fed's attempt to revive the economic growth by bearing fruits. On the contrary, low interest rates are prompting the global investors to look out for alternative investment avenues like emerging markets where the interest rates are high. While the US interest rates are hovering around 1 percent interest rates in India are higher by around 5–6 percent, thus attracting the global investors. The high interest rates are also prompting the non-resident Indians to invest in Indian Government bonds thus pumping foreign exchange into the Indian economy.

The huge current account deficit in the US economy brought about reduction in interest rates. In this atmosphere, the Indian exports made substantial gains and the inflow of dollars intensified. After a large time, the foreign exchange reserves of India rose to levels about $ 90.3 billion and it will cross $ 100 billion at the end of this fiscal. Added to the interest rates factor, reasonable economic growth backed by manufacturing sector, foreign currency reserves and good investment climate have contributed to the appreciation of rupee.

"The future movement of rupee against the dollar depends on many unpredictables like the timing of US recovery, the interest rate policy of the fed, the future investment climate in Europe vis-à-vis US, the political and economic developments in the Arab world". To sum up, it all depends to a large extent on the revival of the US economy. Hence, rupee appreciation against dollar is not because current account surplus, huge foreign exchange reserve, reduction in interest rates, and maintaining inflation within limit, reduction in fiscal deficit, and growth of economy. Even today- despite all these positive signs–the rupee is depreciating against the Yen and Euro.

China's economic growth has been truly remarkable. Its reforms are aimed at encouraging international trade and foreign direct investment. However, India started its reforms much later, and it's behind the curve as compared to China. The Chinese approach to reforms is different from what other nations have done so for. Instead of a top-to-bottom approach, the Chinese opted for a bottom-to-top approach. This enabled the Chinese authorities to gain the support of masses. Having the right approach is a prerequisite for success and that is the key for China's success. As long as the Chinese economy continues to grow, India will be forced to reform to keep up. China has more coherent leadership, is more business-friendly and a much stronger international profile, so it will be way ahead. India has world class intellectual skills and the advantage of English fluency but needs to simplify its business environment. India relies too much on the skills of ability to organize skilled labor to build up enterprises and invest capital. As things stand today, China is way ahead of India in terms of presence in the global market place.

In terms of economic, political and global aspirations, however, China and India are both giants. Each country has a considerable pool of revenues at its disposal. But now, China's exports to the USA suffered because of the prevalence of the deadly disease SARS (Severe Acute Respiratory Syndrome) and this stimulated Indian exports. Prominent in the list of exports was computer software in which Indian companies such as Wipro and Infosys have had an excellent record. The inflow of dollars strengthened the foreign exchange reserves of the RBI, which went on mapping up these inflows at favourable exchange rates.

Let it be understood that the US economy is under pressure and is not growing. Many US large-sized companies have adopted the technique of out-sourcing, which means that instead of importing human labor, foreigners set up offices in India and they get their assignments completed in India at low cost. For it Internet is a helpful device. The Indian IT workers stay in India, work out the assignments during the day (when the Americans are sleep) and transmit their worksheets through the Internet which are on the tables of their counterparts when they arrive in their offices in the US in the morning. Understandably, the American worker is howling against this attack on his labor market. Out-sourcing in short run helps others but in long run it helps India to enhance its productivity.

The RBI has been mapping up the dollar from the market in a bid to eliminate volatility in the Indian foreign exchange market. The appreciation of the rupee against the dollar is no doubt a welcome move but frequent ups and downs can have unhealthy impact on international business environment especially as imports and exports. The RBI has to play a constructive role in this regard, otherwise the country has to face a lot of problems in international finance.

A study of India's long term imports and exports indicates that the trade gap is likely to persist for a long time. Imports will be persistently higher than exports, whatever the rates of exchange for the major currencies. The gap is likely to be narrowed in the coming years through invisible such as IT solutions. There is abundance of brain power to export the software packets in India. Thus, India will continue to have trade deficits for many years to come but the invisible earnings have a bright future.

Will the race against dollar be won by the rupee? Surely, the rupee will have the score over the pound and the Euro as well before shouting " Hurrah". Perhaps the Jubilation bugle has been sounded prematurely.

World Economic Forum (WEF), in its latest Global Competitiveness Report 2001, has used two parameters for measuring the Global competitiveness of the countries in the world. First parameter is Growth Competitiveness Index (GCI). Second parameter is Current Competitiveness Index (CCI). The main purpose of WCR is to evaluate the strengths and weakness of national economies of the world and accordingly, it have got a sample of 75 nations. The GCI evaluates the factors, which contribute in the future process of growth of a country in terms of change in GDP per people. Besides, it also considers level of technology, the quality of public institutions and the macro economic environment. It tells us economic prosperity and rate of improvements of economies in the world. On the other side of it, CCI explores the factors which underpin high current productivity and therefore, current economic progress, also examines from the level of GDP per people.

By the application of both the parameters by WEF has declared Finland as the most competitive nation in the world and accordingly, it ranks first both the indices which means Finland has the potential and prospects over the next five years. (See table 1).

Table 1: Growth Competitiveness Ranking During the Year 2001

Country	*Global Competitiveness Ranking*	*Current Competitiveness Ranking*
Finland	1	1
U.S.A.	2	2
Canada	3	11
Singapore	4	10
Australia	5	9
Norway	6	19
Taiwan	7	21
Netherlands	8	3
Sweden	9	6
New Zealand	10	20
U.K.	12	7
Denmark	14	8
Switzerland	15	5
Germany	17	4
Malaysia	30	37
China	39	47
India	57	38
Indonesia	64	55
Zimbabwe	75	65

Source: Global Competitiveness Report, 2001.

In the terms of GCI the United States of America has slipped to the second place. Japan maintained a low ranking at 21st place down. See Appendix II It is because Japan continuously facing economic stagnation. Similarly, in the case of many developed and developing nations, rankings in terms of GCI have also changed. Some changes are the improvement and some changes are for decline. Finland, Norway, Taiwan, France and China have witnessed improvement in their Growth Competitiveness Ranking while Netherlands, U.K., Denmark, Switzerland, Germany, Malaysia, India, Indonesia, Singapore and Hong Kong have experienced decline. Bangladesh and Nigeria though ranking near the bottom of the GCI scale.

The countries which have a strong and stable macro-economies policies, increase their political and technological capacities definitely find a remarkable place in the GCI.

On the other hand, the Current Competitiveness Index (CCI) explores the forces that underpin high amount productivity and therefore, the current performance, is seen in terms of GDP per people. The CCI reveals, micro economic fundamentals, with one sub-index that concentrates on companies' sophistication and another, on the quality of business environment. These forces indicate why some nations could sustain a higher level of economic prosperity and emancipation than other countries world wide. (See table 2).

In terms of CCI, Finland occupies first rank followed by the United States of America. Then comes Netherland and Germany has fourth place. The most revealing trend is that both Finland and the USA had maintained their respective rankings in the year 2001. Indonesia was assigned the lowest rank. China and Thailand are the other nations with low ranking. India has improved its ranking from 37th in the year 2000 to 36th during the year 2001. Whereas, China one the vital competitors of India has lost its ranking by 3 points, that is, the 44th ranking in the year 2000 to 47th ranking during the year 2001. (See table 3).

Pro-active thinkers feel that competition fosters innovations and support human initiation, than the country going to be a rich country. If a country thinks that competitiveness is bad, the unnecessary duplication of efforts by many companies rather than one, then country is going to be a poor country. India has to believe in this at all costs.

Table 2: Growth Competitiveness Indexes Between 2000 and 2001

Country	*Global Competitiveness Index Ranking*		*Gain/Loss*
	2000	*2001*	
Finland	5	1	+4
U.S.A.	1	2	×1
Norway	15	6	+9
Taiwan	10	7	+3
Netherlands	3	8	-5
U.K.	8	12	-4
Denmark	13	14	-1
Switzerland	9	15	-6
Germany	14	17	-3
France	21	20	+1
Japan	20	21	-1
Malaysia	24	30	-6
China	40	39	+1
India	48	57	-9
Indonesia	43	64	-21

Source: Global Competitiveness Report 2001.

Table 3: Current Competitiveness Index (ranking) During 2000-2001

Country	*CCI 2000*	*CCI 2001*	*Gain/Loss*
Finland	1	1	×
U.S.A.	2	2	×
Norway	20	19	+19
Taiwan	21	21	-
Netherlands	4	3	+1
U.K.	14	15	-1
Denmark	6	8	-2
Switzerland	5	5	-
Germany	3	4	-1
France	11	12	-1
Japan	14	15	-1
Malaysia	30	37	-7
China	44	47	-3
India	37	36	+1
Indonesia	48	55	-7

Source: Global Competitiveness Report, 2001.

India occupies a very low place in international competitiveness rankings. Overall Growth Competitiveness Ranking of the country as per report (GCR for 2001-2002) has slipped from 48 in 2000 to 57 in 2001. In CCR, India has moved up one slot from 37 in 2000 to 36 in 2001.

It is clear that India has been lagging far behind in terms of global competitiveness and this has been because of lesser importance to manufacturing. The attainment of global competitiveness is a painful exercise. But it has to be undertaken at all costs as it is unavoidable. TQM is the only solution left out for Indian companies to enhance the very needed facets namely, improving quality and at the same time cut costs. Under Globalized business environment, this is the immediate are of concern of India.

In the field of economic development independence India has been generally acclaimed for two major achievements. The first is in respect of obtaining a high rate of growth of production of food grains sufficient to meet the growing requirements of an increasing population. The second achievement is in respect of achieving a level, and growth rate, in the index of organized industrial and related production at internationally comparable levels of cost and prices (though not all of them).

The post-independence period from 1947–48 to 1996–97 has witnessed a growth rate of 6.67 percent per annum. From 1950-51 to 1996-97, the growth rate was 7.1 percent per annum.

During the decade of the 1950s the growth rate was 6.82 percent per annum. During the decade of the 1960s it came down to 5.9 percent per annum and during the decade of the 1970s it came further down to 4.26 percent per annum. The declining growth rates were the effects of the adoption of the Mahalanobis strategy. But during the decade of the 1980s, thanks particularly to the policy initiatives of Rajiv Gandhi towards liberalization of imports and redirection of import duties specially in respect of capital goods, the growth rate moved up to 7.54 percent per annum. But owing to severe exchange crisis 1991, and its immediate impact the growth rate came down to 5.97 percent per annum between 1990-91 to 1996–97.

There have been great inter state disparities and differences in the growth rates and composition of industrial output in the last 50 years. The important changes during the last three decades in the relative share in the value added in manufacturing among the different states are given below. Maharashtra (28 percent), West Bengal (22 percent), Gujarat (10 percent), Tamilnadu (7 percent), Bihar (7 percent), UP (6.5 percent), Karnataka (3.1 percent), Assam (3 percent), Andhra Pradesh (2.7 percent), Kerala (2.5 percent), Madhya Pradesh (2.4 percent), Punjab and Haryana (1.9 percent), Rajasthan (1.1 percent), and Orissa (1 percent) in that order, were the leading industrial state in 1960. This order has changed very rapidly over the last three decades. Around 1992-93, the relative shares of the value added for different states was as follows: Maharashtra (22.7 percent), Gujarat (11.3 percent), Tamilnadu (10.3 percent), U.P. (9.1 percent), Punjab & Haryana (6.4 percent), A.P. (6 percent), West Bengal (5.96 percent), Karnataka (5.8 percent), M.P. (5.5 percent), Bihar (4.8 percent), Rajasthan (3.3 percent), Kerala (2.55), Orissa (2 percent) and Assam (1.2 percent).

Maharashtra has suffered a decline in its relative share in more than 5 percentage of points. A.P. has gained in its relative share by 3.3 percentage points. Karnataka has gained in its relative share by 27 percentage points, Gujarat has gained by 3 percent points. Tamilnadu has gained by 3.3 percentage points, Punjab & Haryana together have gained by 4.5 percentage points. M.P. has gained by 3.1 percentage points. U.P. has also gained in its relative share by 2.6 percentage points. Rajasthan has gained by 2.2 percentage points. Orissa has also gained by 1 percentage point. Assam has lost the relative share by 1.8 percentage points.

But the most radical decline in the relative share has been that of West Bengal. It was only next to Maharastra in its industrial status throughout the 1950s and 1960s. But it lost heavily from the 1970s. It has lost in relative share by nearly 16 percentage points. West Bengal was next only to Maharashtra in industrial leadership around the time of independence and till about the end of the 1960s. To what extent idealogical factors are responsible for this big decline in West Bengal's industrial status has to be examined carefully specially by the leftists themselves: In India, economic leftism may not have had much effects at the national level atleast in recent years. But it has certainly harmed West Bengal where it is the predominant ideology. Some rethinking is absolutely necessary in West Bengal State if the situation is not to worsen. It is in the seventies and eighties that West Bengal lost its relative share in a very big way.

Though Kerala's relative share, which was absolutely small, has remained constant over the years, it seems in this state as well, considerable damage has been potentially caused by the force of ideology specially in the matter of industrial relations. From the middle seventies, Kerala has been witnessing, more or less continuously, large inflows of net remittances from abroad. The overall potential of investible funds in Kerala has been quite large. But very little of this potential has gone towards industrial and related development within Kerala. Both labor and capital have been migrating from the State to the other states of India. The level of real wages in Kerala is probably quicker than what can be sustained under potential conditions of high industrial investment in the State. This is a pity because Kerala has advantages in natural, resources, trained manpower, and now, in investible funds. The system of industrial relations may also have to be restructured in this state.

At global level, Marx theory failed, the economic story of the Russia reveals that there is no room for Marx theory. China, today emerging as one of the global leader, it is not because of Marx but because of Keynesian prescriptions. The economic story of West Bengal and Kerala fall in the same line.

By 2005, some 75 percent of China's industrial economy will be in private hands, compared to less than 10 percent in 1980. Today the market almost controls 98 percent of prices, the state only 2 percent. A China-based analyst predicts that unless something is done the pension liability could reach almost 400 percent of GDP by 2030. China, after all, has just passed the US as the world's biggest magnet for foreign direct investment; the world is ignoring the realities of China.

The business world in the 19th century was convinced that Britian was the original workshop of the world; later similar thoughts went about in the US in early 1960s in Japan during the 1970s and South Korea during the 1980s and 1990s. Now the focus has shifted towards China–the new industrial monster.

But India was called the "Golden Birds" in the middle Ages. Arabs, Europeans and warriors and businessmen from many other regions of the world were attracted to it. They all undertook long, adventures journeys to establish relationship with the Country and were successful in their effort. Similar efforts were made by people to reach other parts of the world. Buddhism, Christianity and Islam spread to large parts of the world following establishment of business relationships or political power. In the 19th and 20th century India has been called "a Country inhabited by poor, But at the dawn of the 21st century and the new millennium, it is again star attraction of all the developed nations of the world because of its human resources.

Fortunately, unlike in the pass, India now Commands a new respect among the comity of nations as a growing economic power in this region. Till 1991, economic interactions between India and ASEAN did not flourish especially "during the cold war period, India was regarded by the ASEAN Countries as politically suspect, economically unimportant and at times, militarily threatening. But now India's compulsions of integrating with ASEAN have assumed a new urgency.

Under there circumstances, India's strategic orientation underwent a radical shift and so did ASEAN's view of India moreover, with the decision shift in its economic policy since the launching of the process of liberation action and globalization, India has emerged as one of the fastest growing economics in the world with the potential of becoming a new power house of manufacturing after providing its capabilities in software and information technology.

India keeps the second position next to China in agricultural produce and also keeps the second position next to Brazil in the fruits and vegetables cultivation. Of the total cultivation of the fruits and vegetables 75 percent meant for domestic consumption and the remaining 25 percent remains wastage it is because of lack of cold storage facilities in India. If India has adequate storage facilities then its surplus can be stored and exported and earns Rs.10000 crore per annum through foreign exchange.

Currently the world wheat production is about 550 million tones. Nearly 120 tones of wheat is wheat is traded between nations. Of the total trade, the durum or macaroni wheat accounts for 12 million tones, and the rest is all bread wheat. For reasons of subsidy and other considerations, the area under wheat in the US is coming down. The acreage in China is also declining because of fall in prices. Much of the wheat in the European Union, North America, and Argentina is cultivated under rain-fed situations. Hence, wheat production fluctuates.

In 2001-02, world wheat trade amounted to 107 million tones. The US, Australia, Canada, Argentina and the European Union accounted for 75 percent of the exports. India's share is just 2.5 percent and that too inconsistent. Wheat export from India were placed at 200 000 tones in 1999-2000, which increased to 2.37 million tones in 2000-02, and these may be around 3 million tones in 2001-02.

The major importers are Iran, Brazil, Japan, Algeria, Egypt, European Union, Indonesia, South Korea, Morocco and the Philippines.

Inspite of liberalized trade and mounting wheat stocks, India has not yet emerged as a major wheat exporter. The reason for this is inadequacies relating to research, procurement, marketing, infrastructure and policy. In Feb 2002, Iraq accepted 22000 tones of wheat export from India. The annual exports to this country in future may go up to around 36 Lakh tones. India is keen on export to Iraq because the price realized is lucrative at $203 a tones cost insurance and freight (CIF).

India has emerged as the second largest producers of wheat in the world. It produces 13 percent of world wheat production. Wheat production was only 11 million tones in 1960-61. This rose to 36.3 million tones in 1980-81 and to Rs. 55.1 million tones in 1990-91. It was high at 76.4 million tones in 1999-2000.

There has been remarkable rise in wheat yields over a period. The wheat yield per hectare was only 851 kg in 1960-61. This rose to 1630 kg in 1980-81 and to 2778 kg in 1999-2000. In India, nearly 90 percent of area devoted to wheat crop is having some access to irrigation. The minimum support/procurement price of wheat was Rs. 275 per quintal in 1991-92. This increased to Rs. 475 in 1996-97 and to Rs. 610 in 2000-01. The particular about rice production also shows a rosy picture in the development of agriculture sector in India.

Conclusion

A currency's appreciation/depreciation against other currencies mainly depends upon relative competitiveness in the international market. Competitiveness indicates a country's economic strength and weaknesses. The rupee appreciation against dollar is purely temporary. Even today the rupee is depreciating against major currencies such as the Japanese Yen, Euro and the Pound sterling. Appreciation of the rupee will be the stable and permanent only when if it is on account of competitiveness in the international market. Free and borderless trade is the order of the day. Development of information technology has forced the world to become global village.

Under these circumstances, Keynesian prescriptions are the only way for development of a nation under the capitalistic pattern. There is no flaw in Marx's ideology but the country should go a long way in implementing it is highly impossible, because it is a theoretical frame works. India has the highly sophisticated intellectual skill in the information technology besides; it has a strong agricultural base. Hence a day is working for India to prosperous in an ideally way.

India's compulsions of integrating with ASEAN have assumed a new urgency with the recent failure of the world trade organization ministerial at cancum and the threat issued by the US of bypassing WTO for bilateral trading arrangement India pushing the idea of closer ties with ASEAN and Japan, China and South Korea should see a roadmap being charted for a new economic Co-operation in the Association of South East Asian nations.

REFERENCES

Aglietha, M., (1979), A Theory of Capitalist Regulations–The US Experience, Lexican Press London.

Bruno M. and J.D. Sachs, (1985), Economics of World Wide Stagflation, Harvard University Press, Cambridge, Mars.

Fischer, S.C., (1983), Indexing and Inflation, *Journal of Monetary Economics* 12: pp. 519-542.

Vijay K. Seth, "Flexibility Paradigm and Restructuring of Labour Markets in Developed Marx's Economics" *Journal of Management Research.* Vol. I, No. 4, Sept.-Dec. 2001.

Facts for you (Business & Economics) June 2003.

Chartered Financial Analyst Aug. 2003.

Chartered Financial Analyst April 2003.

The Management Accountant Vol. 38, No. 8, August 2003.

Kishan World, Vol. 13, No. 9, Sept. 2003.

Chartered Financial Analyst Oct. 2003.

The Hindu Business Line, Oct. 22nd 2003.

4

NEW ECONOMIC POLICY: AN OVERVIEW OF EMERGING CONCERNS

P.N.P. Mohamed Sahaputheen &
A. Hidhayathulla

Introduction

Economic liberalism thrives when labour supply is sufficient or workers are weaker and compliant — **Mourice Dobb**

Economic policies of Government of India since 1991 implemented by the then Prime Minister Mr. P.V. Narasimha Rao and championed by Dr. Manmohan Singh are commonly known as New Economic Policy. Its genesis can be traced back to Mrs. Indira Gandhi's period and her successor son's regime marked with industrial delicensing and mild reforms respectively. The constituents of new economic policy are nothing but the pillars of classical economics that occupied economic thinking of 18th and 19th centuries. Going three centuries back, is it new economic policy? It is bringing the old again. What does classical economics say? It epitomizes what LPG says today.

Pillars of Classical Economics

- Economic freedom–Least intervention by the government in the economic affairs of individuals.

- Free trade
- Wide extent of market
- Division of labour

Salient Features of New Economic Policy

- ✓ Liberalisation, deregulation and delicensing
- ✓ Globalisation, foreign investment, and MNCs
- ✓ Disinvestment and public sector reforms
- ✓ Changes in trade and financial policies
- ✓ Devaluation

Sing C. Chew and Robert A. Denemark summarized new economic policy as

- Local government expenditure cut backs
- Monetary devaluation
- Reduction in subsidies for basic staples
- Removal of import quotas
- Tariff reductions
- Interest rate policy reforms
- Revision in agricultural prices
- Reduction in the powers of state marketing boards
- Privatization of state owned enterprises

Why New Economic Policy? —The genesis

A search for ownership of new economic policy will lead one to Structural Adjustment Programmes (SAP). Conditionalities imposed by World Bank in 1982 together with International Monetary Fund in 1986 on third world member nations when they borrow from these institutions are known as Structural Adjustment Programmes. In fact, it seems that third world nations had not approached World Bank or IMF for debt.

In the recycling of petrodollar surplus that was accumulated during 1970s, the private international banks mindlessly and enormously lent to third world. When these banks forced for repayment enmasse, the third world had to appeal for rescheduling of debt service payment (principle with interest repayment) in August 1982. Western economists and private international banks interpreted this as third world debt crisis, as if it were a crisis in the third world economies. In order to perform rescue operation the World Bank and IMF came forward to deliberately help the third world for loan repayment owed to private international banks. While disbursing loans World Bank and IMF required the governments of borrowing nations to carry out drastic policy changes, which are collectively known as new economic policy or economic reforms.

India was almost without any foreign debt in 1982, says Arthur Gunder Frank, peak of so called third world debt crisis but joined the ranks of most indebted third world countries by 1992, peak of implementation of new economic policy. This gives valid scepticsm as to countries might have been made indebted in order to tame them compliable to policy prescriptions. Because in the loan conditionalities of World Bank and IMF market oriented approach has been commonly intertwined. Market orienting the economy by implementing new economic policy has both opportunities and challenges. Whether sinister development predominates over benign consequence must be articulated as it is linked with the life and welfare of the people.

The henchmen of new economic policy advocate that the need for new economic policy arise due to poor performance of the economy under "license-permit raj". License-permit raj was the economic environment featured by stringent licensing procedures, protectionism, subsidies, ceiling on assets size, family fiefdoms, extraordinary concentration of power in the hands of politicians and bureaucrats and corruption. In other words interventionist government is responsible for poor economic growth so new economic policy is needed to dismantle all these controls. Implications of nuances of this neoliberal policy and agencies that suggested these policies and the time that they sequenced are to be addressed in order to understand the concerns that have emerged and started to intensify further during more than two decades of experience with it.

Emerging Concerns

It is a common knowledge that new economic policy creates a liberalized, privatized and globalised economic framework. In this framework market is supposed to determine everything, however in practice market forces of demand and supply are manipulated by a much stronger force the big oligopolistic transnational companies. So in the hands of these forces mankind is likely to suffer a lot. Liberalisation implies governments have no say in the economic affairs of the country. Privatisation implies market has everything to say while globalisation could mean more of liberalization and privatization because of integration with global economy would bring in foreign players.

The first and prominent argument in favour of new economic policy is that it has resulted in moving India in to higher growth trajectory, in the region near 6 percent per annum. True, however some argue that this has been jobless growth. Every one would have been happy with this higher growth rate had it been bestowed equal benefit out of growth for all. This growth ensured maximum profit for funds that float about globally as has been stated in the key reform message of World Bank and IMF. It implies that higher growth rate has not lowered poverty but enhanced prosperity of select few. Top multinational corporations controlling 16 percent of worlds productive assets in 1990 have increased to 33 percent in 2000 with a growth rate of 288 percent between 1990 and 1997 bear out this fact. With this justification of achieving higher growth rate what has happened. Who takes the larger share in the pie? This can be explained by sectoral growth rate of GDP.

Sectoral Changes

Sectoral changes indicate the permeating impact growth has caused on different sectors of the economy. It is a common knowledge that contribution of three sectors of the economy- primary, secondary and tertiary sectors- to the GDP and total employment generation of a nation will undergo drastic changes. So each of the three sectors will register different rates of growth. An analysis of growth rates after implementation of new economic policy would reveal who has gained and lost and by how much.

Year	*Primary*	*Secondary*	*Tertiary*
1985-86 to 1989-90	5.72	8.66	8.83
1991-92 to 1994-95	3.77	8.04	6.40
1995-96 to 1999-2000	1.95	4.99	7.20

Source: CSO.

Table indicates that primary sector growth rate declined from 5.72 to 3.77 and to 1.95 after economic reforms was enforced. Secondary sector too does not take exception to this decelerating trend to come down from 8.55 to 8.04 and to 4.99. Tertiary sector took a dip from 8.83 to 6.40 but gained later to record 7.20 level of growth rate.

Still Indian agriculture supports two third of her population while generating one fourth of total income (GDP). When growth prospects in this sector become gloomy vast chunk of population had been pushed in to vicious living standard, perhaps due to dwindling government support. We could have praised economic reforms if loss in one sector of the economy has been replenished by better one in the next sector. Those ruled out of the benefits of growth in agriculture were declined in the industrial sector, which also recorded dismal growth rate. Tertiary sector after a brief deceleration up to 1994-95 have gained momentum for growth. This being service sector does not possess impetus to generate jobs sufficiently to make good the loss in other sector. However, it significantly contributes to Gross Domestic Product. Hence benefit of growth goes to the people belong to this sector albeit few.

One grave concern due to service sector dominated economy under framework designed by new economic policy is that it gives ample scope for withdrawing foreign investment by private foreign players. Sometimes it could happen in a week's time jeopardizing internal stability of the economy.

Dismal Investment Scenario

One major consequence of new economic policy has been a decline in saving and investment ratios. This is largely because, according to Prof. Biplab Dasgupta of Kolkata University, and M.P. (upper house) a decline in public investment carried out in order to reduce fiscal deficit has not been compensated by a corresponding increase in private investment. Supporters of economic reforms hold the view that liberal economic policy would ensure that future economic growth would result from increased efficiency of investment rather than rises in the level of investment. They meant that investment funds were inefficiently spent once new economic policy is implemented inefficient use of resources would be corrected and efficiency would be restored. The same level of investment would result in more growth. In short, reforms would accelerate growth nevertheless it is unable to bring in more investment.

Professors C.P. Chandrasekhar and Jayathi Ghosh of Jawaharlal Nehru University, however have disproved this notion and showed the rates of investment for India to increase from 20.3 percent in 1990-91 to touch a peak of 26.8 percent in 1995-96 and then declined to stagnate at around 23 percent at the close of the decade.

Government Role Undermined

A major thrust of new economic policy is cut backs in government expenditure for reducing fiscal deficit. There is viable alternative option is available to achieve the same objective that is increasing revenue of the government by taxing those who are able to pay. New economic policy didn't emphasis this aspect. A reduction in government expenditure undermines the role of the state. Role of the state is positively associated with growth when it is undermined economic growth will suffer. And when government is forced to reduce expenditure the axe falls on capital expenditure and social expenditure. Low capital expenditure on irrigation, power and other major rural infrastructure would bring down level of output. Downscale in social expenditure, say on education or health or social security measures has myriad impact besides affecting the quality of human resource of the country.

Agriculture

Notwithstanding every aspect of new economic policy is likely to do agriculture badly, reduction in subsidies, revision in agricultural prices, reduction in powers of state marketing boards and removal of quantitative restrictions have more and direct power to damage agriculture.

Prices of agricultural commodities not only have been lowered but also become unstable on account of dissolution or dilution of powers of state marketing boards. Some commodities has fetched reasonable prices but because of higher minimum support price (MSP) determined by the government. Of late the revision by government of India in MSP has not been reasonable and in Punjab farmers along with the Chief Minister of the state have agitated against central government for a reasonable revision in MSP. The benefit that is due to the MSP has been negated by higher input prices owing to withdrawal of subsidies and in its part withdrawal of power subsidies too pluck out its due from farmers income.

The most serious consequence of reforms in agriculture is gargantuan shoot up in suicides by farmers due to debt and starvation. The toll is to exceed 25000 since 1996 according to estimation by Dr. Vandana Shiva, a development activist. The proponents of new economic policy should keep in mind that

USA is offering $ 300 billion of subsidies to her farmers and entire West has been resolute in guarding subsidies in Cancun WTO Ministerial Conference held on 10th to 14th of September 2003, to the distortion of world trade in agriculture.

Industry–A Sector with Mixed Concerns

Industry is the sector that has been first subjected to new economic policy influence during 1980s. Delicensing and deregulation were the first instruments to dismantle stricter internal controls that led to flexibility in the operations of domestic capital. This period lasted up to 1990 was featured by internal liberalization with effective control by government which yielded 7.8 percent growth in Index for Industrial Production. However, when economic reforms were implemented further in full form in 1990s foreign trade, foreign exchange transactions and foreign investment were liberalized the index for industrial production growth rate fell down to 6.7 percent between 1990-91 and 2000-01.

Prof. C.P. Chandrasekhar and Jayathi Ghosh have explained this trend in terms of two consequences. First, it resulted in some displacement of existing domestic production either directly by imports or indirectly by new products assembled domestically from imported inputs. Second, since it involved closer adherence to fiscal deficit targets in a period of falling tax revenues the stimulus provided to industrial growth by state expenditure was substantially smaller than was the case in the 1980s. Stronger and vibrant economy is possible only with rapid industrial progress because it provides stability to the economy, while agriculture and service sector lack consistency. Such a crucial sector when left unprotected due to changes in economic policies the economy is in great turmoil.

Unemployment

Sinister development of economic reforms is deeply felt in employment front. It is widely argued that new economic policy will generate more employment through liberalized industrial policy and inflow of foreign capital. In reality, however, the most cases of foreign capital inflow take place in the form of merger, amalgamation, joint ventures and other strategic alliances. It implies mere change in ownership not new ventures. For existing firms change hand, the employment level would not surge up.

With the invasion of foreign capital, the labour saving capital-intensive technology too comes in to the developing countries, which have abundant labour supply. This left these countries in a gloomy context of unemployment of the mass. Dr. (Mrs.) Mahajan attributed the following factors to have raised the level of unemployment in the post-reforms period: (a) Competition from multinational corporations due to liberalization (b) closure of factories due to competition and world recession (c) government policy of downsizing public sector labour force through voluntary retirement scheme and ban on fresh recruitment.

New economic policy goes hand in hand with privatization policies, pulling down public investment thereby reducing existing employment opportunities in public sector. Now, that the Indian economy has passed through two decades of changed macro economic setting. As believed by James Madison "institutions that deliver good performance under one setting may no longer deliver once the setting has changed".

In Indian case neither the institutions under old setting under reform regime nor under changed setting have not delivered good, rather deteriorated further. Many sincere attempts have been made recently to assess the propensity of globalisation to generate employment. Worth deserving piece was given by Dubashi, who rightly stated: "Foreign imports have killed off thousands of small and medium industries in India, as many as 4,00,000 according to and estimate. A number of industries have closed down in several cities and towns... Since everybody cannot be a software engineer and take off for Silicon Valley, thousands, if not lakhs of people, have lost their jobs". So, it can be stated that globalisation has not only failed to make the economies vibrant enough to generate more employment but also pushed many off their jobs". Employment elasticity measures employment generation due to a change in policy. So it is used to analyse employment growth rates in India to discuss trend in employment growth during the past two decades.

There has been anomalous growth trend in India as the economy experienced an accelerated growth with a corresponding deceleration in the growth of employment, jobless economic growth as a result of new economic policy. The steady decline in the employment elasticity in all the major sectors of the economic activity except in construction sector explains the fact clearly. The purpose of the concept of employment elasticity is to show by how much the level of employment will rise or fall in response to a given shift in the supply of labour.

Employment Elasticity in Major Sectors

Sector	*1983-84 to 1993-94*	*1997-98 to 2001-02*
Agriculture	0.50	0.50
Mining and Quarrying	0.67	0.60
Manufacturing	0.33	0.25
Construction	1.00	0.60
Electricity	0.50	0.50
Wholesale and Retail Trade	0.60	0.55
Transport, Storage and Communications	0.47	0.55
Financing, Real Estate, Insurance and Business Services	0.90	0.53
Community, Social and Personal Services	0.59	0.50
All Sectors	0.40	0.38

Source: Government of India, Planning Commission, Ninth Five-Year Plan 1997-2002, Volume 1, Table 4.6, p.189.

Employment elasticity for all sectors of the economy declined from 0.40 during 1983-84 to 1993-94 to 0.38 during 1997-98 to 2001-02. The former is the period during which liberalization and privatization policies put in to force and latter is the globalisation era. Hence, it is discernible that these policies failed to generate employment opportunities albeit they deliver good economic growth. Naturally, a scepticsm arises in the minds of every one as to who enjoys the benefit of new economic policy.

Proponents of economic reforms believe that employment would primarily pickup because the output growth is likely to rise up after reforms are taken to roots. Critics, however project that employment would not increase proportionately with growth of output, because of labour saving effects of reforms. Following table gives precise picture of employment growth rate in India during the past two decades.

		Employment	
	Rural	*Urban*	*Total*
Work status/Principal status			
1983-84 to 1993-94	1.74	3.21	2.05
1993-94 to 1999-00	1.23	2.62	1.56

Source: NSS Data.

The content of the table is more than a sufficient evidence to prove the declining tendency of the employment level in terms of principal status. Rural, urban and total employment levels invariably declined as displayed in the table. In the 1990's there were criticisms that export pessimism and inward import substitution policy were responsible for the slow rate of employment growth. It is followed from this that opening up the economy will facilitate trade and growth and all would contribute to more employment. Based on the 55th Round of the National Sample Survey, it is found that there is a sharp decline in the rate of employment generation across both rural and urban areas.

Rural Employment

India is the largest rural economy with a two third of the people to sustain on it. This sector is ironically losing the state support in budgetary and plan fronts. Neglecting this sector is neglecting the vast majority of this nation who are already struggling for their bread. Diversification of employment away from agriculture towards secondary and service sector employment is a positive sign of development. But the main dynamic source of rural employment is the government expenditure in the form of subsidies and rural employment programmes. During the 80's the flow of resources to rural areas raised the rural demand which resulted in the diversification of the self-employed from agriculture to non-agriculture.

But the Macro economic strategy from 1991 has been associated with stagnation of employment generation in the organized sector and declining employment in the public sector. In addition to this reversal process, there have been cuts in central government revenue expenditure on rural development and anti-poverty schemes. There is a substantial reduction in energy and infrastructure investments in rural areas. It is to be noted that financial liberalization measures effectively reduced the availability of rural credit and therefore possibilities for rural enterprise development. Neglecting the rural sector in the economic policies of various governments from 90's is the major cause for the raising rural unemployment.

Poverty Worsened

While India's Gross Domestic Product is growing at 6 percent every year under new economic policy regime it has done little for India's poor shows data evidence. It is worth to mention here that the progress made during 1980's in poverty alleviation was reversed in 1990's the reform and WTO decade.

During 1980's the below poverty line proportion has declined by more than 10 percent and around five crore moved away from the clutches of poverty. An opposite was happened in 1990's. There was no secular decline in either of it. Trend for rural India was worse than urban. Poverty estimates suggest that faster economic growth peer se does not lead to a more rapid fall in poverty. Growth will not reduce poverty (Trickle down theory) is proved again. Workable programmes focused at fighting poverty alone will serve the purpose. Such programmes significantly served in 1980's despite associated leakages. With a view to reducing deficit government expenditure on poverty eradicating programmes has been vastly curtailed in 1990's subsequently the anti-poor trend has set in. Coupled with this the neglect of agriculture, as a part of new economic policy agenda seems to have worsened rural poverty further.

Income and regional inequalities that appear in tandem with poverty also have widened. As a result of new economic policy some states have raced ahead while others had to fall behind. States like Uttar Pradesh and Bihar become poormen's home with little or no economic growth. Orissa, Madhya Pradesh and North Eastern States too have joined the list. Per capita income of people living in other rich states is steadily surging.

Falling Tax Revenues

Tax revenues have tended to fall down as economic reforms intensified. Revenue enhancing tax reforms were allegedly ignored by World Bank-IMF prescribed new economic policy prescriptions. In the name of procedural simplifications tax powers of the Government were scaled down. While freeing international trade and improving market access tariff were reduced to the barest possible minimum. In order to promote investor friendly industrial climate commodity indirect taxes (both excise duty and sales tax) concessions and reductions were constantly on the agenda in the reform driven budgets. Excise duty reduction from 32 percent to 24 percent for soft drinks and computers in the current 2003–04 budget is good case point here. Intra company transactions among multinational companies and their subsidiaries through accounting pricing or transfer prices chunk of corporate income is silently escaping tax liabilities to accumulate in tax havens (low tax nations). All these have fragiled the very root of revenue to the state through tax that has declined from 11.8 percent of GDP during 1985-1990 to 9.95 percent and to 8.89 percent during 1991-96 and 1996-2001 respectively. It is supposed that in order to cope with this declining funds the World Bank and IMF dictates are prescribing targeted cut backs in public expenditure to achieve fiscal deficit below 3 percent.

New Economic Policy–Recent Trends

After more than a decade since new economic policy reformed the Indian economy the instigators behind the policy World Bank and IMF are taking reforms to the states of Indian union to penetrate deep in to the economy. Bringing down government expenditure in the pretext of phasing out fiscal deficit has substantially undermined the role and size of the government. In federal set up some functions of the government are exclusive powers of the state governments. Among those functions some are crucial and if governments' presence is withdrawn from such functions private both domestic and foreign players can venture in and earn enormous profits. For instance, sectors like education, public health, electricity supply etc. are under exclusive control of the state governments. These are monopoly niche areas that multinationals look for. Domestic players, to allure foreign players, are enjoying unlimited profits in these sectors. In order to make state governments compliable the World Bank and Asian Development Bank are adopting state government centered strategy, for which a four point programme is chalked out viz., containing fiscal deficit below three percent of Gross State Domestic Product (GSDP) over 3 to 5 year period, elimination of subsidies including power subsidy, reduction of governments' administrative cost of governance and privatization of state owned public enterprises including disinvestments. These programmes are to be strictly abided by the states aspiring for loan from the international financial institutions. These four points are nothing but the reforms imposed by World Bank and IMF in their Structural Adjustment Loans in 1980's.

Andhra Pradesh, Karnataka, Orissa, Maharashtra, Uttar Pradesh and Tamilnadu are the states queuing for Structural Adjustment Loan from World Bank and Asian Development Bank. The guidelines ate common to all states seeking loan assistance. These loans are different from project specific loan in that it is obligatory on the part of states to achieve broader objectives instead of undertaking a specific project. With the pretext of monitoring and reviewing the adherence to the four point policy prescriptions the World Bank and IMF officials constantly keep touch with state governments and likely to read the budget line by line and dictate terms as they had with central government.

Consequent to the Tamilnadu governments' efforts for obtaining assistance from World Bank, it has slashed subsidies, raised taxes for Rs. 1420 crore in last two years, sells of state owned companies and cooperative sugar mills and cuts perks and pensions of employees. Cut in subsidies and hike in taxes would affect poor and middle class. Privatisation of state owned enterprises and cooperative sugar mills are likely to be a nightmare for lakhs and lakhs of workers. This together with down scaling of government expenditure and size would increase labour supply abundantly that would benefit only foreign private firms that are already rushing for outsourcing their operations in India. This sudden rush of firms could push up wage level to a decent high had these reforms not been implemented. So for workers and ample opportunity for earning handsome wage is lost. Cut backs in pension poses a great threat for lakhs of senior citizen that too their proportion is increasing in the total population as a result of enhanced average life expectancy thanks to medical advancements. Pruning down of pension schemes will also help private pension scheme sellers, which are earnestly eying on Indian geriatric market. Social safety nets even at the dying age too have not been exempted from market and profit point of view of new economic policy. Besides these, the renewed visit of reforms to states would reinforce the already prevailing anguish trend in the country.

Conclusion

The greatest flaw with new economic policy is that it requires implementing nations to adjust their economies to the world economic order designed by the Brettonwoods institutions, World Bank, International Monetary Fund and World Trade Organisation. This order is clandestinely designed to suit the interests of developed nations more specifically the interests of the giant transnational corporations. These institutions never insisted the developed nations to adopt policy changes as it had with other nations. USA is under pressure with one of its worst trade deficits for which the country is blaming China, its largest trading partner. Are Brettonwoods institutions prepared to prescribe any policy change or conditionality to reduce deficit. Country specific, context specific and time specific economic policies that would render good to the entire mass living in a nation alone are need of the hour. Not the one that is dictated by an external agency that is in service of commercial interest.

REFERENCES

Biplab Dasgupta, (1998), Structural Adjustment, Global Trade and the New Political Economy of Development, Vistar Publications.

Chandrasekhar, C.P. and Jayathi Ghosh, (2002), The Market That Failed, Left Word Books.

Kurien, C.T., (1994), Global Capitalism and the Indian Economy, Orient Longman Ltd., Hyderabad.

Mourice Dobb, (1968), Papers on Capitalism, Development and Planning, Routledge and Kegan Paul Ltd., London.

Sing C. Chew and Robert A. Denemark, (1999), The Development of Underdevelopment (Ed.), Sage Publications, New Delhi.

Vaidyanathan, A., (1995), The Indian Economy–Crisis, Response, and Prospects, Orient Longman Ltd., Hyderabad.

Haja Mohideen, A.J. and Hidhayathulla, A. Globalisation and Employment: Dismal Display in India, *Unpublished Seminar Paper Presented in Indo-Canadian Studies Seminar on Globalisation.*

5

ECONOMIC REFORMS AND POVERTY IN COIMBATORE

S.R. Choodambigai

Introduction

It is very difficult to define the term 'Poverty' as there is nothing 'absolute' about poverty and the concept is essentially a relative one. In the materialistic sense, a poor person is one who lacks means to procure necessities of life. Though it appears to be a straight-forward definition, in fact it is not so, because there is no universal agreement on what "necessities" of life are. The situation becomes even more confounded because inadvertently, 'money' is considered synonymous with 'means' in the above definition. It is not the word 'money' but the word 'more money' which implies the concept of poverty. It is always relative, 'A' who is starving is not poor in isolation. He is poor when compared to 'B' who has something to eat. Going a step further 'B' is poor when compared to 'c' who is having not only plenty of food, but also good food. Thus, the concept is purely relative. Drawing a poverty line is more or less an arbitrary proposition. However, for quantifying the extent of poverty, economists adopt some economic indictors or measures to indicate the number of people below the poverty line. Generally, income of the people is taken as the indicator of poverty or affluence. Spending or per capita expenditure is also taken as the indicator of poverty. The 'intake of food' and the 'standard of living' are also taken into consideration in measuring the extent of poverty. Whatever may be the method adopted, the term poverty is not an economic abstraction, but a human condition. It is despair, grief and pain which cannot be measured.

Pt. Jawaharlal Nehru in his famous 'Tryst with Destiny" speech fifty years ago said, "The future is not ease of resting but of incessant striving so that we may fulfill the pledges we have so often taken and one we shall take today. The services of India mean the service of the millions who suffer. It means the ending of poverty and ignorances and disease and inequality of opportunity". Amartya Sen observed "Poverty is a man made phenomenon in the sense that it is the result of the self-interest of the powerful few, who have established a type of socio-economic structure which necessarily creates and perpetuates poverty". Prof. A.K. Sen conceptualized poverty with the help of poor entitlement of living. An entitlement refers to resources, which make the poor capable of getting bundle of commodities in exchange.

Lord Boyd-Orr, the first Director General of FAO was the first person to profound the notion of starvation line in 1945. According to him, a consumption of less than 2,300 calories per person per day was considered as the line of starvation and this idea has been transformed into 'poverty line'. The Indian Planning Commission has defined the poverty line on the basis of recommended nutritional requirements of 2,400 calories per person per day for rural areas and 2,100 calories per person per day for urban areas. The working group consisting of Prof. Gadgil, Dr. V.K.R.V. Rao, Dr. P.S. Lokanathan, Dr. Ganguli and Ashok Mitra worked out the poverty line in India and recommended a standard of private consumption at Rs. 240/- per capita per year at 1960-61 prices as the barest minimum. This means a person consuming less than 67 paise worth of food is considered to be living below the poverty line. Based on this criterion, 58 percent of the population were living below the poverty line during the period 1953 to 1958 and 48 percent of the population were living below the poverty line in 1967-68. According to the estimate of 48th round of NSS during 1991-92 in India around 331.7 millions of people (38.5 percent) are below the poverty line and 272.8 million of them (43.02 percent) are in the rural areas. The poverty line in India is defined with reference to consumer expenditure surveys. As per the Ninth plan, a person is living below the Poverty line when his annual income is less than Rs. 15,480 for urban areas and Rs 13,680 for rural areas.

Absolute poverty is defined by comparing personal or household income or expenditure with the cost of buying a given quantity of goods and services. Relative poverty is defined by comparing that income with the income of others. Subjective poverty is defined by comparing actual income against the income earners expectations and perceptions. There is no scientific and unequivocal definition of who is poor and who is not (Nandlal and Sharma, 1999). As percent UNICEF statistics, out of the total global population of 5.7 billion, 1.55 billion are poor, and their number grows by 25 million every year at the rate of 45 babies born poor every minute. Out of 1.55 billion people languishing in painful poverty, 1/9 billion hail from developing countries, which constituted a third of their population. India alone is the home of 34 percent of the world poor.

The report of the United Nations on the state of the world's health observed that poverty is the biggest single cause of death, disease and suffering. The World Bank defines the world's poor as those who live on less than dollar a day. The Human Development Report 1996 depicted a gloomy picture of the plight of the poor in developing countries. "Around 17 million people die each year from curable infectious and parasitic diseases such as diarrhea, malaria and tuberculosis of the world's 18 million HIV infected people, more than 90 percent live in developing countries. Nearly 130 million children at the primary level and 275 million at the secondary level are still out of school. Nearly 500 million people do not get enough food and about 500 million people are chronically malnourished.

According to the revised estimates of the planning commission (released in December 1996), 37 percent of the population lived below the poverty line in 1993-94. But this estimate is alarming. Between 1983-84 and 1987-88 the poverty ration fell from 45 percent to 39 percent, decline of six percentage points over just four years, whereas between 1987-88 and 1993-94 the incidence of poverty declined by only two percentage points to 37 percent, over a period of six years. In absolute terms, the number of poor increased in 1993-94 from 1987-88. The progress of Nations Reports 1996, released jointly by the Government of India and UNICEF, States that 53 percent of all under-five children in India are underweight which is an indication of malnutrition.

To highlight the views on poverty among different states in India the study provides Table 1 and the incidence of the poverty in India over years in given in Figure 1.

With regard to the causes for poverty first of all, the increasing population in our country stands as a block not only for our technical development but also for an ordinary individual to earn for his everyday life. This is because the growth of production is less than the growth of population. Secondly, technical improvements are quite slow when compared to other countries which in turn causes the mineral resources to remain untapped. This leads to the production of low quality goods. In addition to this, natural calamites play their own role for the deterioration of our country. More over, the standard of education in our country is uncompetable with other highly literate nations and hence we had to face the problem of unemployment. Besides these factors, one of the major problems for India to remain underdeveloped is the most prominent gender inequality.

With this background and attempt has been made by the investigator to make a study on "Economic Reforms And Poverty in India. A case study with respect to selected areas in

Table 1: Percentage of Population below Poverty Line by States in India-1999-2000

State	*Rural*	*Urban*	*Combined*
Andhra Pradesh	11.05	26.63	15.77
Arunachal Pradesh	40.04	7.47	33.47
Assam	40.04	7.47	36.09
Bihar	44.30	32.91	42.60
Goa	1.35	7.52	4.40
Gujarat	13.17	15.59	14.07
Haryana	8.27	9.99	8.74
Himachal Pradesh	7.94	4.63	7.63
Jammu & Kashmir	3.97	1.98	3.48
Karnataka	17.38	25.25	20.04
Kerala	9.38	20.27	12.72
Madhya Pradesh	37.06	38.44	37.43
Maharashtra	23.72	26.81	25.02
Manipur	40.04	7.47	28.54
Meghalaya	40.04	7.47	33.87
Mizoram	40.04	7.47	19.47
Nagaland	40.04	7.47	32.67
Orissa	48.01	42.83	47.15
Punjab	6.35	5.75	6.16
Rajasthan	13.74	19.85	15.28
Sikkim	40.04	7.47	36.55
Tamil Nadu	20.55	22.11	21.12
Tripura	40.04	7.47	34.44
Uttar Pradesh	31.22	30.89	31.15
West Bengal	31.85	14.86	27.02
Andaman & Nicobar Islands	20.55	22.11	20.99
Chandigarh	5.75	5.75	5.75
Dadar & Nagar Haveli	17.57	13.52	17.14
Daman & Diu	1.35	7.52	4.44
Delhi	0.40	9.42	8.23
Lakshadweep	9.38	20.27	15.60
Pondicherry	20.55	22.11	21.67
All India	27.09	23.62	26.10

Source: Planning Commission, Economic Survey, 2000-2001.

Figure 1: Incidence of Poverty In India

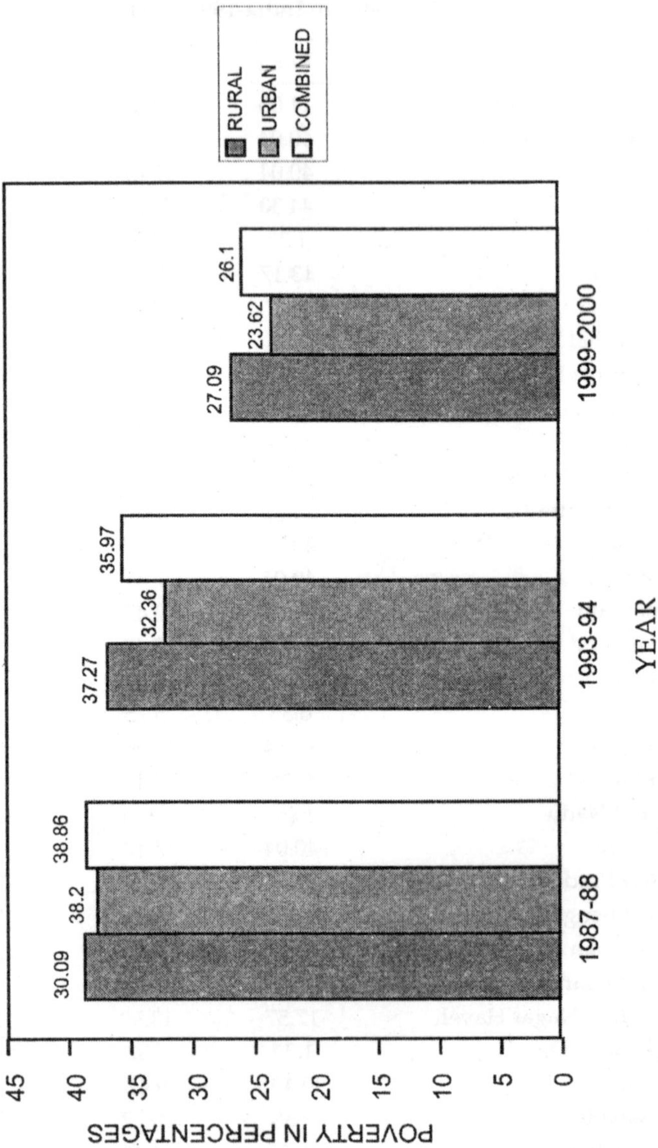

Coimbatore" with the objectives of examining the incidence of poverty in different states of India, investigating the relationship between health, education, gender inequality and poverty in India and locating the effects and changes in Education and Health on the incidence of poverty of the selected samples.

The topic will be discussed with three sections

(i) Reviewing the studies of the economic reforms and poverty reduction,

(ii) Analytical approach to poverty in India,

(iii) Case study on extent of poverty of selected samples in Coimbatore.

Methodology

The investigator selected 15 major states to estimate the extent of poverty in India for the period (1993–94) per which the data is available. Due to the inaccessibility of data for related variables like health, education and gender inequality for the year 1999-2000 which happened to be the latest estimate of poverty, the investigator had done a small sample survey in Coimbatore to supplement the past estimates. [Annexure 1] In Coimbatore district, Vangimanagar of Thondamuthur region and Rangapuram in Ondipudur region were purposely selected for the study because of the proximity of these regions to the investigator. In both the areas, population are deprived of the basic necessities of life and their income also falls below Rs.1,500 per month. An interview schedule was administered among the informants to collect the required information. The secondary data for India on cross-section basis were obtained from the various issues of economic survey, statistical abstracts and manpower profile of India published by government of India, economic division, ministry of finance and institute of applied manpower research, New Delhi.

Hypothesis tested in the course of the study

1. For the analysis of the extent of poverty in India:

   Incidence of poverty would be high if there exist

   (a) Low level of education

(b) Low level of health facilities and
(c) High gender inequality

2. For the case study
Incidence of poverty would be high in areas with
(a) High incidence of illiteracy
(b) High dependency ratio and
(c) Huge amount of debt

Economic growth has been attempted to be measured by economic welfare approach. In this direction, the most widely accepted approach is Physical Quality of Life Index (PQLI), which is based on percentage of literacy rate, infant mortality rate per 1000 live births, life expectancy at birth etc. (Morris D. Morris, 1982).

The investigator also had tried to combine the impact of all this variables and as a result to study the relationship between population below poverty line, education, health and gender inequality of India, multiple regression of the form given below were fitted to the data.

$$PL = a0 + a_1 ED + a_2 HE + a_3 GI + U_i$$

Where PL refers to population below poverty line

ED refers to education

HE refers to health

Gl refers to general inequality

U_i is the random disturbance term and

a_0, a_1, and a_3 are regression co-efficients.

In the case of primary data, to study the relationship between consumption expenditure, per capita income, number of workers in the family, supplementary income and size of the family of the sample households, multiple regression models were fitted to the data for both the regions and the form is

$$Y = \beta_0 + \beta_1 X_1 + \beta_2 X_2 + \beta_3 X_3 + \beta_4 X_4 + U$$

Where Y refers to the total consumption expenditure of the sample households

X_1 refers to the per capita income of the sample households

X_2 refers to the number of workers in the family

X_3 refers to supplementary income of the family

X_4 refers to the size of the family of the sample households

β_0, β_1, β_2, β_3 and β_4 are regression co-efficients and U refers to a constant term.

Gini co-efficient was used to measure the income inequalities in the two regions. The study had applied

Gini co-efficient =1+1n-2n ΣQ_i

where Q_i refers to the ith cumulative proportion of the expenditure classes.

N refers to the number of expenditure classes (i.e. 0-400, 401-600, 601-800, 801-1000, 1001-1200, 1201-1300).

Principal component analysis was used in analyzing the extent of poverty in India to reduce the number of explanatory variables without losing any of it for health and gender inequality i.e., to get the composite index of health and gender inequality,

(i) $HE = a_0 + a_1 X_1 + a_2 X_2 + a_3 X_3 + a_4 X_4 + a_5 X_5 + a_6 X_6$

where

X_1 = infant mortality rate

X_2 = life expectancy

X_3 = number of hospitals

X_4 = number of beds in hospitals

X_5 = persons per bed

X_6 = persons per hospital

(ii) $GI = b_0 + b_1 X_1 + b_2 X_2$

where

X_1 = sex ratio

X_2 = female literacy rate

For the case study, the method of principal component analysis was used to examine the factors influencing the incidence of poverty. The basic variables used for the analysis were as follows:

X_1 = Supplementary income

X_2 = Debt position

X_3 = Dependency rate

X_4 = Education of the head (Dummy variable 0 for illiterates, 1 for primary level, 2 for secondary level, 3 for higher secondary and 4 for college level of education)

X_5 = size of the family

X_6 = number of workers in the family

X_7 = per capital income

SECTION – I

Reviewing the studies on Economic Reforms and poverty reduction

Economic Reforms in India were introduced in 1991 by the Congress (I) government led by Mr. P.V. Narasimha Rao. It spells out a dar strategy for poverty reduction. There are three facets of poverty and they are:

1. Removing income poverty by enhancing opportunity,
2. Facilitating empowerment of the poor and
3. To provide security to overcome risks due to ill health, economic shocks due to natural disasters and violence.

Impact of Economic Reforms

Reforms and Poverty

There is no doubt that economic reforms have been able to promote a relatively higher growth. After the teething troubles of the first two years viz., 1991-92 and 1992-93, the growth rate during 1993-94 to 1997-98 has averaged to more than 7 percent per annum (Table 2). After 1991-92, the momentum of growth has been maintained providing increasing evidence that the growth potential has improved as a result of the reforms initiated in 1991. The growth rate during the Eighth Plan (1992-97) period works out to be 6.8 percent. There is no doubt that after 1992-93 the economy picked up and the growth rate reached and average level of 7 percent during the 4- year period (1994-95 to 1997-98).

Table 2: GDP Growth (at factory cost) at 1993-94 Prices

Year	*GDP (Rs. Crores)*	*GDP Growth Rate*
1980-81	4,01,128	
1990-91	6,92,871	
1991-92	7,01,863	1.3
1992-93	7,37,792	5.1
1993-94	7,81,345	5.9
1994-95	8,38,031	7.3
1995-96	8,99,563	7.3
1996-97	9,70,083	7.8
1997-98	10,16,399	4.8
1998-99	10,82,474	6.5
1999-00	11,48,500	6.1
2000-01	11,93,922	4.0
Annual Average GDP Growth Rate		
1980-81 to 1990-91		5.6
1990-91 to 2000-01		5.6

Source: Complied and computed from CSO, National Accounts Statistics (2000) and earlier issues.

However, thereafter, GDP growth showed signs of deceleration. If we compare the annual average growth rate during the pre-reform period (1980-91) which was of the order of 5.6 percent per annum, then the post-reform decade (1990-91 to 2000-01) also shows the same average annual growth rate of 5.6 percent of real GDP. Obviously, the reform process has not been able to establish its distinct superiority over the pre-reform period. The major issue is to accelerate the growth rate and re-orient the content of reform so that it can make a definite dent on poverty.

(a) Economic Reforms and Reduction of Poverty

At the 41st Annual Conference of the Indian Society of Labour Economics, Dr. S.P. Gupta, member, Planning Commission delivering V.B. Singh Memorial Lecture on November 18, 1999 captioned 'Trickledown Theory Revisited: The Role of Employment and Poverty' surveyed the progress that has taken place in the era of economic reforms after 1991 and the period preceding the reforms. Dr. Gupta brought out the disquieting fact: "In India, the poverty reduction (i.e., reduction of the percentage of people below the poverty line) over 1983 to 1990-91 was around 3.1 percent per annum, but it reversed to 1 percent in the 1990s i.e., between 1990-91 and 1997. In contrast 1983 to 1990-91 was around 5.6 percent, and between 1990-91 and 1997, this is expected to go beyond 5.7 percent".

Dr. Gupta has underlined the pro-elitist basis of economic reforms when he states: "The inverse relationship observed between poverty reduction and GDP growth becomes even more prominent if one obtains the trends over the recent years. For example, between 1993-94 and 1997, the estimates of poverty reduction went down when poverty percentage (i.e., people below poverty line) increased from 35.07 percent to 37.23 percent in the aggregate. This is the period when GDP growth rate increased to around 6.9 percent per annum, the highest ever, witness consecutively for four years in India".

Dr. Gaurav Datt of the World Bank in his article "Has poverty Declined Since Economic Reforms?" has compared the decline in head-count index, poverty gap index and squared poverty gap index for rural and urban India in the pre-reform and the post-reform period. The main conclusions of the study are as under:

Table: 3 Percentage of People Below Poverty Line 1983-1997

Years	NSS Round	Percentage Rural	Urban	Combined	Absolute Numbers (Million)
1983	(38th) LS	45.65	40.79	44.48	322.8
1987-88	(43rd) LS	39.09	38.20	38.86	304.9
1989-90	(45th) TS	33.70	36.00	34.28	276.0
1990-91	(46th) TS	35.04	35.29	35.11	291.0
1992	(48th) TS	41.70	37.80	40.70	348.0
1993-94	(50th) LS	37.27	32.36	35.07	320.5
1994-95	(51st) TS	38.03	34.24	36.98	329.5
1995-96	(52nd) TS	38.29	30.05	36.08	328.0
1997	(53rd) TS	38.46	33.97	37.23	348.8
1998	(59th) TS				
Six months		45.25	35.48	43.01	406.3

LS = Large Sample TS = Thin Sample.

Source: Household Consumption Survey, NSSO, Government of India.

Mid-1980s seems to be a significant watershed in the evolution of living standards in India....while there was a marked decline in both rural and urban poverty rates between 1973-74 and 1986-87, there is an sign of anything comparable.

For the rural sector, the results indicate that while there was a significant trend decline in all the three poverty measures up to mid-1991 (at an annual rate of 2.7 percent for the headcount index, 4.5 percent for the poverty gap and 5.9 percent for the squared poverty gap index), the rate of decline since then is not significantly different from zero.

For the urban sector, in the pre-reform period (1973-74 to 1990-91), the results indicate a declining trend in all the three poverty measures upto mid-1991 (at annual rate of 2.2 percent for handcount index, 2.8 percent for poverty gap and 3.1 percent for squared poverty gap), the same trend is continued even in the post-reform period (1990-91 to 1996-97) and all the three poverty measures register a decline (at and annual rate of 2.2 percent headçount index, 2.65 percent for poverty gap and 3.7 percent for squared poverty gap).

While the urban sector appears to have continued its trajectory of growth and poverty reduction through the 1990s, rural poverty reduction was choked off by lack of rural growth.

GDP Growth, Employment Growth and Poverty

The question arises: why is it that although GDP growth rates have been very high during the recent years (especially after 1993-94), they have not been accompanied by corresponding reduction in poverty. If poverty implies either unemployment or under-employment or absence of good quality employment, then it would be of interest to study the change in employment scenario before and after the economic reforms. Data provided in Table 4 reveals that total employment increased from 3,026 lakhs in 1983 to about 3,568 lakhs in 1990-91 and then improved to about 3,829 lakhs in 1997-98. The rate of growth of employment was of the order of 2.39 percent per annum during 1983 and 1990-91, which was just equal to the rate of growth of labour force during this period. However, it was hoped that if this rate of growth of employment is sustained in the next decade, the country would be able to reduce the backlog of unemployment significantly. But unfortunately, the period of reforms (1990-91 to 1997-98) reveals that the overall growth rate of employment was only of order of 1.0 percent. It may also be noted that since the reform process is limited to the organised sector, more so to the large corporate sector, the growth rate of employment in the organised sector also decelerated to 0.60 percent during 1990-92 to 1997-98 as against 1.73 percent per annum witnessed in the 7-year pre-reform period of 1983-1990-91. This was just one-third of the growth rate of the employment witnessed earlier. There was also a substantial slowdown in the employment witnessed earlier. There was also a substantial slowdown in the employment rate of the unorganized sector to merely 1.1 percent during 1990-91 to 1997-99 as against employment growth rate of 2.41 percent witnessed during the 7-year pre-reform period (1983 to1990-91). This leads one to the natural conclusion that the trickle down effects of the growth process did not benefit the poor. Dr. S.P. Gupta, therefore, states: "All these trends make one rethink the utility of an exclusive policy on 'GDP growth' in resolving poverty or employment. In contrast, it has been observed that high growth in employment in India has almost always been associated with some reduction in poverty. For example, the period of high growth of employment in the 1980s with a comparatively lower GDP growth has witnessed a significant reduction in poverty. In the 1990s as hypothesized, a low growth of employment is seen to be associated with and increase in poverty.

Table 4: Movement of Employment 1983-1997

Years	*Total*	*Organised Sector*	*Unorganised Sector*
1983	3,026.0	240.1	2,785.9
1990-91	3,567.6	270.6	3,297.0
1997-98	3,828.5	282.3	3,546.0
Growth Rate of Employment Annual Average (percent)			
1983 to 1990-91	2.39	1.73	2.41
1990-91 to 1997-98	1.0	0.6	1.1

Source: Computed from data provided by Household Consumption Survey, NSSO, Government of India.

(b) Poverty and employment

It is evident from Table 4 that percentage of people below the poverty line declined from 44.48 percent of total population in 1983 to 35.11 percent in 1990-91 and the absolute number of persons below the poverty line sharply declined from about 323 million in 1983 to 291 million in 1990-91, but thereafter, during the 7 year period since 1990-91 until 1997, the proportion of people below the poverty line went from 35.1 percent to 37.23 percent. In absolute terms, the number of the poor went up from 291 million in 1990-91 to 349 million in 1997. Obviously, the pattern of growth followed after 1991 reduced employment growth rate to 0.6 percent , meaning thereby that employment elasticity which was of the order of 0.41 during 1983 to 1990-91 slumped to an insignificant figure of 0.1 during 1990-91 to 1997-98.

The above analysis stresses a, dire need for changing the gears of the strategy of growth by shifting emphasis from the production of articles of durable consumption like washing machines, colour TVs, refrigerators, air conditioners and cars to articles of mass consumption of wage goods.

Anolytical Approach to Poverty in India

Population below poverty line at All-India level was 1498.26 lakhs (37.27 percent) in 1993-94 which had decreased from 3030.49 lakhs (38.86 percent) in 1987-88. Bihar had the maximum number of population BPL as 262.35 lakhs (58.21 percent and Punjab had the minimum number of population BPL as 4.74 lakhs (11.95 percent) compared to other states like Assam, Harayana and Kerala which have performed satisfactorily during the reference period. On the whole, the percentage of population BPL had declined gradually from (1987-88.) (Manpower profile of India, 1999). (Table 5).

Table 5: Population below Poverty Line Across States in India During 1987-88 and 1993-94

	POPN.BPL (in lakhs)		*POPN.BPL (in percentages)*	
States	*1987-88*	*1993-94*	*1987-88*	*1993-94*
Andhra Pradesh	160.43	106.10	25.86	23.09
Assam	75.75	19.71	36.21	41.46
Bihar	420.93	262.35	52.13	56.44
Gujarat	122.36	34.28	31.54	23.92
Haryana	25.37	11.07	16.64	24.21
Karnataka	158.61	79.86	37.53	33.18
Kerala	88.48	18.96	31.79	26.82
Madhya Pradesh	264.30	158.34	43.07	42.6
Maharashtra	296.27	154.87	40.41	36.43
Orissa	165.93	101.20	55.58	48.41
Punjab	25.17	4.74	13.20	11.08
Rajasthan	142.90	41.73	35.15	27.68
Tamilnadu	231.07	89.95	43.39	36.63
Uttar Pradesh	536.53	303.88	41.46	40.99
West Bengal	283.61	85.21	44.72	35.69
All-India	3070.49	1498.26	38.86	3727

Source: Manpower profile of India, 1999.

The literacy rate at All India Level was at 57 percent, which had male literacy rate as 69 percent and female literacy rate as 44 percent. Among the total literacy rate, Kerala had the maximum literacy rate as 92 percent, which may be due to awareness of the need of education in life, and Bihar and Rajasthan had the minimum literacy rate as 43 percent and 44 percent respectively. (Table 6)

Table 6: Educational Performance of Different States in India during 1993-94

	Literacy Rates (in percentages)		
States	*Males*	*Females*	*Total*
Andhra Pradesh	58	36	47
Assam	78	62	71
Bihar	57	26	43
Gujarat	76	51	64
Haryana	73	47	61
Karnataka	67	46	57
Kerala	95	89	92
Madhya Pradesh	62	85	49
Maharashtra	79	56	68
Orissa	63	39	51
Punjab	68	55	62
Rajasthan	61	26	44
Tamilnadu	78	55	67
Uttar Pradesh	63	33	49
West Bengal	73	53	64
All-India	69	44	57

Source: Statistical Abstracts, 1998.

The male literacy rate was high at Kerala (95 percent) and it was very low at Bihar (57 percent) and Andhra Pradesh (58 percent). The female literacy rate was high at Kerala (89 percent), which was comparatively lower than the male literacy rate in Kerala. The female literacy rate was low at Bihar (26 percent) respectively. (Statistical Abstracts, 1998).

The total number of hospitals was more in Maharashtra (3115) and it was very less in Haryana (78). The Number of beds was more in Maharashtra (78,920) and in Kerala (77,199) and it was very less in Haryana (7028). Population per hospital was more in Bihar (2,63,335) and it was less in Kerala (14,455). Population per beds was more in Madhya Pradesh (3535) and less in Kerala (382). (Table 7).

Table 7: Health Indicators of Different States in India During 1993-94

Major States	*Total Hospitals*	*Total beds*	*Population per Hospital*	*Population per Bed*	*Infant Mortality Rate (per thousand)*	*Life Expectancy at birth (in years)*
Andhra Pradesh	1863	26791	36474	2536	65	61.8
Assam	268	12661	92973	1968	78	55.7
Bihar	328	29090	263335	2969	67	59.3
Gujarat	2370	58984	17765	714	64	61
Haryana	78	7028	216185	2399	70	63.4
Karnataka	293	37929	156452	1209	67	62.5
Kerala	2040	77199	14455	382	16	72.9
Madhya Pradesh	363	18141	186656	3535	98	54.7
Maharashtra	3115	78920	25921	1023	55	64.8
Orissa	284	14494	113519	2224	103	56.5
Punjab	217	14671	95232	1409	53	67.2
Rajasthan	218	20465	206909	2204	84	59.1
Tamilnadu	408	48780	133903	1120	59	63.3
Uttar Pradesh	735	47278	177506	1271	88	56.8
West Bengal	392	54767	97385	507	62	62.1

Source: Manpower Profile of India, 1998.

The Expectation of Life at birth in years was high in Kerala (72.9) and low in Madhya Pradesh (54.7), Assam (55.7), Orissa (56.5), Rajasthan (59.1) and Bihar (59.3) respectively. Infant mortality rate per thousand was more in Orissa (103) and less in Kerala (16).

Overall the Health indicators of Kerala shows greater improvement and this may be due to improvement in health care facilities and various vaccination programmes like polio drops, tetanus, etc. which had been carried out in the state. But these health indicators are very poor in states like Orissa, Bihar, Assam, Madhya Pradesh and Rajasthan. (Manpower Profile of India, 1998).

Sex ratio was high in Kerala (1040) where there was not much female infanticide and better health facilities. Haryana (874) and Punjab (888) had a very low rate of sex ratio. Kerala (89 percent) and Madhya Pradesh (85 percent) had the high female literacy rate. Bihar (26 percent) and Rajasthan (26 percent) had the lowest female literacy rate. (Census of India, 1991 and Statistical Abstracts, 1988) (Table 8).

Table 8: Gender Inequality in India During 1993-94

Major States	*Sex Ratio*	*Female Literacy*
Andhra Pradesh	972	36
Assam	925	62
Bihar	912	26
Gujarat	936	51
Haryana	874	47
Karnataka	960	46
Kerala	1040	89
Madhya Pradesh	932	85
Maharashtra	936	56
Orissa	972	39
Punjab	888	55
Rajasthan	913	26
Tamilnadu	972	55
Uttar Pradesh	882	33
West Bengal	917	53
All-India	929	44

Source: Census of India, 1991 and Statistical Abstracts, 1998.

The relationship between population below poverty line, education, health and gender inequality has been estimated by fitting multiple regression model. The co-efficients of education and gender inequality is negative and for health it is positive.

The co-efficient of education is significant and others are insignificant due to poor health facilities and high gender inequality. 34 percent of variation in poverty level is explained by the education, health and gender inequality. The result confirms Sen's view that increase in educational facilities, health facilities and gender equality would reduce the poverty in a region. Though these variables of social sector are important for poverty eradication economic variables like per-capita income also have an important role in the reduction of poverty level (Kothari et al. 1998).

SECTION – III

The results of the case study are as under:

Majority of the households were Hindus in both regions and most of them belonged to MBCs and SC/ST. In Thondamuthur, 62 percent of the 50 households and in Ondipudur, 76 percent of the 50 households belonged to MBCs and SC/ST. Remaining constitute the backward and forward castes.

The proportion of nuclear families (80 percent) was greater than that of joint families in both the regions.

A major proportion of 68 percent in Thondamuthur and 77 percent in Ondipudur were in the age group 15-99. Dependency rate in Thondamuthur was 32 percent and in Ondipudur it was 23 percent. Dependency rate is negatively related to per capita income.

The sex ratio in Thondamuthur worked out to be 1116 per thousand males and 1161 in Ondipudur. Thus the sex ratio in Ondipudur was found to be higher than in Thondamuthur.

Ondipudur was clearly ahead of Thondamuthur in terms of literacy. A majority of the population (43 percent) in Ondipudur was educated upto the secondary level whereas in Thondamuthur it was only 28 percent and a very high proportion of the population (43 percent) had no formal education.

The average size of the family was 3.65 in Thondamuthur and 3.72 in Ondipudur.

About 46 percent of the household heads in Thondamuthur and 48 percent in Ondipudur were illiterates. The educational level of the household head is positively associated with the dependency ratio. This implies that there would be a high incidence of poverty among illiterates and the less educated.

Majority of the households were receiving income in the range of Rs. 800-1000. The highest income range was Rs.1,200-1,400, which was received by seven families in Thondamuthur as against ten families in Ondipudur.

The data on per capita expenditure showed that majority of (15) families in Thondamuthur and 12 families in Ondipudur were in the expenditure group of Rs. 600-800. The highest expenditure range was Rs.1,200-1,300.

Supplementary income earned also was not much, but only upto Rs.2,500 per month in both regions. In Ondipudur, two of the sample households had also invested for Rs. 25,000. Ondipudur earns more supplementary income than Thondamuthur since majority of them own land, livestock, etc.

The item-wise expenditure showed that in both the regions the highest percentage of income went for food expenditure, which was around 23.49 percent in Thondamuthur and 22 percent in Ondipudur. This proves Engel's law that as income increases, the proportion of expenditure on food decreases.

A multiple regression model was fitted to the data to explain the marginal propensity to consume. It revealed that the marginal propensity to consume was lower in Ondipudur (0.37) than in Thondamuthur region (0.56). It also indicated that about 60 percent of the variations in consumption was due to per capita income, additional income, number of workers in the family and size of family in Thondamuthur whereas these factors caused about 35 percent of the variations in consumption in Ondipudur region.

The debt position of the sample households indicated that about 44 percent of Thondamuthur had heavy debts whereas 61 percent of the sample households in Ondipudur had debts.

The Lorenz curve fitted to measure inequality in income distribution showed that there were considerable inequalities in income in both regions. Initially, the inequality in Ondipudur was higher and at the income group Rs. 800-1,000 inequalities in both the regions are equal. Later, inequality in Thondamuthur raises in the income group Rs.1,000-1,200 where the inequality in Thondamuthur exceeded than that of Ondipudur. (Figure 2).

Figure 2: Lorenz Curve

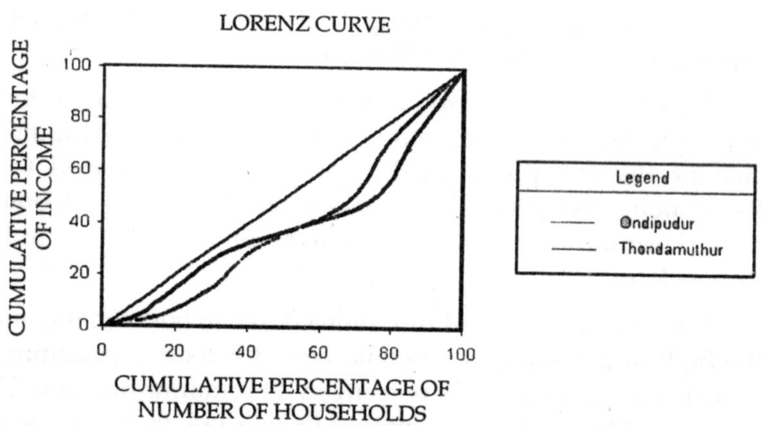

Gini co-efficient was also fitted to measure the level of inequality in both regions. The value of Gini co-efficient was 0.251 for Ondipudur and 0.2515 for Thondamuthur. The greater the value of the Gini co-efficient, the greater would be the income inequality.

The method of principal components analysis was applied to find out the factors affecting the incidence of poverty. It was found that the major factors affecting the level of poverty in both regions were supplementary income, debt position, dependency rate, education of the household head and size of family. These factors together accounted for around 90 percent of the variance in both regions. In this, size of the family caused 10.5 percent of variance in Ondipudur and 8.7 percent in Thondamuthur. These results proved all the three hypothesis of the study that higher level of illiteracy, dependency ratio and huge amount of debt.

The provisions of basic amenities like electricity, toilet., safe drinking water, etc., which are the best indicators of economic development, were very poor in Ondipudur when compared to Thondamuthur. Electricity supply was available only to 62 percent of the household in Thondamuthur whereas 68 percent of the households in Ondipudur had this facility. A mere 14 percent had toilet facilities in Ondipudur as against 28 percent in Thondamuthur. Of the 50 households, only seven had drinking water in their house in Ondipudur whereas 18 households had access to safe drinking water in Thondamuthur.

In Thondamuthur, there was only one high school against five higher secondary schools in Ondipudur. This proves that the educational infrastructure was poor in vangimanagar in Thondamuthur.

In Thondamuthur, about 58 percent were satisfied with the health care facilities while in Ondipudur about 62 percent were satisfied with the facilities available.

Of the 50 sample households surveyed 80 percent possessed ration cards in Thondamuthur whereas 84 percent of the households had ration cards in Ondipudur. In both the regions there were complaints of inadequate supply, irregular supply and long queues. Other than rice, sugar and kerosene, tea was also supplied through Public Distribution System, in Thondamuthur. The commodities supplied in Ondipudur were rice, sugar, kerosene, wheat, and rava. Thus, the functioning of public distribution system was better in Ondipudur region.

There was almost 100 percent awareness among the sample households in both regions about voting rights and vaccination programmes or any such other programmes of the government.

Awareness on family planning programmes and adult education programmes was found to be very poor in Thondamuthur. This may be due to the high illiteracy rate.

Thondamuthur was far behind Ondipudur in terms of infra structure facilities such as transport, telephone booths, post and telegraph office.

Of the 50 households, only 20 percent were satisfied with the functioning of panchayat in Thondamuthur whereas 60 percent were satisfied in Ondipudur.

The results from Lorenz curve (Figure 2) and Gini co-efficient proved that there is higher income inequality in vangimanagar in Thondamuthur than in Rangapuram of Ondipudur which implies that the poverty level is higher in vangimanagar which may be due to poor socio-economic status in terms of literacy, income level, debt position etc. on the other hand, facilities, basic amenities, health care facilities, public distribution system are all functioning better in Rangapuram than in Vangimanagar. The functioning of panchayats was also better in Rangapuram in the sense it provides better drinking water and sanitation facilities.

Based on the research arrived at it is suggested that the strategy to be followed by the second generation reforms should lead to the following ends:

Illiteracy combine with unemployment and low income among the people keeps them in a state of poverty. Therefore, spread of education both at primary level and for adults and imparting skills in particular among the people reducing the dropouts is essential: Development of infrastructure facilities like transport, telecom facilities, post office, etc: Primary health care centers have to be established and vaccination programmes and awareness about infectious diseases, cancer, AIDS, etc. has to be organized; Rural poor should be involved in whenever any programme to help them economically has to be formulated: Voluntary organizations should be encouraged to participate in poverty alleviation programmes: Planning, evaluation and monitoring of poverty alleviation schemes should be given equal weightage in implementing the programmes for the removal of unemployment and poverty. The relationship between planning and control must be watched and secured: Increased public expenditure on social service like health and education is required.

Other steps such as accelerated pace of rural development, planning from below, population control, expansion of communication facilities; more people's participation in the programmes should be taken effectively in the rural sector. The benefits should reach the deprived sections of the population.

Since the social sector occupies a low place in the developmental priorities (Anju Kohli et.al., 2000) in India, extent of Poverty could be reduced by directing more expenditure on Eduction, Health and Gender Equality and by helping the existing institution to deliver services efficiently. Thus, the greater emphasis is on curative rather than preventive measure.

REFERENCES

Anju Kohli, Sadhna Kothari and Neelima Shrivastave, (2000), "Sen's Model of Economic Development-An Inter-State Analysis", *'Economics of Amartya Sen,'* Edited by: Ajit Kumar Sinha and Raj Kumar Sen, Deep and Deep Publications Pvt. Ltd., New Delhi, pp. 182-189.

Dev Mahindra S. and Ranade Ajit, (1998), "Rising Food Prices and Rural Poverty-Going Beyond Correlations", *Economic and Political Weekly,* Sept.-Oct. Vol. 33, No. 39, pp. 2529–2535.

Gaur, K.D., (1968), "Management of Poverty Alleviation in India", Manak Publications Pvt. Ltd., New Delhi, pp. 2-20.

George, T.M., (1999), "Measurement of Poverty and SEN Index", *Southern Economist,* Jan. Vol. 27, No.17, pp. 9-11.

Kannan, K.P., (1995), "Declining Incidence of Rural Poverty in Kerala", *Economic and Political Weekly,* Oct. Vol. 31, No. 41, pp. 2651–2662.

Pradeep Kumar Pande (1997), "Poverty and Female-Headship", *Economic and Political Weekly,* Oct., Vol 31, pp. 893-895.

Sinha J.L. and Gaur K.D., (1999), "Need for New Strategies to Eradicate Poverty", Manak Publications Pvt. Ltd., New Delhi, pp. 18–24.

Subbarao K. and Kakwani N., (1990), "Rural Poverty and its Alleviation in India", *Economic and Political Weekly*, March, Vol. XXV, No. 13, pp. A-2–16.

Vyan V.S. and Pradeep Bhanjava, (1998), "Public Intervention for Poverty Alleviation", *Economic and Political Weekly*, June Vol. 37, No. 14, pp. 2572–2576.

6

AGRICULTURAL GROWTH, EMPLOYMENT AND RURAL POVERTY IN THE ERA OF ECONOMIC LIBERALISATION IN INDIA

K. Dhanasekaran

Introduction

There has been much debate on the impact of structural adjustment and stabilization programmes on rural poverty. International experience of the effects of stabilization and adjustment on the poor has been mixed. The Asian experience suggests that the impact of the post liberalization growth on poverty reduction is greater in situation where in land reforms have been implemented and a high priority has been accorded to physical infrastructure and human resource development. According to Bourguignon and Morrisson (1992), during adjustment there were improvements in the living conditions and consequently decline in poverty in Malaysia, Indonesia and the rural areas of Morocco and Ghana. However, there was deterioration in the living standards in Ecuador, Chile and in the urban areas of Morocco and coted Ivoire. The levels of poverty rose in Chile and Ecuador.

Trader liberalization with its agenda of aligning domestic prices with international prices by removing regulations on external trade such as canalization has the following effects. One effect of removing external is that as international prices are higher than domestic prices, food grain prices in India will increase and consumer will be adversely affected. The other effect of trade liberalization is that higher prices induce a supply response with a resultant increase in labour demand and earnings that offsets the higher price paid for consumption of agricultural product. (Errol D' Souza, 2001). In a developing country like India, with low level of income and high incidence of poverty, reforms adversely affect common people through inflation, which reduces their purchasing power. Hence, it is necessary no examine the impact of trade liberalization on rural poverty.

Data Sources and Methodology

The study is mainly based on secondary data collected from the various quinquennial reports on employment and unemployment published by National Sample Survey Organisation (NSSO). To examine the changing facets of rural employment during the post-reform period, NSS data for 1983, 1993-94 and 1999-2000 were used. Since time series data are not available, the period 1983/1993-94 is regarded as pre-reform period while the period 1993-94/1999-2000 is expected to capture the changes in rural employment brought about by economic reforms. The other secondary data sources are given in the text wherever the data used.

Cropping Pattern and Crop Output

A set of studies indicates that the liberalization of agricultural exports would shift the crop pattern towards high value crops and result in diversion of food grains to livestock feed. This would adversely affect the food security of vulnerable population group (Patnaik 1996). It is also argued that under economic liberalization process food subsidies to consumers for basic cereals have fallen sharply, and this has impacted upon the nutritional intake of the poor (Swaminathan 1996). In India, an overwhelming majority of the farmers are small and marginal and they are not able to take advantage of liberalization and the attractive prices available for export crops.

There is a clear decline in the area under food grains in most part of the country. However, the phenomenon of declining area was observed in several states like Andhra Pradesh, Bihar, Kerala, Orissa and Rajasthan, right from the early 1980s. The process of diversification has been expedited during the post reform period. (Amita Shah 1997). The thrust towards agri-exports during the phase of new economic policy has mainly led to a reduction in the area under all cereals, coarse grains and pulses while increasing the area under oil seeds and other crops.

Although it is very difficult to predict the changes in crop patterns due to liberalization, the available evidence (Table 1) suggests that liberalized environment shifts the cropping pattern in favor of rice wheat sugar cane, cotton and fruits and vegetables. Wheat and rice are the major gainers in terms of area shifts during the post liberalization period and course cereals as a group suffered the greatest loss. The area under wheat increased by 8.5 percent from 1980-81 to 1990-91 and further by 3.7 percent from 1990–91 to 2000–01. Similarly, the areas under rice went up by 6.5 percent from. 1980–81 to 1990–91 and by 3.7 percent forms 1990–91 to 2000-01. In terms of their shares in gross cropped area (GCA), how ever, the changes are not very dramatic. But the changes in area under coarse cereals in relation to their share in GCA are more dramatic. There was a significantly higher fall of 16 percent in area under coarse cereals from 1990-91 to 2000-01 as compared to a drop of 13.4 percent from 1980-81 to 1990-91.

The case of pulses and oilseeds is slightly different as area under these two groups of crops increased by 9.8 percent and 36.9 percent respectively during the 1980s. But, during the 1990s, the area under pulses fell by 19 percent and that under oilseeds by 7.5 percent. A highly significant growth in area

Table 1: Changes in the Cropping Pattern

Crops	1980-81		1990-91		2000-01	
	Area (million ha)	*As a per-centage of the gross cropped area*	*Area (million ha)*	*Area (million ha)*	*As a per-centage of the gross cropped area*	*Area (million ha)*
Rice	40.1	23.2	42.7	23.0	44.3	23.2
Wheat	22.3	12.9	24.2	13.0	25.1	13.2
Coarse cereals	41.8	24.2	36.2	19.5	30.4	15.9
Pulses	22.5	13.0	24.7	13.3	20.0	10.5
Food grains	126.7	73.4	127.8	68.8	119.8	62.8
Oilseeds	17.6	10.2	24.1	13.0	22.3	11.7
Sugarcane	2.7	1.6	3.7	2.0	4.3	2.3
Cotton	7.8	4.5	7.4	4.0	8.6	4.5
Fruits and Vegetable	6.8	4.0	7.6	4.1	10.2	5.3

Notes: 1. Area under fruits and vegetable for 1980-81 and 1990-91 has been calculated using the index numbers of area for these years and actual area under fruits and vegetables in 1991-92.

2. Due to non-availability of data on the gross cropped area for 2000-01, data for 1997-98 has been used.

Source: 1. Agricultural Statistics at a Glance, Ministry of Agriculture, Government of India. Cited in Margin. 2002, pp. 9-10.

under oilseeds, which was witnessed during the 1980's has seen a reversal during the 1990s. On the other hand, area under sugarcane has maintained its growth momentum and exhibited a positive change in the 1990s as well. Area under cotton, which witnessed a negative growth during the 1980s, also exhibited a turnaround of 16.2 percent between 1990-91 and 2000-01.

These shifts in area are partly due to the expansion of irrigation facilities, technological changes and the changes in the institutional set-ups that govern these commodities. The most important cause has been the change in commodity prices, particularly the procurement prices. The trend rates of select crops show that the real prices of cereals have witnessed a positive and significant growth during the 1990s as compared to the negative growth exhibited during the 1980s. In sharp contrast to the changes observed in the case of cereals, the annuals rates of growth in the real procurement prices of oilseeds in particular show reversal in the 1990s in competition to in the 1980s. Some changes in the cropping patterns were, in fact expected after the liberalization of trade. But a great deal of changes witnessed in the recent past is in consequence of the government induced price policy, which is inconsistent with the international price {Table 2, cited in Margin, 2002}.

Table 2: Trend Rates of Growth in Real Procurement Prices of Select Crop (Procurement Prices Deflated by the Wholesale Price Indices For All Commodities)

Crops	*1980-81 to 1990-91*	*1990-91 to 2000-01*
Rice	-1.80	2.85
Wheat	-0.98	2.23
Coarse cereals	-2.32	2.01
Gram	1.79	1.01
Arhar	1.93	1.91
Groundnut	1.43	0.38 (NS)
Rapeseed-mustard	0.20 (NS)	-1.21
Soyabean	-0.75	0.88
Sunflower	3.65	-0.48 (NS)
Cotton	4.21 (NS)	2.46
Sugarcane	0.69 (NS)	1.32

Note: NS Non-significant.

Source: 1. Economic Survey, Ministry of Finance, Government of India.
2. Index Number of Wholesale Prices in India, Ministry of Commerce and Industry, Government of India.

The growth rate of crop production shows deceleration in growth of cereals, pulses, and oilseeds in the 1990s as compared to those of the 1980s. The value of crop production, however, showed higher growth in the 1990s. This was due to higher growth in fruits and vegetables. The share of fruits and vegetables in the total value increased from 17.7 per cent in 1990-91 to 22.7 per cent in 1999-2000 [Table 3, Mahendra Dev

2003]. Rao (1992) views that dryland areas where wages are low and poverty is wide spread may benefit significantly from trade liberalization as they have a comparative advantage in horticultures and livestock production..

Table 3: Trend Growth Rates of Crop Production Sector in 1993-94 Prices

Crop aggregates	*Trend Grown Rates (Percent per annum)*		*Percentage share in total value of crop production*	
	1980-81 to 1990-91	*1990-91 to 1999-2000*	*1990-91*	*1999-2000*
Cereals	3.11	2.26	36.4	34.8
Pulses	1.68	1.15	6.7	5.1
Oilseeds	5.63	2.58	11.0	9.9
Sugar	2.76	2.64	7.9	7.6
Fibers	2.30	2.75	4.3	4.1
Spices	4.46	4.53	2.9	3.4
Fruits and vegetables	2.39	5.99	17.7	22.7
Others	-	-	13.1	12.4
Total value of crop Production	2.67	3.08	100.0	100.0

Note: Trend growth rates are estimated using semi-log function.

Source: Estimated using data from EPW Research foundation (2002). National Accounts Statistics of India 1950-51 to 2000-2001, New linked series with 1993-94 as the base year, fourth edition, Mumbai, Mahendra Dev, 2003.

Growth Rates of Rural Employment and Real Wages

The NSS data, available for 1983/1994, and 1993-94/1999-2000 throw light on rural employment. Table 4 gives a brief profile of rural employment growth for 17 major states of India. It is observed that in the pre-reform period, the growth rates of rural employment in as many as 10 out of the 17 major states turned out to be positive. In other words, a large number of states in India showed a progress in the absolute number of rural employed during the pre-form period. The states that improved the pace of their agricultural employment growth

Table 4 : Growth of Rural Employment (Principal+Subsidiary) In Indian States: 1983/1999-2000

(percent)

States	*Agriculture*		*Manufacturing*		*Community Services*		*Non-Agriculture*		*TotalRural*	
	1983/ 1993-94	*1993-94/ 1999-00*	*1983/ 1993-94*	*1993/ 1993-00*	*1983/ 1993-94*	*1993-94/ 1999-00*	*1983/ 1993-94*	*1993-94/ 1999-00*	*1983/ 1993-94*	*1993-94/ 1999-00*
(1)	(2)	(3)	(4)	(5)	(6)	(7)	(8)	(9)	(10)	(11)
Andhra Pradesh	0.8	0.1	-0.1	-3.2	1.7	1.4	1.1	0.6	0.8	0.2
Assam	N.A	-1.0	N.A.	4.0	N.A.	13.6	N.A	9.5	N.A	1.8
Bihar	-1.7	3.9	-3.7	14.5	-1.4	4.7	-2.5	8.8	-1.8	4.7
Gujarat	-0.4	2.3	5.4	-2.4	1.7	-1.6	3.2	1.4	0.3	2.1
Haryana	0.3	-0.1	-2.3	11.1	2.5	-6.5	2.9	2.5	1.0	0.7
Himachal Pradesh	0.5	-1.6	1.9	3.4	3.7	1.8	5.4	4.7	1.3	-0.1
Jammu and Kashmir	1.0	2.3	0.1	3.9	8.2	0.1	3.5	1.0	1.6	2.0
Karnataka	0.3	0.3	2.0	-3.2	3.7	-4.2	2.3	-0.5	0.6	0.2
Kerala	-2.0	-1.3	-1.9	0.9	0.2	-1.1	0.6	4.1	-1.0	1.3
Madhya Pradesh	0.3	0.2	0.4	4.3	0.4	4.1	0.5	4.8	0.3	0.7
Maharashtra	-0.1	0.4	1.1	0.0	3.6	-3.1	2.0	0.2	0.2	0.4
Orissa	0.7	0.1	-2.2	4.8	-1.3	-1.4	-0.5	3.1	0.4	0.7
Punjab	-2.2	1.5	-2.6	5.4	4.9	-4.0	2.0	3.4	-1.3	2.0
Rajasthan	-0.1	0.1	-0.6	3.5	4.7	-4.1	4.6	2.2	0.6	0.5
Tamilnadu	-0.7	-2.0	1.5	-0.1	0.6	-6.1	1.2	-0.2	-0.2	-1.4
Uttar Pradesh	-0.2	-0.1	-0.7	4.0	1.1	-1.6	1.0	3.6	0.0	0.7
West Bengal	-0.6	0.5	5.3	0.8	2.3	-5.6	3.9	0.4	0.8	0.4
All India	-0.03	0.18	0.72	1.78	1.70	0.32	1.79	2.31	0.33	0.66

Sources: Sarvekshana, April 1998, pp. 28-31; NSSO (1997), NSS Report No. 409, pp. 116-118 and NSSO (2001) NSS Report No. 458, pp. 80-81. N.A.= Not available.

during the post-reform compared with pre-reform period were Bihar, Gujarat, Jammu and Kashmir and Punjab, in the remaining states, agricultural employment growth either slackened or actually declined. For all the states put together, there was no noticeable improvement. For manufacturing, employment growth improved in as many as 11 out of the 17 sates. The picture for the non-agricultural front is also a mingle of improvement and decline or slackness during 1993-94/1999-2000 compared with 1983/1993-94, In overall terms, there was an improvement in the growth rates of employment in manufacturing and in non-agricultural sectors during 1993-94/1999-2000, compared with 1983/1993-94.

Agricultural wages provide importance information on rural poverty. Any decline in rural poverty is discernable only when the real wages increase. Datt and Ravallion (1998) found a strong inter linkage between real wage rates and rural poverty. Real wages are highly correlated with head count ratios. In other wards, wherever incidence of poverty is higher wages tend to be lower and vice versa. A better understanding of recent trends in agricultural wages is important for greater clarity about the nature of rural poverty and the possible means of removing it. Since agricultural labourers are some of the poorest people in the country, a higher wage should result in reduction of poverty. There is significant improvement in real wages rates for agricultural labour. The real wages of rural male labourers increased in the 1990s, (1993-94 to 1999-2000) as compared to that of in the 1980s (1983 to 1993-94) (Sundaram 2001 and Table 5). The increase in real wage rates despite the declining trend in agricultural growth indicates that the expansion of non-form employment might have contributed to the rise in the demand for labour in the non-farm sector mostly in construction, and service sector. Since the wages in the non-farm sector have been considerably higher than the wages in the farm sector, it is inferred that a part of the decline in rural poverty is due to opening up of employment opportunities in the non-farm sector. Thus this evidence indicates that poverty might have declined due to rise in real wages of agricultural lablourers during the economic reform period.

Table 5: Average Daily Wages In Rural India At Constant 1993-94 Price Rate of Growth of Real Wages (Percent Per Annum)

Nature of Employment	*Rural males*		*Rural females*	
	1983 to 1993-94	*1993-94 to 1999-2000*	*1983 to 1993-94*	*1993-94 to 1999-2000*
Manual work agriculture (1-11)	2.74	2.77	3.09	2.93
Casual labour in agriculture (1-11, 13-14)	2.75	2.79	3.09	2.94
Casual labour in non-agriculture (12-14)	2.39	3.70	4.08	4.07

Source: Sundaram (2001).

Rural Poverty

The empirical evidence suggests that the percentage of population living below the poverty live has been declining steadily in recent years (Table 6). The head count ratio (HCR)

Table 6: Estimates of Poverty

Year	*Percent below poverty line*			*Reduction from previous survey (percentage points)*		
	All India	*Rural*	*Urban*	*All India*	*Rural*	*Urban*
1973-74	54.9	56.4	49.0	-	-	-
1977-78	51.3	53.1	45.2	3.6	3.3	3.8
1983	44.5	45.7	40.8	6.8	7.4	4.4
1987-88	38.9	39.1	38.2	5.6	6.6	2.6
1993-94	36.0	37.3	32.4	2.9	1.8	5.8
1999-2000						
30 day recall	26.1	27.1	23.6	9.9	10.2	8.8
7 day recall	23.3	24.0	21.6	12.7	13.3	10.8

Source: Data from 1973 to 1994 was sourced from Economic survey, Government of India. Data for 1999-2000 (30 days and 7 days recall) was sourced from www.indiastat.com.

for rural and urban has gone down in the 1990s. A number of researches during the 1990s have commented on the implications of economic reforms for rural and urban poverty. Tendulkar (1998)s, Datt (1999), Sen (1996) also suggest that the decline in rural poverty, observed during the 1970s and 1980s has been arrested during the reform decade of 1990s. It had also decreased over the 1980s. Even when one does not accept the faster decline over the 1990s, one can conclude that accelerated reforms and deregulation and liberalization of the 1990s have not adversely affected the trend of decline in poverty [Kirit S. Parikh, 2002, p. 3].

Conclusion

In the new economic environment of trade liberalization, there has been a debate whether the reforms have helped to accelerate agricultural output, employment and real wages for the agricultural labour. There is an apprehension that the economic reforms have had an adverse impact on the employment and poverty particularly in rural India. But the empirical evidence suggests that despite the lower agricultural output growth, the poverty has declined in the 1990s as compared to 1980s. The rate of decline of rural poverty was faster during the 1990s than in the 1980s, when economy was on a lower growth path as compared to that of the earlier years. A faster decline in rural poverty during the 1990s can be attributed to higher growth rates of employment in non-agricultural sectors and in real wages. Safety nets played an important role during reform to attack poverty. Rural development programmes affected rural poverty more directly as compared to other safety net programmes during the post reform period. To conclude, agricultural trade liberalization helped to reduce rural poverty in India.

REFERENCES

—— (2002), "Review of the Economy," *Margin,* Vol. 34, No. 23, Jan–June.

Amita Shah, (1997), "Food Security and Access to Natural Resources:

A Review of Recent Trends", *Economic and Political Weekly,* Vol. XXXII, No. 26, June 28–July 4.

Bourguignon, Francois and Morrisson Christian, (1992), Adjustment and Equity in Developing Countries: A New Approach, Development Centre of Organization of Economic Co-operation and Development, Paris.

Datt, G., (1999), "Has Poverty Declined Since Economic Reforms?– Statistical Data Analysis" *Economic and Political Weekly,* December, 11.

Datt, G. and M. Ravallion, (1998), "Why Have Some Indian States Done Better Than Others Reducing Rural Poverty?", *Economica* Vol. 65, No. 257.

Errol D' Souza, (2002), "Reporter's Report on Impact of Economic Reforms on Rural Employment", *Indian Journal of Agricultural Economics,* Vol. 56, No. 3, July-September, p. 605.

Kirit, S. Parikh and R. Radha Krishna, (2002), India Development Report 2002, Oxford University Press, New Delhi.

Mahendra Dev, (2003), "Agriculture, Employment and Social Sector Neglected", *Economic and Political Weekly,* Vol. 38, No. 14, April 5, pp. 1353–54.

NSSO, (1997), NSS Report, No. 409, pp. 116-118.

NSSO, (2001), NSS Report, No. 458, pp. 80-81.

Patnaik, V., (1996), "Export Oriented Agricultural and Food Security in Developing Countries and India", *Economic and Political Weekly,* Vol. 31, No. 37, Special Number, September, pp. 2429-50.

Rao C.H. Hanumantha, (1992), "Integrating Poverty Alleviation Programmes with Development Strategies : Indian Experience", *Economic and Political Weekly,* Vol. 27, No. 48, November 28, p. 2903.

Ravallion, Martin, (1998), "Reform, Food Prices and Poverty In India", *Economic and Political Weekly,* January 10.

Sarvekshana, April 1988, pp. 28-31.

Sen, Abhijit, (1996), "Economic Reforms, Employment and Poverty: Trends and Options", *Economic and Political Weekly,* Special Number, September, p. 2459.

Sundaram K., (2001), "Employment and Poverty in 1960s: Further Results from NSS 55th Round Employment-Unemployment-Unemployment Survey, 1999–2000", *Economic and Political Weekly*, 11 August, p. 3047.

Swaminathan, M., (1996), "Structural Adjustment, Food Security and System of Public distribution of Food," *Economic and Political Weekly*, Vol. 31, No. 26, June 29, pp. 1665-1672.

Tendulkar, Suresh D., (1998), "Indian Economic Policy Reforms and Poverty: An Assessment", in Ahluwalia, Isher Judge and Kittle I.M.D. (eds), India's Economic Reforms and Development : Essays for Manmohan Singh, Oxford University Press, New Delhi.

7

SOCIO-ECONOMIC ASSESSMENT OF ECONOMIC REFORMS ON AGRICULTURE

B. Shyamala

Introduction

The green revolution is one of the biggest success stories of India cited globally, which enabled India to convert from "begging bowl" status to that of self-sufficiency. This impressive transformation was possible due to land reforms, creation of infrastructure such as irrigation, seed production and manufacture of fertilizers, strong Rural and Development systems and HRD. Inspite of the spectacular achievements the green revolution has its deficiency segments. The seed-water-fertilizer technology suffers from two specific lacunae, that is, it is so far available in only two crops viz. wheat and rice and the modern inputs are beyond the reach of small and marginal farmers. It is neither product, neutral nor region neutral and even effects of growth on products, regions and classes of people.

Despite Ten five year Plans and three annual plans since 1950-51 India has faced to solve its basic and number one problem that is feeding the growing millions of population. In recent years, the agricultural problem has become much more severe and intense. The tremendous growth of population from 350 million in 1951, to over one billion in 1999 has increased the demand for food grains. VKRV Rao estimated that with the alarming growth of population, the growth of population, the growth rate of agriculture should be 4 percent where the real growth rate in agriculture is only 2.7 percent only. Against this back drop. New Economic Policy was introduced by the Government of India with its variety of changes down to the grass- root level.

The major objective of this paper is to analyse the overall performance of Indian Agriculture during pre-reform and post reform periods. The specific objective is to analyse some of the variables which contribute to the performance of agriculture in India. The identified economic variables are food grain production. Percapita availability of food, agricultural exports, Food security and social justice in the form of withdrawal of subsidies, agricultural prices, unemployment, decline in production of coarse grains, and so on.

Database and Methodology

The data for the period 1988-89 to 1999-2000 was collected from Economic Survey, Government of India and Hindu Survey of Indian Agriculture. The period under study was divided into Pre-Economic Reform covering 1988-89 to 1993-94 and Post-Economic Reform covering 1994-95 to 1999-2000, in order to know the impact on agriculture. The tools used are percent analysis, compound growth rate, to analyse the data.

Impact on Food Production

India's agricultural sector has a credible record of growth in food grains production. The food grains output is poised to rise 208 million tones in 1999-2000. For the past consecutive years there has been a set back in the overall agricultural production.

The cumulative loss in the index of agricultural production is worked out to about 4.6 percent. The trend in production is given in Table 1.

Table 1 : Trend In Food Production (million tones)

Items	*1950-51*	*1970-71*	*1990-91*	*1999-2000*	*2000-01*
Rice	30	36	43	68	75
Wheat	10	13	25	54	49
Coarse Cereals	39	44	32	53	42
All Food Grains	99	118	124	208	196
	(81.1)	(78.1)	(74.7)	(81.2)	(84.5)
All Non-Food Grains	23 (18.9)	33 (21.9)	42 (25.3)	48 (18.8)	36 (15.5)
All Crops	122	151	16.6	256	232
	(100.0)	(100.0)	(100.0)	(100.0)	(100.0)

Source: Government of India, Ministry of Finance; Economic Survey
Figures in parenthesis indicate percentage.

It is observed that non-foodgrains also show a declining trend from 42 million tones in 1990-91 to 36 million tones in 2000-01. In the case of pulses it was 24 million tones in 1999-2000 and declined to 30 million tones in 2000-01. Excepting rice in all other food grains and non-food grains we can see a declining trend. Moreover the overall crop production also has declined from 256 million tones in 1999-2000 to 232 million tones in 2000-01.

Impact on Percapita Availability of Food

Percapita availability of food is another contributing factor for the performance of Indian agriculture. The net availability of cereals and pulses are funished in Table 2. The percapita availability of cereals increased from during 1981-85, 416.8 to 442b gms during 1996-2000. There is a marginal increase of 25 gms over 20n years. In the case of pulses it declined from 39.3 gms during 1981-85 to 35.9 gms during 1996-2000.

We find a decline in the consumption of pulses by 3.4 gms. Obviously while moving towards food grains security India has succeeded in terms of cereals but has miserably failed to increase in the production of pulses consistant with needs of growing population. In other words the rate of growth of population has outstripped the rate of growth of food.

Table 2: Net Availability of Cereals and Pulses

Year	*Percapita Net Availability (grams / day)*		
	Cereals	*Pulses*	*Total*
1981-85	416.8	39.3	456.1
1986-90	433.9	40.0	473.5
1991-95	446.9	37.5	484.4
1996-2000	442.0	35.9	477.0

Source: Compiled from Economic Survey 1999-2000.

Impact on Indian Food Security

The recent performance of Indian agriculture after the globalization of the farm sector reveals a gloomy picture of the future of food security in India. This is clearly given in Table 3.

Table 3: Performance of Indian Agriculture and Economic Reforms

Performance Indicators	*Pre-Economic Reform 1986-87 to 1990-91*	*Post-Economic Reform 1991-92 to 1995-96*
Gross Terms of Trade Base Average at 1980-81 Prices	92.02	103.36
Gross Value of Aggregate Crop output Average (in million Rs.)	572,980 (+5.79)	671160 (+3.50)
Food grains production Average (in million tones)	160 (+5.70)	181 (+1.84)

Source : Complied and Computed.
Figures in brackets indicate Annual compound growth rate.

It is observed from the table that all the performance indicators show a declining trend. The growth rate of agricultural productions has declined in the post reform period though the overall production has increased substantially the deceleration in production of food grains was of course, a cause of concern because it was lower than population growth rate.

Impact on Agricultural Exports

Despite a severe set back in agriculture in the post reform period Globalization provides on extensive opportunity for farm exports. A number of policy changes have recently been introduced to make agricultural exports more viable. A market determined exchange rate policy has favoured agricultural product exports. Lowering of import duty on capital goods as well as easier availability of credit for exports have also helped.

The Table 4 gives clearly the composition of agricultural export in India and the value of exports in rupee value.

Table 4: Exports of Agricultural and Processed Food Products (in billion Rs.)

Products	*1993-94*	*1994-95*	*1995-96*	*1999-2000*
Floriculture and Seeds	43.3 (1.5)	55.6 (1.9)	103 (1.3)	115.7 (1.2)
Fruits and Vegetables	385.4 (13.5)	433.3 (14.5)	531.2 (6.7)	620.4 (6.3)
Processed Fruits and Vegetables	268.5 (9.4)	348.2 (11.7)	491.6 (6.2)	578.2 (5.9)
Animal Products	374.0 (13.1)	448.4 (15.1)	682.6 (8.6)	931.6 (9.5)
Other Processed Foods	459.7 (16.4)	415.8 (14.0)	1172.0 (14.8)	1325.0 (13.5)
Cereals	1320.9 (46.4)	1236.2 (42.8)	4951.8 (62.4)	6220.0 (63.5)
Total	2851.9	2977.4	7932.3	9790.01

Source: Hindu Survey of Indian Agriculture, (Various issues).

Figures in brackets indicate percentage.

The percent share of agricultural exports in total exports has been increased steadily from 16.4 percent in 1994-95 to 24.4 percent in 1999-2000.

Let us look it today's wellpublicized situation on the food grains front. On the one hand, we have godowns overflowing with grain but on the other, large sections of our population still have one of the lowest percapita calorie consumption. Simply put, this is because these consumers can not afford to buy food at the current prices. When the availability of food grains declines and prices rise as a result of poor crop, a higher proportion of people would be unable to meet the normative level of consumption. This public management of food grains is important for poverty reduction as well as for food security.

Impact on Social Justice in Agriculture

The food security Indians especially the poor is under threat by liberalized economic policies. Indian agriculture is heading for a crisis of food production, food security and rising prices. The export supporting policies have led to a diversion of vast areas of agricultural land for horticulture, aquaculture, orchards and others. Government policy has deliberately encouraged production of commercial crops through increases in subsidies and loans. But at the same time it is to be noticed that other subsidies are totally withdrawn created a havoc in the farm sector.

It is also observed that since 1971 production of food grains especially millets, staple food of the poor had declined from 1.9 million tones to 821,000 tonnes in 1995-96 and further declined to 508,000 tonnes in 1999-2000. The area under coarse cereals had declined by 14.46 million hectares during the same period. Paddy fields are giving way to factories and traditional crops are being replaced by commercial crops. It is observed that there is a marginal increase of 12 million hectares under paddy cultivation over 50 years period between 1950-51 and 2000-01. As a result of this marginal increase, there is little employment for rural poor.

With regard to prices of food grains, the price level in India is higher than international market price. The price index of agricultural products has doubled form 174.4 in 1989-90 to 429.4 in 1999-2000 and agricultural prices as percent of manufactured products has been increased from 103.5 to 127.3 during the same period.

Therefore economic reforms has not yet touched agriculture directly either by opening up trade or by altering the land holding structure. There is no doubt economic reforms pushed up the level of income in the rural sector of the economy. But there have been two discomforting features of the economic reform also, first economic reform has promoted personal inequalities in the rural sector and secondly it has been responsible for widening regional disparities.

Globalisation is considered to be the death penalty to farmers and agricultural labourers. Withdrawal of agricultural subsidies, heavy decline in the price of agricultural products and dismissal of farm supportive Government measures are the main anti-agriculture globalisation policies. The adverse effects of these programmes are not only general set back in production but also the loss of livelihood for farmers and agricultural labourer. Any blow on agriculture severely affects 700 millions in India. The failure of primary sector leaves millions jobless, leading to manifestations of poverty, migration to urban centers and loss of life.

Moreover nearly 160 million people are employed in 21 lakhs Small Scale Industrial units in the country and 60 million people are employed in village and small industries. Withdrawal of safety measures and liberalized import policies make these products to face severe competition from MNC products and ultimately leading to the closure of these units

Let me conclude the discussion on the implications of economic reforms in agriculture. There are two areas we need to "hasten slowly". First, the maintenance of ceiling on agricultural holdings till the pace of diversification in the rural areas is accelerated. Secondly, the policy of food self sufficiency is not to be abandoned till livelihood and consumption pattern change remarkably.

The main ingredients of reforms in agriculture in the future should be:

- Acceleration of the process of liberalizations in domestic markets
- Revision of price support system
- Procurement operations on commercial lines
- Need for stable fertilizer Policy
- Free movement of agri-products to ensure competitiveness in the global market
- Agricultural growth to create a healthy demand for industrial products.

8

AGRARIAN CHANGE AND OCCUPATIONAL DIVERSIFICATION CERTAIN EMERGING ISSUES

B.Vanitha

Agrarian Change

Marxist analysis of agrarian changes focuses on the way the peasant economy changes into capitalist agriculture, which is termed as "Agrarian Question". The alternative path of agrarian development within the framework of Marxist analysis, is of analytical interest in the context of understanding agrarian transformation in countries like India. Byres (1991) attempts to examine alternative paths of agrarian transition. He explains six paths for transitions of which three are familiar, and to this he adds three more which are summed up below.

1. ***English Path*** : This is the classical path where the transition takes place in the shift of land from feudal landlords to capitalists tenants who make possible accumulation from agriculture as a source of capitalist industrial development by employing wage labour.
2. ***Prussian Path*** : It is referred to as 'Capitalism from above' where the feudal land owners reduce peasants into wage labourers–by undertaking investment in agriculture,

appropriate surplus which serve as the source of capital for industrial development.

3. *American Path* : It is described as "Capitalism from below"–where the petty commodity producers, the peasants emerge as peasants producing for profits under state protection. They reinvest the profit in the development of capitalistic agriculture, which also serves as the source of market investment for industry.

4. *French Path* : French peasantry survives side by side with capitalist transformation in the Northern parts but there is no reference to contribution of agriculture to industrial development. The emphasis is on the transition from below.

5. *Japanese Path* : Following the Meiji restoration, the tenants are exploited by landlords with high rents and the state acts as the main agency of accumulation through taxation for industrial investment.

6. *Taiwanese and South Korean Path* : Land reforms of 1940s make peasants free from rents, but through ruthless state taxation, primary accumulation is carried on for industrialization

If we try to apply to these paths to the Indian context, the English path is ruled out as nowhere in Asia any sign of such a possibility of landlord class.

There is no relevance of East of East Asian agrarian transitions to other Asian countries. Japanese path is unique marked by its landlord class. Korean path is influenced by Japanese colonialism. In India the successful capital transformation in the North-West could be through peasant route i.e., capitalist form below (American Path). Such transition could come through peasant struggles and actions against landlords by way of variety of positive actions in favour of the peasant by Indian Government.

Changes in Agrarian Structure and Relations

The post-Independent India had experienced considerable institutional and technical changes which have contributed to the evolving of production conditions in the Indian agriculture. An evaluation of land reforms is important for understanding changes in agrarian structure and agrarian relations. The reference to the reforms are kept to the extent of impact that these had on the process of agrarian transformation. According to Rao (1998) there are four categories of divergent states to capture the land reforms experience in India.

1. Semi-feudal areas like Bihar, where the barriers to reforms inherent in the prevailing structure of society are too strong to be overcome by the efforts of land reforms.
2. 'Green Revolution' areas (e.g. Punjab) where capitalists farming is firmly entrenched and where reforms are needed mainly to improve wages, work environment and economic conditions of labourers.
3. Area (e.g. Karnataka) with less formidable barriers to land reforms and the stronger trust of reforms as compared to semi-feudal areas but having mixed and, on the whole, modest results of reforms.
4. Areas (e.g. West Bengal and Kerala) with strong political mobilization and effective land reforms but where the growth performance has been too weak to compliment reforms to bring about structural change.

Rao on the basis of land reforms experience draws the following conclusions

(a) In none of the four situations did the land reforms help the rural poor in obtaining secure and equitable access to land in the context of growing population pressure on land and keen competition for its control among the different rural strata.

(b) Even in the areas where rural poor are politically well organized as in Kerala and West Bengal, they got only the direct and proximate benefits but did not succeed in bringing an enduring improvement in the economic status.

(c) The dominant rural groups in Bihar, Karnataka and Punjab extended decisive influence in the processes for formulation of land reforms to divert the benefits of the reforms from the rural poor to themselves.

(d) Considerable time and energy has been spend in legislative and implementation aspects of land reforms. The crucial criterion for successful land reforms is the extent to which they form part of cohesive development strategy capable of integrating the objective of growth with those of equity and poverty eradication.

Thus there cannot be a single recipe for all the agricultural ills. Different parts of India are at different levels of agricultural development, which require diverse ownership-tenancy arrangements.

Occupational Diversification

While the land reforms failed to bring about any radical redistribution of land, the introduction of now technology has brought sharper differentiation among peasantry by opening up more profitable opportunities in agriculture to rich peasantry. The rich peasants with better resources, access to information, risk-bearing capacity have benefited in adopting the new technology, which was brought in the name of 'Green Revolution'. The small farmers also ventured to break the barriers by resorting to hybrid seeds on highly usurious borrowing. But with one or two crop failure, these peasants have ended up in enormous debts or dispossessions of all their assets including land and remained as agricultural labourers. Thus the heavy social cost of transition was entirely borne by small-marginal farmers and agricultural labourers. The overall rural workforce increased by about 103 percent during 1951-1991, cultivators increased by about 58 percent, while agricultural labourers increased by a phenomenal 173 percent.

The share to the masses of agricultural sector has shrinked due to casualisation of agricultural workers. Thus there has been fast declining share of agricultural sector in the national product and only a marginal reduction in the share of agriculture in the workforce, (Rao 1994).

Non-Agricultural Employment

There has been pressure of underemployment building up in rural areas. The capacity of agricultural sector to absorb growing labour force in any significant way is suspect and the organized labour sector is also not having any prospect to absorb excess labour force. There is growing concern for the changes in the non-agricultural sector including the activities linked to agriculture. Table 1 shows the distribution of workers in agriculture and non -agriculture in Rural area. (All India)

Table 1: Agriculture and Non-Agriculture Distribution of Workers in Rural Areas -All India

Year		*Agriculture*	*Non-Agriculture*
1973	%	85.6	14.4
	Male	83.3	16.7
	Female	89.7	10.3
1978	%	83.4	16.6
	Male	80.6	19.3
	Female	88.1	11.8
1983	%	81.5	18.5
	Male	77.8	22.9
	Female	87.6	12.3
1988	%	77.8	21.7
	Male	74.5	25.5
	Female	84.7	15.3
1994	%	78.2	21.8
	Male	74.0	26.0
	Female	86.0	14.0
2000	%	76.2	23.8
	Male	74.4	28.6
	Female	85.2	14.8

What is looked for is the declining share of workers in agriculture and it has declined from 85.6 to 76.2 percent between 1973-2000. But the share of employment in agriculture is still remaining very high, which means that the rural labour process in terms of labour market is dominated by agriculture but not limited to agrarian process alone, but linked to off-farm work as well.

Casualistion

Table 2 shows trends in quality of employment in rural areas. The decline in self-employment and increasing casualisation are the two prominent and interrelated trends, which are observed. The process of shift from self-employment to casual labour is due to growing landlessness. There is no place for the notion of one person remaining in one activity, for there is not such single employer or employment available. The diversification of rural labour force is not unidirectional

Table 2: Distribution of Workers by Employment Status in Rural Areas

Category	*1972-73*	*1977-78*	*1982-83*	*1987-88*	*1993-94*	*1999-00*
		Male				
1. Self Employed	65.9	62.8	60.5	58.6	57.6	54.9
2. Regular	12.1	10.3	10.3	10.0	8.6	8.9
3. Casual	22.0	26.9	29.3	31.4	33.9	36.2
		Female				
1. Self Employed	64.5	62.1	61.9	60.9	58.7	57.4
2. Regular	4.1	2.8	2.8	3.7	2.7	3.1
3. Casual	31.4	35.1	35.3	35.4	38.6	39.6
		Persons				
1. Self Employed	65.3	62.6	61.6	59.4	58.0	55.6
2. Regular	9.3	7.7	7.5	7.7	6.4	6.7
3. Casual	25.4	29.7	31.5	32.9	35.6	37.7

but rather one that involves movement back and forth. So whether it is in agriculture or non-agriculture the work at the bottom is characterised by occupational multiplicity with a shift in the character of rural labour from agrarian proletariate to more general rural proletariate. There is growing evidence on the occupational multiplicity of rural labour from a large number of micro studies (Rao, 2001; Unni, 2001; Kumar, 1996; Reddy 2001). If crops fail, since poor, peasantry have no holding power, they have to look for whatever work and wherever accessible. If one men migrate, and do not remit much, women have to enter into agriculture or other work to maintain the household. If distress is too much consumption debt may spark bondage contracts. Children may have to be forced into work. Thus the casualisation often cohabits occupational multiplicity, circulating labour, feminization, child labour, contract labour and bonded labour.

Feminization

Table 3 shows that there has not been any trend in rise in share of rural female work force as their predominant source of work still remains agriculture and their share in the non-farm sector is on the decline. This may be because of the higher wage and skill requirement in the non-farm activity which led to male preference. There are evidences of women entering into agricultural activities left by migrating men or into even temporary bondage in certain circumstances (Unni, 2001).

Table 3: Share of Women in Rural Work force

Nature of work	*1977-78*	*1983*	*1987-88*	*1993-94*	*1999-00*
Agriculture	38.4	39.9	39.1	39.4	38.7
Non-Agriculture	25.9	25.2	25.3	22.9	21.3
All Workers	36.3	37.1	36.1	35.8	34.6

The process of casualisation and the occupational multiplicity has brought the rural labour into much larger informal fold that cuts across rural urban boundaries. This rural labour are circulating in character straddling between rural and urban areas and also between rural and other rural areas. The migrant labourer is often the locus of contract and bonded labourers. Though their moment away from the villages give them and opportunity to assert their right to freedom, it does not always mean migrant labourers escape oppression. The impact of migration on sending and receiving areas is different. In the 'Sending Areas' migration is contributing to a breakdown of isolated nature of rural labour markets and facilitating the development of generalized market for labour. There is upward pressure on wage, which improve the real wage. In the 'Receiving End' the conditions often go against migrant labourer. The migration is a means of turning peasantry into generalized labour looking beyond villages for work, not being able to leave the villages permanently.

High evidence of bonded labour in the agriculture sector is an established fact and it is also true that it has come down drastically in agriculture. But in the non-agriculture sector bonded labour in certain occupations is very rampant which needs special focus. Bonded labour is widely prevalent in stone, slate and marble quarries and brick-kilns wherever these activities exist in the country. It is prevalent in sugarcane industry, among the tribals in Gujarat, in handlooms in Tamilmadu and Andhra Pradesh, It exists in plantations of Assam and West Bengal, in woolen carpet industry in Uttar Pradesh, beedi making in Andhra Pradesh and Tamilnadu and in sea food processing in Kerala. Most of these are migrant agricultural labourers.

The rural labour process in India presents a rude challenge. Emerging tendencies towards improved wages, more freedom, wider mobility, growing external linkages and diversified occupation go along with growing uncertainty of productive employment, increase in instability of employment, growing cost of adjustment, decreasing in protection of workers right and increasing absence of social security. There is a need for more state intervention to provide certain entitlement to work, protect right to work and ensure decent work, and the state is increasingly absent in these roles. This results in enormous human and social costs by way of growing deprivation, which may impede the very growth process.

The New Emerging Issues

The agrarian change in India is one of growing landlessness, high degree of concentration of land, rural inequalities and vast proportion of rural peasantry who have multiple identities. The rural labour process in India suggest the agrarian process is linked with off- own -farm and non -farm work. In this context the emerging issues are

1. What are the characters emerging in non-agricultural activities?
2. What are the economic and social costs of labour adjustments?
3. How to shift these burden of cost off the worker?
4. How far the East Asian experience relevant?
5. What are the Institutional arrangements at different levels required?
6. How to make the institution like Panchayat Raj to play an effective role in planning and organizing productive activities?

The labour organization should shoulder substantial role in labour process in minimizing the burdens on the working class and evolving appropriate mechanism and institutions particularly at the grass root level. Labour mobilization becomes important in protecting the interest of the labourer. How to translate these needs into action? Now the biggest question before us, is how to bring this issues on to the agenda of the state.

REFERENCES

Byres, T.J., (1991), "The Agrarian Question and Differing Forms of Capitalist Agrarian Transition : An Essay with Reference to Asia" in Breman, J. and S. Mundle (ed). Rural Transformation in Asia, OUP, New Delhi.

Byres, T.J., (1999), "Rural Labour Relations in India : Persistent Themes Courmon Processes and Differential Outcomes", *Journal of Peason* Studies Vol. 26, No. 2 & 3, Jan-April.

Breman, J. & S. Mundle, (1991), Rural Transformation in Asia *OUP*, New Delhi.

Breman, J., (2000), "Labour and Landlessness in South and South Asia" in Bryceson, et al. (ed), London.

Bryceson D.F. et. al (ed.) (2000), "Disappearing Pleasantries? Rural Labour in Africa, Asia and Latin America," The Intermediate Technology Group, London.

Jha, (1997), 'Agricultural Labour in India Vikas', New Delhi.

Kumar, B.L., (1996), "Changes in the Composition of Rural Labour Force : Some Evidence from a Village Resurvey" *The Indian Journal of Labour Economics* Vol. 39, No. 4, Oct-Nov.

Mooiji, J., (2000), "Changing Peasantries in Asia" in Bryceson, et. al (ed) op, at.

Rao, V. M. & H.G. Hanumappa, (1999) "Marginalisation Process in Agriculture" Foundation Day Seminar 4-5 Nov, NIRD, Hyderabad.

Rao, V.M., (1988), "Policies for Rural Labour : From Relief to Structural Change" in Radhakrishna. R and A.N. Sharma (ed.) IHD, New Delhi.

Reddy, Narashima, (1998), "Union Intervention in Rural Labour Markets: The Experience of Andhra Pradesh" in Radhakrishna R. and A.N. Sharma (ed.), *'Empowering Rural Labour in India'*, *IHD*, New Delhi.

Sharma, H.R., (2001), "Employment and Wage Earnings of Agricultural Labourers: A State-Wise Analysis" *The Indian Journal of Labour Economics* Vol. 44, No. 1. Jan.-Mar.

Unni, Jeemol, (2001), "Gender and Non -Farm Employment in India"- Workshop on Rural Transformation in India: The Role of Non-Farm Sector, Sept. 19 -21, 2001, IHD, New Delhi.

9

DEVELOPMENTAL MARKETING– A STRATEGIC OPTION FOR RURAL MARKETING

B. Rajasekaran & G. Magesh Kuttalam

Emergence of Indian Rural Market

After independence India decided to adopt a planned approach for developing the economy of this heavily populated country. Economic planning was to bring rapid growth to all sectors and reduce inequalities. It was also believed that this planned approach could play a vital role in capital formation and achieving higher level of investments. This prediction was successful as huge public sector enterprises, heavy dams and buildings, mammoth-financing institutions etc. stand as testimony of government's planned approach. The policy makers also hypothesed that the overall growth in the economy would have "trickle down effect" to all sectors of the society and thereby reduce the inequalities. Unfortunately this was proved partially correct; the urban society where most of the industrial establishments are situated has benefited, whereas the rural, that is basically the agrarian society holding $3/4^{th}$ of the countries population has grown relatively less than that of industrialized urban society. Rural India has witnessed pauperization of its peasantry and migration to industrialized, relatively sophisticated urban parts of the country. With its conservatism and traditionalism along with poor economic growth rate and purchasing power, rural India has a lesser nectar to attract marketers towards them. The scenario of the rural market changed in the sixties with the success of *Green Revolution* and phenomenal increase in the plan outlay for rural development programmes from Rs. 14,000 crore in the seventh plan to Rs 90,000 crore in the current plan. Various assistance extended by United Nations to educate and propagate health and hygiene messages have helped a great deal in increasing the pace of rural economic development. National Council for Applied Economic Research (NCAER) has projected that by 2006-07 the lowest income class i.e. households earning Rs. 25,000/- & below per annum in villages will shrink to 20 percent from 61 percent in 1994-95, the middle income house holds will double over the decade. The six lakh and odd villages housing more than 700 million of country's population with good monsoon is gaining purchasing power and able to free its people from poverty, albeit slowly.

The growth in per capita income and consumption, prosperity and change in life style of the rural market has already started pushing the demand upwards. The producers and marketers are slowly realizing that a huge potential is lying untapped in the countryside. Information about the size of the rural market is attracting not only regional and national players but also international players towards them. Many national and multinational companies have started focusing on this large rural market by conducting studies of the basics and behaviour of this type of market and designing products and services to their needs. Few organizations like HLL, Dabur, TVS etc. have started making a dent and many more are queuing up. More than half of HLL's sale today comes from the rural market. The size of rural market is estimated at around Rs 50,000 crore for FMCGs, Rs 5,000 crore for durables, Rs 45,000 crore for agri-inputs and implements and Rs 8,000 crore for automobiles annually. In spite of this growth, marketers consider rural penetration rate to be slow and low.

Challenges in the Rural Market

Varieties of consumer goods and services right from paper to paint, pin to automobiles, insurance to housing loans and elementary education to entertainments today have a good demand in the countryside, but is not easy for marketers to taste success. A journey into the rural market may not be smooth but bumpy drives with many speed breakers but lot of competitors are behind.

The prime challenges lying on the way of rural marketers are as follows:

(i) ***Fluctuating Economy*** : Economy of the rural market is mainly agrarian in nature. Peasants of the country with small holdings of lands are largely depending on natural factors which cannot be predicted. Demand of the rural market has every chance to lose its consistency due to dependency on seasonality factors and availability of disposable incomes in the hands of customers. This in turn affects the business in many ways.

(ii) ***Geographical Dispersal & Structural Connectivity*** : Villages hold rural population which is small, not contiguous and widely dispersed and hold a less population per square kilometer. The physical and informational reach to the rural market is believed to be a difficult and costly affair. The marketers find it difficult to establish distribution network and cheaper medium for communication.

(iii) ***Rural Behavior*** : Most customers of the rural market behave in a conservative way. They are quite orthodox in their beliefs and attitudes. Influences exerted by those attributes in purchasing have been proved beyond doubt. These strong influences which may be cultural need to be studied and understood by the marketers before designing the products and the strategy for marketing. They do not respond to contemporary calls as like in urban market. Special envoys have to be selected for promoting the products among the rural market, which normally responds to the words of different breeds of idols, colloquially called *Netha* or *Dada*.

(iv) *Exposure to Marketing Stimuli* : The exposure of rural customers with regard to the product, its variant usage, the brand name, advertisement, price, etc. are relatively less. Concepts like Experience Centers (EC), Opportunity to See (OTS), Point of Purchase (PoP) are not tested to the flavor of rural customers. Any product to be successful should be correctly targeted, rightly positioned and repeatedly stimulated apart from choosing an apt segment. Failure of these steps would not facilitate sustained buying behaviour. The stimuli of marketing forces on rural customers are very less, with this weak stimuli marketers cannot aspire for greater success.

(v) *Rural literacy* : The low literacy level also becomes a major hurdle for the marketers. The customer has to be educated a lot about the product, on its usage mainly through visual media. The prejudice in the minds of rural customers has to be diluted and new insights have to be infused which is a herculean task.

Developmental Marketing- An Approach for Success

The challenges lying in the way of rural marketers are tough and many. Marketers operating in a mode which spells success in urban may not fit this rural market. Adoption of new approaches and develop new innovative models is a must for marketers serving the rural market. Poverty of the rural needs to be addressed, the productive and earning capacity of the rural poor has to be increased to enable them to participate in the developmental process and to possess disposable incomes.

Organization interested in the rural market has to adopt *more a developmental marketing approach.* It is more a process of empowering the rural folks financially by enhancing their purchasing power and thereby finding a market for products among them. The beneficiaries of this alliance also act as benefactors. Rural population that is relatively more receptive and would accept any effort that is helpful for their prosperity. Marketers entering Indian rural market can succeed on adopting this *developmental approach.*

Self help Group-An Agent for Developmental Marketing in the Rural Market

Women self help groups (SHGs) have been formed mainly for solving economical and employment problems. Many of such groups with the synergy of members, support from the NGOs' and micro credits given by Government/Banks are functioning in a systematic way and have and have started tasting success. Marketing organizations can use such groups in the villages as their agent in this developmental marketing venture. Similar exercises have been tried by India's largest FMCG Company, Hindustan Lever Limited in the name of *Project Shakti*. The reach and distribution of Hindustan Lever Ltd. products has acquired a further edge with *Project Shakti* because of partnership established with rural SHGs. The project, started in 2001, already covers over 5000 villages in 52 districts of Andhra pradesh, Karnataka, Madhya pradesh and Gujarat, and is being progressively extended. Their vision is to reach over 100,000 villages, thereby touching about 100 million consumers. The SHGs have chosen to distribute HLL's products as a business venture, armed with training from HLL and support from government agencies concerned and NGOs. They claim that a typical Shakti entrepreneur conducts business of around Rs. 15,000 per month, which gives her income in excess of Rs. 1000 per month on a sustainable basis. As most of these women are from below poverty line and live in extremely small villages (less than 2000 population), this earning is very significant, and is almost double their past household income. Definitely, this adds much to the existing business and a major portion of the money in the hands of these rural women would again be diverted for more purchases for self consumption, thereby a beneficiary becomes a benefactor. These self-help groups with local identities promote products better, i.e. the agent of developmental marketing can also put an end to many of the problems faced by the marketer in the rural market.

(i) The members of SHG being local can easily predict the demand, which is seasonal and fluctuating in nature. They can monitor the agricultural productivity and be a useful source of information.

(ii) The group themselves can store the necessary stock and take care of the ware housing operations needed for any business and act as outlets. In short they can be a good channel partner.

(iii) The members being a part of rural community can serve marketers with required information regarding the behaviors/attitudes of rural customers. They can help in designing the behavioral models that facilitate the marketer in long.

(iv) Members of local groups' can be a good vehicle in reaching the rural customers. It will be easy for the local members to identify the probable prospects and their needs; they could act as good advocates/ambassadors in promoting the brand and increase prospects whenever possible. They can provide the customers with needed information and clarify their doubts and also facilitate arrival of a decision.

(v) Since the cohesiveness of the rural people is more, the ability to estimate individual families income and purchasing will be known. This would facilitate decision making on running credit terms to any rural customers.

The group members' local identity, their knowledge on the local market, their entrepreneurial spirits and cohesiveness in the group is a major strength. On the other side organizations aiming at tapping the rural market needs a local partner who is capable of helping them. Identifying the right group and providing proper training and guidance, the SHGs can play the role of distributors' *local level* information system; distribution system communication system and can also act as a catalytic agent. In short they can behave as an agent for development for the village and themselves and as marketers for company and also help develop their community.

REFERENCES

Koontz H. and Weihrich H., (2001), *'Management–A Global Perspective'*, New Delhi : Tata McGraw-Hill Publishing Company.

Kotler Philip, (2003), *Marketing Management*, Delhi : Pearson Education (Singapore) Pvt. Ltd., Indian Branch, Patparganj, New Delhi.

Nair R. Suja, (2001), *Consumer Behaviour-Indian Perspective*, Himalaya Publishing House, Mumbai.

Ramakrishnan Lalitha and Krishnamacharyulu, (2002), *Rural Marketing-Text and Cases*, Pearson Education (Singapore) Pvt. Ltd., Indian Branch, Patparganj, New Delhi.

Kashyap Pradeep, (2003) , *Stealing the Rural Show. Praxis-The Business Line's Journal on Management*, M/s Kasthuri & Sons Ltd., Chennai.

Sundharam K.P.M. and Datt Ruddar, (2003), *Indian Economy*-New Edition, Sultan Chand & Company Ltd., Ramnagar, New Delhi.

Hindustan Levers Distribution Network, Http://www.HLL.Com. copyright 2001, HLL dt. 23/04/04.

10

UZHAVAR SANDHAI (FARMER'S MARKET) IN TAMILNADU–AN ANALYSIS

Punithavathy Pandian & S. Thanasundari

Introduction

Marketing of fruits and vegetables is more complex in nature in comparison with the other field crops because of special traits like highly perishable nature, seasonality and bulkiness, which needs special care and immediate disposal. The Uzhavar Sandhai has assumed more relevance and significance especially in respect of marketing fruits and vegetables. The Uzhavar Sandhai is mainly organised to enhance the farmer's income by preventing intermediaries and distress selling. As the sale at the Uzhavar Sandhai is only for cash the farmers are getting money immediately. This is absent when they sell their produce to the middlemen because most of the traders make delayed payment.

The Uzhavar Sandhai revolves around the farmer and raises the position of farmer-to-farmer seller. The farmer is motivated to bring his produce to the Uzhavar Sandhai as he can directly market it to the consumers. Day in out they come to the market and the market has become their life breath and in turn, the farmer sellers have become the life breath of the market. Hence an attempt has been made to analyse the farmer sellers in selected Uzhavar Sandhai in Virudhunagar and Madurai Districts.

Origin of Uzhavar Sandhai

In order to eliminate the involvement of intermediaries the state government introduced Uzhavar Sandhai (Farmers' market) where the farmers and consumers can have direct dealings. The idea of setting the Uzhavar Sandhai exclusively for selling vegetables grown by the local growers was conceived in the early 1990s by former Union Agricultural Secretary, M.S. Gill. It is reported that 'Kal ghoj', a farmers market, was started way back in 1975 exclusively to sell vegetables and spinach in the former Soviet Union. During a visit to United Kingdom, Mr. M.S. Gill noticed that some of the farmers were selling vegetables and fruits at the roadside on a collective basis at a high profit. The market was very busy. After a detailed investigation, he found that the farmers directly sold their produce to the consumers without the help of intermediaries. Immediately on his return to India, he successfully set 'Apna Mandi' or *'Kisan Mandi'* in Punjab. The first *'Apna Mandi'* was started in Punjab at Chandigarh in 1987, in Haryana at Karnal in 1988. Noticing their success, the Union Ministry of agriculture suggested the idea for starting Uzhavar Sandhais in other states also. Andhra Pradesh took immediate steps to start 'Rythu Bazaar'.[1]

Recently a high-powered European committee visited the largest vegetables market in Tamilnadu, Ottanchatiram for an on the stop assessment of vegetables marketing by the farmers. The committee found that farmers sold their vegetables not only at throwaway prices but also simply dumped unsold vegetables on the roadside for want of transportation. Some growers reported to the committee that vegetables like tomatoes were left in the field itself as even the labour cost for harvesting was not realized.[2] This kind of situation had arisen even in adjoining states like Karnataka, where the growers registered their protest by dumping truckloads of tomato on the national highways due to a glut in the market. Market surplus, high input cost, lack of transportation and exploitation by the middlemen and wholesalers have made vegetable cultivation an unremunerative activity and made farmers lives miserable. Realizing the distress sale of vegetables and fruits, and the middlemen and wholesale traders role in cheating the farmers the committee suggested providing financial assistance of Rs. 300 crores to help the vegetable growing farmers. Even this was not given proper attention by the government at that time and the farmers continued to be exploited by vegetable traders and commission agents.

When the President of the Tamilnadu unit of the Traders Association visited the 'Rythu Bazaar' in Andhra Pradesh, he realized the importance of the concept of a farmers' market. On his return, he reported his conclusions to the Chief Minister, and he was convinced on the feasibility of a farmers' market. The government then identified the sites for Uzhavar Sandhais.

Data

The government established hundred Uzhavar Sandhais in various parts of Tamilnadu. In Madurai and Virudhunagar districts eleven Uzhavar Sandhais were established. At present seven Uzhavar Sandhais are functioning in both in the districts in Virudhunagar, Rajapalayam, Srivilliputtur, Aruppukkottai, Madurai Anna Nagar, Chockkikulam and Palanganatham. One hundred and twenty sample farmer sellers were drawn from all the seven Uzhavar Sandhais. Structured interview schedule were used to collect the relevant information from the sellers. The data were collected during the month of January, February and March 2000.

Analytical Tool

To rank the factors Garettes' Ranking technique was adopted. The formula is

$$\text{Percent position} = \frac{(Rij - 0.5)}{Nj} \times 100$$

Where

Rij = Rank given for ith factor by jth individual

Nj = Number of factors ranked by jth individual

The percent position of each rank thus obtained was converted into scores by referring to the table given by Garret's. Analysis of variance technique was used to list the significant difference between more than two means.

Source of Information

Any new concept needs to be communicated to the group concerned. Successful results can be obtained through proper communication. The communication must reach the right persons, at right time, at the right place and through the right means. The establishment of Uzhavar Sandhai reached the farmers through various media such as All India Radio, newspapers, marketing officials, fellow farmers, pamphlets issued by Uzhavar Sandhais and Television. The sources of information were given to the farmers for ranking. The orders of merit assigned by the farmer sellers were converted into ranks by using the formula. The results of ranking are shown in table 1.

Table 1: Source of Information

No.	*Sources*	*I*	*II*	*III*	*IV*	*V*	*VI*	*Total Scores*	*Rank Position*
1.	All India Radio	15	18	30	10	26	21	6271	V
2.	Local Newspapers	10	33	13	8	20	36	6477	IV
3.	Fellow Farmers	18	25	11	10	30	26	6721	II
4.	Uzhavar Sandhais	33	34	10	9	10	24	6585	III
5.	Marketing Officials	20	27	14	12	14	33	5832	VI
6.	Television	67	12	9	10	11	11	7577	I

Source: Primary Data.

Table 1 reveals that television media played a dominant role in popularizing the establishment of Uzhavar Sandhai. Facts can be grasped more easily through viewing television than any other media. Most of the farmer sellers got the information from their own fraternity.

Decision Making

Decision-making is crucial in marketing. Decision regarding what to sell, when to sell, where to sell, whom to sell must be taken by the farmer sellers. Correct decision must be taken at correct time. Correct decision depends upon the marketing experience and knowledge possessed by the farmer sellers. Some persons may take self-decision; some others may take decision after having consultation with others. In order to find out how they select Uzhavar Sandhai, various decision-making alternatives were given to the farmer sellers for ranking. The alternatives were ranked with the help of Garrete's ranking techniques and given in table 2.

Table 2: Decision Alternatives of the Farmer Sellers in Uzhavar Sandhais

No.	*Sources*	*I*	*II*	*III*	*IV*	*V*	*VI*	*Total Scores*	*Rank Position*
1.	Self decision	20	25	20	25	18	12	6279	IV
2.	Consulting friends	10	20	16	17	38	19	5491	V
3.	Consulting family members	50	27	9	13	15	6	7363	I
4.	Consulting village merchants	25	34	25	13	13	10	6738	II
5.	Consulting the commission agents	8	15	23	23	26	25	5380	VI
6.	Consulting marketing officials	10	40	26	24	13	7	6637	III

Source: Primary Data.

Instead of taking self decision, the farmer sellers give due consideration to their family members. The results presented in table 4 revealed that most of the farmer sellers are taking decision regarding marketing their produces in Uzhavar Sandhai, after having consultation with their family members accompany and assist the farmer sellers in marketing their produces in Uzhavar Sandhais and thus marketing the agricultural produce becomes a family venture in the study area. Hence, consultation with them counts Vijaya Raghavan and Subramanyam (1980) also observed that discussion with family members was the useful method of taking decision.[3] The second rank is given to consultation with village merchants. Outside their family circle, they find it easy to consult with merchants of their own village. Then they consult the marketing officials. The marketing officials are approached to get the particulars regarding the Uzhavar Sandhai.

Reason for Choosing Uzhavar Sandhais

Uzhavar Sandhais provide a place for the marketers of vegetables and fruits to sell their produces directly to the people without recourses to the middlemen. These sandhais are started to establish a direct link between the farmer sellers and the consumers. By eliminating the middlemen, this scheme aims at benefiting both the farmers as well as the consumers. The farmer sellers need not pay rent of the shop allotted to them or commission for selling their goods at the market. The market committee appointed by the state government fixes the prices for the same. The prices are fixed for different commodities on the basis of previous day prices of that commodity in the wholesale market. Garrete's ranking technique is used to find out the primary reason for choosing the Uzhavar Sandhais by the sample farmer sellers. The various reasons are listed in Table 3 along with Garette Ranking.

Table 3: Reasons for Choosing Uzhavar Sandhais by Sample Farmer Sellers

No.	*Sources*	*I*	*II*	*III*	*IV*	*Total Scores*	*Rank Position*
1.	Direct contact with consumer	8	46	29	37	5398	III
2.	Avoidance of middlemen	78	16	14	12	7438	I
3.	Reasonable price	16	24	15	65	4896	IV
4.	No rent for shop and no charge for weighing machine	21	35	56	6	6042	II

Source: Primary Data.

By adopting Garrete's ranking technique it is found that avoidance of middlemen is the first and foremost reason for choosing the Uzhavar Sandhais by the farmer sellers. Most of the sample farmer sellers expressed that avoidance of middlemen is the best advantage of Uzhavar Sandhai. Studies conducted on marketing of vegetables have shown that the exploitation by middlemen resulting in very low share of consumer's rupee. This point is supported by Bhale Rao et. al (1981)[4], Subramanyam (1981)[5] and S. Chowdhury (2002)[6]. Paying rent and establishing a shop is generally out of reach of the small farmers. Getting a place with basic amenities to sell their products without rent is a boon for them. Provision of weighing scales by the marketing committee also relieve them from the botheration of bringing their own scales.

Sales Per Day

The sales per day of the farmer sellers differ from each other. The sales value depends upon the nature of the vegetables sold by the farmer sellers. The details about the sales per day and the nature of vegetables are presented in table 4.

Table 4: Sales per day of the Farmer Sellers

Sales per day	*Number of Farmers*			*Total*
	Local vegetables	*Hill vegetables*	*Fruits*	
Less than Rs.100/-	35 (74.5)	5 (10.6)	7 (14.9)	47 (100)
Rs.101-200/-	21 (55.3)	6 (15.8)	11 (28.9)	38 (100)
Above Rs.200/-	14 (40)	5 (14.3)	16 (45.7)	35 (100)
Total	70	16	34	120

Figures in the parenthesis are percentages.

Table 4 clearly discloses that, 35 (74.5 percent) local vegetable sellers earn less than Rs. 100/- per day. There are 6 (15.8 percent) hill vegetable sellers whose earning ranges from Rs. 101-200/- per day. There are 16 (45.7 percent) fruit sellers who earn more than Rs. 200/- perday. It is evident from this table that the sales of the fruit sellers in Uzhavar Sandhais are higher compared to the sales of other farmer sellers.

Variety of Produce Sold in Uzhavar Sandhais

The varieties of produce sold in Uzhavar Sandhais are classified into three categories such as local vegetables, hill vegetables and fruits. Local vegetables category consists brinjal, tomato, lady's finger, small onion and greens which are grown locally. These vegetables are highly marketed by the farmer sellers in Uzhavar Sandhais. These vegetables are considered as short duration crops grown by the farmer sellers who depend on the sale of these vegetables for livelihood in this study area. During the hot humid rainy season, brinjal is one of the few vegetables available to urban and rural poor at reasonable prices ranging from Rs. 4 to 8/- per kg.. Vegetables such as cabbage, cauliflower, beans potato and carrot are considered as hill vegetables. The climatic condition needed for these vegetables is different from that of local vegetables. Farmer sellers of Kodaikanal market these vegetables. Fruits such as banana, guava, lime, mango and papaya are locally grown and marketed by local growers. The summary statistics regarding the sales per day of these categories of vegetables are given in table 5.

Table 5 : Varieties of Produce sold in Uzhavar Sandhais

Varieties	*Number of Farmers*	*Mean Sales*	*σ (S.D)*	*C.V.*	*F Value*
Small	47	83.46	12.67	15.18	48.461*
Medium	38	163.70	22.12	13.51	
Large	35	287.36	54.35	18.91	

*Significant at 5 percent level.

It is evident from table 5 that, majority of the farmer sellers (58.3 percent) are selling only local vegetables. Hill vegetables are sold by only 16 (13.3 percent) farmer sellers. The average sale of fruits is the highest (193.7) compared to vegetables and hill vegetables. The coefficient of variation is more or less similar in the case of vegetables and hill vegetables. To find out whether there is any significant difference in the average sale value per days among the local vegetables, hill vegetables and fruits, 'F' value is calculated. The insignificant 'F' indicates that there is no difference in the average sale value per day among the local vegetables, hill vegetables and fruits.

Vegetable Cultivation

Vegetable cultivation is made on the basis of soil condition of the agricultural land. Seasonality is on the wane in vegetable cultivation. It has become a common phenomenon to see many vegetables like tomato, brinjal, lady's finger and cabbage being available throughout the year in vegetable markets. This has become possible because of the development of improved varieties/hybrids. In order to increase returns from per unit area of land, and to shorten the period of return to investment intercropping of vegetables is also followed by vegetable growers. Some varieties of greens are grown by the local vegetable growers by adopting intercropping. In fruit orchards especially vegetables are grown to utilize the space available in the initial stage. The important vegetables sold in Uzhavar Sandhais are selected and the details about the number of farmers growing those vegetables are given in table[6].

Table 6 : Number of Farmer Sellers Growing Selected Vegetables in Uzhavar Sandhais

Vegetables/ Fruits	*Number of small farmers*	*Number of medium farmers*	*Number of large farmers*	*Total number of farmers Number*	*Total number of farmers Percentage*
Tomato	42	26	25	93	77.5
Brinjal	39	28	23	90	75.0
Lady's finger	25	24	13	62	51.7
Onion	20	10	15	45	37.5
Potato	18	9	4	31	25.8
Carrot	16	7	6	29	24.2
Banana	6	5	4	15	12.5
Guava	4	6	3	13	10.8
Chillies/Greens	5	4	7	16	13.3

Percentage is calculated out of the total number of farmers.

It may be seen from table 8 that out of the total sample farmer sellers, 77.5 percent reported the cultivation of tomato followed by 75 percent in case of bribjal, 51.7 percent in lady's finger and 37.5 percent in onion. Tomato is widely cultivated because of its demand, because it is profusely used in the Southern Indian cuisine. Among the sample respondents guava cultivators are lesser in number.

Profitability

Profit is the main motivating factor behind any business. Agriculture is not an exception to this. In Uzhavar Sandhais the prices are always higher than the wholesale rate and lesser than the retail rate which benefited the farmers and consumers because of direct selling, zero market margin and nil price spread. (Dharmarajan, 2000, Shanmugam and Kempuchetty, 2000). Rent free shops, free weighing scales and transportation facilities with the elimination of middlemen enables the farmer sellers to get more profit. Information is collected regarding the percentage of profit gained through selling products in Uzhavar Sandhais and presented in table[7].

Table 7 : Percentage of Profit of Farmer Sellers

SI. No.	*Percentage of Profit*	*Number of Farmers*	*Percentage*
1.	Below 10	10	8.3
2.	11-20	14	11.7
3.	21-30	26	21.7
4.	Above 30	70	58.3
	Total	120	100.0

Source: Primary Data.

It is clear from table 7 that 70 (58.3 percent) farmer sellers are getting more than 30 percent as profit in selling their produce in Uzhavar Sandhais. Out of 120 sample farmer sellers 10 (8.3 percent) farmer sellers started that their profit is less than 10 percent.

The farmers who brave the vagaries of monsoon to produce vegetables and fruits, find it difficult to sell the produce at a profitable price. Establishment of U.S. has helped them to overcome the hardships posed by the middlemen. The direct contact with the consumers has enhanced their income. Like any other industry, diversification of products i.e. selling more than two products has resulted in high average sales per day. The Uzhavar Sandhais in general, has done a laudable job in making the marketing easy for the farmers.

REFERENCES

Rajendran, S., "Curtains for Farmers' Market?", *Economic and Political Weekly,* Vol. 36 (29), 2000.

Jeyarathinam, M, "Farmers' Market (Uzhavar Sandhai) in Tamilnadu"- A SWOT Analysis", *Indian Journal of Marketing* Vol. XXXII, No. 8, August 2002, p. 3.

Vijay Raghavan, K. & Subramaniyan, V.S., *Indian Journal of Extension Education,* XVI, pp. 77–81.

Bhale Rao, M.M., Ansari, S.L., and Tyagi, B.P., "Marketing of Vegetables"- A Sample Study, *Agricultural Marketing,* 24 (1) 1981, pp. 27-29.

Subramaniyan, K.V., "Effect of Marketing Costs on Cost of Production and Returns: Case Study of Vegetables", *Agricultural Marketing* 24 (3), 1981, pp. 7–9.

Chowdhry, S., "Co-operative Marketing of Fruits and Vegetables in India: Need of the 21st Century", *Economic Affairs,* Vol. 47, March 2002, p. 56.

Dharmarajan, S., "Rural Marketing–A Tamilnadu Model", *Kisan World,* 27(6), 2000, p. 12.

Shanmugam, T.R. & Kempuchetty, K., "Benefits of Farmers : Markets in Rural Economy of Tamilnadu", *Indian Economic Panorama,* 10 (2), 2000, pp. 29-30.

11

ECONOMIC REFORMS AND FISHERIES SECTOR

K. Karunaharan & C. Thangamuthu

Introduction

Indian fisheries in the pre mechanized period (prior to mid 1950s) was characterized by low fish productivity due to traditional technology and poor standard of living. The infrastructure facilities for landing and berthing were also poor (Anugraham 1940; Selvaraj 1975; Warriar 1967). Constraining the scope for intensive fishing.

During the Second Five Year Plan period, the technology transfer from Norway to India was the major turning point. Later, the globalisation scenario of 1990s onwards was another landmark in changing the profile of Indian fisheries. In this context, the purpose of this paper is to focus how these two economic reforms had their impact on the employment dimension of a select fishing village in Coromandel Coast. The paper seeks to highlights the changing trends in employment opportunities and look for alternative non-fishing employment opportunities.

From the technology dimension, the paper conjectures that the future for fisheries is threatened, signified by the declining trend in per head fish catch. The traditional women employment in fisheries is also declining. Hence there is an impending need for search for non-fishing employment opportunities may be from outside the fishing village, conserve the fishing resources by restricting the outside the fishermen community and also arrest the destructive fishing. It is also suggested to the strengthen the local institutional structure viz, Fishermen Community Panchayat (FCP) and give the responsibility to manage the local fish resources.

Profile of the Coromandel Coast and the Study Village

There are four coastal regions in Tamilnadu, namely, Coromandel Coast, Palk Strait, Gulf of Mannar and West Coast with the coastline of 350 kms., 270 kms., 320 kms. and 60 kms. respectively (GOTN, 1988–89). The Coromandel Coast has six districts including Chennai, Thiruvallur, Kancheepuram, Villupuram, Cuddalore and Nagapattinam (part of this district also spread into Palk strait). In Palk Strait there are four districts (Thiruvarur, Thanjavur, Pudukkottai and Ramanathapuram) of which a portion of Ramanathapuram district has spread into Gulf of Mannar. The Gulf of Mannar districts of Ramanathapuram, Thoothukudi, Tirunelvel,. The West Coast has one district that is Kanniyakumari. The regional classification is based on geographical locations and obviously the district separation is more for administrative purposes, than any economic logic.

There are 591 marine fishing villages (Table 1) spread into 13 maritime districts in above said coastal regions of Tamilnadu. Of them there are 261[1] fishing villages in Coromandel Coast. The study village, Egatoor Karikkattukuppam (E.K. Kuppam) is one among them. In these villages fishing activities are taking place at a small-scale. Hence, the E.K. Kuppam hamlet is purposively selected for the present study (the details about the study village are discussed in the later section). The average distance between the fishing villages in Tamilnadu is 1.82 kms., which means each village has a shore length of less than two kms.

The Coromandel Coast accounts for about 50 percent of the fishing village in Tamilnadu and also around 50 percent of

Table 1: District-Wise number of fishing villages in Tamilnadu, 2000

SI. No.	*Name of the Districts*	*Number of fishing villages*
1.	Chennai	44
2.	Thiruvallur	58
3.	Kanchipuram	44
4.	Villupuram	19
5.	Cuddalore	49
6.	Nagapattinam	51
7.	Thiruvarur	13
8.	Thanjavur	27
9.	Pudukottai	32
10.	Ramanathapuram	184
11.	Thoothukudi	21
12.	Tirunelveli	7
13.	Kanniyakumari	42
	Total	591

Source : GOTN, (2000): Department of Fisheries, Marine Fisherfok Census, abstract, 2000.

the total fishermen households in the State (Table 2). The incidence of men engaged in fishing is marginally higher in Coromandel Coast than the State average per village. In sharp contrast to this, the average number of women in fishing per village is substantially lower (1-31) in Coromandel Coast as against 3.78 in the state. Women are engaged more in fish trading in the Coromandel Coast as against the State average. The net making, however, has not attracted women in the coromandel Coast as it has been the case in the State. Men in fishing trade in Coromandel Coast are outnumbered perceptibly by the State figure.

Employment Dimensions in E.K. Kuppam (the study village)

The total hamlets in Muttukkadu revenue village are eight; the E.K. Kuppam is one among them. The other hamlets in Muttukkadu revenue village are; Kazhipattoor, Vaniyansavadi,

Table 2: Major Socio-Economic Indicators of Fisherfolk In Coromandel Coast and Tamil Nadu, 2000 (in numbers)

Particulars	*Coramandel Coast*	*Tamil Nadu*	*Per village average*	
			Coromandel Coast	*Tamil Nadu*
Villages	261	591	1	1
Number of HHs	59811	143745	229.16	243.22
Total Population	**271502**	**679711**	**1040.23**	**1150.10**
Male	138516	348312	530.71	589.36
Female	132986	331399	509.52	560.74
Total Adult	**170615**	**425882**	**653.69**	**720.61**
Adult Male	89493	222624	342.88	376.69
Adult Female	81122	203258	310.81	343.92
Literate	138410	399067	530.30	675.24
Illiterate	99420	200107	380.91	338.59
Total men in Occupation	**78457**	**194470**	**300.60**	**329.05**
Men in Fishing	70231	170510	269.08	288.51
Fishing Trade	928	3174	3.55	5.27
Net Making & Diving	142	1470	0.54	2.48
Allied	1656	2657	6.344	4.49
Others	5500	16659	21.07	28.18
Total Women in Occupation	**19102**	**37343**	**73.18**	**63.18**
Women in Fishing	344	2237	1.31	3.78
Fishing Trade	16349	23960	69.98	40.54
Net making & Diving	51	2157	0.19	3.64
Allied	544	2063	2.08	3.49
Others	1724	6926	6.60	11.71
Mech. Craft	3135	8009	12.01	13.55
Non-Mc.Craft	20886	41170	80.02	69.66
Gears*	151931	425632	582.11	720.18

Source: Compiled from Marine Fisherfolk Census 2000, DoF, Tamil Nadu.

Note:* Gears are included trawl net, gill net, shore seine and others.

Egatoor, Keel Pakkam, Muttukkadu Colony, Muttukkadu Yellow Board, Muttukkadu (ward no. 8, Muslim residence). The major occupation of above said hamlets are agriculture, agriculture coolie, and coolie is other sectors and small petty traders. Of all the E.K. Kuppam is the only hamlet involved in marine fishing and allied activities.

The total number of respondent's households in the study village is 158 (Table 3). Of the 158 households, 134 households (84.4 percent) are engaged in fishing, six households (3.8 percent) are engaged in fishing related activities such as fish trading, financing and service activities (they do not go for fishing) the rest 18 households (11.4 percent) are neither doing fishing nor in fishing related activities. The non-fishing employment can be classified as government, private, self-employment, real estate broker and casual labour.

Table 3 : Employment Wise Classification of Respondents

Activities	*Number of respondents*	*Percent to the Total*
Fishing	134	84.8
Fishing related	6	3.8
Non-fishing	18	11.4
Total	158	100

Source: Primary survey, 2000.

Note: Non-fishing includes auto driver, grocery merchants, petty shops, etc.,

In the above said employment classification fishing alone has an institutional support from Govt. the other fishing related and non-fishing have no organization in their day-to-day activities.

Table 4 shows that the employment profile of E. K. Kuppam village during the three Census period namely, 1978, 1986 and 2000. The 1986 data were approximate estimation from the previous Census. The female population in the village is greater than the male as per the censuses of 1978 and 2000. Number of persons engaged in fishing has also increased from 137 to 220

Table 4: The Major Socio-Economic Indicators of E.K. Kuppam During 1978, 1986 and 2000

Sl. No.	*Selected Socio-Economic indicators* — *Categories*	*1978*	*1986*	*2000*
1.	Male	268	330	362
2.	Female	277	307	372
3.	Total Population	545	618	734
4.	Number of Families	113	130	171
5.	Average family members			
6.	Illiterate	NA	505	437
7.	Literate	NA	113	297
8.	Number of persons engaged in fishing	137	159	220
9.	Number of persons in allied occupation	1	0	0
10.	Other occupation	0	0	0
11.	Employment in Govt.& Private	NA	NA	13
12.	Total male employment	134	159	233
13.	Number of women in fishing	NA	0	0
14.	Fresh fish trade & Dry fish trade	NA	2	2
15.	Other occupation	NA	7	0
16.	Govt. & Private employment	NA	NA	1
17.	Total Women Employment	NA	9	3
18.	Average monthly income per fisherman	Rs 17, to 475	Up to 6000	NA
19.	Number of Mechanised Boats	0	0	0
20.	Total number of Kattumaram (non mechanised)	142	91	132
21.	Number of canoes	5	2	0
22.	Total number of craft	147	93	132
23.	Total Number of gears	165	120	362

Source: GOTN, Dept. of Fisheries, Fishermen Census, 1978, 1986, 2000.

Note: NA is Not Avilable.

during 1978-2000. No women are involved in fishing. Number of literates have been increasing over the period. The number of kattumaram with out board machine has been increasing. At the same time the use of canoes has been completely stopped. But the net which was used in the canoes is now being used in the kattumaram. The total number of gears almost doubled over the 20 year period from 1978 to 2000.

In 1978, of the total population, 25.13 percent were engaged in fishing which has increased to 29.97 percent in the year 2000.

The employment opportunities for women declined over the period. Women biased activities such as net making and dry fish trade showed a steep fall due to changing technology. And it is true that the women struggle to find out alternate income generating opportunities outside the fishing sector.

In the case of study village, the number of fishing days reduced which made the youth fisherfolk to look for non-fishing employment. Even the non-fishing employment has very little scope in the village. The new prawn trade facilitated by globalisation provides attractive price to the fisherfolk and a good commission for the prawn agents. But the agents give and incentive of advance to the fisherfolk which the latter need not repay. The small women traders are unable to give this incentive amount; hence they are not in a position to compete with them. At present, the only woman prawn trader stopped her prawn trade due to lack of funds (to give incentive advance to the fisherfolk).

The widows are generally given the task of conducting fish-auction at the sea-shore. (This practice is in striking contrast to the general treatment meted out to widows in other occupations. The sight of a widow is considered inauspicious in villages and the widows are not entertained in harvest floor etc.). But, excepting one widow who is engaged in fish auction, other widows had to seek employment elsewhere, on account of declining fish catch. Since fish trading is not familiar, they go for non-fish employment.

If we look into the above aspects of mechanization at the sample village level, the following findings are significant:

1. the traditional cotton net was replaced by synthetic nylon net; Though the Norwegian technology was introduced in mid 1950s, this study village deliberately delayed the

introduction till 1980. The FCP mediated that till every fisherman in the village is able to acquire a nylon net, they shall delay the introduction. These new net materials resulted in changing work relationship. With the nylon net, and individual fisherman can own and operate the net. Hence traditional group fishing with cotton net was given up leading to reduction in man days of fishing. Entry of larger mechanized boats into their fishing ground damaged the fishing ground and reduced the share of their catch. Apart from this entry of deep-sea fishing vessels also shared the fish resources. In the case of women, due to the operation of larger net making industries to support mechanized boat, women employment in net making almost disappeared.

2. The globalisation opened up external market. Even though the price for fish (particularly the prawn) has increased, the availability of fish at the village landing site has reduced. Hence sometimes fisherwomen traders need to approach the nearest mechanized fish landing center for procuring fish for sale in the market. With the influx of export traders in such big centres, the women find it extremely difficult to compete with those export traders.

Mechanisation in Fisheries

According to Bavinck (1998), Blue Revolution as an all-India phenomenon is largely for marine fisheries. Policy makers felt the need for modernisation of fishing in order to meet the food needs of a growing population and also to bridge wide gap which, in their perception, existed between the fish resource and the capacities of the fishing fleet. And they realised that improvement in fisheries might be desirables not only for the sector, but also for the country as a whole.

Mechanisation in significant terms started during mid 1950s. The State Govt. of Tamilnadu collaborated with the FAO in designing a mechanised craft under Indo-Norwegian Project

(INP) one of the first technical assistances that came from a developed country to developing country (Kurien, 1985). As Arundhuti (2001) stated the purpose of Norwegian technology was to raise fish output, improve the quality of processing and marketing and improve living standards of the fisher folk.

In 1907 the first fisheries Department was started in Tamilnadu. The mechanization of fishing boats was undertaken in three stages in Tamilnadu: (i) mechanisation of indigenous fishing crafts, (ii) introduction of small mechanized open fishing boats and, (iii) construction of larger decked fishing boats (Bavinck 1998).

There are three important boats viz; in 1955, Pablo boat of 25 feet, of two tonne fish hold, mainly for gillnetting; in 1962 Illugason boat of 30 feet of , two tonne fish hold and best suitable for Tamilnadu coastal; then Trawler Boat (STB) of four tonne fish hold, with and advantage of winch and cabin attachment. These boats formed core of the technical innovation programme, which lasted until 1980 (Bavinck, 1988).

In 1958 Marina boat building yard was set up and in 1965 Rayapuram boat yard started functioning with labour saving mechanical and electrical appliances. During the period from 1956-57 to 1968-69, subsidy for engine was given to group fishermen as well as individual fishermen. In order to meet the rising demand for boat, three boat building yards were set up in Madras, Cuddalore and Nagapatinam. Government being unable to meet the demand for boats, the private boat building yards came up in Madras, Cuddalore, Tuticorin and Muttom.

Bavinck (1998) has observed that the Blue Revolution unleased new forces and dynamics. The basic problem was that boat fishermen fish in the same place, which artisanal fishermen depended, and this created socio-economic conflicts among them.

There has been an increasing trend in fishermen population and number of mechanized boats in Tamilnadu over the 20-year period, 1978 to 1998. The percentage of active fishermen to the total fishing population has been on the increase during

1990s. Particularly in 1994 the proportion reached a peak level of 43.22 percent, while the corresponding percentage shares from 1978 to 1986 ranged around 21 to 24 percent. The increasing degree of mechanization and bigger boats during the nineties have perhaps necessitated involvement of more men into active fishing. And supply of boats under interest subsidy credit could also be another reason for increase in the proportion of boat-owing fishermen in the total fishing population (Table A3).

According to the Fisheries Department Annual Report (1996-97), the active fisherfolk population has been assessed from registration of boats with Marine Fishermen and Women Co-operative societies. This figure includes fishermen with mechanised boat as well as kattumaram. Hence the scope for some variation between the actual field and the recorded data. Some fishermen might have got themselves registered, but may not be actively engaged in fishing.

Fishing Productivity

Table 5 shows that the per capita fish production (i.e., average production of fish per head of active fishermen) for Tamilnadu is declining since 1986. In 1986, the per capita productivity was around 2.45 tonnes while it slipped down to

Tablè 5: Per Capita Marine Fish Production for Active and Total Fisherfolk Population in Tamil Nadu

Year	*Fisherfolk Population (in numbers)*		**Fish production (in tones)*	*Per capita fish production (in tones)*	
	Total	*Active*		*Total Fisherfolk Population*	*Active fishserfolk*
1986	463800	101869	249576	0.54	2.45
1996	537941	263428	350790	0.65	1.33
1997	545978	261716	356400	0.65	1.36

Source: GOTN, Dept. of Fisheries Statistics (annual report), 1996-97.

Note:* The Fish production years are 1986-87, 1996-97 and 1997-98 respectively.

around 1.33 tonnes in 1996-97 and 1.36 with a slight increase in 1997-98. If the number of total fishermen population (including less active segments like women/children) are taken into account, the aggregate average per capita productivity for the said years was .54 tonnes, .65 tonnes and 65 tonnes respectively. The over all finding is that there has been a decline in per capita fish production for the active fisherfolk. This is indicative of the impending need for shifting from fishing employment to the non-fish sector.

Table 6: Marine Fish Catch from Shore-Seine (Traditional Boat) Net from 1994–95 to 1998-99

Type of nets	*1994-95*	*1995-96*	*1996-97*	*1997-98*	*1998-99*
Catches from seine nets	5436	4441	4713	NA	2056

Source: GOTN, Dept. Fisheries (Annual Reports), 1994-95; 1995-96; 1996-97;1998-99.

As a result of more specialized gears coming into practice, some of the traditional gears such as the shore-seines, boat seines have become less important and are falling into disurse (Sathiadhas, 1997:61; Bavinck, 1998: 57). The catches from these nets too, consequently, show a decline.

If we look for the percentage contribution of Tamilnadu to the total all-India's export in terms of quantity and value, there has been a fluctuation in several years. The share of Tamilnadu's contribution to the total ranged from 6 percent to 25 percent (Table A2). Despite these fluctuations, there is generally a significant contribution of the State to earn foreign exchange. The reasons for the fluctuations are perhaps the changes in prices in the export markets for some of the select species.

Kurien (1989) opines that the prawns have increased in importance to become the 'pink gold' of marine exports from India. In Kerala, according to Kurien, in 1961-62 the beach price of prawns was only Rs. 240 per tonne, i.e., less than price of mackerels which was a low valued species. In 1971-72 prawn price reached Rs. 1810 per tonne, a seven-fold increase.

Tamilnadu's share to the India's total export in terms of value (in contrast with the quantum) has increased significantly thanks to substantial increase in the high value prawn exports from Tamilnadu.

As Bavinck (1998) noted, in 1993 the main income earner was still prawn and it accounted 59 percent of the export volume and 87 percent of earnings. Despite better value of foreign exchange reaching our exchequer, there are likely to be nutritional, and other socio-economic implications causing some structural changes in the production relations in the fisheries sector.

Globalization: Over Exploitation of Fish Resources and Institutional Intervention

The new economic policy can be divided into two parts: (a) Stabilisation policies to correct marco-economic imbalances, and (b) structural reforms to improve the productivity of resources and enhance our export capabilities. The second part encourages fishery sector.

The liberalization of foreign investments has encouraged Indian entrepreneurs to go in for joint ventures in deep-sea fishing. In 1992, 22 foreign companies from South and North Korea, Denmark, Taiwan France, Russia, Latvia, Phillipines, Portugal, USA and Japan have been given clearance to set up joint ventures with Indian companies on deep-sea fishing. Hundred percent export oriented units are given many concessions. Such export-oriented units are fast establishing in sea-food industries (PSBR James and et al., 1993).

Over-fishing of resources had affected the economic status of fisherfolk in many ways. The real per capita incomes of the trawler crew tend to increase at the expense of the traditional fishermen (Kurien and Achari, 1989).

In 1950 no marine fish stocks were known to be over-fished. But in 1974, FAO, UN estimated that almost 70 percent of those stocks were exploited and over-fished. This development point of view. (Editor, 1997). There is a growing concern against the dangers of over-fishing facilitated by modern technology and globalisation.

Kurien (1989) pointed out that the reasons for over-fishing are: (a) Open access nature of the fisheries, (b) use of inappropriate technology, (c) the subsidies and (d) population pressure on in-shore waters.

Ramakrishna Korkandy (1996) has made some pertinent observations on managing the world fisheries vis-à-vis new economic order. The net effect of the trade-off will be less food, more unemployment and more natural resource depletion for the third world countries in the long run. The effects of this unequal exchange are already felt in developing countries like India, where domestic fish prices (in relation to international prices, on many occasions) are raising and ecological imbalances are looming large.

There interlocking factors underlie the over-fishing which have brought the world's fisheries to the brink of biological and economic collapse:

(i) The enclosure of local fishing grounds; (ii) the creation of global markers for fish; (iii) and the build-up of industrial fishing fleets. Fishing grounds which were managed by local communities, often for centuries, have been thrown open to the global economy and over capitalization of assets, rampant overfishing, boom and bust cycles, debt and redundancy. The solutions proposed by apologists for centarlisation and industrialization are to privatize fish stocks and to cut fishing fleets by weeding out the inefficient' fishers that are least to blame for over fishing. Local fishing communities around the world are voicing for alternative measures-for example, by restricting the free play of technologies and bringing fishing grounds back under community control (Simon Fairlic and et al., 1995).

Fish food is an important meat and demand for this product has been increasing every day. The global demand for sea food has been estimated at 110 million tonnes by 2000 AD against the supply of 100 million tonnes (Fisheries World, 1996). But any resource should not be exploited beyond the rate/capacity of natural renewal or replenishment of the stocks. Otherwise the fish resource might cease to be a sustained resource base for the human welfare.

The study village is characterized by a high degree of awareness and concern for conserving the fish resource. Besides taking measures to prevent over-exploitation, the marketing and other social security concerns are taken care of by some institutions, including the FCP evolved at the at the initiative of local community.

There are three agencies/organizations for looking after the fishermen interests at the fishing village level. They are, (i) State Government Organisation including a State Fisheries Department, Fishermen Co-operative societies (FCS) and (ii) Local village Panchayat (State sponsored) and (iii) Fishermen Community Panchayat (FCP). The first two are government institutions and they are involved in giving financial assistance and a few welfare measures during off-season. Apart from financial problem (indebtedness and lack of credit), there are other problems such as social conflict, employment relations, food security and fishing resource conservation.

State Institutions

Tamilnadu Fisheries Department (DoF)

The State Fisheries Department provides subsidy for net, Out board Engine and Kattumaram. The other benefit schemes such as, Death relief fund, off-season relief fund (insurance), housing programmes and other benefits are made available through the Fisheries Department.

Fishermen in the village have registered their names in Fishermen Co-operatives Societies (FCS). Even though there is a scheme of Fisherwomen Co-operative Societies, but it is not in existence in this village since women fishing is absent. The FCS is mediating the Government schemes and provides loans to their members.

Local Village Panchayat

The village panchayat functions as similar in other non-fishing villages. It provides basic amenities to the resident people like road, drinking water, electricity, community toilet and other benefits of Rural development Programmes.

Besides the Government institutions, there is an organization called Fishermen Community Panchayat at the village level. This FCP saves their community people in settling village disputes, off-season relief arrangements and conduct of village festivals.

Non-State Institutions

Pattinavar is the dominant fishing community in Coromandel Coast. Most of the fishing villages have strong **Fishermen Community Panchayat (FCP)**[1]. The fishing communities in India are generally caste-cum-occupation groups. Caste apart from the regulating techniques of fishing, plays and important part in production and marketing organization of the fishing industry. For instance, the Mugavirs, a fishing community in Karnataka in India, have a strong caste Panchayat for the whole district with a hereditary headman who is also the spiritual preceptor (Rajapurohit, 1963).

Fishermen Community Panchayat (FCP) at the Fishing Village Level

Initially (until 1950) the FCP served as a cultural entity, mostly engaged in organization of village festivals, families and social disputes among the fishing community members. It had seldom involved in any significant economic activity that had a bearing on fishing activities. During 1950s the FCP slowly embarked upon some elementary economic rules such as maintaining a registry of fishermen in the village and trying to regulate the fishing activity particularly in terms of fishing net size and the periodicity of its usage. During loan season the FCP used to partly take care of the interest of the needy fishermen, for which donations from the neighbouring industries and businessmen were collected. These "donations" are strictly speaking a misnomer. For instance, in one case, the FCP extracted money as "compensation" for allowing the drain pipe of a neighboring prawn hatchery to pass through seashore. Such forced collections are made for the community welfare. Whenever there was a need for resources for performing temple festivals and functions, the FCP could devise its own method of collecting funds from its own members. Sometimes, the arrange to borrow from the neighboring FCP or a big fish trader. Such loans would be repaid along with interest, from out of the contributions made by the FCP members later on. Thus the FCP emerged largely as an institution of social security and also a stabilizer of social relations. But the role of FCP underwent a perceptible change during the last three or four decades. It is during this period that the advent of Norwegian technology into fishing gear and craft made the fishing a more lucrative economic avenue. Further, thanks to the impact of globalisation and opening up of new markets for special varieties of fish, the export potential widened horizon of market earnings of fishermen. In the backdrop of this changing economic scenario, the FCP deliberately or otherwise focused its attention more towards organizing and regulation marketing of fish catch. The marketing is almost controlled and regulated by the FCP through introduction of new organisation and practices. As part of securing a guaranteed minimum price and also reducing the impact of risk and uncertainty associated with fishing, the FCP arranges for a "community auction" and thereby avoiding internal competition among the fishermen in selling the fish to the traders.

Conclusion

The foregoing analysis thus reveals the following findings:

(i) a substantial growth in fish production at Tamilnadu during nineties as a cumulative effect mechanisation and technological advances.

(ii) the increased fish production is reflected in perceptible jump in export of fish in Tamilnadu during the said period.

(iii) the per capita fish catch (productivity) among active fishermen and total population of fisherfolk have however shown declining trend, signalling over-fishing on the one hand and large number of active fishermen engaged in fishing on the other.

(iv) The phenomenal increase in fish production during 1990s may be mainly explained as a supply response to price increase particularly in the export market in the context of globalisation. The price increases in the export market also should have had their feedback on the domestic fish prices. This compounding effect on fish prices, have possibly resulted in positive response in fish production. The liberalization regime of 1990s has of course given a psychological boost to the exporters. Further, the quality of export has substantially improved thanks to technological sophistication in processing, packaging and marketing strategies inspired by the working style of the MNCs involved in fish culture and exports.

(v) In view of the growing concern for sustainability in fish stock/yield, cautious approach is needed in opening-up the marine fishing to the MNCs, which might extract the fish stock at a rate more rapid than it could be replenished.

(vi) The prevailing employment conditions in the study village project a grim picture. The fisherfolk have been supported by DoF, GOTN but with certain operational limitations.

(vii) The employment potential in fishing has been on the decline on account of, among others, technological changes. For instance, change from cotton net to nylon net has resulted in the disappearance of the erstwhile group fishing which was giving more number of man days of employment. Similarly, women employment in her making also disappeared thanks to mechanised net making. The traditional shore-seine net boats also fast declined. The widows are struggling to find fishing related jobs because of the fall in the volumes of fishing. On the whole, the grim job scenario is reflected in the phenomenon of most of the youth in the fishermen community are searching for jobs in non-fishing sectors.

(viii) In the case of non-fishing employment, the traditional fisherfolk are unable to compete in the job market for want of proper skill / training and lack of exposure. If this trend continues the fisherfolk would be caught between inadequate fishing employment and lack of jobs in non-fishing segment. Hence, it is right time to explore the avenues of non-fishing activities, to conserve the fish resources by restricting destructive fishing and to prevent the entry of non-fishermen community into fishing activity which would deprive the traditional fisherfolk. By providing support to strengthen the FCP and according recognition to its role may go a long way in conservation of fishing.

NOTES

1. The Coromandel Coast excludes 4 fishing villages in Nagapattinam District.
2. The FCP is an exclusive Fishermen Community Panchayat. Functioning as a Non-State Institution to look after fisherfolk's welfare, in terms of fishing, social security, festival celebrations and marketing. It is not an elected body like a State Panchayat. But selection for FCP will be by nomination for more details, refer Bavinck, M. (2001): "*Marine Resource Management –Conflict and Regulation in the Fisheries of the Coromandel Coast*" Sage Publications, New Delhi.

REFERENCES

Anugraham, D., (1940), 'A Study of Madras Fishermen', a Ph.D Diss. University of Madras, Madras.

Bavinck, M., (1998), 'One Sea Three Contender-Legal Pluralism in the In-Shore Fisheries of the Coromandel Coast', a Ph.D Diss., Amsterdam University, Amsterdam.

Editor, (1997), "Overfished Oceans, Booming Fisheries : What Does this Mean for World Food Security?", *News and Views*, October, pp. 1–6.

Fisheries World, (1996), "Marine Fish Marketing Trends in India", No. 3, April, p. 27.

GOTN, (1994), Department of Fisheries, Tamilnadu Fisheries Statistics 1993–94 (Endeavour and Achievement) Madras.

GOTN, (1986), Directorate of Fisheries, A Census of Tamilnadu Marine Fishermen, Madras.

——(1986b), A Status Report on Mechanisation Programme for the Development of Marine Fisheries, Information Brochure 6, Madras.

GOTN, (1994), Department of Fisheries, Annual Fisheries Statistics 1993–94.

GOTN, (1995), Department of Fisheries, Annual Fisheries Statistics, 1994–95.

GOTN, (1996), Department of Fisheries, Annual Fisheries Statistics 1995–96.

GOTN, (1997), Department of Fisheries, Annual Fisheries Statistics, 1997–98.

GOTN, (1998), Department of Fisheries, Annual Fisheries Statistics, 1998–99.

GOTN, (1999), Department of Fisheries, Tamil Nadu Fisheries Statistics (Annual Report) 1998-99.

GOTN, (2000), Department of Fisheries, Tamilnadu Marine Fisherfolk Census Year 2000.

James PSBR and et al., (1993), "Prospects for Marine Fisheries Development in the Economic Environment", *Agricultural Situation in India*, Vol. VI-VIII, No. 5, August, pp. 345-346.

Jhingran, VG. (1991), "Fish and Fisheries of India", Hindustan Publishing Corporation, New Delhi, pp. 577-649.

Karunaharan and Thangamuthu, (2003), " Non-State Institutions and Regulation of Fish Marketing along the Coromandel Coast, Tamilnadu, India", in Rajendra Pradhan (ed.) *Legal Pluralism and Unofficial law in Social, Economic and Political Development, ICNEC, Nepal* (a paper presented in XIII International Congress 7-10 April 2002 in Chiang Mai, Thailand).

Kurien and Achari, (1989), "On Running the Commons and the Commoner the Political Economy of Overfishing", CDS, Tiruvandrum, WP. No. 232, Dec.

Kurien, (1985), "Technical Assistance Projects and Socio-Economic Change: The Norwegian Intervention in Kerala's Fisheries Development Experience", CDS, Tiruvandrum, Wp. No. 205, May.

Marine Product Export Development Authority (MPEDA) (1978), Export Potential Survey of Marine Products in Tamilnadu, Cochin.

Ramakrishna Korkandy, (1996): "Managing World Fisheries Third World Loss", *Economic and Political Weekly,* August 24–31, pp. 2289–2291.

Selvaraj C., (1975), "Small Fishermen in Tamilnadu", Sangam Publishers, Chennai for MIDS.

Simon Fairlie, Mike Hagler and Brian O'Riordan, (1995), " The Politics of Overfishing", *The Ecologist,* Vol., 25, No. 2/3. March-June, p. 46.

Warriar K.M., (1967), "A Socio-Economic Survey of Fishermen in Madras City, Report". Economic Research Centre, Loyola College, Madras.

Table A-2: Export of Sea food products of India and Tamilnadu during 1967-68 to 1996–97

Year	*Quantity of fish production in tonnes*		*% share to the total*	*Rs. in lakhs*		*% share to the total*
	India	*Tamilnadu*		*India*	*Tamilnadu*	
1967-68	21,907	4,631	21.14	1972.00	125.20	6.34
1968-69	26,811	5,220	19.46	2470.00	169.83	6.87
1969-70	31,695	5,942	18.74	3346.00	248.69	7.43
1970-71	35,883	6,329	17.63	3507.00	238.58	6.80
1971-72	35,523	5,511	15.51	4455.00	173.51	3.89
1972-73	38,923	2,571	6.60	5972.00	221.47	3.70
1973-74	52,279	5,719	10.93	8951.00	803.75	8.97
1974-75	45,099	3,922	8.69	6840.00	750.32	10.96
1975-76	54,463	6,389	11.73	12452.92	1668.87	13.40
1976-77	66,750	8,231	12.33	18911.70	2583.95	13.66
1977-78	65,967	8,009	12.14	18095.05	2400.09	13.26
1978-79	86,894	10,033	11.54	23462.27	2870.42	12.23
1979-80	86,401	8,294	9.59	24882.40	2983.27	11.98
1980-81	75,591	6,751	8.93	23484.26	2212.06	9.41
1981-82	70,105	4,833	6.89	28600.54	1782.87	6.23
1982-83	78,175	6,871	8.78	36136.13	2805.46	7.76
1983-84	92,691	16,185	17.46	37302.04	4149.58	11.12

Contd....

Table A-2 (Contd....)

Year	*Quantity of fish production in tonnes*		*% share to the total*	*Rs. in lakhs*		*% share to the total*
	India	*Tamilnadu*		*India*	*Tamilnadu*	
1984-85	86,187	18,792	21.80	38428.07	5128.31	13.34
1985-86	83,651	17,421	20.82	39799.98	6012.53	15.10
1986-87	85,843	18,053	21.03	46067.28	6876.36	14.92
1987-88	97,179	13,361	13.74	53120.00	6619.39	12.46
1988-89	99,777	14,965	14.99	59785.38	10294.39	17.21
1989-90	110,843	18,509	16.69	63499.00	9740.01	14.90
1990-91	139,419	27,340	19.60	89336.98	16588.28	18.56
1991-92	171,820	25,048	14.57	137589.00	23053.00	16.75
1992-93	208,602	30,963	14.84	176743.00	33745.00	19.09
1993-94	243,960	20,473	8.39	250362.00	46188.00	18.44
1994-95	307,337	28,270	9.19	357527.00	75417.00	21.09
1995-96	296,277	–	–	350111.00	–	–
1996-97	395,000	–	–	400760.00	–	–
1997-98	385,820	41,050	10.63	469748.00	122,005.00	25.97

Source: (i) Directorate of Fisheries, A Census of Tamilnadu Marine Fishermen, Madras, (from 1951-52 to 1985-86) and (ii). Govt. of Tamilnadu, Fisheries Statistics (Endeavour), 1994 (from 1986-87 to 1989-90) and 1998 (from 1990-91 to 1997-98).

Note: Seafood export data of both India and Tamilnadu have compiled from Fisheries Statistics Achievement Report 1994 and 1998, from 1967-68 to 1993-94; and rest of the years for India have taken from CMIE, 1998.

Table A-3: Marine Fisherfolk, Active Fishermen Population and Number of Mechanised Boats During 1978 to 1998 in Tamilnadu

Year	*Total Fisherfolk Population*	*Active fishermen*	*Percentage of active fishermen*	*Number of mechanised boats*	*Source*
1978	337713	80035	23.70	2222 (36.01)	MPEDA (1978)
1980	396000	96500	24.36	2750 (35.09)	B.O.P News (1983)
1986	463800	101869	21.95	4000 (25.46)	Status Report (1986)
1991	500000	189000	37.80	6314 (29.93)	TN Fisheries, Achievement, (1998)
1994	522220	225722	43.22	7195 (31.37)	TN Fisheries, Achievement, (1998)
1998	853000	262000	30.71	9896 (26.47)	TN Fisheries Achievement, (1998)

Source: (i) Dept. of Fisheries, (1994), Tamilnadu Fisheries Statistics 1993-94 and 1998, (ii) Govt. of Tamilnadu, Hand Book of Statistics, and CMIE, 1998.

Note: Figures in brackets are number of active fishermen per mechanized boat.

12

PRODUCTION POLICY IN INDIA WITH REFERENCE TO SEED INDUSTRY

T. Senthivel & M. Arumugam

Introduction

Seed is the amazing product of nature and culmination of the life cycle of higher plants. Seed is the basic vital input for crop production. Production of genetically pure and high quality pedigree seed is requiring high technical skills and financial investment. The high quality seed is the blue print of the agrarian prosperity. In the past 50 Years, Indian agriculture has made enormous strides for raising food grains production from 50 million tonnes to over 200 million tonnes. Sustained increase in agriculture production and productivity is dependant, to a large extent, on efficient system for timely supply of quality seeds to farmers.

The seed sector has made impressive progress over the last three decades. The area under certified seeds has increased from less than 500 hectares in 1962-63 to over five lakhs hectares in 1999-2000. The quantum of quality seeds has crossed 100 lakhs quintals. The Seed Act 1966, seeds (control) order 1983 promulgated there under, and the new policy on seeds development, 1988, from the basis of promotion and regulation to the seed industry.

Aims and Objectives

In order to achieve the food production targets of the future, a major effort will be required to enhance the seed replacement rates of various crops. This would require a major increase in the production of quality seeds, in which the private sector is expected to play a major role. At the same time, private and public sector seed organization at both central and state levels, will be expected to adopt economic pricing policies which would seek to realize the true cost of production. The creation of a facilitative climate for growth of a competitive and localized seed industry, encouragement of import of useful germplasm, and boosting of exports are core elements of the agricultural strategy of the new millennium.

Biotechnology will be the key factor in agricultural development in the coming decades. Genetic engineering/ modification techniques hold enormous promise in developing crop varieties with a higher level of tolerance to biotic and abiotic stresses. At the same time, concerns relating to possible harm to human and animal health and bio-safety, as well as interests of farmers, must be addressed. Globalization and economic liberalization have opened up new opportunities as well as challenges. The unnecessary regulations to be dismantled, it must be ensured that gullible farmers are not exploited by unscrupulous elements.

Major Thrust Areas

A. Varietal Development and Plant Variety Protection

The development of new and improved varieties of crop plants and availability of such varieties to Indian farmers is of crucial importance for a sustained increase in agricultural productivity.

1. A Plant Varieties & Farmers' Rights Protection (PVP) Authority will be established which will undertake registration of extent and new plant varieties through the plant varieties registry on the basis of vertical characteristics.

2. The registration of new plant varieties by the PVP Authority will be based on the criteria of novelty distinctiveness, uniformity and stability.
3. Registration of all plant genera of species as notified by the Authority will be done in a phased manner.
4. The rights of farmers to save, use, exchange, share (or) sell farm produce of all varieties will be protected, with the proviso that farmers shall not be entitled to sell branded seed of a protected variety under the brand name.
5. Regular interaction among the Private and Public Researchers, Seed Companies/Organizations and developing Agencies will be fostered to develop and promote growth of a healthy seed industry in the country.
6. To keep abreast of global developments in the field of plant variety protection and for technical collaboration, India may consider joining Regional and International organizations.

B. Efficient Seed Production

To meet the nations' food security needs, it is important to make available to Indian farmers a wide range of seeds of superior quality, in adequate quantity on a timely basis, public sector seed institutions will be encouraged to enhance production of seed towards meeting the objective of food and nutritional security.

B.I Government Seed Production System

The Indian Seed programme adheres to the limited three generation system of seed multiplication namely, breeder, foundation and certified seed categories. Nucleus seed is the seed produced by the breeder seed.

1. Breeder seed is the seed material directly controlled by the originating or sponsoring breeder or Institution for the initial and recurring production of foundation seed.

2. Foundation seed is the progeny of breeder seed. Foundation stage II may also be produced from foundation seed stage I.
3. Certified seed is the progeny of foundation seed or the progeny of certified seed. If the certified seed is the progeny of certified seed, then this reproduction will not exceed three generations beyond foundation stage I.
4. Truthful seed production category should not be encouraged. Only tagged seeds alone be permitted for sale in markets.

B.II Public/Private Sector seed production

1. Public sector seed production agencies will continue to have free access to breeder seed under the National Agricultural Research System.
2. Private seed production agencies will also have access to breeder seed subject to terms and conditions to be decided by Government of India.
3. State Agriculture Universities/ ICAR Institute will have the primary responsibility for production of breeder seed as per the requirements of the respective states.
4. Special attention will be given to the need to upgrade the quality of farmers' saved seeds through interventions such as the seed village scheme.
5. To put in place an effective seed production programme, each state will undertake advance planning and prepare a perspective plan for seed production and distribution over a rolling (five to six year) period, Seed banks will be set up in non-traditional areas to meet demands for seeds during natural calamities.
6. As hybrids, have the potential to improve plan vigour and increase yield, support for production of hybrid seed will be provided.
7. The storage of seed at the village level will be encouraged

to facilitate immediate availability of seeds in the event of natural calamities and unforeseen situations.

8. Seed growers will be encouraged to avail of seed crop Insurance to cover risk factors involved in seed production.

C. Quality Assurance

For obtaining assured seed quality the following points should be considered.

1. The seeds Act will be revised to regulate the sale, import and export of seeds and planting materials of agriculture crops including horticulture and supply of quality seeds and planting materials to farmers through our the country.
2. The National Seed Board (NSB) will advise the government on all matters relating to seed planning and development. The NSB will function as the apex body in the seed sector.
3. The NSB will undertake registration of kinds/varieties of seeds that are to be offered for sale in the market, on the basis of identified parameters for establishing Value for Cultivation and Usuage (VCU) through testing/ training.
4. The NSB will accredit ICAR, SAUS, public/private organizations to conduct VCU trials of all varieties for the purpose of registration as per prescribed standards.
5. The NSB will prescribe minimum standards of germination, genetic characters, physical purity, seed health etc.
6. Registration of seed processing units will be required if such units meet the prescribed minimum standards for processing the seeds.
7. Seed certification will continue to be voluntary. The certification tag/label will provide and assurance of quality to the farmers.

8. The NSB will accredit individuals (or) organizations to carry our seed certification including self-certification on fulfillment of criteria as prescribed.

9. To meet quality assurance requirements for exports of seeds. Seed testing facilities will be established in conformity with ISTA and OECD seed certification programmes.

10. Farmers will be encouraged to use certified seeds to ensure improved performance and output.

11. Farmers will retain their right to save, use, exchange, share or sell their farm seeds and planting materials without any restriction. They will be free to sell their seed on their own premises only.

12. Stringent measures would be taken to ensure the availability of high quality of seeds and check the sale of spurious or misbranded seeds.

D. Seed Distribution and Marketing

For promoting efficient, timely distribution and marketing of high quality seed through out the country, a supportive environment will be provided to encourage expansion of the role of the private seed sector. Efforts will be made to achieve better coordination between state governments to facilitate free Interstate movement of seed and planting material through exemption of duties and taxes.

1. A National seed grid will be established as a data-base for monitoring of information on requirement of seed, its production, distribution and preference of farmers on a district wide basis.

2. Distribution and marketing of seed of any variety, for the purpose of sowing and planting will be allowed only the said variety has been registered by the National Seed Board.

E. Infra Structure Facilities

1. Modernisation of seed processing facilities will be encouraged interms of modern equipment and latest techniques, such as seed treatment for enhancement of performance of seed etc.,
2. Conditioned storage for breeder and foundation seed and aerated storage for certified seed would be created in different region.
3. By developing suitable infra structural facilities seed quality can be maintained and in turn the seed will perform well in the field and increase the production and productivity.

F. Transgenic Plant Varieties

Bio technology will play a vital role in the development of the agriculture sector. This technology can be used for not only to develop new crops/varieties, which are tolerant to disease, pests and abiotic stresses, but also to improve productivity and nutritional equality of food. All genetically engineered/ varieties will be tested for environment and bio-safety before their commercial release, as per the regulations and guidelines of the environment protection ACT (EPA) 1986.

1. Seed of transgenic plant varieties for research purpose will be imported only through the National Bureau of Plant Genetic Resource (NBPGR) as per the EPA, 1986
2. After the transgenic plant variety is commonly released, its seed will be registered and marketed in the country as per the provisions of the seed act.
3. All seeds imported into the country will be required to be accompanied by a certificate from the competent authority of the exporting country regarding their transgenic character.
4. Packages containing transgenic seeds/planting materials, if and when placed on sale, will carry a label indicating their transgenic nature.

G. Import of Seeds and Planting Material

1. The objective of the import policy is to provide the best material available any where in the world, to Indian farmers to increase crop productivity, farm income and export earning. While ensuring that there is no deleterious effect on environment, health and bio safety.

2. While importing seeds and planting material, care will be taken to ensure that there is absolutely no compromise on the requirement under prevailing plant quarantine procedures, so as to prevent entry into the country of exotic pests, diseases and weeds detrimental to Indian agriculture. Eg. Parthenium weed.

3. All imports of seeds will require a permit granted by the plant protection advisor to the government of India, which will be issued with in the minimum possible time frame.

4. All import of seeds and planting materials, etc. will be allowed freely subject to existing policy guidelines and the requirement of the plants, fruits and seeds (regulations of import into India) order 1989. Import of parental lines of newly developed varieties will also be encouraged.

5. Seeds and planting materials imported for sale into the country will have meet minimum seed standards of seed health, germination, genetic and physical purity as prescribed.

6. All importers will make available a small sample of the imported seed to the gene bank maintained by National Bank for Plant Genetic Research (NBPGR).

7. The existing policy, which permits free imports of seeds of vegetables, flowers and ornamental plants, cuttings, saplings of flowers, tubers and bulbs of flowers by certain specified categories of importers will continue.

8. After the arrival of consignments at the port of entry, quarantine checks would be undertaken, which may include visual inspection, laboratory inspection,

fumigation and grow-out tests. For the purpose of these checks, samples will be drawn and the tests will be conducted concurrently.

H. Exports of Seeds

The following points may be considered with regard to export of Indian seeds.

1. Government will evolve a long term policy for import of seeds with a view to raise India's share of global seed export from the present level of less than 1 percent to 10 percent by the year 2020.
2. The export policy will specifically encourage custom production of seeds for export and will be based on long term perspective, dispensing with case to care consideration of proposals.
3. Establishment and strengthening of seeds export promotion zones with special incentives from the government will be facilitated.
4. Promotional programmes to improve the quality of Indian seeds to enhance its acceptability in the International market will be taken up.
5. Testing and certification facilities will be established in conformity with international requirements.

I. Promotion of Domestic Seed Industry

1. Incentives will be provided to the domestic seed industry to enable it to produce seeds of high yielding varieties and hybrid seeds at a faster pace to meet the challenge of domestic requirements.
2. Seed Industry will be provided with a congenial and liberalized climate for increasing seed production and marketing, both domestic and International.
3. Emphasis will be given for improving the quality of seeds produced and specials efforts will be directed towards improving the quality of farmers' saved seeds.

4. Financial support for capital investment, working capital and infrastructure strengthening will be facilitated through NABARD/ Commercial Banks/Co-operative Banks.
5. Tax rebate/concessions will be considered on the expenditure incurred on in-house research and development of new varieties and other seed related research aspects. In order to develop a competitive seed market, the states will be encouraged to remove unnecessary local vacation on sales of seeds.
6. To encourage seed production in non-traditional areas including backward areas, special incentives such as transport subsidy will be provided to seed producing agencies operating in these manginalised areas.
7. Reduction of Import duty will be considered on machines and equipment used for seed production and processing which one otherwise not manufactured in the country.

Conclusion

The government of India trusts that the National Seeds Policy will receive the fullest support of State Governments/ Union Territory Administration, State Agricultural Universities, plant breeders, seed producers the seed industry and all other stake holders, so that it may serve as a catalyst to meet the objectives of sustainable development of Agriculture, food and National security for the population, and improved standards of living for farming communities.

The National Seeds Policy will be a vital instruments in attaining the objectives of doubling food production and making India hunger free. It is expected to provide the impetus for a new revolution in Indian Agriculture, based on an efficient system for supply of seeds of the best quality to the cultivator. The National Seeds Policy will lay the foundation for comprehensive reforms in the seed sector. The policy will also provide the parameters for the development of the seed sector in the Tenth and subsequent plans.

The new policies should emphasis mainly the development of transgenic plant materials, export of quality seeds, efficient and modern infra-structural facilities and true marketing channels. This will ultimately stepup the productivity of each crop varieties and pave way for increasing the standard of living.

REFERENCES

Manual of Seed Certification Procedures-Directorate of Seed Certification, Coimbatore. 2002.

Seed Industry in India: Poised for a leap-Article by Pushparaj Singh, 2000, Freelance Journalist India.

www.seedtamilnadu.com/ nsp.htmls.

13

SMALL SCALE INDUSTRIES UNDER LIBERALISATION

M. Soundarapandian

Introduction

Over the past five decades, Government policies have been formulated to develop a framework for the revival and development of cottage, tiny, rural agro and small-scale industries. With a view to determining the types of industrial units which needed special support, it was considered necessary to develop and appropriate classificatory definition for SSI units under the industries (Development and Regulation) Act, 1951. The periodic revisions in the definition of SSI, as made by the Government of India, are summarized in Table 1.

The SSI sector in India covers a wide spectrum of industries categorized under small, tiny and cottage segments ranging from small artisans/handicraft units to modern production units with significant investments. This sector has acquired a prominent place in the socio-economic development of the country as it not only acts as a 'nursery' for the development of entrepreneurial talent, but also produces a wide range of product, exceeding 7500.

The term Small Industry evokes different meanings for different agencies. The Planning Commission, Government of India, views the entire Village and Small Industries (VSI) sector

Table 1 : Definition of Units of SSI

Year	*Capital*
1950	Capital Assets not exceeding Rs. 5 Lakh.
1958	Capital investment of less than Rs. 5 Lakh.
1959	In Capital investment, value of machinery to be taken at original price paid irrespective of it being new or old.
1960	Gross value of fixed assets upto Rs. 5 Lakh.
Original Value of Plant and Machinery Only	
1966	Upto Rs. 7.5 Lakh
1975	Upto Rs. 10 Lakh
1980	Upto Rs. 20 Lakh
1985	Upto Rs. 35 Lakh
1991	Up to Rs. 60 Lakh
1997	Up to Rs. 3 crore
1998	Upto Rs. 1 crore

as a part of the SSI sector. The National Sample Survey Organization under the Central Statistical Organization (CSO), Government of India, defines the entire industry sector in terms of organized and unorganized segments, as well as in terms of industrial enterprises run by households and non-households. The Central Excise Department, on the other hand, distinguishes SSIs on the basis of the annual turnover of the units (up to a maximum limit of Rs. 3 Crore). The industrial policy planners in the Small Scale Industries Board define SSI on the basis of investment in plant and machinery (an upper limit of Rs. One crore).

Growth and Performance

Earlier the SSI sector was promoted and protected by the Government because to some of its inherent advantages. The over protected measures were: subsidized industrial shed rent, subsidization of electricity rates, interest rates and reservation.

But now due to liberalization and into World Trade Organisation (WTO), the Small Scale Industries have to be strong enough to complete not only the internal market but also the enterprises of foreign countries.

After implementation of New Economic Policy in India, the Liberalisation, Privatisation and Globalisation (LPG) Policy has put this Small Scale sector in a difficult position. The Government of India took the following steps under liberalization era:

- Devaluation of Indian Currency in 1992
- Reduction in the import tax drastically
- Dereservation of 15 items during 1997
- Removal of quantitative restrictions in 1999
- Reducing the investment limit of Rs. 1 crore
- Dereservation of 15 more items in 2001-02 budget
- Foreign Direct Investment Ceiling

Despite, the SSI sector had achieved the tremendous growth during the liberalisation period in India. The performance of the SSI sector during the economic reforms period is given in Table 2.

From the Tables 2 and 3, it is clear that the growth rate of the SSI units had declined from 6.14 percent in 1993-94 to 4.92 percent in 2000-01, but the number of SSI units increased from 19.4 lakhs units in 1990-91 to 33.7 lakhs units in 2000–01.

Regarding the production level of SSI sector during the economic reforms period was Rs. 209300 crores in 1992–93 and it increased to Rs. 645496 crores in 2001. The growth rate of production was only 7.1 percent in 1993-94 and 8.09 percent in 2000-01. The employment level generated by SSI sector was 125 lakhs percent in 1990-91.

After ten years of privatisation period, the employment of SSI sectors was increased only upto 185.64 lakhs percent in 2000–01. The growth rate was also 3.97 percent in 1993-94 and 4 percent in 2000–01.

Table 2: Performance of SSI Sector

Year	*Number of units*		*(Nos. In Lakh)*	*Fixed*
	Regd.	*Un-Regd.*	*Total*	*Investment*
1	2	3	4	5
1990-91	NA	NA	19.4	NA
1991-92	NA	NA	20.82	NA
1992-93	16.48	5.98	22.46	NA
1993-94	17.76	6.12	23.88	NA
			(6.14)	
1994-95	19.44	6.27	25.71	NA
			(7.66)	
1995-96	20.18	6.40	26.58	NA
	(3.81)	(2.07)	(3.88)	
1996-97	21.82	6.50	2.03	64839
	(6.69)	(1.56)	(5.46)	
1997-98	22.82	6.62	29.44	70891
	(5.59)	(1.85)	(5.03)	
1998-99	24.06	6.74	30.80	77531
	(5.43)	(1.81)	(4.62)	
1999-00	25.26	6.86	32.12	82411
	(4.99)	(1.78)	(4.29)	
2000-01	26.14	6.98	33.12	89276
	(5.78)	(1.750)	(4.92)	
2001-02	27.31	7.11	34.42	NA
			(4.92)	
2002-03	28.49	7.23	35.72	NA
			(3.8)	

Source: Annual Reports, Ministry of SSI, New Delhi, 2002-03.

The level of export of SSI products had increased from Rs. 17784 crores in 1992-93 to Rs. 59978 crores in 2000-03. Even though, there is a growth of 5 times in export of SSI products, the growth rate of the export had fallen year by year.

Table 3: Growth of SSI Sector

Year	*(Rs. In crore) Production*		*Employment (No. in Lakh)*	*Export (Rs. Crore)*
	(at Current prices)	*(at Constant Price of 1993-94)*		
1	2	3	4	5
1990-91	155340	NA	125	9763
1991-92	178699	NA	130	13883
1992-93	209300	225626	134.06	17784
1993-94	241648	241648	139.38	25307
		(7.10)	(3.97)	
1994-95	298886	266054	146.56	29068
	(23.69)	(10.10)	(5.15)	
1995-96	362656	296385	152.61	36470
	(21.34)	(11.40)	(4.13)	(25.46)
1996-97	411858	329935	160.00	39248
	(13.57)	(11.32)	(4.84)	(7.61)
1997-98	462641	357749	167.20	44442
	(12.33)	(8.43)	(4.5)	(13.23)
1998-99	520650	385296	171.58	48979
	(12.54)	(7.7)	(2.62)	
1999-00	572887	416736	178.5	54200
	(10.03)	(8.16)		
2000-01	639024	478456	192.23	NA
	(11.54)	(6.08)	(3.9)	
2001-02	670316	451033	192.23	NA
	(8.03)	(8.23)	(3.5)	
2002-03	742021	514292	199.65	NA
	(7.5)	(7.5)	(3.9)	

Source: Annual Reports, Ministry of SS, New Delhi, 2002-03.

Table 4 reveals that the growth of the number of SSI units was the maximum during VII plan and minimum during VIII plan and employment was at its peak during VI plan and lowest in VII plan. During the first two years of IX plan (1997-99) the addition was 9.24 percent and 9.5 percent respectively in the number of units and further employment offered. Following the liberalization policies of 1991 during the last decade of 20th century the small industries sector accorded 60.87 percent growth yielded 38.82 percent additional employment.

Table 4: Progress Under Five Year Plans

Period	*No. of Units (Percentage)*	*Employment (In Lakhs)*
VI Plan (1980-85)	90.84	35.21
VII Plan (1985-90)	93.91	24.58
VIII Plan (1992-97)	42.85	21.25
1978-88	254.05	98.14
1988-98	187.59	56.26
1991-99	60.87	38.82

Source: Annual Reports, Ministry of SSI, New Delhi.

Implication

The positive impact of globalisation policy on the Indian Economy are: E-Prosperity, accumulation of foreign exchange, prudent discipline in the banking sector, fiscal discipline, development of the capital market and improvement in the balance of payments position, etc. The other side of the globalisation policy on SSI is analysed below:

Competitiveness

With globalisation, the SSI sectors are now more exposed to serve competition both from larges scale sector, domestic, foreign and growth Multi National Companies. The competitiveness in Indian Industries is so servere as a result of abolition of industrial licensing and restrictions on MRTP companies, liberalization of foreign investment, import of foreign technology, removal of quantitative restriction on industrial goods, reduction of import rates etc. Inspite of 11 years of industrial reform, India's Competitive advantage is not sufficiently felt in the international market.

Sickness and Financial Crunch

The number of sick units in the SSI sector increased from about 2.2 lakhs units in 1991 to 2.6 lakhs in 1995 and declined to about 2.2 lakh by 1998. This is against an increase in the total number of SSI units from 19 Lakh units to more than 34 lakh units during 1991-2001. But the proportion of sick units to totals units had declined from 11.35 percent in 19.91 to 7.25 percent in 1998. The high rates to taxes, delayed and inadequate credit, marketing difficulties and labour problems are the major problems for the sickness of SSI units.

In 2000, the increase in SSI credit was to the extent of Rs. 3114 crore. In 2001, the credit of SSI sector has increased by Rs. 2657 crore. However the share of credit to SSI sector as a percentage of net bank credit has decreased from 17.5 percent (March, 1998) to 14.2 percent (March, 2001). Under privatization policy, if there is any retard in the functioning of the public sector banks, it will reduce the social responsibility in lending to SSI sectors.

Reservation Policy

The policy of reservation was initiated in 1967 with 47 items. As on date 799 items reserved in this sector. Reservation grants protection ton small-scale units against large/medium scale undertakings including multi-national who are not allowed to manufacture these items except under 50 percent export obligation.

In order to provide statutory backing to the small-scale sector, the IDR Act was amended in March 1984 empowering the Government to reserve items. The change in IDR Act, 1951, necessitated the constitution of an Advisory Committee on Reservation in March 1984.

This Committee has met 20 times and the last meeting of the Committee was held on 3rd Feb 2001. On the recommendation of this committee, the Government de-reserved 15 items from the list of items reserved for manufacture in the small scale sector vide notification S.O.2

(E) dated 1.1.2001 and S.O. 603 (E) dated 29.6.2001. Some of the key items dereserved vide these notifications are readymade garments, toys and leather goods. Similarly, vide Notification S.O.1013 (E) dated 9.10.2001, the investment ceiling of 41 reserved items belonging to hosiery knitwear and hand tools has been raised from Rs. 1 crore to Rs. 5 crore to help in modernization and improving quality of products.

The available data shows that 28 percent of the total production originated from the reserved items. 24 percent of the SSI units manufactured reserved items. 11 percent of the items manufactured in SSI sectors are reserved. It may be also noted that 60 percent of the exports of SSI sectors comes from the reserved items.

Quantitative Restrictions

According to the Export-Import policy of 2001-02, the Government of Indian removed import licensing quota curbs, known as quantitative restriction on 58 items reserved for the SSI sector. With the removal of quantitative restrictions, goods from the outside world are now marketed in India. This had raised the basic questions about the role for SSI reservation. In many labour intensive areas, with great export opportunities SSI reservation in India is handicapping the development of efficient economics of scale, while firms in countries such as china are able to complete effectively in the international and in the Indian market.

Future of the SSI

Based on the past studies and the performance growth of SSI sectors with the implications of the New Economic Policies, the following trends of the SSI will be estimated in India

- A customers driven economy will compel medium and large industries to offload more manufacturing and services to the SSI's.
- Total quality management in SSI will play and important role and greater emphasis will be placed on product quality and perfections.

- There will be and exponential growth in productivity by the application of advanced to technology. This would reduce cost and increase the margin of returns.
- Government grants, subsidies, reservation etc., will disappear and small industries sector will react to market forces more sharply.

Strategies

The government may adopt the following suitable strategies for the development of SSI under the liberalization era.

- The credit limit under the Credit Guarantee Fund Scheme may be enhanced to Rs. 50 lakhs per borrower of SSI units.
- The excise exemption limit can be increased to 2 crores for small scale entrepreneurs.
- The scheme of Technology upgradation and Management Programme (UPTECH) are to be implemented to the viable small scale industrial units. The awareness may be created about the credit linked capital subsidy scheme of the Government of India.
- The Government should create industrial and Science parks with best possible infrastructure.

Conclusion

Globalisation and change in technology are emerging as the major forces that will modify and mould the environment for small business and entrepreneurship over the next decade which will witness the emergence of more competitive and efficient SSI sector. The role of the Government will be that of a facilitators for providing support to SSI in the era of Globalisation. The Government would increasingly focus its energies towards providing human resources development support along with establishing quality certification facilities and dissemination of information.

REFERENCES

Annual Reports, Ministry of Small Scale Industries, Government of India, 2002-03.

M. Soundarapandian, (ed) 'Small Scale Industries', Vol-I and II, Concept Publications, New Delhi, 2002.

M. Soundarapandian, (ed) 'Rural Industries in India,' Mohit Publications, New Delhi, 1998.

M. Soundarapandian, 'Rural Entrepreneurship,' Kaniskha Publishers and Distributors, New Delhi, 1999.

M. Soundarapandian, 'Rural Industries Under Liberalisation,' Dominant Publishers, New Delhi, 2003.

14

MANUFACTURING POLICY FOR CHEMICAL FERTILIZER INDUSTRY

T.T. Ranganathan

Introduction

The importance of the fertilizer sector in India needs to hardly be emphasized as it provides a very vital input for the growth of Indian agriculture and is an inevitable factor that has to be CD reckoned within the attainment of the goal of self-sufficiency in food grains. The fertilizer sector would cover not merely the fertilizer industry but also certain activities in the agricultural sector, which are very intimately linked with the production and distribution of fertilizers. The fertilizer industry has to cater to the needs of the farmers who are the most important consumers of the fertilizer industry

The incoherent and tentative policies of the government are the main causes for the ill health of the fertilizer in India today.

The eighties maked, the golden era in the history of fertilizer industry in India. A stable and conductive policy environment in both the nitrogenous and phosphatic segments had given a big boost to domestic production capabilities on one hand and consumption of fertilizers on the other. This in turn, contributed immensely to rapid increase in production of food grains and other agricultural commodities.

In pursuance of the policy objective of providing fertilizers to farmers at and affordable price, while ensuring and adequate return on investment to the entrepreneurs, the Retention Price cum Subsidy Scheme (RPS) was introduced in 1977. Under the scheme, the difference between the statutorily notified sale price and the retention price (cost of production as assessed by the Government plus a reasonable return on net worth) is paid as subsidy. The retention prices are fixed unit-wise taking into account the cost of the project, vintage of the plant, feedstock, consumption of norms etc.

Under RPS, as the selling price was controlled at a low level, the excess of reasonable cost of production and distribution which was higher due to over all inflation and increasing prices of inputs including hydrocarbons, was reimbursed as subsidy to the producing units.

The fertilizer industry has been subjected to price and distribution controls. In August 1992, potassic and phosphatic fertilizers were decontrolled and the retention pricing scheme thus got confined only to urea. The question, whether the fertilizer sector should be fully decontrolled or not, has to be examined thoroughly in the era of liberalization.

While drawing up a long term fertilizer policy, it is necessary to appreciate certain issues relating to production, consumption and distribution. The fertilizer subsidy which forms and important ingredient of the budget is also matter to be dealt with in the proper perspective.

Consumption of Fertilizers

The consumption of fertilizers is as important a factor as their production. There should be appropriate balance in the consumption of different fertilizer nutrients. The appropriate NPK ratio under Indian soil conditions is stated to be 4:2:1. In 1991-92, the year immediately preceding the decontrol of phosphatic and potassic fertilizers, the NPK ratio was 5.9:2.4:1. Consequent on decontrol of phosphatic and potassic fertilizers, the NPK ratio got distorted to 9.68:2.94:1 in 1993-94. The same has somewhat improved to 7.9:2.8:1 in 1997-98. The farmers have to be educated in the matter of nutrient balance, which is of great long term significance for the Indian agricultural economy. Apart from the need for increase in the consumption of fertilizers in appropriate ratio, there is a need to evenly spread the consumption of fertilizers all over the country. The studies have shown that lack of irrigation and lack of credit were the two main stumbling blocks that came in the way of maximizing consumption of fertilizers. It would not be possible to have major irrigation projects in future because of financial constraints. Further, the emphasis is shifting in favour of watershed concept. In order to encourage consumption of fertilizers in rainfed areas, it would be useful to have a national project for fertilizer use.

Quantum of Subsidy

A study of the data regarding the farm subsidies and food grains productivity in certain selected countries would go to show that the quantum of subsidy in term of US $ (as value of agricultural production) per capita and per hectare of arable land is very much less as compared to that of some of the advanced countries. However, a developing country like India cannot afford to spend huge amounts by way of subsidy. It is obvious that in the interest of overall agricultural development and to keep the fiscal deficit within manageable. Infact, the level of subsidy on fertilizers has reached a level of As 13,975 crore (Budget Estimate for 1999-2000D). This level of subsidy does not seem to be any more sustainable.

On the fertilizer subsidy front too, which was the trigger point for all the mess, there has been utter disappointment. The subsidy payments zoomed from Rs. 4400 crores in 1990-91 to about Rs. 11,400 crores during 1998-99. During the current year, even as provision in the budget is a staggering Rs. 13,250 crores. On current indications, the likely actuals may well be above Rs. 15,000 crores. This level of subsidy dies not seem to be any more sustainable.

The long term fiscal policy document (1987) has stipulated that in order to keep the non-Plan revenue expenditure within 12 percent of the GDP, the expenditure on food and fertilizers subsidy should not exceed 1 percent of the GDP, as the non-Plan revenue expenditure on defence and interest payments is inflexible. Hence, the fertilizers subsidy has decreased from 0.87 percent of the GDP in 1992-93 to 0.59 percent of the GDP in 1996-97.

Indigenous Production-Policy of Self-sufficiency

The Government has all along followed the policy of self-sufficiency. The policy of attaining self-sufficiency has been influenced by the availability of the three main nutrients required for the various crops apart from the need to protect the domestic industry and the logistical difficulty in importing the entire requirement. Of the three main nutrients that are required, nitrogen, phosphate and potash, indigenous raw materials are available mainly for nitrogen.

The Government policy aimed at attaining the maximum possible degree of self-sufficiency in the production of nitrogenous fertilizers based on indigenous feed stocks. The country is self-sufficient to the extent of 90 percent in the case of nitrogenous fertilizers. In the case of phosphates, the paucity of indigenous raw materials is a serious constraints in achieving the goal of self-sufficiency. The Government has, therefore, adopted a mixed strategy by going in for a combination of domestic production based on indigenous/imported rock phosphate and imported sulphur, domestic production based on imported intermediates like ammonia and phosphoric fertilizers is met through the first two options. Similarly, in the case of potash, there are no known commercially exploitable reserves in the country and the entire requirement of potassic fertilizers both for direct application as well as for manufacture of complex fertilizers is met through imports. The philosophy of self-sufficiency in the case of nitrogenous fertilizers has proved to be a pragmatic one because imports of urea were costlier as compared to indigenous production till recently. Further, any significant increase in the quantum of imports would have further pushed up the price of nitrogenous fertilizers in the international market.

Policy Changes in the Last Few Years

On account of steady pricing policies pursued by the Government of India, there has been a significant increase in consumption and production of fertilizers. In a major policy initiative taken in 1992, with a view to reducing the subsidy, all the phosphatic and potassic fertilizers were decontrolled. Consequently, the prices of these fertilizers increased sharply leading to fall in their consumption. In order to cushion the impact of increase in prices of these fertilizers and to arrest decline in their consumption, the Government of India introduced a concession scheme from 1992-93 itself at the rate of Rs. 1,000 PMT. The scope and coverage of concession scheme have been significantly enhanced in subsequently years. As a result of these measures, there has been an increase in consumption of DAP and MOP. As a result of these measures, the NPK ratio has improved from 9.68:2.94:1 in 1993-94 to 7.9:2.8:1 in 1997-98.

Against this background, a High Powered Fertilizer Pricing Policy Review Committee (HPC) under the Chairmanship of Professor C.H. Hanumantha Rao, former Member, Planning Commission, was set up on 27.1.97 to review the existing system of subsidization of urea and suggest and alternative broad-based scientific and transparent methodology.

The HPC in its report, submitted to the Government on 3.4.98, has explored a number of options for determining producers' price such as the existing RPS with some modification, group retention price, uniform administered price and market oriented system. The HPC has expressed the opinion that the Retention Pricing Scheme suffers from many infirmities in as much as it is non-competitive, administered in nature and also a combination of norms and actuals.

Long Term Policy for Fertilizer Industry

Economic liberalization and reform are the two keynotes of the Government's political philosophy, which has embraced almost all sector of the economy. The Telecom, Power and

Petroleum sectors have also felt the impact of this policy. Even in the case of the fertilizer sector, and attempt to introduce liberalization has been made since August 1992. It is obvious that the fertilizer sector has to fall in line with the rest of the economy. Total decontrol would, therefore, have to be the ultimate goal for, this sector.

It must, at the same time, be necessary to ensure that the transition to the era of total decontrol would have to be achieved in a phased manner so that there are no political and economic problems during the period of transition. Total decontrol may imply a high rise in the price of fertilizers, which the farmers, especially the small and marginal ones, may not be in a position to afford. One of the aims of total decontrol is to contain the burden of subsidy. In the anxiety to reduce the burden of subsidy, however, one cannot afford to ignore the socio-economic aspects of the problem, which are very serious indeed. About 70 percent of the fertilizer is being used in 100 out of 426 districts, chiefly on irrigated cereal crops, sugarcane and cotton.

Hence, It is high time that the Government breaks from the mind-set of the past and tasks a holistic and coordinated look at the problem of ballooning fertilizer subsidy.

The radical approach is thus likely to prove counter-productive. A phased programme for attaining total decontrol is thus considered absolutely essential. It is proposed that the ultimate goal of total decontrol be achieved in three phases ? as per the time frame and the details given in succeeding paragraphs.

During Phase I of the programme (2000-2002), Government had taken up the following to achieve the New Fertilizer policy.

Removal of Aberrations and Deficiencies

(i) Reassessment of capacity and modulation of offtake depending upon i.e. reassessment of capacity to be adopted and the effective cutoff date for the purpose of recovery of excess subsidy.

(ii) Increase in price of urea at regular intervals. (As price of urea in India was the cheaper (in December, 1998 Dollar term) being 88.14 US $ PMT as against that of 119.32 US $ in Bangladesh, 191.3 US $ in Malaysia, 160 US $ in Thailand. But the consumption of urea per ha. is generally higher in these countries than India.

(iii) Improving the implementation of the concession scheme by delay in the announcement of the rate of concession of every season and to be removed.

Initiation of New Measures to Move Towards Decontrol

(i) The problem of feedback- the demand for natural gas will increase but the domestic production is less.

(ii) Feasibility of a coal based technology-In order to reduce the import of feed stock, adoption of coal based technology is explored.

(iii) Promotion of joint ventures- Fertilizer plants to be setup in countries where natural gas is abundant.

(iv) Decision on fertilizer pricing policy i.e. adoption of uniform Normative Referral Price (NRP) based on Long Run Marginal Cost (LRMC) policy after dismantling RPS scheme.

(v) Not to encourage new capacities for the production of urea.

(vi) Encouraging private sector rather then public/ cooperative sector in fertilizer production.

(vii) Closure of Government owned sick units.

(viii) New capacity can be created at Eastern and Southern Zone which are deficit.

(ix) Estimate Demand and Supply on Long term basis.

(x) WTO related matters also be considered i.e. like removal of quantitative restrictions on various items including fertilizers.

(xi) Extension concession scheme to biofertilizers i.e. encouraging the use of bio fertilizers.

During Phase II (2002-2004), the following policies will be taken.

(i) Based on the demand and supply, new capacity has to be created as long term perspective.

(ii) To protect indigenous industry and to fulfill the commitment made to WTO, upward revision of custom duty also be made.

(iii) New initiatives will be developed to settle the disputes between the fertilizer producers and agencies such as GAIL, UNGC with regard to quantitative and qualitative issues relating to supply of natural gas, petroleum naphtha prices.

(iv) Concession scheme to urea also be extended irrespective of their feed stock.

(v) NPK ratio in fertilizer consumption is being encouraged based on soil testing.

(vi) Promotion of eco-friendly use of fertilizer as N and P are the most dominant polluter of soil, water and atmosphere.

During Phase III (2004-2007), the following policies will be taken up

(i) Total decontrol with a view to allow operation of free market force could be introduced

(ii) Concession to urea to be withdrawn

(iii) The Government will take the role of monitory and fiscal measures, so as to the greater exposure to global competition and perform the role of monitoring the trends of consumption, prices, availability, determining custom duty, providing infrastructure like laying down the pipelines, erecting terminals for receiving LNG etc. and also facilitate proper policy formulation.

The Government had taken long term policy on the fertilizer sector to combate the crisis created by the ballooning of fertilizer subsidy. This may be stable and conductive policy for this vital sector having strong linkage with country's food security and overall agricultural prosperity.

REFERENCES

"Long Term Policy on the Fertilizer Sector," Ministry of Chemicals and Fertilizers, Dept. of Fertilizers, Government of India.

"A Long Term and Stable Policy-Still Exudes Fertilizer Industry" Dr. Uttam Gupta, Chief Economist, *Agriculture Today*. Vol. II, No. 5, Dec. 1999.

15

NON-FARM EMPLOYMENT IN THE DROUGHT-PRONE RURAL VILLAGES OF TIRUNELVELI DISTRICT, TAMILNADU

K. Pazhani

Introduction

Planned economic development implies the use of available resources in such a way to maximize the rate of growth of production to provide maximum welfare to the society. It can be achieved only when various plans for the creation of employment opportunities are implemented with its full spirit to fulfil the social objective of providing optimum employment. But most of the developing countries like India are unable to solve this problem and have its repercussions on the economy. In its economic aspect, the existence of large numbers of unemployed people means a tragic waste of human resources and the resultant deprivation of society of the goods and services the unemployed could produce.

India faces severe unemployment problem in both rural and urban areas. By 1991, the country work force had grown to 401 million and is expected to be 519 million in 2010 (World Bank, 1998). International Labour Organisation (ILO) estimated that 8 million jobs were lost during first two or three years after reforms in 1991. The High-Level Committee on Agricultural Credit through Commercial Banks (1997) remarked, "Although the population depending on agriculture continues to be around 62 percent, the share of agriculture in national income has fallen from 50 percent to around 30 percent. This situation will have its direct impact on the employment generation in agriculture. At this juncture, a study of this nature becomes pertinent to provide a possible solution to the policy-makers to solve the employment related problems in the rural non-farm sector.

To cope with the ongoing changes in the international arena in the name of liberalization and globalization, India has also made drastic changes in its economic policies in the form of privatization in different sectors of the economy. But trade liberalization is supposed to allow resources to move from productivity protected sectors to high productivity sectors. But what is export markets in areas of comparative advantage (such as agriculture) are effectively closed, or credit is not available (or available only at exorbitant interest rates) to create the new export-related jobs. Then workers simply move from, low-productivity protected jobs to unemployment. Growth is not enhanced, and poverty is increased (Stiglitz, 2003). Several studies on rural non-farm employment (Bhalla, 1997; Acharya and Misra, 2000; Chadha, 2002; Sheila, 2002; Mahajan, 2002) reveals that there has been employment diversification in rural areas during the post-reform period.

Nature of Employment

According to Sen (1982), one is entitled to one's own labour power, and thus to the trade-based and production-based entitlements related to one's labour power. But, people in the rural areas have only labour to sell but very often fail to find a willing party to employ them. This situation has made the labour force to accept any type of work at very low wage. If there are more number of self-employed and regularly employed work force it will accelerate the growth of output, income and improvement in the standard of the living of the people.

Table 1 reveals that the percentage of 'self employed male and female shows a declining trend while the percentage of casual labour employed shows an increasing trend. Further, the percentage of regularly employed male and female workers also shows a declining trend. More self-employment and more regular employment means more food, more clothing, housing, social amenities, increased education and welfare. But, trends in the nature and growth of employment depicts an unhealthy development of the economy, which will pave the way for concentration of more and more wealth in few hands, social injustice and growing number of people below the poverty line due to heavy population pressure.

Table 1: Sex-wise Distribution of Nature of Employment In Rural India

(Percentages)

Year	*Male*			*Female*		
	Self employed	*Regular employed*	*Casual labour*	*Self employed*	*Regular employed*	*Casual labour*
1972-73	65.9	12.1	22.0	64.5	4.1	31.4
1977-78	62.8	10.6	26.6	62.1	2.8	35.1
1983	60.5	10.3	29.2	61.9	2.8	35.3
1987-88	58.6	10.0	31.4	60.8	3.7	35.5
1993-94	57.9	8.3	33.8	58.5	2.8	38.7
1999-00	55.0	8.8	36.2	57.3	3.1	39.6

Source: Different Quinquennial Reports on Employment and Unemployment of NSSO, GOI.

Non-agricultural activities in many developing countries often account for as much as 50 percent of rural employment and a similar percentage of house-hold income. This distribution varies across countries and regions, with rural Africa considered to have the most diversified non-agricultural activities, followed by Latin America, East Asia, and finally, South Asia (Reardon et al., 1998). This is the situation prevailing in most of the States in India. This situation may be attributed to the failure of the Government to frame suitable policies to generate employment opportunities to eradicate unemployment and poverty to improve the standard of living of the people.

Growth of Employment and GDP

The Central and State Governments of India have been taking strenuous efforts through various plan to implement self-employment schemes such as TYRSEM (1970), IRDP (1980), DWCRA (1983), wage employment schemes like JVVT (1989) EAS (1993), IAY (1996), MWS (1996), CRSP (1986) and also Special Area Development Programmes (SADP) such as DPAP (1973) and WGDP/ HADP (1975) to generate more employment to improve the economic conditions of the poor. These programmes will act as inducing factors for the rapid economic development of India, if the growth of GDP is having a corresponding increase in the growth of employment opportunities.

Table 2 depicts deceleration in the growth of employment and acceleration in the growth of GDP. This situation may be attributed to factors such as, rapid mechanization of agriculture after the Green Revolution, rapid industrialization to produce export surpluses, improvement in the productivity per unit of labour, establishment of export-oriented unit to produce on a large scale unaccompanied by generation of employment, adoption of labour-saving devices in manufacturing, mining and construction industries.

Table 2: Growth of Employment and GDP During The Five Year Plans

Plans	I	II	III	IV	V	VI	VII	VIII	IX
GDP*	3.7	4.2	-3.8	3.4	5.0	5.5	6.7	6.5	7.3
Growth of Employment	0.39	0.85	2.03	1.99	1.84	1.89	1.38	1.13	1.14

Source: Plan Documents.

*Annual Growth Rate at Constant Price.

Rural Non-Farm Employment

Most of the studies on migration suggested for the creation of employment opportunities in the rural areas to arrest rural-urban migration. But factors like population growth, frequent failure of monsoon and the resultant fall in the surplus labour absorbing capacity of agriculture, decline of rural industries increased the problem of unemployment in the rural areas. Works like dissilting of tanks, digging of canals are also done by machines. This situation has made the people to find supplementary employment if not alternate employment in the rural non-farm sector. Absence of income from agriculture compelled even female work force to find jobs to share their responsibility in the household. This led to the emergence of many rural employments to the rural poor. They are tailoring, beedi making, safety-matches, cotton mills, fish processing, bottle making, construction works, petty shops, clerical works in hospitals, etc. Similarly, male work force that are mostly in agriculture began to work in quarries, construction works, sand-mining, textiles, lime-stone factory, making charcoal, bore-well construction, driving etc.

In a capital-starved country like India, inadequate financial facilities impede economic development to a greater extent. Employment generation in the rural non-farm sector (RNFS) is no exception to this sorry state of affair. The importance given to NFS by the various financial institutions of our country is given in Table 3. It shows that there has been an increasing trend in the distribution of loans to non-farm sector by different financial institutions except in 1997-98. Non- farm sector loans have increased by 98.96 percent during 1998-99 compared to the year 1993-94. The Land Development Banks alone have disbursed more than 50 percent of the total loans during 1996-97 and 1997-98. The overall average loans advanced by these agencies per year came to Rs. 152.81 crore. The Land development Bank's share per year has surpassed this overall average by Rs. 119.2 crores while the share of other agencies has remained far below the overall average. Most of the loans sanctioned by these banks to NFS development benefit the rich

Table 3 : Bank-wise Distribution of Non-farm Sector Loans from 1993-99

Rs. in crores

	Banks				
Year	*Commercial Banks*	*Land Development Banks*	*State Co-op. Banks*	*Regional Rural Banks*	*Total*
1993-94	89.56	146.17	44.2	49.01	328.94
	(27.2)	(44.4)	(13.2)	(14.9)	(100.00)
1994-95	111.98	155.22	69.91	73.97	411.08
	(27.2)	(37.8)	(17.0)	(18.0)	(100.00)
1995-96	64.07	221.33	61.03	113.93	460.36
	(13.9)	(48.1)	(13.3)	(24.7)	(100.00)
1996-97	69.69	329.60	89.26	156.13	644.68
	(10.8)	(51.1)	(13.9)	(24.2)	(100.00)
1997-98	88.64	333.51	70.85	123.66	616.67
	(14.4)	(54.0)	(11.5)	(20.1)	(100.00)
1998-99	135.48	292.8	70.71	155.47	654.46
	(20.7)	(44.7)	(10.8)	(23.8)	(100.00)
Total	760.95	1632.07	498.92	775.58	3667.52
	(126.83)*	(272.01)*	(83.15)*	(129.25)*	(152.81)*

Source: NABARD, Mumbai.

Figures in parentheses indicate percentage to total.

*Average per agency per year.

who have land and buildings. Employment generation has not so far been considered as a criterion for sanctioning loans by these agencies.

Co-operative institutions are specially established to extend liberal credit for agricultural and rural development. NABARD is providing refinance facilities and advised them to diversify their lending practices. This induced the Agriculture and Rural development banks to lend to non-farm sector (NFS) and small road transport operators (SRTO) in addition to lending to farm sector.

Table 4 reveals that there has been a declining trend in the loans advanced by the PCARDBs for agriculture and allied activities. But NFS has received more than 38 percent of the loans advanced by these banks except in 1994-95. This is a healthy sign for development of the rural economy. But, unfortunately, these loans are availed by the propertied class, which is used to exploit the poor in the rural areas. It has led to too much of unemployment in the rural non-farm sector.

Table 4: Purpose-wise Advances of PCARDBs in Tamilnadu from 1994-99

(Rs. in lakhs)

Sl. No.	*Purpose*	*Year*				
		1994-95	*1995-96*	*1996-97*	*1997-98*	*1998-99*
1.	Agriculture and Allied	8935.58 (59.56)	10415.37 (55.16)	1127.97 (54.86)	10794.34 (56.34)	11883.85 (55.92)
2.	Non-Farm Sector	5132.06 (34.21)	7291.86 (38.62)	7810.79 (38.00)	7553.66 (39.42)	8307.44 (39.09)
3.	Others	934.21 (6.23)	1176.03 (6.23)	1466.80 (7.14)	811.6 (4.24)	1060.19 (4.99)
	Total	15001.85 (100.00)	18883.26 (100.00)	20554.56 (100.00)	19159.60 (100.00)	21251.48 (100.00)

Source: Various SCARDBs' Annual Reports.

Employment Scenario in Tamilnadu

The working population in Tamilnadu rose from 202 lakhs in 1981 to 242 lakhs in 1991 census displaying an annual increase of 1.82 percent against the population growth of 1.44 percent per annum. The work participation rate moved from 41.7 percent to 43.3 percent between 1981 and 1991. Employment in the organised sector remained stable at 25.6 lakhs in March 1998 as well as March 1997. The growth of employment decreased by one percent in the public sector and went up by 2.44 percent in the private sector in 1997-98. This situation may be attributed to the policy of privatization followed by the Government of Tamilnadu.

A total of 7 lakh persons seeking jobs have registered during 1997-98 as against 6.51 lakh persons during 1996-97. The applicants in 'Live Register' at the end of March 1998 were 39.32 lakhs. The placements which stood at 27604 in 1996-97 rose to 34974 in 1997-98. The centrally sponsored schemes like IRDP and DWACRA provided employment to 180696 and 27483 persons respectively in 1997-98. Employment to the tune of 558.29 lakh mandays was created under Employment Assurance Scheme (EAS).

Tables 5 and 6 reveal that though there are a positive change in non-farm employment of men in the rural areas there has been wide variations in it. This situation may be attributed to the failure of monsoon in major part of the state and also prevalence of persistent drought in most of the southern districts of Tamil Nadu. Further, utilization of more amounts of labour-saving devices in agriculture and decline of cottage and small scale industries. (See Appendix-I)

Table 5: Non-farm Male Employment to Total Employment in Tamilnadu and India (percentage)

Nation/State	*1961*	*1972-73*	*1977-78*	*1981-88*	*1993-94*	*1999-00*
India	16.3	16.7	19.5	25.5	26.0	28.6
Tamil Nadu	20.7	24.6	26.0	34.8	36.0	31.8
Percentage (Plus or Minus)	–	15.85	5.69	33.85	3.45	11.67

Source: *Southern Economist*, September 1, 2003, p. 14.

Table 6: Non-farm Female Workers as Percentage to Rural Workforce 1971 to 1999-2000

Nation/State	*1971*	*1981*	*1991*	*1993-94*	*1999-00*
India	12.96	12.73	13.10	13.8	14.6
Tamilnadu	15.47	13.43	15.50	21.5	24.1
Percentage (Plus or Minus)	–	-13.19	15.41	38.71	12.09

Source: Southern Economist, September 1, 2003, p. 14.

Review of Related Studies

According to *Desai* (1983), successive plans of development has not generated gainful employment for all the net addition to the labour force and continue to add to the backlog of unemployed persons. To him, a permanent solution can only be achieved through the development of a system of scientific, diversified and assured agriculture, the building up of a wider range of small and processing industries in rural areas, rural electrification, growth for new skill and general economic and industrial development.

Todaro (1985) has clearly examined the dimensions as well as the analytics of the employment problem in developing nations. To him, substantial unemployment in LDCA economies has been one of the most striking symptoms of their inadequate development. He has recommended factor-price modifications as an important means of generating more employment opportunities. *Vaidyanathan* (1986) viewed the level of rural employment in non-agricultural activities to be a function of (i) the level of rural demand for non-agricultural goods and services produced locally: (ii) the level of extra-local demand for rural products (services); and (iii) location, scale and technology of activities catering to these demand.

Dev (1990) has studied the factors determining inter-regional variations in the share of non-agricultural employment. To him, manufacturing was the major sector in terms of its share in rural non-agricultural employment. He has concluded that there is no alternative to diversification of employment from agriculture to non-agriculture in rural area to raise the level of living of the rural Population. According to *Unni* (1991), non-agricultural activities in rural areas play a vital role in providing simple consumer goods and services to the rural households. She has analysed the factors which affect the inter-regional variations in non-agricultural employment.

According to *Siddappa* (1994), the non-farm sector is a significant sector in reducing the pressure on farm sector and also substantial increase in farm productivity. The NFS absorbs the unemployed and under employed rural labour force and augments the household income and employment. The increased income of the rural poor may be bringing them in more equal distribution of income. *Namasivayam* (2000) has mentioned that subsidy is one of the means of reducing the inequalities in income and wealth distribution among the rural non-farm households and to improve the financial position and raise their income level above the poverty-line.

Nagaiya (1999) has analysed the trend in RNFS employment in India and Andhra Pradesh. He has suggested that development of infrastructure in rural areas and small towns as sine qua non for RNFS development. In his paper, *Sudhakar Reddy* (2000) dealt with the seasonal variations in RNFS employment, impact of Rural Non-Farm income on distribution, determinants of RNT activities, employment and income.

According to *Pirabu* and *Thangamuthu* (2003), agriculture sector alone cannot provide the ultimate solution for rural poverty, unemployment and under employment. Growing non-farm employment contributes to the rural employment and addresses the basic problems of unemployment and poverty to a considerable extent.

Objectives and Methodology

The overall objective of the study is to know the reasons for the preference of non-farm employment instead of traditional employment in the agriculture and allied activities. The specific objectives are:

(i) to know the different types of NFS employment available and the nature of employment provided by them;

(ii) to study the impact of rural non-Farm sector on employment and income of the sample households;

(iii) to know whether there is gender discrimination with regard to hours of work and wages and salaries;

(iv) to analyse the emerging characteristics after the change of employment from farm sector to non-farm sector; and

(v) to suggest possible remedies to reduce if at all completely eliminate the problems related to employment in the rural non-farm sector.

The study is conducted in Tirunelveli district of Tamilnadu. The district consists of 10 Taluks, of which Radhapuram taluk is purposively selected for the present study. Absence of secondary data related to non-farm activities in this drought-prone taluk made the researcher to select five villages from among 49 revenue villages in the Taluk. 20 samples were selected from each revenue village to get a total of 100 samples. By using a well-structured questionnaire required data were collected from the sample households through personal interview for the year 2001-2002. All the children below the age of 15 and elders above 60 years are considered as dependent people. Their number is excluded while calculating employed or unemployed people in the sample households.

Description of the Study Area

Tirunelveli district is on the southeastern portion of Tamilnadu. It covers and area of 6823 sq. kms. It lies between 8.05′ and 9.30′ of the Northern Latitude and 77.05′ and 70.25′ of Eastern Longitude. Out of the total population of 25,01,832 in the district, as per 1991 census, 1,70,86,556 (68.3 percent) live in rural and 7,93,176 (31.7 percent) live in urban areas. The density of population per sq. kms was 367 as against 429 for the state.

Agriculture is the main source of income of the people in this district. 91.3 percent of the total working population is cultivators. Out of the total area of 143691 hectares is the district 33472 hectares were cultivated more than once. Among the total irrigated areas, well irrigation covers 40061 hectares (39.58 percent), tanks 43758 (43.24 percent) and canals 17384 (17.18 percent) hectares. Cement, cotton textiles, wheat products and manufactures of chemicals are large-scale industries. Important village industries are handloom, poultry farming, brick making, lime burning, mat weaving and jaggary production. This district is famous for the production of numerous varieties of handloom clothes, fine mats of Pathamadai.

Out of the 19 blocks in this district, Radhapuram Block, the drought prone area has been selected for the present study. 84 percent of the population is living in the rural areas. This block is having 11175 (15.54 percent) hectares of cultivable land, of which only 3778 (33.8 percent) hectares are net area sown. This situation may be attributed to failure of rainfall and the average rainfall lying below the normal rainfall in this district. The normal rainfall for the year was 888.7 mm where in Radhapuram Block it was 463.7 mm. This is one of the important reasons for the preference of non-farm employment in the study area.

Discussions and Findings

This part of the paper deals with the analysis of primary data collected for the purpose and the emerging policy implications. The study reveals that out of 489 sample population from 100 sample households, 281 (57.46 percent) are male and 208 (42.54 percent) are female. The average family size is 4.89 (approx. five) members. It ranged from a minimum of two and maximum of eight members in a family. Female literacy rate (90.38 percent) is higher than male literacy rate (89.98 percent). The earner-dependent ratio is 0.84 (approx. One). Out of 266 employed 138 (51.88 percent) are female and 128 (48.12 percent) are male. In 27 families, women are engaged only in household activities. In the remaining 73 families, 52 families sent two to four women from each family for employment of various types whereas in 21 families one woman is working in the NFS. This situation proves study report of FAO that of all the hours worked throughout the world, women contributed about two-thirds (Antony, 1985).

Reasons for Moving to Non-Farm Employment

Like migration, mobility of labour from one job to another has become a continuous process due to various reasons.

Moving to non-farm employment in the rural areas has been sometimes conceptualized as a relief to the strain and tensions associated with bigger family size, number of dependents, absence of stable income from agriculture and other sources. The above said factors elicit multiple responses that include moving to non-farm employment and involvement of more female work force in such employments.

Table 7 reveals that drought, absence of water in the well, family expenditure and debt burden are the major reasons for moving from farm sector employment to non-farm sector employment. Sixteen percent of the interviewed families revealed such a movement due to drought and unstable farm income. In five out of seven categories of reasoning, respondents revealed absence of water in their well as the main cause. It necessitates policy measures to improve ground water level in the study area.

Table 7: Reasons For Moving to Non-farm Employment

Sl. No	*Reasons*	*Number of Families*
1.	Drought	7
2.	No well water	15
3.	Drought + Unstable farm income	16
4.	No well water + Family Expenditure	25
5.	No well water + Debt	8
6.	No well water + Family Expenditure + Debt	24
7.	Drought + No well water + Family Expenditure + Debt	5
	Total	100

Source: Survey data.

Emergence of Sub-sectors

A shift of rural workforce to the non-farm sector has paved the way for the emergence of three types of sub-sectors. They are:

1. *High share sub-sector*—Beedi-making, tailoring, textile works, brick-making.
2. *High growth sub-sector*—Sand-mining, Limestone-mining and construction works.
3. *Emerging sub-sector*—Charcoal preparation, quarrying, fish processing, firewood cutting.

Impact on Employment and Income

The persistent drought has been adding fuel to the already burning problems associated with employment in the rural areas. The changing agrarian relations have rendered many jobless and make them to find jobs elsewhere. The available non-farm employment sources are beedi-making, tailoring, textiles, sand-mining, construction works, quarries and also charcoal making. Thus, the growth or rural non-farm sector employment can emanate from both agriculture and the undesirable situations prevailing in the rural areas.

Table 8 reveals that out of 266 employed 138 (51.58 percent) are women and 128 (48.12 percent) are men. This situation will depict a backward sloping supply curve since more number of women is employed to get additional income in addition to the income earned by the head of the family. 92.48 percent of the employed are in self-employment and temporarily employed. More than 80 percent of the female workforce is

Table 8: Sex-wise Classification of Nature of Employment

Sl.No.	*Sex*	*Nature of Employment*			*Total*
		Permanent	*Self-employed*	*Temporary*	
1.	Male	12 (9.38)	27 (21.09)	89 (69.53)	128 (100.00)
2.	Female	8 (5.80)	28 (20.29)	102 (73.91)	138 (100.00)
	Total	20 (7.52)	55 (20.68)	191 (71.80)	266 (100.00)

Source: Survey data.

engaged in beedi-making since it provides regular employment of at least 5 or 6 days work per week, provident fund provisions, bonus, medical care and also scholarship to their children who are studying in schools and colleges.

Non-farm activities are particularly important for those rural households with little or no land (Reddy, 2000). But in the study area, even people with more land are benefited because of non-farm sector employment. The study reveals that participation in non-farm sector activities has increased the average income per household from Rs.18,100 to Rs.39,400. This may be attributed, especially women to the increasing number of employed per household in the non-farm sector.

Table 9 reveals that the NFSE has reduced the inequalities in income distribution. The Gini co-efficient of the above frequency distribution reveals that inequality in income distribution is less (0.25) in the post-NFSE than the pre-NFSE (0.85). This situation may be attributed to the increase in the number of employed including women in the former case and in the latter case only landowners used to get income.

There is gender discrimination in the payment of wages in the NFSE. If a male worker gets Rs. 120 for nine hours duty,

Table 9: Classification of Respondents on the Basis of Income Before NFSE and After NFSE*

Income Group (Rs. in '000)	*Number of Families*	
	Before NFSE	*After NFSE*
0-10	17	3
10-20	50	8
20-30	24	19
30-40	6	22
40-50	1	20
50-60	1	16
60 & Above	1	12
Total	100	100

Source: Survey data.

*Non-Farm Sector Employment

women get only Rs. 60. This is the reason why employers prefer women to work in their enterprises.

Emerging Characteristics

The emerging trend in the rural non-farm sector is increasing number of employed women who otherwise will remain without employment. This situation has changed the preference of the society to have more female children since they are income yielding assets. They prefer jobs which requires less hours of work and assured income. Women, who are in household activities only, began to get themselves involved in hazardous occupations like quarrying, wood-cutting. People have changed their attitude to go for works which requires less or no skill accepting very low wages in order to maintain their family in the absence of income from farm activities.

Policy Implications

The Central as well as the State Governments have been implementing various programmes for the generation of employment to eliminate poverty and to improve the standard of living of the people. But they have not generated employment enough to meet all the requirements of the net addition to the labour force. The following are policy implications emerging out of the present study.

1. The authorities concerned have to take necessary steps to control growth of population in order to reduce the pressure of population on the farm sector and also the existing unemployment and underemployment in this sector. The services of non-governmental organizations and the NSS volunteers of schools and colleges may be better utilized to create awareness about the evils of population explosion.

2. There is and urgent necessity to generate more non-farm sector employment since self-employment such as beedi-making provides employment to women and male work force is not having gainful employment opportunities

except works in lime-stone mines, sand-mining, firewood cutting etc.

3. The Central as well as the State governments have to formulated new policies for making an effective use of unutilized and underutilized manpower and also available other resources.
4. Banks and other financial institutions should be instructed to lend liberally for projects in the rural areas by considering employment generation potentials as a criteria for availing loans.
5. Considering the total population and the number of unemployed, underemployed and also disguised unemployed, more funds have to be allocated for the purpose of employment generation in the rural non-farm sector.
6. Non-availability of infrastructures-basic, banking, marketing, transport and communications is a cause for the non-availability of non-farm sector employment through the establishment of various types of industries. The Governments should take adequate measures to provide necessary infrastructure adequately.
7. Non-farm sector cannot develop on its own. Its development in many areas depends on the development of the farm sector. Steps should be taken to provide canal irrigation facilities wherever possible which indirectly improves ground water level and sustained development of farm sector and paves the way for the development of many agro-based industries to generate employment opportunities to the people in the rural areas.

Conclusion

The study reveals that persistent drought conditions prevailing in the study area have made the people to do any work, whether it is self-employed or casual in nature. Paucity of investible funds, absence necessary skill and training also contribute their share for the non-availability of non-farm sector employment adequately to rural populace of our country. Acceleration of construction works and construction of tanks and others may be encourages since it involves government fund and require large number of lab our force. Various research and development works have to be undertaken to know the causes fro persistent drought conditions in this part of country and find solutions to it so that the life our brethren in the rural areas could be save at least in the near future.

REFERENCES

Amartya Sen, (1982), "*Poverty and Famine : An Essay on Entitilements and Deprivation*", Oxford University Press, Delhi.

Barathan, D., (2001), Economic Growth and Decline of Poverty in the Post Reform Period, *Southern Economist*, Vol. 40, No. 15 & 16.

Blaug, Layard and Woodhall, (1969), "*The Causes of Graduate Unemployment in India*", Allen Lane the Penguine Press, London.

Boothalingam, M., (1995), "Rural Non-Farm Sector and Co-operatives-A Case Study of Karnataka State Co-Operative Agriculture and Rural Development Banks", *Land Bank Journal*, Vol. XXXIII, Issue IV.

Dinabandhu Mahal, (2000), "Diversification of Lending under Non-Farm Sector Financing in India", *Land Bank Journal*, Vol. XXXIX, Issue II.

Hanumantha Rao and Rajalakshmi, K., (2002), "Structure of Employment and Casualisation in Rural India during Pre and Post-Reform Regime", *Journal of Rural Development*, Vol. 21, No. 1.

Joseph E. Stiglitz, (2003), "Poverty, Globalisation and Growth: Perspectives on some of the Statistical links" *Southern Economist*, Vol. 42, No. 10.

Laxmaiah, G., (2002), "Reforms and Employment Problems in India: An Overview", *Southern Economist*, Vol. 40, No. 20.

Michael P. Todaro, (1985), '*Economic Development in the Third World*', Orient Longman, London.

Mahendra Dev, (1990), "Non-Agricultural Employment in Rural Employment in Rural India: Evidence at a Disaggregate level", *Economic and Political Weekly*, Vol. XXV, No. 28.

Nagaiya, D., (1999), "Rural Non-Farm Sector in Andhra Pradesh Trends and Directions for the Future", *Journal of Rural Development,* Vol. 18, No. 1.

Ravindra Pirabu, R. and Thangamuthu, C., (2003), "Non-farm Employment Among Schedule Caste Households in Tamil Nadu: A Study" *Southern Economist,* Vol. 42, No. 9.

Sindappa, (1994), "Rural Banks and Non-Farm Sectors in Rural Development-A Case Study of T.G. Bank in Karnataka State", *Land Bank Journal,* Vol. XXXIII, Issue I.

Sudhakar Reddy, E. (2000), Rural Non-Farm Employment in Developing "Economies-Theoretical Formulation and Empirical Evidence", *Journal of Rural Development,* Vol.19, (1).

Vaidyanathan, A., (1986), "Poverty and Unemployment in Rural India: A Study of Spatial and Temporal Variations", *Economic and Political Weekly,* Vol. XXI, No. 2.

Valsamma Antony (2002), "The Prospects and Growth of SSIs in India: An Overview", *Southern Economist,* Vol. 41, No. 1.

Unni, Jeemol, (1991), "Regional Variations in Rural Non-Agricultural Employment-Exploratory Analysis", *Economic and Political Weekly,* Vol. XXXVI, No. 3.

Annual Report 1999-2000, NABARD, Mumbai.

66th and 67th Annual Report, TNSCARDB Ltd., Chennai.

68th, 69th and 70th Annual Report, TNSCARDB Ltd., Chennai.

'Tamilnadu-An Economic Appraisal 1997-98', Government of Tamilnadu, Chennai, 2000.

APPENDIX –1

A model for generating employment opportunities during drought

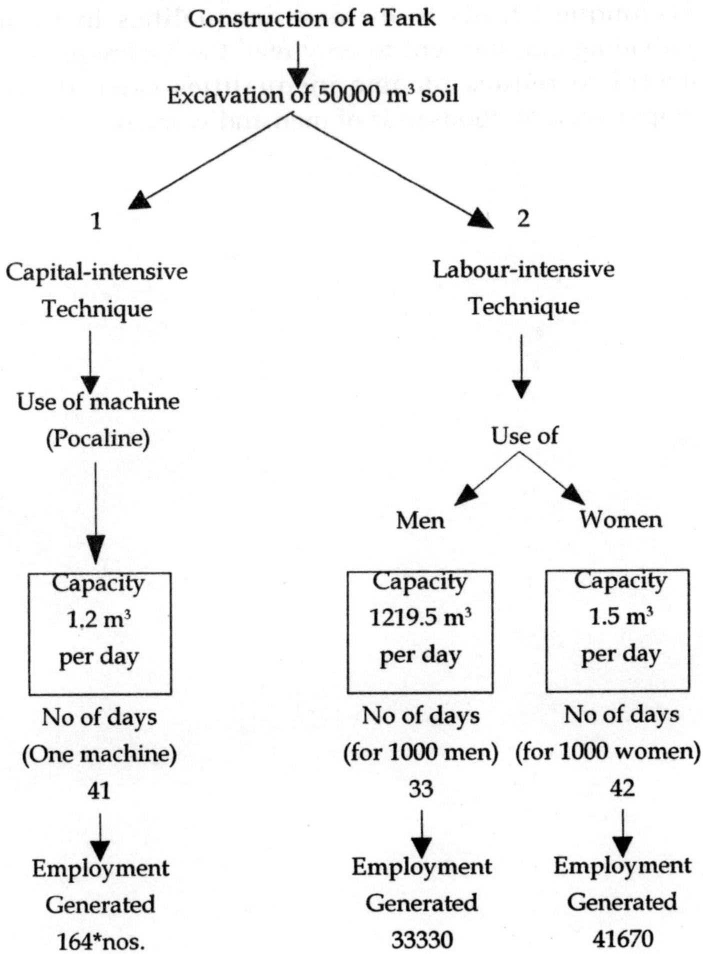

*The required number of labour per days is Two Pocaline operators, one Pocaline cleaner and one watchman. For 41 days, total labour employed comes to 4 x 41 = 164.

The technique II (labour-intensive) is suitable to apply in the study area where getting employment is a difficult task due to continuous drought for the past one decade. We can better use both men and women since both are trying their level best to earn income for household daily expenses. While Technique I leads to increase inequalities in income by providing employment to only few, the Technique II will be useful to reduce income inequalities since it provides employment to thousands of men and women.

16

RURAL LABOUR, INVESTMENT AND PROFIT IN TINY SECTOR– A STUDY

S. Radhakrishnan &
K. Balasubramani

Introduction

World Trade Organisation conference held on 13.09.2003 at Cancun, Mexico, end in futile as they were not signed any agreement. The reason is the developed countries granted more subsidy on export of agriculture products and as the result the under developed countries are not able to compete with them. Further, all the proposals discussed in conference were in support of developed nations. It is clear that liberalized economic policy is to ruin the agro-based and tiny sector in the under developed countries like India. India propose to achieve 8% GDP growth during tenth plan. In the year 2000-2001, the total GDP is 6.0 out of which contribution by agriculture and allied activities is only 0.9. This was decreased from 9.6 in the year 1996-97. In India, where agriculture is the prime occupation, GDP of Agriculture and allied activities must have major share in total GDP.

In this context a study is undertaken to identify the relationship among rural labour, employment and profit in tiny sector. Employment, earning, investment, profit and other variables are studied in this study.

Profit

Profit is the engine that drives the business enterprise to achieve its objectives and is the reward for entrepreneurship.[1]

Application of Profit in Financial Management

The term "Profit" is viewed by different people in different perspective. For example, from the point of view of Financial Management profit is the test of efficiency and measure of control, to the owners, a measure of worth their investment, to the creditors, the margin of safety, to the employees, source of fringe benefits, to the government, the measure of taxable capacity on the basis of legislative action, to the customers, demand for price cut, and finally, to the country, and index to the economic progress, national income generated and rise in the standard of living.[2] A business enterprise is, thus, able to discharge its obligations to the various interested segments of society only through profits. It is, therefore, imperative that profit should be basic thing for which the business undertaking should strive in the interest of their all round development.

Profitability

Profitability is the basis of determining the functional efficiency of any business activity. Profit maximisation is the primary objective of all activities in a business enterprise.

Objective of 'Profit Planning' are

1. To obtain annual earnings before tax of: Twenty percent of net capital employed, i.e. on total assets less liabilities 16 percent on share holders-equity.
2. To improve profits after taxes by at least 10 percent a year.
3. To pay shareholders an annual return of 15 percent on shareholders equity after retaining 50 percent net earnings in business.[3]

According to Marx's theory, profit is the surplus emerging out of the expropriation of fruit of labour by the capitalists.

Profit is classified into the following concepts:

(a) Gross profit,

(b) Operating profit,

(c) Profit before depreciation,

(d) Profit after tax.

These concepts create some ambiguity in selecting the right procedure for estimating the efficiency of business. Gross profit is the surplus of sales value of the output over variable cost of production. Its significance, from management point of view should be sufficient to cover operating expenses and leave a net profit.

Operating profit is obtained after subtracting depreciation personnel and other expenses from gross profit.

This is a measure of operational efficiency of the business and it is usually referred to as Profit before Interest and Taxes (PBIT), Net profit after payment of interest but before tax is known as Profit Before Tax (PBT). Net profit after payment of tax is Profit After Tax (PAT). Thus PAT is the amount ultimately available to the enterprise for appropriation either for dividend or for retained earning or for both.

In financial management rather than profit maximization, it is maximization of wealth, which is emphasized as the goal of business.[4]

Profit serve as a yardstick for judging the competence and efficiency of the management.

The profit is affected by the several factors. Some of the important factors are as follows:

1. Selling price of the products
2. Volume of sales
3. Variable cost per unit
4. Total fixed costs

5. Sales makes (or mix) of different products. The management can achieve their Target Profit goal by varying one or more of the above variables.[5]

There is a considerable academic debate about the impact of working capital on the profitability of a firm. One school of thought argues, that fixed capital only plays a very significant role in profit generating process. Moreover, they also suggest that there may be negative relationship between working capital and profitability. The other school of thought argues that unless there is a minimum level of investment in the working capital which provide a provide a promising vehicle for increasing profitability, output and sales cannot be maintained. In this sense, working capital acts as an explanatory variable in profit function of a company industry. Obviously a large number of considerations play significant role in the development of arguments and counter arguments in this regard. The profitability risk trade off, cost of factors in relation to investment in current vis-à-vis fixed assets, financing through long term versus short term sources are the common ones.[6]

Statistical Tools

Inter temporal comparison of performance needs estimate of variations in various factors over a period of time. For this purpose some of the statistical tools are used. They are

(a) Mean average,

(b) Simple averages of annual growth rate,

Availability of Data

The profit here taken from the audited balance sheet of the institutions under study. Net profit alone is taken for this study purpose.

Inadequacy of Data

Industry wise and product wise data on profit and value of production are not available.

Data Analysis

The particulars of profit on value of production for the five institutions are given in Table 1.

Inference

Earning profit is essential for survival and sustainability of business. In the case of Khadi and Village Industries, profit maximisation is not the main aim. As already stated, the main aim of Khadi and Village industries activities are to generate employment in the rural areas. It does not mean that no profit should be earned. It was not possible to earn huge profit.

The net profit earned and the value of production i.e. output of the five institutions under study are given in the following Table 1.

Table 1: Profit on Value of Production

(Rs. in Lakhs)

Sl. No.	*Name of the Institution*	*Net Profit Mean Average*	*VP Mean Average*	*Percentage of Net Profit on VP*	*Rank*
1.	GKVIPCT	1.79	171.29	1.05	III
2.	MNSS	0.80	42.97	1.86	II
3.	GSS	(-) 0.13	14.73	(-) 0.88	V
4.	KSS	1.46	68.54	2.13	I
5.	TNSS	0.56	63.54	0.88	IV
6.	Total	4.48	361.07	5.15	
7.	Mean	0.90	72.21	1.03	

Mere perusal will reveal that the average profit earned by the five institution is less than one lakh and the percent share on Value of Production (output) is 1.03 MNSS and KSS contributed nearly 2 percent on Value of Production GSS contributed nothing towards profit because of its internal management problem.

Profit alone cannot be used as a tool to measure the efficiency of the Khadi and Village Industries activities, as its main objective is to generate employment. The reasons for low growth rate and meagre profit may be some of the following:

1. Long duration of operating cycle.
2. Low turnover of capital.
3. Cash cycle is high and hence shortage of credit..
4. No marketing facilities.
5. Sales effected only during rebate period of 90 days in a year.
6. Low productivity as there is lack of machine and tools.
7. Unskilled or semi-skilled workers yield less production with low quality.
8. Lack of application of modern scientific management.
9. Depend mainly on Government fund and rebate concession for sale.
10. Stiff competition from Handloom and Mill sector.
11. Lack of compatibility with other sector in market.
12. Lack of mass media advertisement fro its products.
13. Lack of Swadeshi spirit among the people to buy the products made by their own fellow beings.
14. People comparing the quality of Handmade Khadi and Village Industries products with mill made products.

Further Research Suggested

Industry wise, product wise research can be undertaken at the micro level in Khadi and Village Industries Institutions.

Investment and Employment in KVI Institutions

Investment and Employment in KVI

KVI activities need less per capita investment. KVIC is the major financial agent to finance the KVI activities.

KVIC extends financial assistance to both KVI in the form of grant and loan. Khadi industries receive grant and loan without interest. The financial assistance consists of Capital expenditure loan for acquiring of fixed assets and working capital for day to day operation in this activities. The loan issued for VI carries an annual interest of 4 percent. In case the above loan is not sufficient the institution can avail bank finance at higher interest rate but the difference between two interest rates will be given by KVIC to the institutions under interest subsidy scheme.

Chief rationale for the development of KVI is their contribution towards generation of employment opportunities in a thickly populated country. Thanks to relatively simple technology adopted in these activities, a worker uses tools and equipments of modest value.

Statistical Tools

Inter temporal comparison of performance needs estimate of variations in various over a period of time. For this purpose some of the statistical tools are used. They are

(a) Mean average,

(b) Simple averages of annual growth rate,

Data Available on the Issues

For the purpose of capital cost, investible funds of the institutions have been used. Investible funds consists of capital fund, accumulated profit, capital expenditure loan and depreciation reserve Value of investible funds as in 1986-87 has been accepted as starting point. Net additions to investible funds in the subsequent years have been deflated to the price level of 1986-87. Thus cumulative value of investment in the price level of 1986-87 could be obtained for the twelve-year period under study. For each year amount of investment has been divided by number of workers and average capital cost per work place is obtained.

Inadequacy of Data

Industry wise and activity specific data on employment and investment are not available.

Data Analysis

Chief rationale for the development of Khadi and Village Industries is their contribution towards generation of employment opportunities in a thickly populated country. Thanks to relatively simple technology adopted in these activities, a worker uses tools and equipments of modest value. Thus capital cost per work place is very low in these activities. Variations in average capital cost have been measured in simple annual averages, during the twelve year period. Thus particulars of investment and employment for the five institution are given in the following Table 2.

Table 2 : Mean Average of Investment and Employment

Employment in No.
Investment in Lakhs

S. No.	*Name of the institution*	*Mean average of employment*	*Mean average cost of investment per work place*
1.	GKVIPCT	1703	12.287
2.	MNSS	720	6.418
3.	GSS	125	19.393
4.	KSS	1102	6.361
5.	TNSS	1033	8.070
	Total	4683	52.474
	Mean average	937	10.495

Inference

As already pointed out Khadi and Village Industries activities are not required much capital investment. As it is labour oriented the cost of capital per work place will be less. As per the study (refer Table). The mean average of capital cost per work place of the five institutions is Rs. 10,495/-. Total employment generated by the institutions is 4683. The mean average of capital cost per workplace of the five institutions are given in the following Table 3.

Three institutions invested less than ten thousand per work place. One institution is just above the average of Rs. 10,495/-.

It is concluded that KVI activities are labour oriented and need less capital investment per work place.

Table 3:

Sl. No.	*Name of the Institutions*	*Per capita Investment*
1.	GKVIPCT	12.287
2.	MNSS	6.418
3.	GSS	19.393
4.	KSS	6.306
5.	TNSS	8.070
	Total	52.474

Wage and Employment in Khadi and Village Industries Institutions
Wage and Employment in KVIC

It is needless to say that KVI activities are labour intensive. It uses simple machine and tools and employs people from rural area who are mostly illiterate. The KVI activities are able to provide employment to the people of all ages, in case of Khadi all family members including children, adults, housewives and age-old people contribute according to their ability. The process of pre-spinning, spinning and weaving etc., engages people of all ages. Hence Gandhiji took up this khadi activity for giving employment to the rural masses who are illiterate mostly and otherwise no work to do to earn their daily bread. In the pre-independence period and immediately after the commencement of KVIC, khadi was the major production of KVI sector and provide more employment to the people. It was estimated that in the year 1955-56 khadi production was 76 percent on total value of KVI production, and the employment has 51.85 percent. Further as this activities are labour intensive the share of labour input or of labour on total value of khadi production is estimated from 47 to 50 percent. The average annual per capita earning of khadi is around Rs. 13,000/-. Due to overcome the problem of working capital in khadi sector more village industry activities are undertaken. Consequently, the share of percentage of khadi and total value of production is now reduced to 13 percent.

Table 4 : Fund Released from KVIC to Both Khadi & Village Industries Employment, Wages

Year	*Employment (Lakh in person)*	*Wages paid*	*Percapita earning (per annum) (Rs in thousand)*
1	2	3	4
1988-89	42.87	546.98	1.276
1989-90	46.26	674.30	1.458
1990-91	48.57	784.06	1.614
1991-92	50.16	888.54	1.771
1992-93	52.50	1013.63	1.931
1993-94	52.28	1140.65	2.141
1994-95	53.46	1269.37	2.374
1995-96	56.72	1363.85	2.405
1996-97	58.17	1532.85	2.635
1997-98	56.50	1546.34	2.737
Total	518.49	10760.57	20.342
Mean	51.85	1076.06	2.034

Perusal of particulars of wages and salary reveal trends obtained in the earning by workers over a period of time in the context of changes in level of operations and capital cost.

The computation of wages, salaries covers data on wages, salaries, provident fund contribution by management expenses on labour welfare. Relevant particulars for the KVIC for the period of ten years can be found in table 5. Per capita wage in current price is Rs.1,761.

Statistical Tools & Problems

Inter temporal comparison of performance needs estimate of variations over a period of time. For this purpose some of the statistical tools are used. They are

(a) Mean average,

(b) Simple averages of annual growth rate,

Table 5: Average Earnings on V.P. and Per Capita Earnings

Sl. No.	*Name of the Institution*	*Mean average of employment*	*Mean average of Per capita earnings (Rs. in Thousands)*	*Mean average of earnings (Rs. in lakhs)*	*Mean average Value of production (Rs. in lakhs)*	*Share of percentage of average earnings on V.P. 5/6*
(1)	(2)	(3)	(4)	(5)	(6)	(7)
1.	GKVIPCT	1703	3.075	52.26	171.29	30.50
2.	MNSS	720	2.693	19.41	42.97	45.17
3.	GSS	125	2.556	3.31	14.73	22.47
4.	KSS	1102	3.454	38.18	68.54	55.70
5.	TNSS	1033	3.051	31.47	63.54	49.51
6.	Total	4683	14.829	144.63	361.07	203.35
7.	Mean		3.167		72.24	40.05

Source: Appendix A-13.1 to A-13.5, A-6.1 and Chapter-V.

The wage here taken from the audited balance sheet of the institutions understudy. Employment here taken from the annual reports of the institutions.

Industry wise and product wise data on wage and employment are not available.

The particulars of wage and employment for the five institutions are give in the following Table 5.

Inference

Major share of value of production is spared by labour, in Khadi and Village Industries activities. This statement is proved by this study. Average earnings, and value of production of the five institutions are given in Table 9.32. Institution wise particulars are given in Appendix A-13.1 to A-13.5. The average earning of the five institutions is Rs.144.63 lakhs for the employment of 4683 and per capita earning is Rs. 3.167. The percentage of wage on Value of Production is around 40 percent. Hence, it is well known that Khadi and Village Industries programme is mainly for the worker (or) poor artisans and not for augmenting wealth by earning more profit.

REFERENCES

Mohammed Rafiqual Islam, "Profitability of Fertilizer Industry in Bangladesh", *The Management Accountant,* Vol. 35, No. 5, May-2000, p. 338.

Solomon Ezra and Pringle, "An Introduction to Financial Output", Good Year Publishing, Santa Monica-1977, p. 404.

Amit Mallick and Debasish Sur, "Working Capital and Profitability: A Case Study in Interrelation", *The Management Accountant,* Vol. 33, No. 11, November-1998, p. 43.

Khadi and Village Industries Commission, "Statistical Abstract in Khadi and Village Industries", KVIC, Mumbai-1998.

17

KHADI AND VILLAGE INDUSTRIES DURING POST REFORMS

R. Seerangarajan &
P. Muruganandan

Introduction

India is to find employment to 26 million educated unemployed and 44 million less educated unemployed; totally 70 million persons. In addition to this another 200 million non-employed women are engaged in household non-paid work who are not willing to go out of their houses seeking paid jobs. These 200 million are to find job within their house premises. About 66 percentage of the labour-force who are engaged in agriculture are seasonally unemployed. They account to 22 million agricultural workers. Apart from agriculture, about 300 million workers are to find job from non-agricultural or agricultural related rural industries and services. The organised large scale industrial sector employ only 3 percent of the labour force; the remaining 97 percent of the labour force are engaged only in unorganized or less organised Cottage and Village Industrial Sector, and in organised small and ancillary sector. The manpower employable capacity is more for cottage and village industries. Therefore, India's problem of unemployment can be solved only through rural industrialization that too on Gandhian approach or vision. The Gandhian vision means, employment oriented, self reliant, resource based, having the man as the center of all activities The Gandhian vision of rural industrialization envisages capacity utilization of manpower, developing resource based activities in villages, promoting self-reliant economy with Swedeshi spirit; dignity of labour; developing scientific attitude and technological skill for improving productivity. In this regard the Government of India was established Khadi and Village Industries Commission in 1957 for creating awareness on KVIs to the new entrepreneurs. The All India Khadi and Village Industries Commission and the State Khadi and Village Industries Boards make all efforts to enhance the spread of village industries. The Sarvodaya and Gandhian institutions have established tie-up and networking with the District Rural Development Agencies through their area approach. Special programmes for scheduled castes and scheduled tribes are extended throughout the country. The Village Industries provide employment to 56 lakh persons directly, another 40 lakhs may come under indirect employment. The indirectly employed population are mostly women. Such workers are engaged in collection and drying of cereals and pulses, collection of oil seeds from forest areas, herbs from forests, picking up and cleaning of cotton, bleaching of cloth, collection of fibrous plants for processing and coir production, selling of finished products through shops of their own etc. There must be about 10 million persons engaged under organised village industries supported by the Khadi and Village Industries Commission and Boards. During 2001-02 the KVIs has produced goods worth Rs. 7551.52 crores and it has exported goods worth Rs. 21.62 crores.

Small Scale Industries In India

The policy of the Government of India may have to sufficiently protect the small scale industrial sector from the ill-effects of globalization of economy and liberalization of international marketing. In 1994-95, there were 25.71 lakh small scale industrial units; this has increased to 26.72 units in 2000-01 which is not an appreciable growth. The employment position in private organised sector was 75.52 lakhs in 1983. This has increased to 177.30 lakhs in the year 2000-01 which is a good trend; but still the small scale organised sector engages only 17 percent of the industrial labour force. About 80 percent of the labour force are in the unorganized sector of traditional industries. Modernization of units, skill development training, technological improvement would be highly essential in the traditional sector of industries. At the end of the Seventh plan period, the small scale sector of industries of all kind, both private, public or societies provided employment to 12 million persons. This has increased to 18 million at the end of the Ninth plan period.

The export position in the case of small scale industries has not made any change in the last 10 years. At the end of the 7th Plan period, the SSI sector contributed for about 40 percent of the export. The same volume of export or in a range of 35 to 40 percent is maintained at the end of the Ninth Plan period. Unless the export position improves, the employment status of this sector cannot improve considerably. The local consumption for about 80 percent is only from the small scale sector. The government of India policy intends to liberalize this sector from stringent regulations and strong bureaucratization for tapping its growth potential. The Government may lay down procedures to cut the red-tapism, bureaucratic delays and reduce corruption in the grant of concessional credit to SSI units. There are cases where a small scale unit becomes virtually a subsidiary of a large company with a share holding of 24 percent with their nominees acting as benami owners. In many places big units are interested to use the small units only as sub-contracting agencies for small jobs. In such situations, the big units do not encourage the small units to function independently.

Challenges Before Small Enterprises:

Dismantling of quantitative restrictions on imports of 1429 items, lowering of tariffs on imports, Open General License (OGL) for the reserved categories of 812 items, reduction in subsidies for exports, lack of access to industrial credit, marketing bottlenecks, compliance with cumbersome procedures, technological obsolescence, harassment by inspecting functionaries, out dated labour laws, operational inflexibility, lack of warehousing facilities, lack of awareness of the policy of the Government and inadequate training arrangements are some of the challenges before the small scale sector.

The Problems of the Small Scale Industrial Sector

(i) *Shortage of Raw Materials :* Shortage of raw materials is a problem in the case of small scale industries. In hand loom industry, yarn supply is a big problem. This industry uses mill yarn. The mills would prefer to supply yarn to the mills in bulk. Such a bulk supply is easy for them to avoid overhead charges. In the case of hand loom industry retail supply is to be undertaken by some agency. The weavers co-operative societies are doing this work. Most of the weavers Co-operative societies are not managerially sound. They are often run by special officers superceding the Boards of Directors. The administrative structure will have to be strengthened to solve this problem. Similar problem of storage of raw materials exist in the case of sugar industry. Sugarcane availability is season; and hence for certain months the mills are closed without operation. During this period of closure the workers may suffer without work. The same problem exist with the agro-processing industries who draw seasonal raw materials from agriculture.

Untrained or unskilled labour or inadequately trained or less motivated labour is a problem in small scale industries. Mostly the labourers in small enterprises get trained only after joining the industries. The reason is, there are no sufficient number of training centers in each industry. Even supervisory staff join their positions only with mere theoretical knowledge. Skills are gained only out of experience in the work spots. Training programmes both pre-position and in-service are to be thoroughly planned in each industry by its Federations or Associations.

(ii) ***Provision for Industrial Education and Training*** : The workers of an industrial unit need education continuously and periodical training need to be arranged. Enough research has gone in to every industry and the industries have the advantage of scientific knowledge and technology. These specialized research have taken place in industrially advanced countries. The advantages have not percolated adequately to the developing countries. The globalization and liberalization process must facilitate percolation of scientific industrial knowledge and technical know-how into the areas of economically developing countries. The modern practices of the various production methods must reach each and every unit of the industry concerned. The workers of any corner of a country must get adequate facilities for updating their training on new technology.

(iii) ***Inadequacy of Finance*** : The liberalization process under WTO agreement will create competitiveness between industrial concerns of different countries. The industrial units who involve themselves in the world trade need to strengthen their infra-structure, production technology and marketing network, for which there should be enough be enough financial support. The Small Industries Development Organization through the Reserve Bank of India and Small Industries Development Bank of India may plan for meeting out this need.

(iv) ***Regulations*** : Cumbersome procedures are to be discussed with the entrepreneurs and the Government authorities, and to be relaxed to the facilitate the small enterprises. Regulations should not tighten the hands of the new entrepreneurs.

(v) ***Other Problems*** : There are other problems which will affect the performance of small enterprises in the process of liberalization, which are to be carefully attended.

Problems such as bureaucratization, location disadvantages, non-implementation of reservation policy, non-competitive nature of the industry, technological obsolescence, less attention of supporting institutions on sick units, non-membership and less contact with the industrial associations, lack of access to institutional credit, marketing bottlenecks, harassment by inspecting functionaries, out dated labour laws, inadequate warehousing facility, relaxation from export-import policy under Open-General License (OGL), Competition resulting from liberalization measures, lifting quantitative restrictions affect the small scale industries.

Objectives of the Study

The specific objectives of the study are:

(i) To analyse the production and sales performance of KVI products.

(ii) To examine the export performance of KVI products.

(iii) To identify the employment provided by KVI products; and

(iv) To suggest suitable measures for the development of KVI products.

Period of the Study

The study covers for a period of ten years from 1992-93 to 2001-02.

Table 1 reveals that the production performance of Khadi and Village industries. In terms of Khadi, the highest production has recorded in 1998-99 (Rs. 635.89 cr.), and the lowest was recorded in 1992-93. In terms of village industries, it has shown a increasing trend from Rs. 2876.82 cr. in 1992-93 to Rs. 2140.52 cr. in 2001-02. In the case of growth rate it has declining from 12.42 percent in 1992-93 to 9.07 percent in 2001-02 with and average growth of 11.43 percent. In order to improve production of KVIs, it should adopt proper production planning and improve the quality with rich designs.

Table 1: Production of Khadi and Village Industries

(Rs in Crores)

Sl. No	Year	Khadi	Village industries	Total	% Growth rate
(1)	(2)	(3)	(4)	(5)	(6)
1.	1992-93	353.48	2523.34	2876.82	-
2.	1993-94	357.27	2876.87	3234.14	12.42
3.	1994-95	389.71	3234.34	3624.05	12.05
4.	1995-96	522.23	3504.22	4026.45	11.10
5.	1996-97	626.40	3889.85	4516.25	12.16
6.	1997-98	624.10	3895.21	4519.31	0.07
7.	1998-99	635.89	4476.48	5112.37	13.12
8.	1999-2000	551.94	5613.41	6165.35	20.60
9.	2000-2001	431.57	6491.69	6923.26	12.29
10.	2001-2002	411.00	7140.52	7551.52	9.07
	Average				11.43

Source: KVIC Annual Reports.

Table 2 explain the sales performance of KVI products. In terms of Khadi, the highest sales has recorded (Rs. 745.90 cr.)

Table 2: Sale of KVI Products

(Rs. in Crores)

Sl. No	Year	Khadi	Village industries	Total	% Growth rate
(1)	(2)	(3)	(4)	(5)	(6)
1.	1992-93	387.13	2810.12	3197.25	-
2.	1993-94	409.24	3232.01	3641.25	13.89
3.	1994-95	490.85	3578.33	4069.18	11.75
4.	1995-96	567.36	3861.78	4429.14	8.85
5.	1996-97	581.10	4242.89	4813.99	8.69
6.	1997-98	745.90	4319.38	5065.28	5.22
7.	1998-99	647.83	4953.18	5601.01	10.58
8.	1999-2000	631.79	6137.41	6769.20	20.86
9.	2000-2001	570.55	7384.55	7955.10	17.51
10.	2001-2002	518.25	8383.49	8901.74	11.90
	Average				12.13

Source: KVIC annual Reports.

in 1997-98, and the lowest was recorded (Rs. 387.13 cr.) in, 1992-93. Due to high cost and more maintenance than polyester cloth the khadi sales was recorded declining trend, for the survival of khadi, it is our duty to create awareness on Khadi among the people. In this regard, attractive advertisement may be given by the famous politicians, film stars and cricket players, In the case of village industries, it has maintained increasing trend from Rs. 2810 cr. in 1992-93 to Rs. 8383.49 cr. in 2001-02. In order to improve the sales of KVI products, the present marketing practices should be modified with the modern marketing strategy.

Table 3 indicates that the employment provided by Khadi and village industries. It has provided 52.50 lakh employment in 1992-93 to 62.64 lakh employment in 2001-02 during under study. The negative growth rate has been recorded during 1997-98 (-2.87) with an average growth of 2.01 percent.

Table 3 : Employment of Khadi and Village Industries

(Rs. in lakhs)

Sl. No	*Year*	*Khadi*	*Village industries*	*Total*	*% Growth rate*
(1)	(2)	(3)	(4)	(5)	(6)
1.	1992-93	-	-	52.50	-
2.	1993-94	-	-	53.28	1.49
3.	1994-95	-	-	53.46	0.34
4.	1995-96	-	-	56.75	6.15
5.	1996-97	-	-	58.17	2.50
6.	1997-98	14.01	42.49	56.50	(-) 2.87
7.	1998-99	13.85	44.44	58.29	3.17
8.	1999-2000	12.35	46.88	59.23	1.61
9.	2000-2001	9.56	50.51	60.07	1.42
10.	2001-2002	8.48	54.16	62.64	4.28
	Average				2.01

Source: KVIC Annual Reports.

Table 4 express the export performance of KVI products. The export of KVI products has shown a up and down trend.

The highest export value of Rs. 29.65 cr has recorded during 1999-2000 and the lowest of Rs. 18,40 cr was recorded during 2000-01. In the case of growth rate, during 2000-01 it has recorded negative growth rate of (-) 37.94 with an average growth of (-) 11.67 percent. This indicates that the necessary steps should be taken by the Government of India to capture more foreign markets. For the development of export of KVI, it should be produced good quality with rich designs.

Table 4: Export Performance of KVI Products

(Rs. in crores)

Sl. No	*Year*	*Export value*	*% Growth rate*
(1)	(2)	(3)	(4)
1.	1998-1999	24.69	-
2.	1999-2000	29.65	20.09
3.	2000-2001	18.40	(-) 37.94
4.	2001-2002	21.62	17.50
	Average		(-) 11.67

Source: KVIC Annual Reports.

Findings of the Study

- In terms of khadi, the highest production has recorded in 1998-99 (Rs. 635.789 cr.), and the lowest was recorded in 1992-93. In terns of village industries, it has shown a increasing trend from Rs. 2876.82 cr. in 1992-93 to Rs. 7140.52 cr. in 2001-02. In the case of growth rate it has declining from 12.42 percent in 1992-93 to 9.07 percent in 2001-02 with an average growth of 11.43 percent.
- The highest sales has recorded (Rs. 745.90 cr.) in 1997-98, and the lowest was recorded (Rs. 387.13 cr.) in 1992-93. Due to high cost and more maintenance than polyester cloth, the khadi sales was recorded declining trend, for the survival of khadi, it is our duty to create awareness on Khadi among the people. In this regard, attractive advertisement may be given by the famous politicians,

film stars and cricket players. In the case of village industries, it has maintained increasing trend from Rs. 2810 cr. in 1992-93 to Rs. 8383.49 cr. in 2001-02.

- It has provided 52.50 lakh employment in 1992-93 to 62.64 lakh employment in 2001-02. during under study. The negative growth rate has been recorded during 1997-98 (-2.87) with and average growth of 2.01 percent.
- During 1998-99 Khadi and Village industries goods has exported worth Rs. 24.69 cr. and it has exported goods worth Rs. 21.62 cr. in 2001-02. The highest export was (Rs. 29.65) recorded during 1999-2000.

Suggestions for the Development of KVIs

- Restrictions are to be imposed on imports to save the native industries. Duties are to be levied on imports that are being dumped at extremely low prices because of the subsidies they are receiving from their Governments. The export oriented units need special attention on priority basis in aspects such as: finance, technology upgradation, availability of raw materials, quality assurance, packaging, marketing intelligence and infrastructure. There should be consortia of export units in every region. The small enterprises are to be facilitated to participate in international exhibitions. Marketing intelligence is to be promoted. Facilities are to be created to have tie-up with importers of other countries. There is a very high export potentiality in areas such as auto-parts and accessories, electronics and electrical equipments, motor cycle parts, computer software, textiles, leather goods, food processing industries, and garments. Export competitiveness can be created for Indian products through ensuring qualities, developing infra-structure, productivity of labour, creation of a brand image. Special Economic Zones (SEZ) are to be created in Gujarat and Tamilnadu for promoting export potentialities. And special attention must be made in SEZs in areas like flexible nature of labour laws, high quality infra-structure, removal of bureaucratic hurdles.

- Voluntary institutions must be encouraged to start small scale industrial units with financial assistance and infra-structure facilities. Some of the enthusiastic institutions may run a cluster of industrial units for utilization of resources and for providing employment to the local educated and unemployed.

- Village panchayats may create marketing complex in their own areas for facilitating local marketing. Comparatively it will be easy for the Village Panchayats to develop infra-structure for marketing and thus, they will be able to generate income sources. The Panchayat Unions/ Samithis may promote rural industrual estates with 10 to 20 sheds for facilitating new entrepreneurs to establish industries. The Panchayat Samithis may draw finance directly from SIDBI for infra-structure development in rural industrial estates.

- The District Development Councils may have to periodically discuss the District plan and review the progress of work. The General Manager, District Industries Centre will become answerable to the District Development Council.

- Nowadays advertisement play a key role for sales promotion. So that the Khadi and Village Industries should explore attractive advertisement with the famous film (or) cricket stars. This strategy should help to improve the sales performance of the KVI products.

- In order to protect Khadi and Village Industries, the research organizations like, CSSR, ICSSR, and KVIC etc., should come forward to provide fellowships to Rural Industries and Management Graduates for doing research and development on this field. This will improve the management practices as well as quality of the KVI products.

REFERENCES

Francis Cherunilam, "Village, Small and Ancillary Industries: The New Policy", Himalaya publication, 1997, pp. 211-212.

Chabra, N.N., "Rural Industries", *Kurukshetra,* Vol. XLVI, (5), Feb. 1998, pp. 20-26.

KVIC Annual Report, Khadi and Village Industries Commission, Mumbai.

Reddy, P.N. Principles of Business Economics: Pricing Policy and Methods, S. Chand & Company Limited, New Delhi, 1995, pp. 207-209.

Rao, R.V., "Cottage and Small Scale Industries and Planned Economy", Sterling Publications, Mumbai, 1999.

18

ENTREPRENEURSHIP DEVELOPMENT IN SMALL INDUSTRIES UNDER LIBERALISATION

N. Meenakshi Sundaram & E. Anand

Introduction

The recent development in economy and the policy of Liberalisation has created many challenges in the business, small industries and industrual area. Nearly 70 percent of the population lives in villages in India. Rural India is characterized by mass poverty, under employment and unemployment besides large-scale migration to urban areas, small and cottage industries play an important role in the developing countries. In India there has occurred a rapid growth of Rural Industrial sector.

Large Level computerization and automation has also introduced a major changes in the nature and type of employment from that in traditional production and business environment and also in the small Industries. Where entrepreneurs are employed in large number in small, medium and large scale industries and business. The IX plan emphasized the need to pay attention to planned state intervention to provide greater opportunities for education and employment to entrepreneur.

Entrepreneurship Development Institute of India (EDII)

EDII is a National Organisation sponsored by all India financial institutions and the Government of Gujarat. It has emerged from the centre for Entrepreneurship Development of the Gujarat Industrial and Technical cousultancy organisaton. It conducts research, training and institution building activities for encouraging the participation of backward regions and special target croups to entrepreneurship. Its entrepreneurship development programme consists of :

(i) Selecting potential entrepreneurs.

(ii) Achievement motivation training.

(iii) Product selection and project report preparation.

(iv) Business management training.

(v) Practical training and work experience.

(vi) Post training support and follow up.

The programme run by EDII is said to be the oldest, largest, most comprehensive, best organised and the most successful entrepreneurship development programme in the country.

Institutional Set Up

In order to accelerate the small industries development, Government at the central state levels have set up a number of development agencies / institutions such as District. Industries Centres (DICS), Small industries Service Institute (SISI) and small Industries Development organisations etc. All India Financial Institutions–IDDI, IFCL, ICICI have promoted/ sponsored a number of Technical consultancy organisations (TCOS) to assist small entrepreneurs in different ways. In 1986, the small Industries Development Fund was set up in IDBI in order to assist small scale, village and cottage industries and tiny sector units in the rural areas. Recently, the Small Industries Development Bank of India (SIDBI) has been established to help small-scale units. In addition to these institutions there are agencies like National Science and Technology

Entrepreneurship Board, Khadi and Village Industries commission, commercial banks, EXIM bank and Co-operative Banks who undertake promotional activities aiming at facilitating industrial development.

Institutional Frame Work

To provide financial assistance to entrepreneurs the Government has set up a number of special financial institutions besides commercial banks. They may be classified in to two categories.

1. All India Financial Institutions
2. State Level Financial Institutions

The State Level institutions are further divided into two categories, State Financial Corporations (SFCs) and State Industrial and Investment Corporations. Besides the two types of institutions, in some states there are State Industrial Corporations which are engaged in the development of the industrial estates and providing financial assistance like equity support. The All India Level Financial Institutions are as follows.

(a) Industrial Finance corporation of India.

(b) Industrial credit and Investment Corporation of India.

(c) Industrial Development Bank of India.

(d) Industrial Reconstruction Bank of India.

(e) EXIM Bank of India.

(f) Unit Trust of India.

(g) LIC, GIC, etc.

(h) National Small Industries corporation.

(i) Small Industries Development Bank of India.

New Entrepreneur Development Agency

The New Entrepreneur Development Agency has been created in order to assist educated unemployed graduates to set up SSI units in urban and metropolitan areas. The Agency will close candidates only from among those sponsored by Government Institutions and Agencies like SISI, DICs, University Employment Guidance Bureau. The selected candidates will be assisted in selecting the projects suitable to their aptitude and backgrounds. The candidates on identifying the projects will undergo an Entrepreneur Development Programme to be conducted by Agencies like SISI, ITCOT, etc. Practical training will also be arranged in industries, wherever possible.

Projects with credit requirements up to Rs. 5 lakhs are only eligible for finance under the scheme. 100 percent finance will be provided in the beginning and the margin will be built up to 20 percent over a period of times depending on the profitability of envisaged project. Assets created with bank finance and personal quarentees of parents will be sufficient securities for the loans given. The maximum amount of loan will be Rs. 5 lakhs and the repayment of term loans will be based on the profitability projection and within seven years. The interest rate for medium loan is 13.5 percent p.a. and for working capital 14 percent p.a. up to Rs 2 lakhs and 15.5 percent p.a. above Rs. 2 lakhs up to Rs. 5 lakhs.

Need for Training and Development

The objective of entrepreneurial training is to develop motivation and competence necessary for successful lunching, management and growth of the enterprise. Entrepreneurial development is relatively a recent phenomenon as compared to executive development.

The objectives of an entrepreneurial development programme (EDP) may be divided into two categories short - term objectives, and long -term objectives.

Short-term Objectives

Short–term objectives imply the objectives, which are to be achieved immediately after the completion of the programme.

Preparing a personality for the entrepreneurial venture, making him competent to scan the environment and situation within the existing regulatory frame work are the short-term. Objectives short-term objective is to help a participant in the fixation of his/her goal of life as entrepreneurisation.

Long-term Objective

In the long run, an entrepreneurial development programme seeks to equip the participants with all the skills required for the establishment and smooth running of business ventures.

The objectives of an entrepreneurial development programme are as follows:

(i) To enlarge the supply of entrepreneurs for rapid industrial development.

(ii) To develop small and medium enterprises sector which is necessary for employment generation and wider dispersal of industrial ownership.

(iii) To industrialise rural and backward regions.

(iv) To provide gainful self-employment to educated young men and women.

(v) To diversify the sources of entrepreneurship

(vi) To improve the performance of small scale industries by developing managerial skills among small entrepreneurs.

Advantages of Entrepreneurship Development

1. Help in the rapid economic Growth and industrialization of the country and create the necessary infrastructure for economic development.
2. Promote redistribution of income and wealth.
3. Earn returns on Investment and thus generate resources for development.

4. Create employment opportunities.
5. Promote balanced regional development.
6. Assist the development of small scale industry.
7. Promote import substitution, save and earn foreign exchange for the economy.
8. Act as a countervaiting to over an put up and effective competition to undertakings in the private sector.
9. Gain control over the commanding heights of the economy.

Small Industries Under Liberalisation Era

In the era of liberalization and globalization the products and services are required to be qualitative and quantitative if one has to survive in the open competition. With the new economic policy a virtual economic revolution is taking place. Not only foreign companies are entering India, but Indian companies are also expanding diversifying and are going global. In the fast moving scenario, Indian entrepreneurs need to synchronise and keep the pace with the developing world. Suitable changes in the Entrepreneurship Development programmes are to be made to train the entrepreneurs, not only to manage the change but also innovate to effect the change.

New technology based firms are now playing an important role in development of the country. New generic technologies, especially in the areas of biotechnology, new materials, information technology and telecommunication offer a wide spectrum of opportunities for new knowledge based small industries, new technology based firms are generally small units which help the new industries based on radical technology innovations. They have high commercial and technical risks because of the changes effecting the sector. However, these units can be successfully managed by new entrepreneurs. In order to give greater thrust to the development of new technology based firms, the concept of Science and Technology Entrepreneurs Park (STEP) was evolved in India. The STEP provides trainings in the area of science and Technology for potential entrepreneurs in emerging fields in small and ancillary sectors.

Entrepreneurs in Small Industries

The small entrepreneurs of the rural and urban area can engaged in the production and marketing consumable goods which can be produced with lesser capital. The following are some of the cottage and small-scale industries suitable for small entrepreneurs:

Ghani Oil Industry

Edible oil is a part of our day to day food and there is great demand for edible oil in India.

1. Raw materials: Edible oil seeds (Locally available).
2. The capital requirement for the above industry will be Rs. 60,000/-.

Agarbathi Industry

Burning of bathis (udubathis) in religious and social functions is a practice in India.

1. Raw Material: charcoal power, sandal wood powder, gigathu, markiolundu powder, aromatics and other perfumes.
2. Total requirement of capital for this industry will be Rs. 45,000/-.

Honey Procession

Honey is the nature's gift which has got high market demand. There for the entrepreneur can make high profit in this business.

1. Raw materials: Raw honey.
2. Total capital required for this industry will be Rs. 1,00,000/-.

Cleaning Powder

The cleaning powder is mainly used to clean the house hold utensils, enamel vessels etc., there is a very good market demand for this product.

1. Raw material: Calcite powder, soda ask acid slurry, sodium meta silicate, Trisodin phosphate etc.
2. Total capital required for this industry is Rs. 50,000/-.

Bakery

Bakery products is a part of our day to day food. There is a good market demand for this product.

1. Raw material: Maida, Sugar, Yeast, Salt, Bread improver, Acetic acid, Milk powder, Egg, Water Firewood/Fuel and Fat.
2. Total capital required for this industry is 30,000.

Paper Bag and Cup

Paper cup is such a commodity, which now a day plays an indispensable role in our life. It is used in tea shop, functions, shop and weddings. Therefore the entrepreneur can make high profit in this business.

1. Raw materials: Scoring and punching, cycling machine, paper cutting machine and accessories.
2. Total capital required for this industry is Rs. 1,00,000.

Detergent Cake

The Detergent cake is mainly used to clean the cloths.

1. Raw materials: Stone powder, soda Ash, china clay, STPP, TSP, Acid slurry, sodium silicate, starch, perfume and colour.
2. The capital requirement for the above industry will be 1,00,000/-.

Detergent Powder

Washing cloth is necessary to remove dirt. So, there is a very good market demand for this product.

1. Raw materials: Washing soda, Sodium Sulphate, Dalumide, Colour, Salt, Perfume, Water, Caustic lye, and Acid slurry.

2. Total capital required for this industry is Rs. 50,000/-

Black Phenyle

The Black phenyle is mainly used to clean bath room and Toilets.

1. Raw materials : Rosin, Castor oil, Cresote oil, Caustic soda solution and water.
2. Total capital required for this industry 25,000/-

Computer Aided Textile Design Unit

Designing cloth is very important element for increase production and sales operations.

1. Raw materials: Monitor, C.P.U. Key board, Mouse, Dot Matrix Printer, Scanner, UPS and software.
2. Capital required for this unit is Rs. 50,000/-.

These are many more cottage and small industries which suitable to small entrepreneurs such as shampoo, liquid blue, Pappad making, Pickles, Leather and Bio-gas etc. These industries are capital cheap and labour intensive. Since all these goods are consumable items, which are required for our day to day life, they can be easily marketed in the local area. Therefore, in the era of Liberalisation a lot has been done in the country to develop new entrepreneurs through training and at present most of the states are involved in the entrepreneurship development programmes. So, the above mentioned cottage and small industries suitable for small entrepreneurs.

Conclusion

In the era of Liberalisation the New technology based firms are now playing an important role in development of the country. New generic technologies, especially in the areas of biotechnology, new materials, information technology and telecommunication offer a wide spectrum of opportunities for small industries. New technology based firms are generally small units which help the new industries based on radical technology innovations. They have high commercial and technical risks because of the rapid changes effecting the sector. In this context the entrepreneurial training is a vital force in the promotion of small enterprises in the economy. So, more training programmes should be initiated in region-wise, business wise and Industry wise by including dynamic factors like information sharing and the provision of infrastructural facilities.

REFERENCES

Menon P.K.B., *"Entrepreneurship Development Small Enterprises Development Management and Extension Journal."* Vol. XXIII, No. 1, March 1999.

Narendra Kumar D., "Women Entrepreneurship Development in India, problems and prospects" Indian Institute of Public Opinion.

Gupta C.B., "Entrepreneurial Development" Sultan Chand & Sons, New Delhi, 1999.

Srivastava S.B., "A Practical Guide to Industrial Entrepreneurs" Sultan Chand & Sons, New Delhi, 1999.

Government of India, "Entrepreneurship in Small Scale Industries, Ministry of Industry" New Delhi, 2000.

19

IMPACT OF ECONOMIC POLICY ON SERVICE SECTOR

R. Ramkumar Prabu &
H. Samvel Thavaraj

India's Business Environment

Despite growing trade and investment, foreign companies in India consider it a challenging business environment. Major problems include infrastructure shortages and expense; red tape and transparency issues, intellectual property protection and the backlog in the court system.

Since the early 1990s, trade reform has been India's most substantial and successful area of economic reform; trade now represents about 30 percent of India's GDP, up from only 15 percent before reforms. Despite on going trade reforms, India still imposes many restrictions and its average tariffs remain high by regional standards. Nevertheless, exporters are finding new opportunities as import barriers fall in previously protected markets.

New Economic Policy

When asked about the impact on the socio-economic conditions of various sections of the society of the economic policy, the Committee were informed that under the new economic policy, the role of the Government and Public Sector are getting redefined. Requirement of manpower of the Government Department is being reassessed and fresh recruitment in Government Departments and institutions is kept limited to the minimum essential needs.

Commencing from 1991, India has been going through process of economic reforms and liberalisation. The reforms have embraced almost all aspects of the country's economy. These reforms fall under two basic categories:

(i) Liberalisation measures and
(ii) Macro-economic reforms and structural adjustments.

Under the Liberalisation Measures

New Industrial Policy

- Liberalisation of industrial licensing
- FERA Liberlisation
- MRTP Liberalisation
- Curtailment of public sector

New Trade Policy

- Lowering of import tariffs
- Abolition of import licenses
- A more open exim regime
- Convertibility of rupee
- Encouragement to exports
- Encouragement to foreign exports
- Integrating India's economy with the global economy

Under the Macroeconomic Reforms and Structural Adjustments

Macro Economic Reforms

- Fiscal and monetary reforms
- Banking sector reforms
- Capital market reforms

Structural Adjustments

- Phasing out subsidies
- Dismantling of price controls and introduction of market driven price environment
- Public sector restructure disinvestment
- Exit policy

Objectives of the NEP

All the measures together aim at modernizing the country's industrial system, removing unproductive controls, encouraging private with the global economy. In one word, all round opening up of the country's economy has been the aim of the new policies and measures and these are collectively referred to as the New Economic Policies (NEP).

India's Growth and Reform Outlook

- India has grown robustly since its early 1990s reforms and in early 2001, the Government announced further fiscal, labour market, trade, foreign investment, privatisation and government administration reforms; if implemented, these could return India to previous real GDP growth peaks of 7 to 8 percent per year.
- However, since the mid 1990s, governments of India's large decentralized democracy have found it difficult to achieve consensus for further rapid reform.
- A more likely scenario is continuing incremental reform; together with past reforms and on going trade liberalization commitments, this should ensure India maintains 5 to 6 percent growth over the medium term.
- However, at a time when much of Asia outside China faces slow growth or contraction, India's growth prospects look relatively robust.
- Due to reforms, India's 'middle class' is expanding rapidly; about 60 million people now live in households

with income over US $6000 per year, compared to only about 25 million in 1994-95.

Socio-economic Impact of the New Policy

As regards the economic impact of the new policy, it was stated that the new industrial policy is aimed at development of the national economy as a whole. As a result of this policy, there have been changes in the foreign investment, industrial development, infrastructure development, as well as reforms in the financial sector and public sector. In the Budget speech for 2001-02, it has been stated that economic reforms began in 1991, the economy has grew at an average rate of 6.4 percent per a year since 1992-93 in comparison to 5.8 percent recorded in the 1980s. Further, poverty had shown declining trend from 36 percent in 1993-94 to 26 percent or less now.

When asked to explain whether profit making public sector undertaking are being disinvested, the Department of Disinvestment in a written note have stated that the decision of the Government for disinvestments of its equity in any public sector enterprises is governed by the declared disinvestment policy. This policy of the Government is applicable to all public sector enterprises, irrespective of the fact whether it profit making or loss incurring.

The public sector enterprises have been classified as strategic and non-strategic as indicated below:

(i) The Strategic Public Sector Enterprises would be those in the areas:

Arms and ammunitions and the allied

Atomic energy (except in the areas related to the generation of nuclear power and applications of radiation and radio-isotopes to agriculture medicine and non-strategic industries).

Railway transport

(ii) All other public sector enterprises would be non-strategic. For the non-strategic Public Sector Enterprises, the reduction of Government share to 26 percent would not be automatic and the manner and pace of doing so would be worked out on a case-to-case basis. A decision in regard to the percentage of disinvestments i.e. Government share going down to less than 51 percent to 26 percent would be taken on the following considerations:

(a) Whether the industrial sector as a countervailing force to prevent prevent concentration of power in private hands, and

(b) Whether the industrial sector requires a proper regulatory mechanism to protect the consumer interests before Public Sector Enterprises are privatised.

This is the overall impact of the new economic policy in the Indian economy. The study focus on the impact of new economic policy in the service sector especially in the major services like telecommunications, banking, educational and insurance.

New Telecom Policy 1999

Importance of Telecommunications

The Government of India (Government) recognizes that provision of world class telecommunications infrastructure and information is the key to rapid economic and social development of the country. It is critical not only for the development of the Information Technology industry, but also has widespread ramifications on the entire economy of the country. It is also anticipated that going forward, a major part of the GDP of the country would be contributed by this sector. Accordingly, it is of vital importance to the country that there be a comprehensive and forward looking telecommunications policy which creates an enabling framework for development of this industry.

Need for a New Telecom Policy

In addition to some of the objectives of NTP 1994 not being fulfilled, there have also been far reaching developments in the recent past in the telecom, IT, consumer electronics and media industries world-wide. Convergence of both markets and technologies is a reality that is forcing realignment of the industry. At one level, telephone and broadcasting industries are entering each other's markets, while at another level, technology is blurring the difference between different conduit systems such as wire line and wireless. As in the case of most countries, separate licenses have been issued in our country for basic, cellular, ISP, satellite and cable TV operators each with separate industry structure, terms of entry and varying requirement to create infrastructure. However, this convergence now allows operators to use their facilities to deliver some services reserved for other operators, necessitating a relook into the existing policy framework. The new telecom policy framework is also required to facilitate India's vision of becoming an IT superpower and develop a world class telecom infrastructure in the country.

Objectives and Targets of the New Telecom Policy 1999

The objectives of the NTP 1999 are as under:

- Access to telecommunications is of utmost importance for achievement of the country's social and economic goals. Availability of affordable and effective communications for the citizens is at the core of the vision and goal of the telecom policy.
- Strive to provide a balance between the provision of universal service to all uncovered areas, including the rural areas, and the provision of high-level services capable of meeting the country's economy;
- Encourage development of telecommunication facilities in remote, hilly and tribal areas of the country;
- Create a modern and efficient telecommunications infrastructure taking into account the convergence of IT,

media, telecom and consumer electronics and thereby propel India into becoming an IT superpower;

- Convert PCO's, wherever justified, into Public Teleinfo Centres having multimedia capability like ISDN services, remote database access, government and community information systems etc.
- Transform in a time bound manner, the telecommunications sector to a greater competitive environment in both urban and rural areas providing equal opportunities and level playing field for all players;
- Strengthen research and development efforts in the country and provide an impetus to build world-class manufacturing capabilities.
- Achieve efficiency and transparency in spectrum management.
- Protect defence and security interests of the country.
- Enable Indian Telecom Companies to become truly global players.

New Policy Framework

The New Policy framework must focus on creating an environment, which enables continued attraction of investment in the sector and allows creation of communication infrastructure by leveraging on technological development. Towards this end, the New Policy Framework would look at the telecom service sector as follows:

- Cellular Mobile Service Providers, Fixed Service Providers and Cable Service Providers, collectively referred to as 'Access Providers.'
- Radio Paging Service Providers.
- Public Mobile Radio Trunking Service Providers.
- National Long Distance Operators.
- International long Distance Operators.

- Other Service Providers.
- Global Mobile Personal Communication by Satellite (GMPCS) Service Providers.
- V-SAT based Service Providers.

Impact in Telecom Sector: An Overview

The $8 billion telecommunications sector in India has undergone a major transformation in the past couple of decades. From a complete monopoly of the public sector, the telecom industry has witnessed the breaking down of monopolies and significant policy reforms, favouring the entry of private players. The private sector has been allowed make a foray not only into value-added services, such as cellular and paging services, but also the basic telephony services.

Reforms have taken place in the telecom sector in three phases.

The first phase began in the 1980s, when in 1984, private manufacturing of customer premise equipment was given the go-ahead.

- Proliferation of individual STD/ISD/PCO network took place throughout the country by way of private individual franchisees.
- Also, two large corporate entities, the Mahanagar Telephone Nigam (MTNL) and Bharat Sanchar Nigam (BSNL), were created out of the department of telecommunications (DOT) to handle the sectors of Mumbai and Delhi respectively.
- A high-powered telecom commission was set up in 1989 and Videsh Sanchar Nigam (VSNL) was made the international service provider catering to all telecom services originating from India.

The second phase of reforms in the telecom sector commenced in 1991 with the announcement of the new economic policy.

- To begin with, the manufacturing of telecom equipment was delicensed in 1991, while radio-paging services were opened up in 1992.

- In 1994, the basic telephony sector was opened up by providing licences to six companies to operate in the basic areas. These companies were: Bharti Telenet, Essar Commvision, Shyam Telecom, Hughes Telecom, Tata Teleservices and Reliance Telecom.
- The National Telecom Policy in 1994 emphasised on Universal Service and Qualitative Improvement in telecom services.
- While an independent statutory regulatory was established in 1997, the internet services were opened up in 1998.
- Since then, more companies have been given the go-ahead to enter basic telephony, such as Reliance, Tatas, HFCL, Bharati, Aircel, Digilink and Birla AT&T.

The third phase of reforms in the telecom sector began in the late 1990s, with the announcement of the New Telecom Policy in 1999.

- The underlying theme of the reform process of NTP was to usher in full competition through unrestricted entry of private players in all service sectors.
- The policy favoured the migration of existing operators from the era of fixed license fee regime to that of revenue sharing.
- The duopoly rights of the MTNL and VSNL (VSNL's monopoly ended in April 2002 when the sector was thrown open to the private sector) were discontinued to herald the era of unlimited competition in the industry.
- The policy further outlined the strengthening of the regulator, opening up of International Long Distance (ILD) and National Long Distance (NLD) services to the private sector and the corporatisation of telecom services.
- The year 2001 witnessed the entry of private operators in basic telephony and NLD services and the

introduction of a fourth player in every cellular circle. With these reforms, the telecom sector is witnessing a new trend of growth.

The basic services sector has completely changed. In 15 state capitals, telephone is now available on demand, teledensity has doubled, exchanges have become digital electronic and WLL (Wireless in Local Loop), i.e., limited mobility has been allowed. In the area of cellular services, licenses have been granted to four operators in each circle, while the services are being run in eighteen telecom circles and four metro cities. The current subscriber base in the cellular market has risen to 5 million. While 460 Internet Service Provider (ISP) licences have already been granted, more than 240 clearances have been issued to set up their own international data gateways.

However, with technological advancements in any sector, controversies are bound to follow. The entry of more WLL operators on the scene with low costs has threatened the survival of cellular players who entered at a peak time. As a result, in January 2002, cellular operators, based on the global system for mobile communication (GSM), threatened not to offer interconnectivity to WLL operators and block calls unless the government solved the issue of access charges.

At the time of the introductory launch of its WLL services (Reliance India Mobile) in December 2002, Reliance Infocomm promised national roaming facility to its customers. As WLL services are meant to offer limited mobility, the advertisements put the cellular operators in a fix. According to them, the offering of roaming services was a clear breach of existing regulations.

The Cellular Operators Association of India (COAI) even moved the Telecom Disputes Settlement and Appellate Tribunal (TDSAT) accusing WLL operators for violating license conditions and orders of the tribunal by offering roaming facility. However, Reliance Infocomm later clarified that the company had planned to offer multiple subscription to customers. Hence, the roaming facilities being offered were well within the WLL license.

In line with the above the above issues the specific targets that the NTP 1999 seeks to achieve and making the sector to have changes

- Make available telephone on demand by the year 2002 and sustain it thereafter so as to achieve a teledensity of 7 percent (7 telephone connections per 100 people) by the end of this calendar year and 15 percent by the year 2010.
- Encourage development of telecom in rural areas making it more affordable by suitable tariff structure and making rural communication mandatory for all fixed service providers.
- Increase rural teledensity from the current level of 0.4 to 4 by the year 2010 and provide reliable transmission media in all rural areas.
- Achieve telecom coverage of all villages in the country and provide reliable media to all exchanges by the year 2002.
- Provide Internet access to all district headquarters.
- Provide high speed data and multimedia capability using technologies including ISDN to all towns with a population greater than 2 lakh.

Conclusion

According to a press note from Cellular Operators Association of India (COAI) the total subscribers base has reached 1.83 crore at the end of September 2003 after an addition of 9 lakh subscribers in September alone. This shows how telecommunication sector is being tuning towards an aggressive growth.

The advancement that is due the technological innovations in this sector has improved the structure of the banking. The reforms in the telecom industry has thrown up the doors to the network banking.

New Economic Policy in Banking

The Reserve Bank of India (RBI) is India's central bank. Though the banking industry is currently dominated by public sector banks, numerous private and foreign banks exist. India's government-owned banks dominate the market. Their performance has been mixed, with a few being consistently profitable. Several public sector banks are being restructures, and in some the government either already has or will reduce its ownership.

Private and Foreign Banks

The RBI has granted operating approval to a few privately owned domestic banks; of these many commenced banking business. Foreign banks operate more than 150 branches in India. The entry of foreign banks is based on reciprocity, economic and political bilateral relations. An inter-departmental committee approves applications for entry and expansion.

Capital Adequacy Norm

Foreign banks were required to achieve an 8 percent capital adequacy norm by March 1993, while Indian banks with overseas branches had until March 1995 to meet that target. All other banks had to do so by March 1996. The banking sector is to be used as a model for opening up of India's insurance sector to private domestic and foreign participants, while keeping the national insurance companies in operation.

Banking

India has an extensive banking network, in both urban and rural areas. All large Indian banks are nationalized, and all Indian financial institutions are in the public sector.

RBI Banking

The Reserve Bank of India is the central banking institution. It is the sole authority for issuing bank notes and the supervisory body for banking operations in India. It supervises and administers exchange control and banking regulations, and administers the government's monetary policy. It is also responsible for granting licenses for new bank branches. 25 foreign banks operate in India with full banking licenses. Several licenses for private banks have been approved. Despite fairly broad banking coverage nationwide, the financial system remains inaccessible to the poorest people in India.

Indian Banking System

The banking system has three tiers. These are the scheduled commercial banks; the regional rural banks which operate in rural areas not covered by the scheduled banks; and the cooperative and special purpose rural banks.

Scheduled and Non Scheduled Banks

There are approximately 80 scheduled commercial banks, Indian and foreign; almost 200 regional rural banks; more than 350 central cooperative banks, 20 land development banks; and a number of primary agricultural credit societies. In terms of business, the public sector banks, namely the state Bank of India and the nationalized banks, dominate the banking sector.

Local Financing

All sources of local financing are available to foreign-participation companies incorporated in India, regardless of the extent of foreign participation. Under foreign exchange regulations, foreigners and non-residents, including foreign companies, require the permission of the Reserve Bank of India to borrow from a person or company resident in India.

Regulations on Foreign Banks

Foreign banks in India are subject to the same regulations as scheduled banks. They are permitted to accept deposits and provide credit in accordance with the banking laws and RBI regulations. Currently about 25 foreign banks are licensed to operate in India. Foreign bank branches in India finance trade through their global networks.

RBI Restrictions

The Reserve Bank of India lays down restrictions on bank lending and other activities with large companies. These restrictions, popularly known as "consortium guidelines" seem to have outlived their usefulness, because they hinder the availability of credit to the non-food sector and at the same time do not foster competition between banks.

Indian vs Foreign Banks

Most Indian banks are well behind foreign banks in the areas of customer funds transfer and clearing systems. They are hugely over-staffed and are unlikely to be able to compete with the new private banks that are now entering the market. While these new banks and foreign banks still face restrictions in their activities, they are well-capitalized, use modern equipment and attract high-caliber employees.

Government and RBI Regulations

All commercial banks face stiff restrictions on the use of both their assets and liabilities. Fourty percent of loans must be directed to "priority sectors" and the high liquidity ratio and cash reserve requirements severely limit the availability of deposits for lending. The RBI requires that domestic Indian banks make 40 percent of their loans at concessional rates to priority sectors' selected by the government. These sectors consist largely of agriculture, exporters, and small businesses. Since July 1993, foreign banks have been required to make 32 percent of their loans to these priority sector. Within the target of 32 percent, two sub-targets for loans to the small scale sector (minimum of 10 percent) and exports (minimum of 12 percent) have been fixed.

Foreign banks, however, are not required to open branches in rural areas, or to make loans to the agricultural sector. Commercial banks lent $8 billion in the Indian Financial Year (IFY, April-March) 1997-98, up sharply from $4.4 billion in the previous year.

Need to Ponder

Debates on India's slowdown focus on the manufacturing sector which is dangerously misleading: one of the biggest areas of worry about India's economic slowdown is being ignored- the systemic flaw of India's banking sector. Stories about the real health of Indian banks get less publicised because banks are still overwhelmingly owned, controlled and directed by the government, i.e., the ministry of finance (MoF). Banks have no effective mouthpiece either.

Grey Future

One more reason being the opacity of the Reserve Bank of India. This does not mean a forecast of doom for the Indian banking sector the kind that has washed out south east Asia. And also not because Indian banks are healthy. We still have no clue about the real non-performing assets of financial institutions and banks. Many banks are now listed. That puts additional responsibility of sharing information. It is now clear that it was the financial sector that caused the sensational meltdown of some Asian nations. India is not Thailand, Indonesia and Korea. Borrowed investment in property in India is low and property prices have already fallen, letting out steam gently. Our micro-meltdown has already been happening.

Conclusion

Still, there are several other worries about the banking sector, mainly confusion over ownership and control. Sometime soon India will be forced to apply the norms of developed countries and many banks (including some of the biggest) will show very poor return ratio and dozens of banks will be bankrupt. When that happens the two popular reasons to defend bad banks will disappear. These are: one, to save face in the remote hope of that fortunes will 'revive' and two, some banks are too big to be allowed to fail, fearing social upheaval. As professionalism has crept in these fields the outcome was better managers to the society, the result is commercialization of education through the new educational policy.

New Educational Policy

Educational policy and progress have been reviewed in the light of the goal of national development and priorities set from time to time. In its Resolution on the National Policy on Education in 1986, an emphasis on quality improvement and a planned, more equitable expansion of educational facilities and the need to focus on the education of the girls was stressed.

About a decade ago and a half later, the National Policy on Education (NPE-1986) was formulated which was further updated in 1992. The NPE 1986 provides for a comprehensive policy framework for the development of education upto the end of the century and a Plan of Action (POA) 1992, assigning specific responsibilities for organizing, implementing and financing its proposals.

Structure and Progress of Education in India

The focus in on the broad dimensions and magnitude of the structure, organization and progress in education. Further it also highlights growth and priority areas in education in India that point to the challenges of the future. There are about 888 thousands educational institutions in the country with an enrolment of about 179 millions. Elementary Education System in India is the second largest in the World with 149.4 millions children of 6-14 years enrolled and 2.9 million teachers. This is about 82 percent of the children in the age group.

Expension of Professional Education

Professional Education is an omnibus term. It can encompass Degree, Diploma or Certificate courses offered not only by universities and "recognized" institutions, but also programmes or courses for training organized by employers such as Banks, Insurance Companies and many others organizations. Today, a wide variety of training programmes are being run by every one of the All India and Central Services as well as the State Services.

When we are looking at the "universe" of Professional Education, we cannot ignore the large number of enterprises in the realm of Training Industry. Some of these, such as NIIT or APTECH, have played a major role in operationalising the use of computers and imparting training in, marketing, financial management to create competence in the competitive scenario ushered in by globalisation.

Impact of NEP in Education

The Challenge to Education a document produced by the Ministry of Education of the Indian Government states that "the whole process of higher education has become warped, disoriented and dysfunctional, producing a number of unemployable young men and women." It may appear odd to quote this as an opening statement of an essay on India's higher education system, but there is no other objective way of introducing the subject.

The statement and what follows refer to post-secondary college and university systems, and excludes non-university and professional institutions of higher education. In India, higher education is faced with deteriorating conditions resulting from expansion and worsened by an affiliation system and shrinking resources.

Lately, these and other issues, such as

- Declining quality,
- Inadequate facilities, and
- A mismatch between education and human power requirements,

Have become crucial themes in current social and political debate. However, this is nothing new-a number of education commissions and committees appointed since the country became independent in 1947 have identified these maladies and made recommendations to revamp the system.

Commercialisation of Education

Consequences & Cures

(A) What is Commercialisation of Education?

Does it mean that?

- When a person's chances of enrolment in a quality educational institution depends upon how much cash he or she can put up.
- When fees for attending educational institutions rise to a level beyond the capacity of families in the middle-income group.
- When the cost of education precludes the participation of persons belonging to the disadvantaged sections of society whose hope for breaking out of the mould of social or economic inferiority lies in self-improvement and upliftment through education.
- When processes of enrolment in education lead to the segregation of the rich and the poor.
- When education, as an undertaking, becomes so profitable that it starts attracting entrepreneurs interested mainly making money, with no commitment to the ideals and objectives germane to the development of functionally empowered and self-sustaining individuals capable of facing the challenges of unanticipated problems and situations.
- When, for permission for setting up facilities for education, it becomes customary to pay substantial sums for the privilege of permission.
- When providing education becomes a mechanism in the hands of the more affluent societies for drawing talented children away from the social and economic responsibilities arising from the area, region or country of their birth.

(B) What is the logic for intervening with state policies to put a stop to commercialisation?

(C) If the institutions established by commercially oriented private entrepreneurs are to be discouraged, how will the gap created by the closure of commercial institutions or the hiatus created by the exclusion of such entrepreneurs from the educational field be made up be state or other non-commercial enterprises?

(D) In this age of globalisation and aggressive foreign enterprises backed by powerful foreign powers, how will the state control the entry of high cost institutions offering foreign degrees generally favoured by aspirants trying desperately to go and work abroad?

Financing for Education

Now, about the shrinking finances for higher education: in India, except for a couple of private universities, all universities are financed by the national or a state government.

- The colleges are also largely funded by government.
- The students pay a nominal fee that constitutes less than 10 percent of the budget of the institution.
- Thus, higher education is currently heavily subsidized. Faced with a severe resource crunch, the government and the University Grants Commission (UGC) are encouraging colleges and universities to generate their own funds and ultimately become self-reliant (a utopian idea.) Developments during the last two or three years indicate that the government is seriously considering privatizing higher education.

The issues relating to the resource crunch and, in general, the funding of higher education in the Indian context have brought into focus a vital issue of university-industry interaction. At present, there is hardly any interaction between the two, except for the management faculties of half a dozen universities.

As mentioned, changed economic policies have resulted in globalization and liberalization in trade and industry, resulting in the need for more trained human power and an increase in research and development. (India invests only one percent of what Japan devotes to research and development). Many multinationals and joint ventures have already launched projects that demand employment in a particular sector. University-industry interaction, therefore, has become a very important aspect of higher education. We must not miss the opportunity of such interaction.

Another recent development is the reiteration of the need for vocational education at the higher education level. There is a feeling that general undergraduate education in India imparts perfunctory knowledge of a few subjects, with the result that students neither develop employable skills nor become fit for self-employments.

To enhance employability, in 1994-95 the UGC launched a scheme of vocationalization of first-degree education as recommended by the T.N. Dhar Committee (1993). Until now, formation of vocational skills has been a neglected area in India's higher education system. The present scheme offers a better opportunity for employment without undermining the existing undergraduate academic programs. (The policy makers have realized that any disruption in the existing structure is going to be resisted.

It is hoped that the scheme of vocational education does not become another example of well-intentioned but badly managed and poorly implemented programs. The most important aspect of this program is the training of the students at the plant. This, so far, has been a weak link in the Indian system.

Conclusion

The university system in India is not in a central position, hence it is not able to give direction either to the society or to the government, rather it is at the receiving end. The latest proof of this is the formation of the National Assessment and Accreditation Council (NAAC) at the initiative of the UGC, which is all the same an exciting development. Established in September 1994, the NAAC would function as an institution for grading institutions of higher education and their programmes. It would help the institutions to realize their stated objectives, encourage self-evaluation, help improve .eaching and research, and introduce other reforms.

The establishment of the NAAC is a laudable step toward quality assurance and would make the system more transparent and accountable. Because the new entry of multi nationals in the insurance sector which led to the intake of the professionally qualified people for the betterment of their operation in India. Erstwhile there was only one giant LIC of India run for its money had been forced to face the influence of new entrants in the insurance market.

New Economic Policy in Insurance

Giving an insight into the trends that could be expected in the insurance sector, "One of the major concerns in this area has been that private players, particularly foreign players, will grab a large market share. This hypothesis has been disproved in emerging markets worldwide. It has been found that, typically, foreign insurers take only a small share of an individual country's market."

Taiwan, where foreign companies managed a share of 3 percent seven years after the sector was liberalized, and Korea, where it was 1 percent after 20 years.

The report is based on research conducted by KPMG in India and abroad and on insights gained through working with clients in different markets. It examines the key issues, and outlines possible trends, opportunities and challenges for the insurance sector in India once it opens up for private participation.

The KPMG report makes the following observations with regard to the insurance sector in India:

- The threat of new players taking over the market has been overplayed;
- Nationalised players will continue to hold strong market share positions, but there will be enough business for new entrants to be profitable;
- Opening up the sector will certainly mean new products, better packaging and improved customer service;

- A middle market approach tapping segments and niches that are currently underserved will prove profitable for new entrants;
- New companies often overestimate the need for insurance expertise, assuming that a joint venture is the most appropriate type of alliance, when in fact many forms are possible; and

  Both new and existing players must explore new distribution and marketing channels.

Impact of NEP in Insurance : An Overview

Change is Imminent

For the uninitiated, the National Insurance Company Ltd., New India Assurance Company Ltd., Oriental Insurance Company Ltd. and United India Insurance Company Ltd. are the four insurers who underwrite risks other than life and, apart from governing them, their holding company GIC restricts itself to accepting aviation risks.

After several years of debate a consensus has been reached amongst the political parties, barring the leftists, on liberalizing the sector. The recent government move to allow registration of insurance companies by the registrar of companies is proof of current political thinking on this subject.

It is expected that the Insurance Regulatory Authority Bill will most likely to get Parliament's approval once a new government is installed at the centre. Meanwhile, the Insurance Regulatory Authority, or IRA, is busy preparing the ground rules to hasten the entry of private players.

Indian Giants are Pygmies

Already several Indian corporate groups have signed joint venture agreements with foreign insurance giants. When one compares the financial strength of foreign insurance companies with that of their Indian partners, the local partners look like pigmies. In fact, even the "big" domestic insurance companies look small too.

Consider this. Standard & Poor's ranks the Rs. 2,000-crore premium income United India a mere 150th amongst the top 200 global business insurers, based on 'non-life net premium written'.

So what does liberalization of the sector portend for public sector insurers?

According to estimates, once the private sector is allowed, the nationalized insurance companies would initially loose about 15 percent of their business. Clearly, the loss will be heaviest at the top end of their business portfolios. And, once de-tariffing (freeing rate controls) is done, the public sector companies are likely to loose more in any rate war that ensues.

Precious Time Lost

Faced with this obvious threat, GIC in its submission to the government's standing committee on finance suggested consolidation of its current operations in one of the following ways to strengthen the government-owned insurance companies:

- merger of all four companies into one.
- all four companies to be made independent.
- continue with existing structure with cross holdings.
- allow one company to take care of the insurance requirements of corporate sector and others to carry on personal lines of business, and
- each company to operate on a regional basis.

This blueprint for restructuring general insurance suggests creation of speciality offices to focus on particular lines of business. Though the vision document advised a three-phased restructuring exercise couple of years ago, GIC is yet to implement the major prescriptions, and has lost precious time.

Unless the concerned officials in New Delhi pull up their socks and reorganize the sector, the insurance companies will have a tough time in the future. Right now, GIC's suggestion of merging its four subsidiaries into one and hiving off its reinsurance business as a separate outfit looks to be winning formula.

A Question of Redeployment

It is more important to have a broad-based autonomous board of directors which is free to take decisions on product design and pricing, organizational restructuring, etc.

What about the trend of global insurance majors merging? "The world over mergers are for reducing manpower and costs. However, here one cannot think of cutting down on human hands."

All India Insurance Employees' Association, advocates amalgamation of all four insurance companies into one. "as far as we are concerned, merger of branch offices to cut down costs is welcome. However, the general insurance industry is registering an annual growth rate of 15 percent. And growth needs human hands to service the clients;"

The new holding company could, in turn, offload its stakes in the merged entity to the public at a premium at a suitable time. Remember, the Union finance ministry recently asserted that the government will not infuse any additional capital into GIC or its subsidiaries. Why, the government could, at some stage later, offload its stake in GIC Holdings and complete the cycle of restructuring.

Simultaneously, GIC should not forget that financial institutions are moving towards the concept of universal banking, and are offering all kinds of financial services under one roof, organisations like ICICI, the Industrial Development Bank of India, and the State Bank of India have announced plans to start insurance operations.

Both ICICI and IDBI grabbed banking licences when the Centre decided to allow new-generation private banks, while GIC, unfortunately, failed to even apply for one. ICICI, apart from banking sector is also a major player in the non-banking financial services segment.

Conclusion

The consolidated figures of GIC and its subsidiaries support such a view. Provisional figures for the year 1998-99 show GIC's free reserves as Rs. 6,450 crore, net worth as Rs. 7,361 crore, technical reserves as Rs. 14,087 crore, investment income as Rs. 2,350 crore, and total investments Rs. 19,000 crore,. All this on a paltry equity of Rs. 375 crore! A relatively large organisation like this will be in a better position to leverage its investment portfolio to attract business.

The other major benefits that would accrue if the GIC network merges into one entity are: higher underwriting and risk retention capacity; increase in reinsurance premium; reduction in reinsurance outflow; healthy solvency margins; settings; setting right the asset/liability mismatch, and reduction in costs.

For example, one visible avenue for savings is the rent outflow. Currently all four insurers and GIC operate from about 4,150 offices, most of them rented ones. If they merge, the duplication of branches would vanish, resulting in huge savings.

General Outlook of the Overall Impact of NEP

All over and above the recent issue in the service sector shows the following:

- India's booming services sector continued its steady growth in the April-June quarter of the current fiscal year, boosting the overall economy, said a survey report.
- According to the Confederation of Indian Industry (CII) survey, cellular phones, construction industry and hotel industry helped the services sector to post an impressive growth in the April-June quarter over a year-ago period.
- The cellular phone services sector registered a subscriber growth rate of 115 percent in the quarter ended June 30, 2003, over the same period in the last fiscal year, said the survey.

- "The present growth rate is expected to continue over the next few months," said the CII report.
- Sanctions or home loans registered a 35 percent growth while disbursements registered a growth of 34 percent in April-June 2003 over the same period in fiscal 2002-03.
- "The outlook for the next six months is positive and growth for both sanctions and disbursements are expected to be more than 35 percent," said the survey.
- "The industry rallied forcefully after the Iraq war and tourist arrivals are expected to rise up to 15-20 percent more in the next six months. Occupancy in hotels is also expected to grow by 15-20 percent in the coming months."

Conclusion

As we have been influenced by economic changes in our day to day life, it raises a question of whether we have a raise in the standard of living or not? The answer may be different according to the individual perceptions and the experience we are facing. Even there is a significant positive impact, there are controversies bound to follow which lead to some threats in every fields.

20

DEVELOPMENT OF HEALTH CARE DURING REFORMS REGIME

K. Nageswara Rao

Introduction

Generally, economic reforms refer to the special efforts aimed at the removal or economic imperfections in an economy. In other words, economic reforms relate to the short term changes for better economic environment and have to refrain from operation quickly. Paradoxically, refreshed economic reforms are pursued with new vigour and strength even after a decade. Hence academicians are perturbed at the treatment meted out to the very nature and basic feature of economic reforms.

A decade of economic reforms opened up the Indian economy and provided for better prospects of economic growth and development. However, it remains a matter of judgement to establish whether economic reforms succeeded in achieving the de sired objectives. Those who initiated these reforms are now advocating a rethinking on new grounds. It is a fact that the effects of reforms are not up to the mark and the economic progress has been slow and discontinuous. However, the first generation reforms set in motion the structural reforms that brought changes in our system.

Purpose of the Study

Development of health status can't be viewed only in the national context, but should also be seen in regional dimensions. Status exhibits marked differences in the health indices, availability and access as well as economic indices. Hence, the Ninth Five Year Plan document stated that all states may experiment and evolve appropriate mechanisms and see how the funds could be utilized locally to improve available facilities and quality of the health care provided. In this context, it is attempted in this study to analyse the development of health status with the existing health care facilities available to the people in Andhra Pradesh State.

Statement of the Problem

World Health Organization Study Group on "Measurement of the Levels of Heath" pointed out that the comprehensive health indicators are, (1) Crude birth Rate (2) Death Rate and (3) Infant Mortality Rate. It is recognized that the health status is related to and is determined by numerous factors such as per capita income, way of life, marital status, housing, sanitation, water supply, infrastructure social organization, structure of the region, nutrition, level of education, health facilities provided by the Government, political and administrative set-up, geography, climate, religious beliefs etc,.

However, (1) the per capita income (2) expenditure on public health (3) the number of hospitals and (4) the bed strength per million population in the hospitals are selected in this study to analyse the health status of the people in Andhra Pradesh.

Objectives

The important objectives of this study are:

1. to examine the trends in the indicators of health status.
2. To analyze the trends in the determinants of health status and
3. To estimate the effects of determinants of health on the indicators of health status namely

(a) birth rate

(b) death rate

(c) infant mortality rate.

Methodology

In the light of the objectives mentioned above, the data relating to the health indicators are collected from official source for the period from 1986-87 to 1999-2000. The movements in these health indicators are examined by fitting a trend equation Yt = a+bt for each of these three indicators during 1986-2000.

Similarly, the data relating to the determinants of health status are collected from official sources for the period 1983-93 with 1980-81 base and for the period 1983-2000 with 1993-94 base. The movements in these determinants of health status are analysed by fitting a trend equation mentioned above.

Assuming that the three indictors of health are influenced by the four determinants selected in this study, the selected variables are classified into:

Dependent Variables	**Independent Variables**
(Indicators of health status)	*(Determinants of health status)*
1. Birth rate (y_1)	1. Per capita income (X_1)
2. Death rate (y_2)	2. Expenditure on public health (X_2)
3. Infant mortality rate (y_3)	3. Number of Hospitals (X_3)
	4. Bed strength (X^4)

In order to estimate the effect of determinants of health status on each of the indicators of health status, a multiple regression of the following form is used:

$$Y = a + b_1 X_1 + b_2 X_2 + b_3 X_3 + b_4 X_4$$

Limitations

It is acknowledged that separate data relating to the selected variables for rural and urban areas may provide a more clear and detailed understanding of the trends in health status in Andhra Pradesh. Similarly, data relating to the selected variables for longer period may present some more changes in their movement. Further, inclusion of data on the expenditure on medical services by the private sector and facilities extended in the urban areas may also reveal different trends in the health indicators.

Demographic Features of Andhra Pradesh

According to the projections of 2001, with a population of 7.64 crs. Andhra Pradesh accounts for 7.54 percent of totals population of the country. The projected annual exponential growth rate of population in Andhra Pradesh during 1991-2001 is 2.01 percent against 2.14 percent for India. The density of population of the state per sq. km is 242 persons.

According to the projections nearly 70.0 percent of the population in the state live in rural areas. The literacy rate is 44.09 percent against 52.21 percent for the country. The percentage of population aged 0-6 years to total popt lation in Andhra Pradesh is 14.99 while the total workers as percentage to total population is 42.80.

The per capita gross state domestic product of Andhra Pradesh increased from 3.7 percent during 1980-81 to 3.7 percent during 1996-97. The projected average annual per capita consumption expenditure in Andhra Pradesh in 1996-97 is Rs. 4634.40 in rural areas and Rs. 7483.20 in urban areas.

Analysis of Health Status in Andhra Pradesh

The data on the indicators of health status on Andhra Pradesh during 1986-99 are shown in table 1. During the period under study the birth rate declined significantly by 10.10 percent while the death rate also climbed down from 9.9 to 8.2 percent. Another significant feature of health status is a significant fall (16 births) in the infant mortality rate per 1000 live births. Expansion and extension of health facilities to improve their accessibility and availability yielded positive results.

Table 1: Indicators of Health Status in Andhra Pradesh

Year	Birth Rate			Death Rate			Infant Mortality Rate		
	Rural	*Urban*	*Combined*	*Rural*	*Urban*	*Combined*	*Rural*	*Urban*	*Combined*
1986	32.4	28.7	31.6	10.7	7.1	9.9	87	59	82
1987	30.9	28.2	30.3	10.7	7.3	9.9	84	58	79
1988	27.6	26.3	27.4	10.9	7.4	10.2	89	63	83
1989	26.3	24.4	25.9	10.2	6.7	9.5	88	53	81
1990	26.6	25.1	26.3	9.7	6.8	9.1	73	56	70
1991	26.5	24.4	26.0	10.5	6.7	9.7	77	56	73
1992	25.1	22.3	24.5	10.1	6.0	9.2	78	42	71
1993	24.6	23.5	24.3	9.7	5.6	8.6	70	46	64
1994	24.1	22.9	23.8	9.0	6.5	8.3	69	52	65
1995	24.8	22.5	24.2	9.2	5.9	8.4	74	43	67
1996	23.5	20.6	22.8	9.2	5.9	8.4	73	38	65
1997	23.1	20.5	22.5	9.1	5.9	8.3	70	37	63
1998	22.8	20.9	22.4	9.7	6.0	8.8	75	38	66
1999	22.0	20.6	21.7	9.0	5.7	8.2	75	37	66

Source: Government of Andhra Pradesh, Economic Survey 2000-2001, pp. 162-163.

However, a closer examination of the data reveals that urban-rural variations in the health status are significant. The higher rate of literacy, higher levels of per capita income, larger expenditure on public health, improved medical facilities both in the public and private sectors contributed to an improvement in the health status in urban areas. On the other hand, lower rate of literacy, lower per capita income, inadequate network of community and primary heath centers and sub-centres for providing health services, inadequate health care infrastructure the indifference of the government to appoint medical officers in rural areas resulted in a relatively lower health status in rural areas of Andhra Pradesh.

Table 2 presents the data relating to the determinants of health status in Andhra Pradesh during 1986-2000. It is seen that per capita income increased by 6 times while the expenditure on public health increased by more than 4 times during 1986-2000. This shows There is a positive relationship between per capita income and expenditure on public health. However it is distressing to know that the number of hospitals remained the same while the bed strength per million population declined significantly during 1986-2000. Hence, one is inclined to conclude that the increase in the health status of Andhra Pradesh is, to a larger extent, due to the expansion and extension of medical facilities in the private sector. Of course, one cannot deny the fact that the literacy programmes, family welfare, women and child welfare programs contributed for a decline in the birth rate and infant mortality rates in Andhra Pradesh.

Trends in the Indicators of Health Status in Andhra Pradesh

Table 3 presents the results obtained from the trend equations fitted to the data on the indicators of health status and determinants of health status in Andhra Pradesh during 1986-2000.

Birth rate (y_1) declined at a rate of 32.82 percent per annum on an average while the infant mortality rate (y_3) went down out and average annual rate of 7.57 percent. This can be

Table 2: Determinants of Health Status in Andhra Pradesh

Year	*Per Capita income current prices (Rs.)*	*Expenditure on public health (Rs. in Lakhs)*	*Number of Hospitals*	*Bed strength per million Population*
1986-87	2394	3776	1983	502
1987-88	2869	4700	1994	501
1988-89	3584	5570	1910	495
1989-90	4054	5733	1996	492
1990-91	4728	6252	1998	491
1991-92	5556	7483	1915	483
1992-93	5718	8246	1878	465
1993-94	7442	9686	1947	485
1994-95	8763	11235	1951	479
1995-96	10018	10954	1988	466
1996-97	11224	13594	1990	447
1997-98 (R)	11683	14102	1987	459
1998-99 (R)	13865	14751	1983	451
1999-2000 (Q)	14715	16599	1989	456

Note: Figures of Per Capita income for the years 1987-88 to 1992-93 are at old series (Base: 1980-81) and for the years from 1993-94 to 1999-2000 are at New Series (1993-94 Base years).

Source: Government of Andhra Pradesh Economic Survey 2000-2001 for co 1.2.

Government of Andhra Pradesh ANDHRA PRADESH BUDGET. In brief, for various years for col. 3.

Government of Andhra Pradesh STATISTICAL ABSTRACTS of A.P., for various years for col. Nos. 4 and 6.

Table 3: Results of Trend Values (1986-2000)

Health Indicators

1. Birth rate (y_1) = 25.26 - 0.3282 t
2. Death rate (y_2) = 9.04 - 0.0739 t
3. Infant Mortality Rate (y_3) = 71.07 - 0.7571 t

Determinants of health Indicators

1. Percapita income (y_1) = 7615.57 + 489.7252 t
2. Exp. on Health (y_2) = 9477.21 + 485.3197 t
3. No. of Hospitals (y_3) = 1964.92 + 6.8846 t
4. Bed Strength (y_4) = 476.57 – 2.1049 t

attributed to the effective implementation of birth control programmes and women and child care programmes in Andhra Pradesh. A decline in the average annual death rate of 7.39 percent indicates the improvement in the medical and health facilities provided in the state.

The trend relating to the per capita income (x_1) is positive and significant at an annual average rate of Rs. 489.72. This upward movement in the per capita income indicates an improvement in the standard of living of the people in the state. Similarly, the expenditure on public health (x_2) showed and increasing trend at and annual average of Rs. 485.32. This hike in the expenditure on public health indicates the commitment and determination of governmental efforts to improve the working expenses to provide medical facilities in the state.

Through the trend relatively to the number of hospitals (x_3) and bed strength (x_4) has been negative, their annual average decline is insignificant. This indicates the governmental inability to meet the (fixed) capital requirements of public health needs. This signals the fact that private sector has been instrumental in promoting the health status in Andhra Pradesh in the wake of liberalization and privatisation. These trends imply considerable improvement in health status in Andhra Pradesh during 1986-2000.

In order to analyse the influence of the determinants of health status on the indicators of health status, each indicator of health status is regressed separately on all the determinants of health status during the periods 1986-93 and 1993-2000 and the results are obtained.

(a) Birth Rate (y_1)

It is observed that increasing per capita income (x_1) and expenditure (x_2) on public health have pulled down the birth rate (y_1) in Andhra Pradesh during 1986-93. In other words, Birth rate varied inversely entire per capita income and expenditure on Public health. This favourable trend in the birth rate may be due to an improvement in the standard of living including improved consumption, increased awareness to family planning programmes. Further, better infrastructural and health services provided by increased expenditure on hospitals also have contributed to the fall in the birth rate. During 1993-2000 the expenditure on public health continued to pull down the birth rate.

(1986-'93) (period) $y_1 = 69.9642 - 0.0001(x_1) - 0.0018(x_2) - 0.0104(x_3)$
(1.7152) (0.0039) (0.0044) (0.0259)

$R^2 = 0.8524$

(1993-'00) (period) $y_1 = 12.2542 + 0.0001(x_1) - 0.0005(x_2) + 0.0064(x_3)$
(0.1466) (0.0001) (0.0001) (0.0079)

$R^2 = 0.9928$

(Figures in the parentheses are t values)

(b) Death Rate (y_2)

Per capita income, expenditure on public health and the number of hospitals influenced the death rate negatively and resulted in a fall in the death rate. This favourable effect is due to the improved standard of living including better consumption. The increased per capita income enabled the people to take disease preventive measures. Further, the increasing expenditure on public health ensured better medical and health services to reduce the death rate. The number of hospitals also have contributed to a decline in the death rate during 1986-2000.

(1986-'93) (period) $y_2 = -16.7010 - 0.0003(x_1) + 0.0003(x_2) - 0.0075(x_3)$
(0.1670) (0.0004) (0.0004) (0.0025)

$R^2 = 0.9928$

(1993-'00) (period) $y_2 = 54.7170 - 0.0002(x_1) - 0.0003(x_2) - 0.0071(x_3) - 0.0244(x_4)$
(0.1770) (0.0001) (0.0001) (0.0096) (0.0147)

$R^2 = 0.7515$

(Figures in the parentheses are t values)

(c) Infant Mortality Rate (y_3)

Infant mortality rate has been influenced by per capita income, expenditure on public health and also buy the other two selected determinants. Apart from the improvement in the economic conditions of the people and the expanded on public health, facilities including the number of hospitals and the bed strength per million population have been the important factors that reduced the infant mortality rate marginally in Andhra Pradesh during 1993-2000.

(1986–'93) (period) $y_4 = 74.1790 - 0.0037 (x_1) + 0.0008 (x_2) - 0.0477 (x_3) + 0.2176 (x_4)$

(4.8555) (0.0109) (0.0125) (0.0025) (0.5672)

$R^2 = 0.7409$

(1993-'00) (period) $y_3 = 74.4870 - 0.0015 (x_1) - 0.0015 (x_2) - 0.0044 (x_3) - 0.0045 (x_4)$

(1.4780) (0.0097) (0.0010) (0.0795) (0.1229)

$R^2 = 0.5972$

(Figures in the parentheses are t values).

Figures of the Study

The rapid decline in birth rate indicates the effectiveness of birth control programmes and family welfare efforts made by the Government in the last two decades. The decline in the death rate indicates the improved quality of health facilities that control the deaths from communicable diseases. However, the stagnant or marginally negative infant mortality rate during 1990-2000, particularly in rural areas, is a matter of greater concern that needs to be addressed immediately.

In accordance with the growth of State Domestic Product of Andhra Pradesh the per capita income is increasing over a period leading to and increase in the expenditure on public health. However, the growth rates of the number of hospitals constructed and beds provided are not proportionate to the rate of the growth of population.

The growth of percapita income of the people reflected in the overall improvement in the standard of living which includes improvement in food consumption, greater awareness for longer life, small family norm, and the availability of social overheads and health services pushed the birth rate downwards.

The growth rate expenditure on public health and the number of hospitals did not succeed in reducing the birth rate particularly in the rural areas of Andhra Pradesh as their budget allocations are found proportionately inadequate, particularly.

Though per capita income influenced the death rate to decline, the rate of decline was not significant. Perhaps, the present level of per capita income is the minimum required to cause a decline in death rate. Hence, a higher rate of percapita income seems to be necessary to bring down the death rate considerably in future, particularly in rural areas.

The influence of per capita income and number of hospitals in Andhra Pradesh on the infant mortality rate, though not significant, is debatable. As observed from Table 1 the infant mortality rate is high in rural areas, which implies that the availability of medical services are inadequate and unsatisfactory.

Suggestions

Family welfare programmes and birth control programmes are to be continued on a massive scale to keep the birth rate declining.

Large scale availability of effective public health facilities in rural areas is important to raise the life expectancy.

Government shall modify its health policy to ensure medical services in rural areas by appointing and insisting the medical officers to work in the primary health centers on a regular basis.

Private corporate sector is to be encouraged to provide health services, in rural areas at a reasonably subsidized cost.

Health insurance schemes are to be grounded in rural areas by the private sector managed health care units.

The proportion of expenditure on public health and provision of beds in the hospitals need to keep pace with the requirements of the growing population.

Women welfare schemes and nutritional programmes are to be executed effectively to pull down the infant mortality rate, particularly in rural areas.

In order to promote the health status in Andhra Pradesh all public health programmes including medical, water supply, sanitation, nutrition, child care, women development, family welfare etc. are to be implemented in an integrated manner.

REFERENCES

World Bank, World Development, 1991, Over view, Paths to Development, Oxford University Press, New York, p. 4.

Investing in People, Nutrition and Life Expectancy, *Ibid,* p. 53.

World Health Organisation, *Wttochronicle,* 31, p. 267.

Government of India, Economic survey, 2001, pp. 5-116.

World Health Organisation (1957) Technical Report Series, No.137.

K.N. Reddy and Selvaraju, "Determinants of Health Status in India, an Empirical Verification", IEA Conference Volume, 1994, Mumbai, p. 31.

Tata Services Ltd., Statistical Outline of India, 2000-2001, Mumbai, Dec. 2000.

Bureau of Economics and Statistics, "Statistical Abstract of A.P.", Government of Andhra Pradesh 2000.

Dr. N. Manonmoney, " An Economic Analysis of Health Status in Tamilnadu", Indian Economic Association Conference Volume, February, 1994.

21

AN EVALUATION OF THE ROLE OF REGIONAL RURAL BANKS (RRBs) IN RURAL CREDIT

V.S. Ganesamurthy & V. Nachimuthu

Introduction

India is a land of village where nearly 72 percent of the population lives in villages. Agriculture is the main occupation of rural people. Rural Economy can grow if only agricultural sector grow. Credit is one of the important input for agriculture Timely supply of credit will help to achieve higher production and income to the farmers.

There are many Institutional and Non-institutional sources supplying agricultural credit. Among the Institutional sources Commercial Banks, Co-op Banks, NABARD and Regional Rural Banks are important. Regional Rural Banks came into existence based on the specific recommendation made by the working group on rural banks appointed by the Government of India in 1975.

Considering the functional gaps and credit gaps in the existing credit agencies, the working group recommended this new type of institution to provide rural credit. The government of India passed an Act in Feb 1976 for setting up Regional Rural Banks mainly "with a view to developing the rural economy by providing credit for the purpose of development of agriculture, trade, commerce, industry and other productive activities in rural areas, credit and other facilities, particularly to the small and marginal farmers, agricultural labourers, artisans, small entrepreneurs and for matters connected therewith and incidental thereto.

Growth of RRBs

During the first year, six regional banks were sponsored by the public sector banks. During 1977, 34 banks came into existence. By march 1979, 16 more rural banks were established. Regional Rural Banks have been set up by the joint efforts of the Centre and State Governments and commercial banks. As at the end of Jun 1981, a total number of 102 Regional Rural banks covering 172 districts in 18 state were working in the country, The total number of branches of these banks were 3598, which was 10 percent of the branches of all commercial banks.

At the end of Jun 1981, total deposits with Regional Rural Banks amounted to Rs. 253 crs and their advances Rs 302 crs as much as Rs.261 crs (91 percent) was provided to small and marginal farmers, landless labourers and rural artisans.

Statement of the Problem

The introduction of New Economic Policy (NEP) has changed all sectors viz, agriculture, industry and service during the last 12 years. The developed countries are depending upon their service sector. But developing countries like India, China, Pakistan are depending upon the agricultural sector. These countries should take the efforts for agricultural development to earn more income , to produce more production and to promote social and economic changes. Then only the rural areas will develop and provide employment, production and income for rural peoples.

In this paper the authors attempted to evaluate the role of RRBs in rural credit. For the purpose of analysis the latest two years data were collected from RBI Bulletin for the year 2000-2001 and 2001-2002. the performance of RRBs were analysed by taking variables like banking indicators, no of branches, rural-urban purpose wise outstanding loans and advances and the financial ratios were also used for the study.

Table 1: No. of Branches of RRB in India

Sl. No.	*Year*	*No of Branches*
1.	As on 30.6.2001	14452
2.	As on 30.6.2002	14473

It is clear from the above table that the number of branches of Regional Rural Banks have steadily increased during the study period.

Table 2: Population of India 2001.

1.	Rural	741660293 (72,21 percent)
2.	Urban	285354954 (27.78 percent)
	Total	102715247 (100.00 percent)

Source: Census of India 2001.

From this table it is clear that nearly 72 percent of population lives in Rural areas.

Table 3 reveals important banking indicators of RRBs Liabilities and assets for the year 2000-2001 and 2001-2002. The liabilities, which is included aggregate deposits (Demand & Time deposits was Rs. 30051 Cr. Borrowings and other Demand & Time Liabilities was to the tune of Rs.30051 Cr, Borrowings and other Demand & time liabilities was to the tune of Rs.1225 cr. The assets which is included Bank credit, Investment (Govt. & Other approved Securities) and Cash balance was Rs.13454 Cr out of this bank credit alone stood at Rs. 12663 Cr.

Both Demand and Time deposits registered an increasing level in absolute term as Rs.6499 crs and Rs.7716 crs during the study period and Time deposits increased Rs. 30528 crs and Rs. 35504 crs in the year 2000-2001 and 2001-2002 respectively.

Table 3: Important Banking Indicators of RRBs

(Rs. In Crores)

S. No	*Items*	*Mar 2000*	*Mar 2001*	*Mar 2002*	*Variation 2001-2002*
1.	Liabilities to the Banking system	183	177	188	11 (6.2)
2.	Liabilities to others	31306	38696	44873	6177 (16.0)
	2.1 Aggregate deposits	30051	37027	43220	6193 (16.7)
	(a) Demand Deposits	5105	6499	7716	1217 (18.7)
	(b) Time Deposits	24946	30528	35504	4976 (16.3)
	2.2 Borrowings	52	24	12	-12 (-50.0)
	2.3 Other Demand & Time liabilities	1203	1645	1641	-4 (-0.2)
3.	Assets with Banking system	13454	16973	18509	1536 (9.0)
4.	Bank Credit	12663	15579	18373	2794 (17.9)
5.	Investments	6009	7546	6772	-774 (-10.3)
	(a) Govt Securities	1223	1588	1915	327 (20.6)
	(b) Other approved securities	4786	5958	4857	-1101 (-18.5)
6.	Cash Balance	343	441	472	31 (7.0)

Source : Reserve Bank of India Bulletin 2002.

The bank has reduced its borrowing liability from Rs.52 crs in the year 1999-2000 to Rs 12 crs in the year 2001-2002. The growth rate has shown the negative trend percentage i.e. 50.0 percent when compared with the year 2000-2001.

In absolute terms the bank credit has shown an uptrend during the study period. The bank has extended more credit to rural development during the study period. In absolute terms the bank credit increased for the rural development. In the year 200-01 47.5 of credit was given to agri, and theremainging 52.5 percent was given to rural development. But in the next year 2001-02 the share of agri credit has declined from 47.5 to 45.7. Where as the total non-agri credit has increased from 52.5 to 54.3 percent.

Owing to the decline in investment, especially in approved securities, which has declined from Rs.5958 crs to Rs.4857 crs in the year 2001-2002 to 2000-2001. It showed a declining trend in 2001-2002. The cash balance of the bank has steadily increased from Rs. 343 crs to Rs. 471 crs for the study period.

From the analysis of banking indicators of RRBs, it clearly shows that the bank has acquired more assets during the study period than its liabilities. Hence the banks' financial position has development through various banking activities.

Table 4 explains that purpose-wise outstanding, loans and advances of RRBs for 2000-2001 and 2001-2002 are analysed.

Table 4: Purpose-wise Outstanding, Loans and Advances of RRBs

(Rs. in Crores)

Sl.No.	*Particular*	*As at end March*	
		2000-2001	*2001-2002*
1.	Short-Term (Crop Loans)	2865	3670
2.	Term-Loan for agri & allied activities	3339	3547
3.	Indirect Advances	23	N.A.
	Total Agriculture	6227 (47.5)	7217 (45.7)
4.	Rural artisans, village and cottage industries	773	561
5.	Other industries	664	246
6.	Retail trade and self employed etc.,	2073	1951
7.	Other purpose	3372	5819
	Total Non-Agriculture	6882 (52.5)	8577 (54.3)
	Grand Total (Agri + Non-Agri)	13109 (100.0)	15794 (100.00)

Source: Reserve Bank of India Bulletin 2002.

Agricultural loans are short-term (crop loan) term loan for agri & allied activities and indirect advances. Non-agricultural loans are comprised with rural artisans, village and cottage industries, other industries, Retail trade and self employed etc and other purposes.

In terms of percentage, bank has reduced agricultural loans and advances from 47.5 percent in 2000-2001 to 45.7 percent in 2001-2002. But Non-agricultural loans and advances has increased from 52.5 percent in 2000-201 to 54.3 percent in 2001-2002.

From the table 4 we may interpret, that bank has provided more loans and advances to non-agricultural purposes than agricultural purposes, which may be due to the effect of globalisation and privatisation policies. Further due to failure of monsoon, crop failure, low return from agri may be the reasons for the shift from agri to non- agricultural credit.

Table 5 analyses that the financial performance of RRBs through their Income and Expenditure for the years 2000-2001 and 2001-2002.

Table 5: Financial Performance of RRB

(Rs. In Crores.)

Items	*2000-2001*	*2001-2002*
A. Income	4859.83	5564.19
(i) Interest Income	4625.94	5191.46
(ii) Other Income	233.89	372.73
B. Expenditure	4259.19	4956.31
(i) Interest Expenditure	2965.53	3329.15
(ii) Provisions & Contingencies	129.56	166.20
(iii) Operating expenses	1164.10	1460.96
(iv) of which wage bill	1004.50	1264.24
C. Profit		
(i) Operating profit/Loss	730.20	774.08
(ii) Net Profit/Loss	600.64	607.88
Total Assets	49641.39	56803.84

Source: Reserve Bank of India Bulletin 2002.

RRB has earned most of their income from "Interest" through bank credit. The small amount of income contributed by other income souces which include bank charges, service charge etc. The income of the bank has increased from Rs.4859.83 crs in 2000-2001 to Rs.5564.19 crs in 2001-2002.

On the other hand, the expenditure of the bank has incurred by interest given to depositors and it was followed by operating expenses of the bank, Of which, the bank has allocated approximately 90 percent for salary. The provisions and contingencies has incurred from Rs.129.56 crs in 2000-2001 to Rs.166.20 crs in 2001-2002. It stood Third position among the different type of expensive

The bank operating profit has increased from Rs.730.20 crs to Rs.774.08 crs in the years 2000-01 and 2001-2002 respectively. Net profit also showed an up trend in the study period. From the table one can infer that the financial performance of RRB has showed an increasing trend and total assets has also grown to a remarkable extent.

Table 6 shows the calculated financial values for the years 2000-2001 and 2001-2002. When we compare the last two years ratios, there was a significant improvements in their performance at net profit ratio, income ratio, other income ratio, expenditure ratio, operating expenses ratios, wage bill ratio and provisions and contingencies. Among them, expenditure, operating expenses and wage bill should be reduced through avoiding and controlling some expenses.

Table 6: Financial Ratio's of RRBs

	Ratios	*2000-2001*	*2001-2002*
(i)	Operating Profit	1.47	1.36
(ii)	Net Profit	1.21	1.07
(iii)	Income	9.79	9.80
(iv)	Interest Income	9.32	9.14
(v)	Other Income	0.47	0.66
(vi)	Expenditure	8.58	8.73
(vii)	Interest Expanded	5.97	5.86
(viii)	Operating Expenses	2.35	2.57
(ix)	Wage Bill	2.02	2.23
(x)	Provisions and Contingencies	0.26	0.29
(xi)	Spread (Net Interest income)	3.34	3.28

Source: Manually computed from Data (Ratios to Total Assets).

On the other hand, operating profit , net profit, interest income, interest expended and spread (net interest income) ratios accounted a declining performance during the last two years of the study period. Therefore, it is clearly shows that the income of the bank has declined whereas the expenses of bank has increased. Hence the policy measures has undertaken in respect of RRB through the permission to relocate loss-marking branches to do better business in location centers and conversion of loss-making banks into satellite/mobile offices. Without these changes, the performance of service area had salutary effect on the financial performance of RRBs. Since RRBs are started only in backward areas the loan recovery position is very weak and it has affected the performance of the RRBs.

Policy Suggestions

On the basis of the analysis of the study, the authors have suggested the following remedial measures,

- The performance of RRBs should be improved through establishing more branch offices in rural areas.
- The bank should provide more loans and advances to agricultural activities.
- RRBs should help to poor agricultural farmers through rural agricultural co-op centers.
- RRBs has to minimize the expenditure in wages and administrative activities.
- The bank can provide farm loans for the purchase of implements.

REFERENCES

Bhattacharya S.N., "Rural Economic Growth in India : In Theory & Practice," Minerva Printers, Delhi, 1986.

Mongia J.N., "Banking Around the World" Allied Publishers, New Delhi, 1985.

RBI Bulletin, Various Issues.

Murty S., "Financial Sector Reforms and Economic Growth in India" RBSA Publishers Jaipur (India) 302003, 1997.

22

SECOND GERNERATION REFORMS: EDUCATION SCENARIO AND DIRECTIONS

T.V.Anandi

"The objectives have to be more people related rather than commodity related and Economic Policies will have to particularly focus on those who are worst off in society"

—Amartya Sen

Introduction

Education, particularly higher education as the instrument of individual, societal and economic transformation is well recognized now more that ever. It is the lifeline of development, be if spiritual or economic, scientific or technological, national or global. Cultural development and national integration are most easily achieved by education the masses. Education is a human right, literacy provides access to knowledge, development of skills and thereby brings about the awareness of rights and responsibility in every individual and the community as a whole. In the 21st Century countries will be measured by the education and health status of their population and not by GDPs ad GNPs.

Education is a process of making an all round development in human beings. It is and essential condition for economic development. Education develops skills, knowledge, efficiency and abilities, which are necessary for economic development. In short development of any country depends on the development of human resources. India has embarked on a process of economic reforms since 1991, Marketisation, Liberalisation, Privatisation and Globalisation have been the key words of Economic Reforms. In the first generation of reforms there was a concentration of measures relating to fiscal discipline, deregulation and reduction of physical and tariff barriers relating to imports and exports. The second generation of economic reforms seems to be concerned with continuation of the first generation reforms and its re-enforcement through disinvestment in financial an non-financial public enterprises and opening of the agricultural economy, in addition to the rest of the economy to multinational and other enterprises in the developed countries in order to give effect to the stipulation of the World Trades Organisation.

Education does not seem to find any place in these reforms. Actually economic reforms and educational reforms should go hand in hand. There can be no rapid economic development without a sound base of education. Education is essential, though not a sufficient, condition for economic development. However, because of fragmented thinking and approach, out policy makers seem to have failed to closely link-up educational reforms with economic reforms.

In this paper and attempt is made to discuss the effects of globalisation only on education. The general objective of this paper is to assess the performance of the Indian Economy in the field of education and to suggest policy directions for the second generations reforms. It would be of interest to understand as to how the expenditure on education has changed in the post reform period vis-à-vis the pre-reform period so as to examine the need for making correction in the second generation reform.

SECTION – I

Educational Performance During Pre-reform and Post-reform Period

India's performance in education over five decades has been mixed impressive achievements on the one hand and conspicuous failure on the other. Following features of India's educational scenario are worthy of attention.

1. The Indian education system is characterized with the severe degree of under-investment. Developing country's spend more public money on education than in India. Some example:

   Sweden 8.4, Zimbabwe 8.3, Maldives 8.1, Canada 7.6, New Zealand 7.3, Kenya 6.8, Cuba 6.6, Australia 6.0, France 5.8, UK 5.4, Iran 5.9, India 3.6. Japan, Korea, USA and Germany 6 to 8 percent

2. Although in absolute terms, the increase in expenditure on education in India during the 50 years of Independence is impressive. The real increase in expenditure for the student has been rather very modest.

   1950s & 60s favourable period on education. 1980s-education experienced at a reasonable at a reasonable high rate of growth.

   There has been increase in the allocation for education in the 1990s. but at the same time, this has been curved by economic policies of stabilization and structural adjustment, that seemed to have very seriously affected the allocation of education.

3. The priority for education reflected in the proportion of national income allocated to education increased from about one percent at the time of independence to about 3.5 percent in recent years.

   By the year 1981, educational expenditure had risen to a level of 3.0 percent of GDP as against 0.68 percent in 1951 and 2.41 percent in 1971. During 1981 to 1991, a gradual increase in educational expenditure was witnessed and it reached a peak level at 4.39 percent of GDP in 1990. there after, this percentage has shown a gradual decline from 4.39 percent in 1990 to 3.76 percent in 1994 and further to 3.62 percent in 1977. This indicate a lower priority given to education in the post reform period compared with the perform despite the fact that the government has been proclaiming that it intends to increase it to 6 percent of GDP. Dr. V.R.Panchamukhi has calculated the average annual growth rate of per pupil expenditure in education in the pre-reform and post reform period.

Average Annual Growth Rate of per Pupil Expenditure in Education

	Pre reform period	*Post reform period.*
Elementary education	6.9	1.2
Secondary education	5.0	0.0
University education	0.2	-4.4

Source: EPW, March 4-10-2000 p. 839.

The above table indicates that there has been a serious deterioration in per pupil expenditure in education in all sectors of education. In the sphere of elementary education, the annual average growth rate of expenditure stumped from 6.9 percent during the pre reform period to nearly 1.2 percent during reform period. In secondary education, there was zero growth rate of per pupil expenditure and in university education this growth rate became negative to the extent at 4.4 percent in the post reform period.

A review of expenditure on education in the pre-reform and post reform period reveals that

- Instead of educational expenditure moving towards the target of 6 percent of GDP in to post reform period it declined to 3.62 percent
- Per pupil expenditure education level, more especially at the elementary education level has shown seriously deterioration in the average growth rates.

4. The relative importance given to education in the five year plans has been declining gradually over the years.
5. Primary education was given a boost in the seventh and the eighth plans. But this boost seems to have been made possible by severe cuts in plan resources for secondary and higher education.
6. The capital expenditure on buildings, libraries, equipment, furniture etc. form a very small proportion. 2 percent of total expenditure on elementary education. Many schools are in the open space, inadequate room, some without black boards reflects a severe degree of under investment in asset formation in education.

From the table it is very clear that the plan expenditure on various sectors of education expect elementary receives less attention and so the resources received by them are decreasing after the new economic policy.

SECTION – II

Policy Directions For Second Generation Reforms

The real wealth of a nation is its people. To make a country's development the obvious indicators are the wealth of the nation, the prosperity of its people and its standing in the international forum. The second generation reforms should correct some of the bad effect of the first generation reforms, especially on education. There is need for preparing and agenda and action plan regarding second generation reforms to go further in achieving the liberalization, privitalisation and globalisation (LPG) in India. To solve the crisis in education, an integrated plan needs to be implemented to restructure the entire system of education.

- There should be strong support from the policy makers and chief administration for globalisation, to make Indian education as a major source of foreign exchange, to improve quality of Indian education, to spread Indian culture and value.

Plan Expenditure on Different Sectors of Education

(Percentage)

Sectors of Education	*I plan 1951-55*	*II plan 1956-61*	*III plan 1961-66*	*Plan holiday 1966-69*	*IV plan 1969-74*	*V plan 1974-79*	*VI plan 1980-85*	*VII plan 1985-90*	*1990-92*	*VIII plan 1992-97*	*IX plan 1997-2002*
Elementary	56	35	34	24	30	35	33	37	37	47	58
Secondary	13	19	18	16	18	17	21	24	22	18	13
Adult	-	-	-	-	-	-	9	6	9	9	3
Higher	9	18	15	24	25	22	22	16	12	8	12
Technical	13	18	21	25	13	12	11	14	17	14	12
Others	9	10	12	11	14	14	4	3	2	4	2
Total	100	100	100	100	100	100	100	100	100	100	100

Source: Various issues of Economic Survey and National Account Statistics of India.

- Steps should be taken to make the parents of school going children aware of the importance of education. In all states, the mid day meal programme must be implemented in full vigour. Then only, the aim of universal education can easily be achieved.
- Higher education is paramount importance for economic and social development. Institutions of higher education should have the main responsibility for equipping individuals with advanced knowledge and skills required for position of responsibility in government, business and the professions.
- State and society should perceive higher education not as burden on federal budgets but as a long term domestic investment in order to increase economic competitiveness, cultural development and social cohesion.
- A minimum level of learning is required for creating awareness about goods/services available in the international market.
- The entire educational system has progressively come under government regulation and control as a result the system has lost flexibility, initiative and invectiveness. So essential in the fast changing world of today the process of liberalization of education should be begin.
- The share of expenditure on education should be raised to the recommended level of 6 percent from the present level, then only the educational sector can avail all the facilities required for quality education.
- New financing techniques should be encouraged to correct the unacceptable decline in allocation for higher education in the plans. In the case of higher education, the network of IITs, IIMs, IISs, NCST etc. should be expanded and present intake of these institutions should be increased to cater the needs of the economy.
- The syllabus in schools and colleges should be restructured to impart to students to each stage of

education-the ability to forge on his own self-employment schemes. The allocation of investment in primary, secondary and higher education should be such as to socially optimize the rate of return on the investment.

Co-ordinated, penetrating and pragmatic policy in turn with the overall educational reforms is essentially needed. So Liberalization, Privatisation and Globalisation will make the economy emerge as an Asian tiger for the next millennium.

23

CHANGING SCENARIO IN SMALL SCALE INDUSTRIES DUE TO NEW TELECOM POLICY

P. Sundara Pandian &
J.Kamatchi Eswaran

Introduction

Over the last 3 years, India has slowly but surely liberalized its telecom services market. Today India is one of the most deregulated telecom markets in the world and provides opportunities for both foreign operators and equipment suppliers.

Till 1991, provision of all types of domestic telecom services was a monopoly of the Department of Telecommunication (DoT). The state owned Videsh Sanchar Nigam Limited (VSNL) was the monopoly carrier of international traffic.

In 1991, as part of the new industrial policy unveiled by Narasimha Rao-led Congress Government, the DoT for the first time invited private participation in telecom services. The process started with tendering of licenses to provide cellular mobile service in the four metropolitan cities of Delhi, Mumbai, Kolkata and Chennai. In the next round of licensing the government has awarded cellular licenses for circles, which broadly corresponded to states[1]

The license was awarded to three circles. They were Circle A, Circle B, Circle C.

Circle A comprises of Maharastra, Gujarat, Andhra Pradesh, Karnataka.

Circle B comprises of Kerala. Punjab, Haryana, UP-west, UP – east, Rajasthan.

Circle C comprises of Himachal Pradesh, Bihar, Orissa, Assam, UP-North, UP-South.

The following table brings the number of cellphone subscribes for various periods in the metros and the three circles.

Cellphone Subscriber Base in Our Country

Area	*January[2] 2000*	*January[3] 2002*	*April[4] 2002*	*April[5] 2003*
Metros	7,12,792	22,54,000	26,99,000	45,84,000
Circle A	5,17,407	19,64,000	21,88,000	46,03,000
Circle B	3,98,928	13,06,000	15,87,000	36,02,000
Circle C	39,568	2,01,000	2,39,000	5,46,000
Total	16,68,695	57,25,000	67,13,000	1,33,35,000

Source: Secondary Data.

Statement of the Problem

Cellphone is a modern communication media between the people. The people prefer it because it is point to point communication in a very quick way. By using this facility we can save large amount by eliminating traveling cost, time etc. Cellphones are now used all over the civilized world and particularly by the business community. Now-a-days, In India small scale industries are very much benefited with the help of mobile communication. In Tami Nadu, auto drivers, call taxi drivers, commission agents are having cellphones. In the last two years the cellphone users growth shows a phenomenal increase of 100 percent. It, therefore, calls for a critical study of role of cellphone communication in small scale industries growth due to the usage of cellphone. Hence, this study has been undertaken to throw the light on the role of cellphone in business and the activities for which the cellphone used by the subscriber in the study area namely Virudhunagar. The study area Virudhunagar has large number of SSI units.

Scope of the Study

1. The union consisted of the subscribers of cellphone who is having a business unit in and around Virudhunagar.
2. The subscribers under various plans/schemes of SIM card providers are taken into account.

Primary Data

The present study is an empirical one based on survey method. First hand data were collected from the field through questionnaire and observation.

A number of discussions were held with knowledgeable persons such as academicians, businessman, for designing the questionnaire and stating the research problem.

Sampling Design

The universe comprises of cellphone subscribers in Virudhunagar. The sampling unit was an individual cellphone subscriber who is having a business unit, who may possess any number of cellphone connections. In Virudhunagar there are four service providers, viz., BPL, Aircel, Airtel and BSNL. BPL company has 4200 subscribers and the Aircel company has 3150 subscribers and Airtel company has 750 subscribers and BSNL has 1200 subscribers. A sample of 100 cellphone subscribers was decided for the survey.

Limitations of the Study

The data gathering instrument is another source of error. The interview schedule used for this study despite pretesting, does remain a source of errors. The wordings of the question could not always be easy to understand by the respondents more over, the translation of the question in Tamil could create response errors especially ambiguity in understanding the question as well as the answer.

The subscribers used as respondents in the study does not maintain any original records. So they had to recall from their memory and furnish readymade information for the queries put forth by the researcher with fear. Hence, the data collected were subject top recall bias.

Occupation of the Respondents

The cellphone is widely used by the businessman irrespective of the nature of their firm. The survey has brought to a sharp focus on the occupation of the respondents.

Occupation of the Respondents

Occupation	*No.of respondents*	*% of Total*
Traders	61	61.00
Manufacturers	26	26.00
Services	13	13.00
Total	100	100.00

Source: Primary Data.

Growth of Business to the Usage of Cellphone

Most of the business units are getting their cellphone connections mainly to improve their business irrespective of the size of the business units. Now-a-days, in the small scale industries, every person in the concern will have a cellphone connection. Unlike in other parts of the country, the number of fisherman using cellphones in Kerala is comparatively higher. Over 20,000 subscribers in the state are fishermen. The fishermen, while on the sea, could sell their catch and that is the kind of advantage traders and businessman were looking for[6]. Nearly 20 percent of the traders felt their business has grown very considerably and nearly 15 percent of the traders felt their business has grown very little. Nearly 16 percent of the manufacturers felt their business has grown very considerably and nearly 20 percent of the manufacturers felt their business has grown very little. Nearly 16 percent of business who are doing service felt their business has grown very considerably and nearly 16 percent of the respondents felt their business has grown very little.

Growth of Business Due to the Usage of Cellphone

Occupation	*Very Consi-derably*	*% of Total*	*Consi-derably*	*% of Total*	*Little*	*% of Total*	*Very Little*	*% of Total*	*Total*
Traders	12	19.67	25	40.98	15	24.59	9	14.76	61
Manufacturer	4	15.38	11	42.30	6	23.07	5	19.25	26
Service	2	15.38	5	38.47	4	30.76	2	15.39	13

Source: Primary Data.

Usage of Cellphone in Business Activities

Every business unit can use their cellphone in various activities like purchasing, sales, finance and miscellaneous. An effort has been made in the study to find the respondents frequency of using cellphone in above activities.

The survey date reveals that for purchasing, 64 respondents (64 percent) had very frequent usage and 36 respondents (36 percent) had used very rarely. For sales, 83 respondents (83 percent) had very frequent usage and 17 respondents (17 percent) had very rarely. For finance, 12 respondents (12 percent) had very frequent usage and 88 respondents (88 percent) had very rarely. For miscellaneous purpose, 78 respondents (78 percent) had very frequent usage and 22 respondents had very rarely.

Fall in a DoT Bill Due to the Usage of Cellphone

In Virudhunagar, most of the business units are having business transaction with all the major towns in Tamil Nadu. Most of the towns in Tamil Nadu come under the coverage area of simproviders. So these areas are treated as local calls and the subscribers are benefited by the slash in STD charges.

Usage of Cellphone in Business Activities

Activities	Very Frequently		Frequently		Neither Frequently nor Rarely		Rarely		Very Rarely	
	No.of respon-dents	*% of total*	*No.of respon-dents*	*% of total*	*No.of respon-dents*	*% of total*	*No.of respon-dents*	*% of total*	*No.of respon-dents*	*% of total*
Purchase	40	40	24	24	18	18	15	15	3	3
Sales	66	66	27	27	4	4	3	3	–	–
Finance	–	–	12	12	9	9	30	30	49	49
Miscellaneous	–	–	78	78	13	13	–	–	9	9

Further they can easily contact the persons who are having the cellphone in the first attempt. So this may reduce the bill. Nearly 60 percent of the respondents felt that there is a fall in DoT bill due to the usage of cellphone.

Fall in DoT Bill Due to the Usage of Cellphone

Response	*No.of respondents*	*% of total*
Yes	59	59
No	41	41
Total	100	100

Source: Primary Data.

Reduction in Traveling Expenses

Because of the usage of cellphone, business man's travelling expenses may be reduced. This is due to the needed person is contacted at the right time. So, it will reduce the unnecessary travel. Further the travelling can be well planned. 62 percent of the respondents felt that their traveling expenses were reduced due to the usage of cellphone.

Reduction in Travelling Expenses due to the Usage of Cellphone

Response	*No.of respondents*	*% of total*
Yes	62	62
No	38	38
Total	100	100

Source: Primary Data.

Conclusion

Now-a-days cellphone is one of the vital element for business. It serves a lot to increase the business. With out it, the business unit may feel like a handicap. In the modern days business people and high executives become addict to the cellphone. From the survey, it is very clear that most of the businessman felt that their business has increased considerly because of using cellphones. It has become a treasure for medium and small scale business unit. Most of the business unit felt that their DoT bill and their traveling cost reduced considerably due to the usage of cellphone. (As most of the business units are dominated by single persons in SSI units, cellphones helped them tremendously) so, due to the New Telecom Policy 1994, the growth of small scale industrial units are rapid and phenomenal.

NOTES

1. P. Balakrishna, "India's Transformation", *SPAN*, September/October, 2001, pp. 42-43.
2. ***Computers Today,*** November, 2000.
3. *Business Line,* February, 12, 2002, p. 5.
4. *Business Line,* May, 10, 2002, p. 7.
5. *The Hindu,* May 14, 2003, p. 16.
6. G.K. Nair, Mobine on the high seas, Business Line, March 12, 2002, p. 5.

24

NEW STRATEGIES OF DAIRY COOPERATIVE DEVELOPMENT IN DINDIGUL DISTRICT IN THE ERA OF ECONOMIC LIBERALIZATION

Samwel Kakuko Lopoyetum

Introduction

Dairy Cooperative System

In developing countries like India and Kenya there is paramount need to permit cooperative dairy sector to perform its functions and decision-making process with greater autonomy and independence, particularly in the era of LPG. The vision 2010 advocated by the National Dairy Development Board NDDB (Hq. based in Anand) should aim at fostering the required planning, execution and control of activities with micro level approach in the era of LPG, and economic Liberalization the dairy cooperative sector needs to improve the quality of its products and utilize many other relevant modern marketing strategies. As a whole, the dairy cooperative sector needs to improve the quality of its products and utilize many other relevant modern marketing strategies. As a whole, the dairy cooperative sector would assume themselves as dynamic force in enhancing rural industrialization and commercialization of dairy activities in rural areas. The promotion of farmers socio-economic welfare and livelihood, would need self-governance of dairy cooperative societies and they can tie over the harsh realities of open market environment and huge competition unleashed by the LPG era. It is worthy to blend the opportunities brought about by the free market economic system and makde availability of their products felt in the market. They must take advastages of economic Liberalization (EL) and globalisation of the national economy. In the era of open market economy, dairy cooperative sector must improve its productivity and profitability to survive, offer affordable services to members, as such can ultimately lead to sustainability of dairy cooperative industry in the era of liberalization and globalization.

Indian dairies are often being referred to as primitive and unable to manufacture modern processed dairy products. The liquid milk demand of urban consumer is met by reconstituted milk powder imported from various sources. Moreover, the per capita availability of milk has increased from 112 gms in 1970-71 to 203 gms in 1997-98 and stands at 214 gms/day as against 300 gms/day recommend by Indian Council of Medical Research (ICMR).

Moreover, a large number of internal and external problems are directly affecting dairy cooperative sector such as: the animal productivity remains very low averaging 1.5 litres/day, low purchasing power of the vast majority of the consumer, dairy sector is not producing milk and milk products meeting international standards. Again, constraints such as inefficient milk production, inefficient milk procurement, inefficient transportation, non-adopting of modern milk processing, system inefficient storing and distribution system has extremely affected the dairy cooperative sector. Similarly, unimproved cattle herd, poor herd quality, low milk yield, lack of fodder (cattle feed). Inadequate veterinary services, low viability and low profitability have hampered the growth and development of dairy cooperative sector.

Most of the milk is in the hands of very small and economically poor/weaker milk producers located in rural areas, with small land holdings. Dairy farmer depends on seasonal agricultural crops for their fodder and cattle feeds. Milk production is subsidiary occupation and provides employment, opportunity dairy cooperative sector is faced with inadequate technical skills, which leads to low milk productivity, inadequate support for marketing and distribution of milk and milk products. Ultimately, inadequate technical support for breeding and health cover, and also milk shall remain a perishable commodity if not stored properly during the marketing and distribution process.

Thrust Areas of Dairy Cooperative Sector

The total milk production increased from 78 million tonnes in 1999-2000 to 81 million tonnes in 2000-01, the milk powder (including infant milk food) increased from 2.25 lakhs tones in 1999 to 2.30 lakhs tones in 2000, production of condensed milk increased from 11,000 tones in 1999 to 11050 tones in 2000. more than 7000 dairy cooperatives organizations are covering over 7000 villages and dairy cooperative organizations which are run by the women constituting now 21 percent of the total dairy cooperative societies and set to increase by 2010. The main thrust areas remain to be (i) The dairy cooperative enterprises shall be socio-economic tool for the removal of poverty (ii) dairy cooperative enterprises shall provide ample opportunities, and chances for self – employment and gainful employment (iii) It provide income generation opportunities to the marginal, small dairy farmers and rural community, (iv) It act as a dynamic socio-economic mixed shield and for better improvement of the weaker section of the community. (vi) rural dairy cooperatives shall continue to provide and supply fresh milk to urban milk consumers. (vi) It provides adequate milk to improve nutritional standards of the human being, particularly children and old-age groups.

An overview of Dairy Co-operative Societies in Dindigul District

Composition of Livestock Population in Dindigul District

In Dindigul District, there are 369843 dairy animals (composed of cattle 264282 and buffaloes-105561), sheep-

259455, Goat–166963, poultry–465763 cross–breed cows the exotic cows–186. This district is rich in livestock wealth and animal assets. There are 42 veterinary dispensaries stocked with AI facilities and equipment, there are 128 centres supplying frozen semen. These centres are not adequately serving all the dairy farmers, in fact there is a shortfall of more than 16 dispensaries and shortfall of AI facilities to the level of 1.7 lakhs. The Jersey breeds are found in the plains areas and Holstein, Friesian animal population in Kodaikanal, whereas Buffaloes are found all over the District. There is shortage of fodder production in the District, therefore, dairy cooperative union and primary milk producers cooperative societies must improve the supply of fodder& innovate better ways of fodder production activation through establishment of feed factory and fodder tanks.

Need for Diversification of Business Activities at District Milk Union

The Dindigul District Milk Producers Union must diversify its operations and functioning. It must improve the availability of cross-breed, animals high yielding animals, must intensify and extensify Artificial Insemination (AI) services, must improve the provision of concentrates feeds, improve fodder production and milk collection operation, improve milk distributions, venture into production of different milk collection operation, improve milk distributions, venture into production of different milk products, improve organization of most of the PMPCS & must provident adequate technical inputs. The union is collection milk from its members and selling unprocessed milk (whole milk) to meet the share of milk demand in Dindigul and other parts of the District. By effectively and efficiently collecting milk from PMPCS, they are boosting their business performance and profitable working of the primary milk produces cooperative societies. They must initiate programmes to enhance milk production in the District through effective and efficient dairy extension services, dairy animal breeding etc., in collaboration with the Department of Animal Husbandry. The most efficient and effective ways of harnessing the livestock wealth in Dindigul District can be though cooperative sector, private sector, self-help and voluntary business organizations. It would generate adequate income and gainful employment to the enormous number of dairy farmers in the District. The cattle feed is largely based on the enormous number of dairy farmers in the District. The cattle feed is largely based on the crop residues, open grazing system, collection of fodder from places and obtaining concentrate feeds from the PMPCS. The union must adopt the backward and forward linkages and fill gaps between demand and supply of milk in the District. It must sensitize dairy farmers on the cost of production of milk, seasonal fluctuations, the quaintly and quality of the milk produced. The union must arrange for prompt payment i.e.., weekly or fortnightly as desired by the PMPCS andensure lower rate of concentrated cattle feed than the private supplies/businessman. In procurement and marketing operations of milk union, the critical areas are milk quality control, packaging of milk and milk products, branding, advertisement, milk pricing, milk payment and milk processing. The union must ensure that all these factors are effectively and efficiently managed and controlled.

The fundamental dairy statistical development indicators of the District under study are presented in the subsequent tables (1-4). It is essential to present these statistical details so that, business performance of the Dairy Cooperative Societies can be ascertained and linked to these crucial dairy development indicators, thereby ascertaining the growth of its operations and business performance during a particular period of time.

When we consider Dindigul District, the study reveals that there are numerous milk producers cooperative societies (MPCS) which were established in the region. It is essential to mention about the growth of the human population. The human population pattern in this district is very distinctive. Urbanisation is picking up very fast and it rendered the highest in Kodaikanal area followed by Dindigul block. Whereas, the population increase (change) was noticed more in Kodaikanal

Table 1: Block Wise Distribution of Societies at Dindigul District

Sl. No.	Name of the Block	Functioning Societies				Dormant Societies				Total			
		SC	W	G	T	SC	W	G	T	SC	W	G	T
1.	Nathan	-	-	16	16	-	-	6	6	-	-	22	22
				(7.96)	(6.84)			(6.52)	(5.08)			(7.51)	(6.25)
2.	Sanarpatti	1	2	26	29	-	-	6	6	1	2	32	35
		(12.5)	(8.00)	(12.93)	(12.39)			(6.52)	(5.08)	(10.00)	(4.08)	(10.92)	(9.94)
3.	Dindigul	1	-	5	6	-	3	7	10	1	3	12	16
		(1.25)		(2.49)	(2.56)		(12.5)	(7.61)	(8.48)	(10.00)	(6.12)	(4.10)	(4.54)
4.	Vedasandur	-	2	20	22	-	1	11	12	-	3	31	34
			(8.00)	(9.95)	(9.40)		(4.17)	(11.96)	(10.17)		(6.12)	(10.58)	(9.66)
5.	Gugeliumparai	-	-	14	14	-	3	3	6	-	3	17	20
				(6.96)	(5.98)		(12.5)	(3.26)	(5.08)		(6.12)	(5.80)	(5.68)
6.	Vadamadurai	-	4	6	10	-	3	3	6	-	7	9	16
			(16.00)	(2.99)	(4.27)		(12.5)	(3.26)	(5.08)		(14.290)	(3.07)	(4.55)
7.	Thoppampatti	-	1	33	34	-	3	10	13	-	4	43	47
			(4.00)	(16.42)	(14.53)		(12.5)	(10.87)	(11.02)		(8.16)	(14.67)	(13.35)
8.	Athur	1	3	12	16	1	3	16	20	2	6	28	36
		(12.5)	(12.00)	(5.97)	(6.84)	(50.00)	(12.5)	(17.39)	(16.95)	(20.00)	(12.25)	(9.56)	(10.23)

Contd....

Table 1: (Contd....)

Sl. No.	Name of the Block	Functioning Societies				Dormant Societies				Total			
		SC	W	G	T	SC	W	G	T	SC	W	G	T
9.	Palani	-	2	15	17	-	-	5	5	-	2	20	22
			(8.00)	(7.46)	(7.26)			(5.44)	(4.24)		(4.08)	(6.83)	(6.25)
10.	Oddannchatram	-	-	10	10	-	-	2	2	-	-	12	12
				(4.97)	(4.27)			(2.17)	(1.700)			(4.10)	(3.41)
11.	Kodaikanal	-	-	6	6	-	-	1	1	-	-	7	7
				(2.99)	(2.56)			(1.09)	(0.85)			(2.39)	(1.99)
12.	Reddiyar Chatram	1	4	9	14	-	1	10	11	1	5	19	25
		(1.25)	(16.00)	(4.480)	(5.98)		(4.170)	(10.87)	(9.32)	(10.00)	(10.20)	(6.48)	(7.10)
13.	Nilakottai	3	3	17	22	-	3	5	8	3	6	22	31
		(37.5)	(12.00)	(8.46)	(9.40)		(12.5)	(5.43)	(6.78)	(30.00)	(12.25)	(7.51)	(8.81)
14.	Batlagundu	1	4	12	17	1	4	7	12	2	8	19	29
		(12.5)	(16.00)	(5.97)	(7.26)	(50.00)	(16.16)	(7.61)	(10.17)	(20.00)	(16.32)	(6.48)	(8.24)
	Total	8	25	201	234	2	24	92	118	10	49	293	352
		(100)	(100)	(100)	(100)	(100)	(100)	(100)	(100)	(100)	(100)	(100)	(100)

Source: Complied from the records of Sub Registrars's co-operatives (Dairy) at Dinduigul (1999): by M. Seethalakshmi

Figures in the parenthesis represent percentage, SC: Schedule Caste. W: Women, G: General, T: Total.

(14 percent) followed by Palani (10 percent) and then Dindigul (8 percent) and other blocks (8 percent). In effect, there is and urgent need to encourage the new formation of strong and viable Primary Dairy Cooperative Societies (PDCS), strengthening and improvement of the working conditions and enhancement of profitability, viability, sustainability and business results of primary milk producers cooperative society to feed the increasing population with milk & milk products. There is an urgent need for inculcating the collective efficiency in primary milk producer's cooperative organizations and District Milk Producers Cooperative Union. Dairy sector is known for granting permanent income and generate employment opportunities to the small, marginal farmers. Dairy cooperative organizations encourage members to supply milk through cooperative societies and , they mobilize necessary

Table 2: Block-Wise Distribution of Membership (1999)

Sl. No.	*Name of the Block*	*Membership*					
		Male		*Female*		*Total*	
		No	*%*	*No*	*%*	*No*	*%*
1.	Natham	6215	61.39	3909	38.61	10124	100
2.	Sanarpatti	7642	60.70	4947	39.30	12589	100
3.	Dindigul	1253	55.79	993	44.21	2246	100
4.	Vedasandur	3654	65.79	1900	34.21	5554	100
5.	Gugeliumparai	2692	70.51	1126	29.49	3818	100
6.	Vadanadurai	595	46.63	681	53.37	1276	100
7.	Thoppampatti	7122	67.23	3465	37.73	10587	100
8.	Athur	1665	60.53	1079	39.47	2734	100
9.	Palani	2151	59.37	1472	40.63	3623	100
10.	Oddannchatram	3230	65.25	1720	34.75	4950	100
11.	Kodaikanal	2550	61.52	1595	38.48	4145	100
12.	Reddiyar Chatram	1244	60.07	827	39.93	2071	100
13.	Nilakottai	9507	56.49	7323	43.51	16830	100
14.	Batlagundu	12365	55.35	9975	44.65	22340	100

Source: Complied from the records of the Sub Registrar of Cooperatives (dairy) at Dindigul (1999) by M. Seethalakshmi.

support from dairy farmers and associations,. The PMPCS can ultimately improve the socio-economic conditions of the dairy members. It is an effective agent of socio-economic conditions of the dairy members. It is an effective agent of socio-economic transformation of both rural and semi-urban areas of developing countries such as Kenya and India. Tables 1-4 shows details regarding the, blockwise distribution of societies, blockwise distribution of membership, the growth trend in membership and shares of DMPC Union, Business Performance and working capital performance of DMPCU & PMPCS.

Table 3: Growth Trend in Membership and Shares Capital of Dindigul Milk Producers Cooperative Union

Sl. No.	*Year*	*Membership*		*Share capital (Rs. In Lakhs)*	
		DMPCU society	*PMPCS (Individual)*	*DMPCU*	*PMPCS*
1.	1995-96	217	103911	7.90	4.76
2.	1996-97	236	102309	7.25	4.91
3.	1997-98	233	104679	6.51	5.16
4.	1998-99	268	175366	4.44	3.64
5.	1999-2000	223	85695	4.44	3.96
Average		235	94992	6.11	4.49
Average per society		235	426	6.11	0.02
Annual Growth Rate (AGR percent)		-	-	-15.88	-4.04

Source: Complied from the records of the Sub Registrar of Cooperatives (dairy) at Dindigul (1999) by Karnnakaran.

During 1998-99 the union refunded the share capital obtained from the Government.

Self–Help Groups and Dairy Business Activities in Dindigul District

Nearly all Self – Help groups are promoting socio- economic development in Dindigul District by making a lot of contribution towards generation of income & employment opportunities. The SHGs promoted by NABARD and launching of specific programmes for women empowerment and capacity building measures have provided active partnership support among developmental agencies. There were 3485 Self-Help

Table 4 : Business Performance & Working Capital of Dindigul Milk Produces Cooperative Union (DMPCU) & Primary Milk Producers cooperative Societies (PMPCS)

Sl. No.	*Year*	*Working Capital*		*Business performance in value of sales execute (Rs. in Lakhs)*	
		DMPCU	*PMPCS*	*DMPCU*	*PMPCS*
1.	1995-96	1326.86	52.33	1396.76	267.62
2.	1996-97	1399.64	54.05	1439.82	324.33
3.	1997-98	1433.41	56.80	1575.71	292.06
4.	1998-99	1493.01	40.05	2017.93	242.81
5.	1999-2000	1556.58	43.59	1577.39	209.51
Average		1441.90	49.36	1601.53	269.27
Average per society		1441.90	0.22	1601.53	1.21
Annul Growth Rate (AGR percent)		2.95	-4.01	2.29	-0.01

Source : Complied from the records of the Sub Registrar of Cooperatives (dairy) at Dindigul (1999) by Karunakaran.

Groups operating with 53380 women as members. The creamery unit run by Chemparutti Self-Help Group are promoting and doing dairy Business activities by obtaining loan under SGSY schemes to undertake keeping of milk animals and dairy business activities. These SHG are engaging in the income generating activities and providing employment to its members. They undertake training activities for its members. Their members take their own milk produce which are produced to the creamery centers, where they are paid on the basis of cream extracted from whole milk. The value of cream is noted in the register on daily basis and the account is maintained by the members in specific banks and repayment of loan is fixed by the group i.e. Rs. 1000 per member. They provide a number of prompt services to members such as;

(i) Member's doorstep delivery of the cattle feed concentrates and other essential services.

(ii) They reduce the transportation cost which would have been exorbitant to the members.

(iii) Payment of milk is on the basis of butter fat content (cream content).

(iv) They offer very good price for milk supplied to the creamery centre.

(v) No delay of payment of milk price, therefore they adopt timely settlement of dues (Source: Field Investigation).

Pallapatty Primary Milk Producers Cooperative Society (PMPCS)

The Pallapatty Cooperative Milk Producers Society Ltd (PPCMPS) was registered on 20-11-1961 initially it functioned as milk supply society. It was amended by the Registrar of Cooperative Society, Tamil Nadu and named as Cooperative Mil producers Society in 1987. The prime reason for forming this society was to reduce or remove the fraudulent practices of the private milk business vendors supplying adulterated milk to consumers and paid low prices to the milk producers. The main objective of this society is to encourage members to venture in to dairying enterprises in extensive manner and increase milk production. The milk producers would get good milk prices through cooperative society. The cooperative society aims at developing dairy enterprises and better dairy husbandry to milk producers. The society provide large number of services to milk producers. The society admits only genuine milk producers who owned milch animals and agreed to sale their milk through cooperative society. They prohibit milk vendors from becoming members of the cooperative milk produces society.

Methodology

This research study is based on descriptive method. Both the secondary and primary data were used in this study. The primary data were collected from members of Palapatty PMPCS. The primary data connected to socio- economic mix of dairy farmers were collected from members, such as benefits from society and services obtained from dairy society. Comprehensive interview schedule were prepared and administered to the respondents. Conventional statistical tools like averages, percentages, chi-square etc. were applied in this study.

Reasons for Setting up the Pallapatty Primary Milk Producers Cooperative Society (PPMPCS)

The major reason for setting up the PPMPCS is to remove the fraudulent practices of private milk vendors who were engaged already in milk business and they have been supplying not only adulterated milk to the consumers but also paid low price to the milk producers.

Objectives of the Society

The important objective of the society is to encourage dairy members to take up dairying activities extensively and to increase milk production and to enable the dairy members to sell their milk at a reasonable milk price rate through their primary milk producers cooperative society. Further, it has the objective to develop dairy units and to carryout the Extension activities of dairy farming, animal husbandry and other important activities connected to dairying business activities.

Liability of the Society

The liability of the members of the society is limited to the share capital contributed by its members.

Membership Position

As per the bye-law only genuine milk producers who owned milch animals and who agreed to sell their milk through the primary co-operative milk society are allowed to be the members of the society. There is explicit provision in the bye-law to prohibit the milch vendors fro becoming dairy members. The bye-law has also prescribed the individuals maximum limit for share –holding to 100 shares or Rs.1000/-

Any one who is over eighteen years of age respectively in the area of operation can become a member of the primary cooperative milk society and person who is a minor or unsound mind cannot be admitted as a member.

Table 5: Profitability PPMPCS

Years	*Profit*	*GR*
1995-96	0.28	-
1996-97	0.09	-67.86
1997-98	0.34	277.78
1998-99	0.55	61.77
1999-2000	0.73	32.73
Average	0.39	-
CGR	21.25	-

The above table clearly indicates that the society has continuously been earning profit. The profit level shows an increasing trend except in the year 1996-97. The average profit of the society for a year worked out to Rs. 39,000/-. The average growth rate was found to be 21.25 percent. It may be inferred that this society has a chance or providing dividend to its dairy members even in the era of economic liberalization characterized by cutthroat competition.

Procurement of Milk

Milk collection (Procurement) is the major activity of the dairy cooperative society. Milk is collected twice in a day i.e., morning and evening. The society procures milk from its members. The society takes various measures to find out the level of Butterfat content.

The quantity of milk and butter fat content of the milk procured will determine the selling price. The procurement and selling prices are determined on this basis. The procurement of milk shows an increasing trend. The average morning milk procurement was 1836 liters and the evening is 1929 liters. The yearly growth rate was found to be 5.10 percent in the morning and 3.53 percent in the evening. The procurement function is done by the society promptly. The members also prefer to supply only the pure milk to the cooperative society than to the private traders/vendors.

Sale of Milk

Sale of milk is the prime function of the society. The society is allowed to sell the milk to the local consumers and then to the District Dairy Union.

Table 6: Sales Performance

(Lts)

Years	*District Co-operative Milk Union*	*Local Sales*	*Total*	*GR*
1995-96	700	1835	2535	-
1996-97	632	1872	2504	-1.22
1997-98	429	2008	2437	-2.68
1998-99	458	2147	3605	47.93
1999-2000	436	2488	2924	-23.29
Average	531	2070	2601	-
CGR	-9.05	6.29	2.89	-

Table 7: Annual Sales Performance

(Lts)

Years	*District Co-operative Milk Union*	*Local Sales*	*Total*	*GR*
1995-96	2.56	6.69	9.25	-
1996-97	2.31	6.83	9.14	-1.19
1997-98	1.56	7.33	8.89	-2.74
1998-99	1.67	7.84	9.51	6.97
1999-2000	1.59	9.08	10.67	12.19
Average	1.94	7.56	9.49	-
CGR	-9.05	6.29	2.89	-

The above table exhibits the sale of milk in liters by the dairy society. The sale of milk is done through two ways. One is through the District Co-operative Milk Producers union and through local sales. The sale of milk to District union is showing increasing trend year after year except the year 1996-97 and 1998-99 and the local sales is showing increasing trend. The dairy society authorities are giving more attention to local sales than dispatching milk to the District Milk Cooperative Union. Even in the era of economic liberalization characterized with free market the primary dairy cooperative societies are increasing their local sales and at the same time supplying milk to the dairy milk union for further processing.

Veterinary Services and Artificial Insemination (AI)

All the medical care, veterinary services sands artificial inseminations (AI) are provided by the dairy cooperative society. The members, at the times of need may get services through the local veterinary doctors.

The society provides prompt artificial insemination to cattle. The doctors visits the dairy societies weekly once, if emergency services in needed, the cattle owners will consult the government veterinary hospitals. The society provide insurances of milch animal, dairy loan, fodders. In the era of economic liberalization, there is and urgent need to provide opportunity to the Self-Help Groups (SHGs) and private sector to deal with Artificial Insemination services.

Table 8: Services Offered by the Dairy Society

Details of Services offered	*No. of Members*			
	Male	*Female*	*Total*	*percentage N=60*
Artificial Insemination (AI)	31	29	60	100
Fodders Supply	20	16	36	60
Veterinary care and services	31	29	60	100
Milch animal loans	21	25	46	77
Insurance Cover	31	29	60	100

It is observed from the above table that artificial inseminatin (AI) veterinary care and services and insurance are services availed by the sample respondents. Loans for the purchase of milk animal and fodders are availed by 77 percent of the dairy farmers respondent and 60 percent avail fodder supply from society. Hence, it can generally be inferred that majority of the dairy society members are availing all the services offered by the Primary milk producers cooperative society.

Table 9: Trend of Medical Care and Artificial Insemination (AI)

Years	*Medical care and artificial Insemination*	*GR*
1995-96	356	-
1996-97	343	-3.65
1997-98	360	4.96
1998-99	258	-28.33
1999-2000	218	-15.50
Average	307	-
CGR	-9.34	-

The above table indicates the trend of providing medical care and artificial insemination facilities. It is showing declining trend during the study period except in the year 1997-98. Average growth rate is declining with the rate of –9.34 percent. Hence, it is inferred that dairy members are inclined to change over from modern methods of insemination to traditional method of breeding or natural method insemination.

Table 10: Breed of the Animals

Details	*No. of Members*		
Local cows breed	1	-	1(2)
Jersey breed	25	25	50(83)
Sindu breed	6	4	9(15)
Total	31	29	60(100)

Figures in parenthesis are percentage to column total.

The study reveals that 83 percent of the sample respondents are having more number of Jersey breeds of cows than Sindu (15 percent) and local breed (2 percent). Hence, it may be inferred that most of the members are having high quality grades of cows. The hypothesis here, is that there is no association between the types of milch animal breed and Gender.

Since the calculated value (0.56) is less than the table value (5.99) at 5 percent significant level the hypothesis is accepted. There is no association between the types of milch animal breed and gender perspective.

Number & Type of Milch Animals

Dairy animals play and important role in dairy farming business. The cow owned by milk producers depend on their convenience and management of the animals etc. The cows kept by the members are of three kinds.

Viz. 1. Local breed 2. Jersey breed 3. Sindu breed

They also practice zero-grazing system of keeping dairy animals.

Butterfat and Dairy Characteristics of Jersey Cow

Jeysey is the smallest of the dairy breeds. Needs more liberal feeding practice. It needs good pastures and liberal feeding for good returns. The breed is very Pre-Potent when crossed upon common cattle or grades of other breeds. The cross-breeds will be strong and milking qualities are good. Heifers mature young and come to into milk at the age of Twenty-four to twenty six months. The most prominent and best known characters of Jersey milk are the high percentage of BF easy creaming of milk. It has large fat Globules the Butterfat varies between 4.5 and 6.5 with and average of about 5.3. The total solids are high in keeping with the fat content averaging 14.9 percent. The fat on an average constitutes 34.5 percent of the total solids and good quantity of milk. The economy of fat production is good in Jersey cow compared with other breeds. The economy of fat production is to be attributed to two factors. (1). Fat represents a greater proportion of the solids than in other breeds i.e. less skim milk is produced to the pound of fat. (2) Small proportion of the ration used for maintenance of the cow.

Table 11: Milch Animals Units

Details	*No. of members*		
	Male	*Female*	*Total*
Only one dairy cow	10	16	26 (43)
2-4 dairy cows	4	-	4 (7)
Above dairy cows	17	13	30 (50)
Total	31	29	60 (100)

(Figures in parenthesis are percentage to column total).

The above table reveals that 50 percent of the sample respondents are having 4 cows, 43 percent of the residents are having only one cow and only 7 percent of the respondents are having more than 4 cows. It is inferred that majority of the respondents are having more than 2 to 4 cows for the purpose of increasing their earning capacity and Employment generation.

The hypothesis is, there is no association between number of milch animal and the gender of the respondents. Since the calculated value (18.33) is more than the table value (5.99) at 5 percent significant level. The hypothesis is rejected. Hence, it is inferred that there is some associating between number of milch animal and gender of the respondents. The female practise zero-grazing with less milch animals than male counterparts.

Table 12: Value of Milch Animal

Details	*No. of members*		
	Male	*Female*	*Total*
Rs. Less than 10,000	11	15	26(43)
10,000-20,000	8	7	15(25)
Above 20,000	12	7	19(32)
Total	31	29	60(100)

(Figures in parenthesis are percentage to column total).

The above table shows that 43 percent of the sample members are having cows of value less than Rs. 10,000, 25 percent are having Rs. 10,000 to 20,00 value of cows and 32 percent of the sample members are having more than Rs. 20,000 value of cows. Therefore, it may be inferred, that most of them are more conscious on buying high quality cows without being discouraged by the cost of the improved breed of milch animals.

Table 13 : Milk Yield Per Cow

Details	*No. of members*		
	Male	*Female*	*Total*
Less than 5 liters	10	16	26(43)
5-10 liters	7	5	12(20)
Above 10 liters	14	8	22(37)
Total	31	29	60(100)

(Figures in parenthesis are percentage to column total).

From the above table it is concluded that 43 percent of the sample members are producing less than 5 liters of milk from a cow, 37 percent of the respondents are producing above 10 liters and 20 percents of the sample members are producing 5 to 10 liters of milk. Therefore, it may be inferred that fairly large number of dairy farmers are getting less than 5 liters per cow.

Monthly Earnings & Income

Income level is the deciding factor of standard of living and quality of life. Whether the milk production and dairy business activities are giving sufficient income for their daily needs or not? Whether it is economical to keep the dairy cows or not? It is always common that, they depend on dairy business activities and animal husbandry simply because it is their way of life. This attitude must change, so that they can face economic liberalization with confidence and commitment and reap the benefits of economic liberalizations.

The dairy farmers access to food, economic status, access to various infrastructure facilities are greatly depended on the income status of the dairy farmers. Moreover, an immediate access to namely, health, education, transport and communication are based the income factor.

Table 14: Monthly Earning & Income

EarningDetails	*No. of members*		
	Male	*Female*	*Total*
Less than 300	3	2	5(8)
300-600	13	20	33(55)
Above 600	15	7	22(37)
Total	31	29	60(100)

(Figures in parenthesis are percentage to column total).

The above table shows that 55 percent of the sample dairy members are earning Rs. 300-600 per month, 31 samples members earn above Rs. 600 and only 8 percent of the sample members earn less than Rs. 300. Therefore, it may be inferred that by concentrating on milk Production and dairy business activities could earn higher income but not above Rs. 600 per month.

The hypothesis that there is association between monthly earning & income and gender. Since the calculated value (4.54) is less than the table value (5.99) at 5 percent significant level, the hypothesis is accepted. Therefore, there is no association between monthly earnings and gender of the sample respondents. However, more number of male respondents earn above Rs. 600 than female.

Table 15: Expectation of Dairy Members

Sl.No.	Details of Expectation	No.of members (N=60)
1.	Prompt of milk price	48 (80)
2.	Arrangement of loan facilities	26 (43)
3.	To conduct co-operative election	15 (25)
4.	Expansion of local market sales	30 (50)
5.	Restructuring & revising the milk price once in six months	55 (92)

The expectation of dairy farmers was gauged and tabulated. It is understood that majority (92 percent) of the respondents emphasized on the restructuring and revising the milk price once in six months, 80 percent of the respondents required prompt payment of milk price, 50 percent of the respondents demanded and expected expansion of local market sales, 43 percent of the respondents demanded the arrangement of loans facilities and 25 percent of the respondents are interested and expecting the conduct of election. Therefore, most of the respondents are demanding & expecting milk price restructuring & reviewing. It is followed by expectation and demand for prompt payment of milk price. Generally, dairy farmers are more conscious on their milk price than other factors such as cost of milk production.

Significant

Factors responsible for gearing up dairy cooperative sector to face economic liberalization and globalization

The dairy cooperative sector must gain dynamic competitive advantages in an open market economic system in order to meet the challenges posed by globalization and economic liberalization. Thus, this study has identified the following factors which are significant for gearing up the growth and development of dairy cooperative sector such as.

(i) The natural importance given to milk products consumption with the rising income levels of rural and urban communities from time to time.

(ii) The largest cattle population (wealth) and ability of women- folk, Energetic youth getting involved in the better animal husbandry practices.

(iii) More importance is given to the quality of milk and higher prices for hygienic milk on t he basis of Butter Fat and SNF Components.

(iv) The New Generation Dairy Cooperative Farmers (NGDCF) are highly educated making use of latest

Table 16: Services Marketing Mix of Milk Cooperative Processing Industry : Strength and Weakness in the era of Economic Liberalization

Services Marketing Mix	*Strength*	*Weakness (w)*
1. Product	Multi product, Availability of raw materials (milk), Establishment of control laboratory (Commissioner of Milk), Not adulterated milk, product availability is average.	Quality of product are low, percentage of BF is very low, inadequate milk products, less standardization of milk, milk yield is very low, quality of milk is very low, no knowledge of the mild products, sell of liquid milk, inadequate quality control measures, lack of new product development, innovation, no branding, no attractive package, no functional value, moderate quality, awareness of products low.
2. Price	Policy of prompt payment, policy of payment on BF/SNF, revision of the procurement price (Buffalo & Cow milk), different selling price metre	Inadequate price, absence of competitive price policy, lack of consistent price structure, haphazard controls and subsidies, milk is sensitive to price, rural markets desire low to medium price products.
3. Place (distribution)	Supply of inputs at the door step, milk procurement and marketing of milk, sale of milk, wholesales, dealers through retail outlets, dependents on the village shops, shandies, transportation is average.	Cost of collection of milk is very high, long distances, places, untimely delivery, insufficient transport facilities, poor distribution, unconnected distribution network, no market segmentation.
4. Promotion	Financial Assistance (NDDB), existence of federation to do promotion, Introduction of schemes OFI, OFII, OFIII, vision 2010,	Improper linkage to banding and financial institutions, inadequate advertisement and publicity limited funds for advertisement, less sales

Contd....

Table 16: (Contd....)

Services Marketing Mix	*Strength*	*Weakness (w)*
	sales promotion measures are effective, use of traditional media (Puppetry, street theatre.)	promotional measures, not gives importance to customers / relationship, personal selling is expensive, prevalence of more language and dislects.
5. Participation (People)	Producers oriented, supervision and control of societies as per their own laws, technical expertise i.e., NDDB staff, NDRI	Untrained and non professionals, illiterate, traditional, superstitious, poverty of diary farmers, lack initiatives, indebted farmers, no proper training to employees, political interference's, appointment of special officers, excess staff, lack of techno- logical know – how, not familiar milk products, dairy terminology used difficult.
6. Processes	Additional facilities given by NDDB, subsidy given by the government, adaptation of new technology, use of better dairy processing system	Products manufactured far from the point of production se of less sophisticated machines, accumulated losses, increase in raw materials costs, delayed audit, unhygienic dairy conditions, inadequate use of modern technology, lack of innovation.
7. Physical Evidence	Assets/Own building, infrastructure, equipment's.	Inadequate machines and equipment, poor infrastructure for processing , transportation system is expensive

Source: Dr. S.K. Lopoyetum (2002) GRI.

information and technology, adopt advancement of science and technology. They will take dairying operations as full time business activity.

(v) The vertinary services, Artificial insemination and health cover of animals are privitised and the Government veterinary hospitals are providing free animal health services.

(vi) The WTO and international organizations are following very stringent quality requirement for export purposes, which can enhance dairy performance in Indian rural economy.

(vii) The removal of subsidies by western countries can provide chance to India dairy industry to compete in the world dairy market. India and New Zealand are two countries without subsidies and gradually withdrawing.

(viii) The basic food segment will grow by 100 percent by 2005 and add RS 25 lakh households, therefore, shifting to higher levels of food consumption patterns centrally, deviating from ordinary food substance to processed foods.

(ix) The extended shelf-life of dairy products by using advanced methods of food preservation and cost effective packaging, controlling the quality of milk products would have a bearing in the Twenty First Century or new Millennium.

Impact and Implication of Dairy Cooperatives in the era of Economic Liberalization and Globalization

A very large number of dairy farmers are directly involved in the Dairy Cooperative Societies (DCS) would double in the 21st century with the emergence of New Generation Dairy Farmers. There was phenomenal increase in milk production by treble to 663 million tones between 1970 and 1995, which would be enhanced in the forthcoming decades. There would be Declined dependence on imported dairy commodities. There is huge prospects of sustainable growth and generation of adequate rural employment in the 21st century. Transfer of income from urban to rural areas/equitable distribution of incomes would be streamlined in the years to come. There is spin off rural economic development through operations floods programmes of NDDB i.e, OF I OF II OF III and other new dairy development programmes such as vision 2010. By creating technological consciousness and awareness among 75 percent of 'OF' beneficiaries who are landless, marginal and small farmers dairy sector is moving forward in a big way in the era of economic liberalization and globalization. In fact, the vision 2010 plan of NDDB is geared towards production of milk and milk products in different milk shed areas and dairy regions of the country in large quantities in the forthcoming years.

Consequent to modernization and advancement of science and technology in the 21st century, there will be tremendous social empowerment and emancipation of rural poor leading to significant improvement in their socio-eco-political environment. Women particularly, would be the largest beneficiaries of the 21st century dairy cooperative sector. Presently, the animal husbandry and dairying industry contribute to about 8-10 percent to the GDP of the country, which would be enhanced in the ensuing decades. The creation of efficient milk processing capacities and growth of dairy equipment industry has helped in the development of dairy cooperative industry. In fact, India has also exported expertise in dairy cooperative enterprise to countries such as Sri lanka (Kiriya Milk Industries of Lanka Limited), setting up of modern dairy processing plant in Kyrgyz republic. Also, Zimbabwe and Kenya are nowadays keen in borrowing the 'Anand pattern/ model' and in due course of time they will follow suit.

Cleaning and Sanitization of Dairy Equipments at both District Union and Primary Milk Producers Society Level

In the era of LPG it is essential to maintain hygienic conditions in the dairy units else their products may not be accepted at the world standard level. Sanitary and photo-sanitary (SPS) measures (non-tariff measures) must be given top priority by the dairy cooperative organizations. Even the WTO and the European Union countries insist on bacteria - free milk and milk and milk products. The dairy cooperative sector must be conscious of quality standards acceptable in global dairy market.

In addition to tariffs barriers, there are many non-tariff barriers over which directly and indirectly affect dairy industry in India. The non-tarriers are imposed under Technical Barriers to Trade (TBT) and even European Union insists that milking cows must be mechanized to avoid contamination and use portable water in dairy processing factory. They must also use filtered air, steel machinery, and advance methods of Dairy Technology. In this way, they are protecting human health, animal health, plant life and environment at large.

Here, the question of cleanness and sanitization assumes great significance. Therefore, sanitization or sterilization implies destruction of all pathogenic and non-pathogenic organism from the milk (dairy) Equipments. The milk containers or equipments may contain soil/milk products residues. These residues, may be due to water previously used or dust, dirt or other foreign materials, liquid milk films, air-dried milk, heat precipitated films, heat-hardened films, milk-stones and miscellaneous foreign matter. The most serious problems in the rural areas are milk-stones accumulation in the milk containers / equipments. The milk -stone is the accumulation of dried milk solids and salts from hard water & washing solutions. It consist largely of calcium phosphate, milk proteins, precipitate coagulated and baked-on by heat. The milk-stone consist of moisture 2.7 percent to 8.7 percent, Fat 3.6 to 17.7 percent, Protein 4.4 to 43.8 percent, Ash 42 to 67.3 percent. The rural dairy farmers can be educated and trained on sanitization process. They must leave the surface of the milk containers free as possible from milk residues & viable organisms. They can use detergents (two or more types of detergents) such as Alkalis (Sodium Hydroxide/Sodium Carbonates, Phosphates, Bicarbonates), Acids (Phosphoric,

Tartaric, Citric, Gluconic, mild Acids for milk–stone removal, use of not more than 1 percent of Conc. of Nitric acid in stainless steel surfaces). It is essential to prepare chemicals with higher clearing efficiency.

Methods & Procedure for Sanitization which can be Opted by the Dairy Cooperative Societies to Produce Hygienic and Good Quality Milk

The procedure of sanitization depends on the hardness of water and type of the soil prevailing in the region. There are three methods of washing viz. Hand–Washing, Mechanical Washing (Can- washing & Bottle–washing) and cleaning-in-place or In–place-cleaning (IP). In India, most dairy organizations use sodium carbonate which lower the cleaning efficiency than tri-sodium silicate. The procedure for sanitization which can easily be followed by dairy cooperative units are:

(i) Drain and Remove all the loose and other matter from the milk containers / equipments.

(ii) Do pre-rising with cold or tepid water to remove remaining milk solids.

(iii) Use hot water rinsing to remove traces of detergents.

(iv) Sanitizing to destroys all pathoges and almost all Non-pathogenic organism.

(v) Draining and drying must be done to prevent bacteria growth and corrosion. Never use Towel cloth of any kind, provide adequate drying and ventilation process to the containers and equipments.

Bench Marking Strategies and Methods of Improving Dairy Cooperative Development

The District Dairy Cooperative Development Strategies can be undertake at Two levels viz at DMPCS & AT PMPCS. The strategies must be based on (i) Procurement and marketing strategies (ii) Processing and operational strategies (iii) Organizational control & management (iv) Uses of better

Strategy of milk production and productivity of animals (v) better strategies of animals feeds and fodders (vi) Use of better dairy extension services and animal health cover (vii) Adoption of Anand pattern of dairy cooperatives (viii) Strategy of prompt milk payment (ix) Effective and efficient use of common community grazing land. (x) Improvement of milk quality by giving proper education and training to the dairy farmers. (xi) Providing financial assistance and loan facilities to the dairy farmers.

Best Strategies and Approach to Enhance Management & Operations of Dairy Processing Cooperative Societies and Milk Producers' Cooperative Societies

The best strategy may be defined as the best plan of action to achieve the specified objectives under competitive circumstances particularly in the era of economic liberalisation and to lagislation. Strategies are dynamic in nature and subject to modification. It is a continuous process. The term strategy has military connotation and used widely in the field of management and administration of business, because they are fought like wars and counter-wars in different environmental situations. The following are some of the most viable strategies, which can be adopted by cooperative marketing and dairy processing organizations. (1) The researcher is advocating for efficient and effective organization and methods (O & M) in dairy cooperative sector. (2) Modernization of dairy cooperative sector by using the latest methods of Manufacturing and processing of milk. (3) Use of Appropriate and Intermediate Technology. (4) The NDDB & Federation and Unions can have dairy business on joint ventures & collaboration basis. (5) Promotion of Inter-Cooperative Dairy Products Export Trade, (6) use of improved storage and grading system, (7) Use of low cost packaging and effective labeling, practices (8) Dairy cooperative must aim at cost focus strategy, (9) Dairy cooperative can adopt focused niche market strategy in domestic market and external markets. (10) Application of product differentiation strategy as marketing strategy of dairy cooperative sector. (11) Enhancement of competitive and adoptive approach, (12) Adoption of value addition techniques, especially in cooperative products and services, (13) Inculcating the culture of professionalism and enhancing human resource development in dairy cooperative organizations. 14) Promotion of dairy business diversification, (15) Implementation of internal checks and controls, (16) Use of information technology (IT) and communication, (17) Creativity and innovative Strategies, (18) NDDBs and Federation of dairy unions can adopt consultative strategies strictly on business terms (19) Adoption and use of 4 Ps marketing strategies and 7 ps service marketing strategies by all dairy cooperative units, (20) Computerization and Automation of Dairy Cooperative processing manufacturing sector, (21) Integration and collaboration strategy (strategic alliance) of dairy cooperative at local level, regional level, state level, national level and international level. 22) Use of management quality circles (MQC) and 23) Finally exploration of the use of viable combination strategy.

REFERENCES

Ananthakrishnan, C.P., Pandmanabhan, P.N., (1992), "Dairy Farming and Milk Production", Shri Laxmi Publications, Madras.

Attwood, D.W., Naviskar, B.S., (1998), "Who Shares? Cooperatives and Rural Development", Oxford University Press, Delhi.

Kulandaisamy, V., (1982), "Cooperative Dairying in India", Rainbow Publication, Coimbatore.

Maxcarenhar R.C., (1988), "Strategy for Rural Development-Dairy Cooperatives in India", Sage Publication, New Delhi.

Deepak Shah and Ashok Shah, (1996), Impact of Dairy Cooperative on Marketing Pattern of Milk-A Case of Study, *Indian Cooperative Review* 33 (3).

Shiyani R.L., (1996), "An Economic Inquiry into the Impact of Dirty Cooperatives on Milk Production", *Indian Journal of Agricultures Economics* 51 (3).

Subburaj B.S.K. Loyopetum and R. Karunakaran, (2001), "Members Perception on the Social Impact of Dairy Cooperative Societies in Dindigul District; A Survey" *Indian Cooperative Review,* 39 (1).

Katar Singh of Mukunda Dar, (1982), "Impact of Operation I at the Village Level-Research Report", Anand IRMA.

Gupta S.K., "Dairy Next Millennium the Challenges" *Yojana* Vol. 43 (11) Nov. 99.

Anjani Kumar, (1998), "Milk Production Function and Factor Demand in Milk Production", *The Bihar Journal of Agricultural Marketing,* Vol. VI, No. 4, October.

Shrode R.B., (1999), "Dairy in India" *Rural India* Vol. 62 (9).

Singh Mohar, et al., (1998), "Constraints Faced by the Dairy Seeking Information Regarding Improved Dairy Formig Practices" *Rural India,* Vol. 61 (9-10).

Nath Abbay et al., (1998), "Milk Procurement A Challenge for Personnel of Milk Union" *Rural India,* Vol. 61 (6).

Koli, P.A., (2000), "Can Milk Cooperative Sustain in 21st Century" *Indian Cooperative Review,* Vol. XXXVIII, No.1.

Hage, N.C., (2001), "WTO Challenges for Indian Dairy Farmers", *Yojana.*

Mohinder Singh & Anil Kumar, (1996), "Technological Interventions in Rural Dairy Development; A Study", *Kurushetra.*

Selvaraj, V., (2002), "Marketing of Dairy Products Through E-Commerce", *Kissan World,* Vol. 29.

Subburaj, B., "Indian Dairying-Its Prospects", *Tamil Nadu Journal of Cooperation,* March 1997.

Subburaj, B. Ravichandran, K. and Samwel Kakuko Lopoyetum, (2003), "Appropriateness of Management Strategies; Are they Myth to Cooperatives" *The Cooperator,* Vol. 40, No. 8.

Iyer L.L., (1973), "Fifty years of Dairy Development in India Tasks Ahead" *Indian Dairy Man,* Vol. 25, No. 12.

Suryamurthy, (2001), "Milk Marketing Strategies" *Tamil Nadu Journal of Cooperators,* Vol.1, No. 8.

Samwel Kakuko Lopoyetum, (1999), "Indo-Kenya Dairy Cooperative

System; Scope for Dairy Cooperative Development and Replicability Strategy of Indian Model in Kenya" Cooperative Perspective, *Journal of Cooperative Management*, Vol. 34. No. 3.

Samwel Kakuko Lopoyetum, (1999), "Computer Application in the Management Administration of Cooperatives" *Tamil Nadu Journal of Cooperation*, Vol.91, No. 4.

Srinivasan Gowda, M.V., (1994), "Cooperatives in the New Economic Scenario, Agenda for Liberalization", *Southern Economist*, p.21.

25

ECONOMIC REFORMS AND EMERGING ISSUES ON RURAL DEVELOPMENT

I. Sundar

Introduction

Rural development, uplift of rural people and more specifically, the alleviation of rural poverty continue to be the central concern of development planning in India. It could be noted that in India nearly 70 percent of the population depend on agriculture and its allied activities for their livelihood either directly or indirectly. However, there is a growing concern on rural development in India in consequence of implementation of New Economic Policy since 1991. There is a growing concern on GATT on Indian agriculture and rural development. Borrowing from International Monetary Fund and acceptance of GATT and treaties of WTO has imposed a check on agricultural subsidies. The new economies reforms have introduced in India in consequence of GATT and WTO agreement and treaties. This paper devotes to analyze the impact of the economic reforms in rural development.

Economic Reforms and Agriculture

The state intervention in agriculture could be analyzed carefully. The structural adjustment measures and government economic interventions have some influence over the others. It includes providing non-marketable facilities, marketable facilities, price distortions and regulations to subsidies and levies. When adjustment is the results of true price system i.e., a price system that correctly reflects the scarcities in the economy, the necessity of providing market facilities and removing price inhibition or regulations is far less evident than otherwise. It could be noted that in developed countries, also while a vital role is played by private sector in production and of marketing agricultural products, the role of the state is also essential in determining floor and ceiling prices for agricultural commodities, stock piling of excess quantities and providing a legal framework for all transactions, especially relating to land ownership. In these countries, a sort of division of labour between state and private enterprise has been put into operation. Developing countries should draw lessons from this particular division of labour.

The effectiveness of the market mechanism in promoting agricultural development is a major concern in the era of economic reforms. Developed countries also well recognized that the state has to intervene in the agricultural markets with a view to ensure reasonable returns and stable income to the farmers. Market interventions by the government in the agricultural sector are quite common in all types of economies from Japan and South Korea to France, Switzerland and America.[1] The justification of state intervention in agricultural products and credit markets is all the more strong in the context of Indian agriculture suffering from inadequate development of infrastructure and strong and pernicious linkages between rural credit, labour and product markets.[2]

It is a known that the agricultural price policy pursued in India has worked against the interests of Indian farmers as the internal prices are isolated from the international prices and in fact Indian agriculture is subjected to disprotection in contrast to the high protection enjoyed by the Indian industries.[3]

Regarding agricultural prices there is a need to analyze to what extent farmers we rely on price incentives to increase agricultural output. It is observed that in the case of individual crops Indian farmers have been found to be quite responsive and price policy can he used to bring about shifts in cropping pattern in favour of preferred crops. The aggregate supply response of agriculture is debateable one. The available studies indicate fairly low aggregate supply elasticity of agriculture[4]. In the Indian context, therefore, importance of non-price factors like appropriate technology, institutional changes and infrastructure play and important rile in agricultural development.

There is a need to analyze to what extent international prices can be used as a reliable guide for determining agricultural policy. It is well known that the international prices of agricultural goods do not reflect free market prices and are highly distorted and volatile. As Dantwala has rightly remarked, apart from international prices there are several relevant factors, which should guide agricultural policy viz., agro-climatic potential of different regions, technological horizon of different crops, domestic demand and supply in the context of balance of payment constraint.

Moreover, high agricultural prices would benefit only the surplus producing farmers, who constitute a small proportion of Indian farmers. A large majority of farmers still produce food grains for domestic consumption and are either outside the framework of the market mechanism or are forced to resort to distress sales.

The main advantage of successful structural adjustment is the disappearance of economic problem involved in the distinction between current and shadow prices. By imposing real exchange rates, major cause of difference between social utility values and current prices is removed. The removal of distortive tax and subsidies as well as imposition of modern tax system such as the value-added to tax obeys the same logic. Privatization of activity undertaken by the State trading organizations removes some price distortions though it can also have side-effects such as depriving farmers of free access to technical information. If such side-effects are undesirable, they may be corrected by relevant projects. In addition, there are situations where public interventions are obviously necessary, independently of any structural adjustment programme.

Economic Reforms and Subsidies

The supply of key agricultural inputs like fertilizers, canal water and electricity at subsidized rates is and essential part of the strategy of agricultural growth with low output prices. The input subsidies have to be given in the light of its impact on agricultural and growth and not from the narrow view point of reduction in fiscal deficit alone. Increase in irrigated area and fertilizer use have been the critical variables in sustaining the green revolution in the country. The decline in fertilizer consumption consequent upon a sharp rise in fertilizer prices, would affect the foodgrain production. The reduction in net income of farmers, consequent on sudden withdrawal of subsidies, would also affect private investment in agriculture.

The small and marginal farmers would be particularly adversely affected, since they are not in a position to benefit from higher output prices due to lack of marketable surplus. Reduction in fertilizer intake by them would affect available food supply to them through lower production. Thus, they will be subject to a double burden. It is good that the Eighth Five Year Plan document recognizes the likely adverse effect of reduction of fertilizer subsidy on agricultural production and consequences of its inequities for the small and marginal farmers.[5]

It would also be pertinent to add here that not all the losses in supply of agricultural inputs can be treated as a subsidy to the agriculturists. Nearly half of the fertilizer subsidy goes to support the fertilizer industry. In fact, fertilizer-grain price ratio is relatively unfavourable to the Indian farmers as compared to the ratio prevalent in other countries. There is also considerable overstaffing, inefficiency and theft in the working of irrigation Departments and State Electricity Boards, which need to be attended to. Finally, one should recognize the 'public good' nature of infrastructural facilities like irrigation and rural electricity, which have a favourable impact not only on the agricultural sector but the rural economy as a whole. There is thus a good case for limited and targeted subsidies for land and water development programmes to boost agricultural output and incomes.[6]

Economic Reforms and Rural Credit

The analysis of the implications of financial sector reforms on agricultural development deserves due attention on the part of the present study. The expansion of commercial banks in the rural areas and emphasis on priority sector lending since the nationalization of major banks in 1969 have played an important role in increasing institutional credit availability in rural areas and supporting the spread of the green revolution. The reorganization of the financial system on market-oriented policies will affect the flow of credit to the rural areas. The Narasimha Committee has recommended that the share of priority lending should be brought down from the present 40 per cent level to 10 percent in near future and eventually phased out. The Committee has also recommended phasing out of concessional rate interest on priority sector loans. Fears have been rightly expressed among economists that these measures would have a serious deleterious impact on agriculture and rural development.

The inhibition in credit supply and domination of large farmers in availing the benefits of credit programmes is the common phenomena in India. It is proponents of financial sector reform put, misuses some important points. They are (i) sudden contraction of availability of commercial bank credit to the large and medium farmers would impair agricultural growth and reduce the supply of foodgrains, thereby causing general economic disruption[7] and (ii) The growth of institutional credit advanced to small and marginal farmers has been higher and they now account for over 40 percent of total institutional credit and 62 percent of short-term credit, far in access of their share in area they operate. In fact, the commercial bank credit is more equates as compared to the cooperative credit.[8] Further, the greater reliance of the small and marginal farmers on non-institutional sources at exorbitant interest rates should not be used to justify the hike in interest rates by commercial banks. Rather, they have to be taken out of such exploitative linkages through increasing their access to institutional credit at reasonable rates.

The rapid growth of agricultural and non-agricultural segment of the rural economy would require a larger flow of institutional credit than in the past. The banking and cooperative credit agencies have to gear themselves up to meet this difficult challenge.

Economic Reforms and Price Policy

It is evident that the government has liberalized international trade in foodgrains allowing domestic prices to international levels. Currently, prices of wheat, coarse grains and pulses in India are roughly 10 percent more than the international prices and rice prices 30 percent less. However, the agreed GATT Agreement is likely to push up relatively the prices of wheat and coarse cereals by 5 percent whole bringing down the rice prices. Hence the liberalization of agricultural trade in the post GATT scenario may involve a rise in the domestic relative prices of food grains by about 15 to 20 percent. The effect of such a price rise, as measured by calculation of price elasticities, would be the reduction of consumption of the poor while leaving that of relatively affluent unaffected. Export surpluses of food grains could be at the cost of the poor consuming significantly less than even the inadequate amounts they consume today. It should be noted that while the effect of exporting food grains upon domestic prices and availability is direct and , therefore, more obvious, similar results would occur even if other non-food cash crop exports were encouraged, in so far as these imply acreage shifts away from food grains rather than substantially increasing total supply.

The outcomes of price policy depend upon a number of factors, viz., (i) the exporters of a product, whether they are self-employed small peasants or capitalists, (ii) the commodity exported, whether staple food other poor or not, (iii) proportion of the poor in different sectors, (iv) weight accorded to the poor in overall policies, and (v) effects of contraction in expenditure. If the exporters are poor and small peasants, adjustment through devaluation will benefit the poor. When the commodity exported is staple food of the poor, prices will rise and the poor will be the suffers. The contractionary effects of adjustment will hurt the poor as a consequence of contraction of public investment associated with further contraction of private investment. When the effects fall on social expenditure, the poor are the victims of a decline in health and education services.[9]

Effects of Economic Reforms and Rural Employment

New economic policy has effects on rural employment. These effects occur in the form (i) withdrawal of subsidies on inputs in agriculture, and (ii) liberalization of industrial and trade policy.

Many studies have mentioned the well known fact that within agriculture, there are heavy subsidies for fertilizers, power and irrigation. These subsidies contribute to huge fiscal deficit and, therefore, it is proposed to withdraw these under NEP. These subsidies create inequality between regions and distort the allocation of resources. Even then, they have a role to play in increased employment and output within agriculture. The cost of inputs to the farmers is reduced, which in turn contributes to intensive uses of land. This has got direct and indirect benefits on employment. Larger input-use leads to generation of employment, which is a direct benefit. However, indirect benefit is achieved through employment generated by additional output.

Hence withdrawal of subsidies for inputs in agriculture would reduce employment in agriculture sector, It happens in the form of (i) price elasticity of input use, (ii) elasticity of employment to yield and (iii) elasticity of crop yield to input use.

Fertilizer is one of the most important inputs and the subsidies are most prominent in this respect. It has been found that in many states of India, elasticity of crop yield to fertilizer use is positive and the price elasticity of fertilizer use is negative.[10] A relative rise in the price of fertilizer may induce substitution by organic manure, which is good for sustainable agriculture development; and has to be deliberately promoted. Arise in produce price along with a rise in fertilizer price could arrest the increase in the relative price of fertilizer and work against disincentives to use. But the rise in produce price is not less inequitable than subsidy on fertilizers. The non-price factors such as improved access to credit and improved fertilizer prices. Thereof, if the flow of benefits from subsidies is considered, there is a case for reduction of subsidy and use of non-price factors for promoting fertilizer use. As a result of reduction of fertilizer subsidy, there can be some employment uses. However, there is need for a phased withdrawal of subsidies in agriculture.

The internal and international competition improves efficiency because of liberalization and the domestic gross capital formation is also increased due to Foreign Direct Investment (FDI), which in turn are expected to step up growth rates and also employment, depending upon the changes in technology and their effects on elasticity of employment to output. The multi-national corporations have displacement effects on employment, It is observed that (i) the MNCs employ techniques which are more capital-intensive than domestic enterprises, and (ii) the chance that a local project would have emerged in the absence of direct foreign investment. It is evident that the techniques employed by MNCs are more capital-intensive than those employed by local enterprises. In the case of second issue, this is least likely in areas where local firms do not have access to knowledge. The more capital-using techniques of MNCs will have some adverse effect on employment. The adverse effect of technology, consequent on entry of MNCs, could be compensated only by additions to investments and rate of growth far higher than what could be obtained without such investment. Such compensated benefits are likely to be realized in short and medium terms. Therefore, one would expect the rate of labour absorption in the sector to decline.

Liberalization of trade is unlikely to expand agricultural and rural exports in the absence of development of infrastructural facilities for export markets. The short-term effects on employment are unlikely to be favourable even if exports are stopped up through promotion of agro-processing, since the employment intensity of modern processing is likely to be less than the corresponding intensity of traditional industry. Modern agro-processing development depends on the following features. Modern processing develops a whole range of new industries, resulting in addition to aggregate employment. Then the modernization of agro-processing should result in more efficient use of raw material and also contribute to utilization of by-products, which remain unutilized. Both these effects are likely to be observed in the long run, but in the short run one should expect a reduction in employment as traditional processing is replaced by modern processing.

Economic Reforms and Rural Poor

The effects of structural adjustment could fall on the rural poor in the programme following ways: (i) some people are direct victims of structural adjustments such as employees of rural health and school teachers in village retrenched as a consequence of cut back in public expenditure in the areas of health and education. They are called new poor (ii) some individuals and families whose income are so low that price increases by structural adjustments pushed these below the border line. Hence they are border line poor rushed to the poverty and (iii) some of the people are extremely poor even before the adjustment programmes. The concern here is with all the categories of rural poor not just the newly poor or the border-line poor pushed into the power.

Economic Reforms and Cooperatives

Cooperatives have been functioning in the country for the past one century with primary objective of promoting socio-economic well-being of rural people. However, in the course of time cooperatives have become highly bureaucratized, weighed down by inefficiency and inertia. In the changed context of economic liberalization, rural cooperatives must infuse some amount of corporate culture in their activities. The cooperatives must be debureaucratized and managed professionally and must make more profits as their members stand to gain by accrual of dividend and interest incomes. Given tremendous scope for export of agricultural products, strengthening of cooperatives to go beyond primary production and develop processing and marketing will be immensely profitable as in the case of cooperatives in western agriculture. Farmers must pool funds and expertise and run the cooperatives. Specialized agricultural cooperatives such as sugar and milk, characterized by voluntary participation and open-market orientation, must be encouraged for other commodities. At the same time, established cooperatives may loosen up and diversify into producing a diverse range of products and services from electrical equipment and machinery to construction and transport. Besides conventional share holding, employment/ supply shares may be issued to raise funds against assurance of providing employment or accepting supply of materials from shareholders. NABARD may play a leading role in refinancing the rural cooperatives for running enterprises of the sort indicated above.

Agricultural producers must be encouraged and guided to form growers' cooperative organization to undertake export of fruits, vegetables and flowers which may significantly enhance their earnings. Grape growers' associations in Maharashtra are noteworthy in India. In order to export high quality eco-friendly products, members of growers' association need to be trained on organic farming, cultivating of insect and disease-free plants and trees, improved pruning and staggered harvesting techniques and packaging of products. Domestic competition will need to be fostered on a much larger scale in industries supplying inputs to agriculture and processing and buying its outputs. The growers' cooperative organization must arrange to ensure supply of timely inputs and develop common facilities such as precooling centers and refrigerated transport before airlifting to long distance domestic and foreign destinations. Agricultural exports will have multiplier effects on rural employment as higher earnings by agricultural producers due to exported is likely to induce more capital formation at farm level and intensification of agriculture production. Besides, investment on building, marketing and processing of infrastructure will add to rural employment. In this connection export potentials for super-fine rice are very promising. Cooperative organization must concentrate in creating these facilities either as private or cooperative units. The satellite technology has given us an excellent opportunity to make weather forecasts, and to get updated on national and international marketing conditions. Cooperative organization must educate farmers to regulate production and market supply, thus minimizing the impact of weather and market risks. The location of facilities must be closer to production centers of different commodities to ensure better access by all producers, irrespective of their size. Training members of cooperative organization on grading by quality, size and other features, pre-packaging and packaging will enhance time and efficiency in moving products from farm gates to processing or export points. Cooperative organization may be offered special concessions and economic incentives to embark on these tasks. Revitalising and reorienting rural cooperatives is one way of strengthening agriculture cooperative organization.

Economic Reforms and Biological Software

There is a growing familiar of biological software throughout the world such as tissue culture seedlings, bio-fertilizers, bio-pesticides, vermicultured manures and nitrogen fixing plants. Now the firms have concentrated on banana, floriculture, sugarcane and plantation crops and have put up green houses to introduce hardness in the tissue cultured plants. The firms can be encouraged to locate tissue culture units and green houses in the rural areas, relatively nearer to markets and closer to highways. This will create tremendous potential to provide jobs to rural youth, with little amount of training. One must note that the estimated potential of global demand for tissue culture products is Rs. 45,000 crores annually. Groups of farmers and small scale entrepreneurs, particularly educated of bio-pesticides. Production of bio-fertilizers is another area, promotion of which will generate rural employment. The agricultural products emanating from use of bio and organic fertilizers offer bright export possibilities. Production of hybrid seeds in the case of rice and select oilseeds are potential activities, which will add value to landless families. The rural entrepreneurs have hesitation to launch production of bio-fertilizers may be ascribed to lack of technical guidance. State Agricultural Universities have a crucial role to play in this process. There is a concern on lack of adequate practice among our farmers on bio-controlling of plant pests due to lack of awareness, knowledge and want of linkages with laboratories. The present move of the government to set up Small Farmers' Agribusiness Consortium is a welcome step.

Economic Reforms and Wasteland Development

Corporate firms are interested in forestry and horticultural production. They have shown interest to manage larger areas of wasteland by planting trees to meet their raw material demand. This is a good opportunity for the government to involve rural poor in this process. In this connection large areas of wastelands can be entrusted to corporate firms on a long lease to undertake forestry and horticultural production. In turn corporate firms can allot plots of wasteland to tribals and agricultural labourers with a buyback arrangement of tree and horticultural products for defined production periods. The firm may supply required inputs and extend technical guidance to those households who can contribute labour and manage trees besides enjoying the consumption of by-products such as grasses and leaves as fodder and loppings as fuel. The benefits at harvest time can be shared between the rural households and firms. Social benefits, which may flow out of this programme, will be enormous in terms of economic and environmental benefits.

Conclusion and Policy Measures

It could be seen clearly from the above discussion that there are problems and prospects of economic reforms on rural development. In order to overcome the negative impact of economic reforms on rural development, the following policy measures can be considered.

1. There is a need to maintain the functioning of public distribution system as it provides basic needs goods at low price to the poor rural household. Hence, it should not be disturbed in the name of market mechanism.
2. There is a need to conduct research study on impact of new economic policy on rural development. This helps to modify the new economic policy to cater the needs of the rural people.
3. The export led agricultural growth may create regional disparities. Hence, efforts should be made to reduce the incidence of regional disparities in the process of development through proper government intervention.
4. The liberalization policy should not affect the food security of millions of Indians.
5. The import of low priced food product should be discouraged as it affects the price of food produced by the Indian farmers since they are unable to meet the cost of production. So they are forced to sell their produce at low price, consequent upon local competition.
6. The government should not follow the disinvestment policy in agriculture and rural development as they affect the life of millions of India.
7. In order to develop agriculture, there is a need to follow agro-climatic regional approach for efficient allocation of resources and higher resource productivity.
8. The post harvest technology to be promoted not only for agricultural production, but improving the qualitative characters also which enhances its sale ability.

9. The competitive power of the small farmers could be enhanced through cooperative marketing.

10. In order to prevent the problem of rural unemployment, the import of agricultural technology should be discouraged.

11. The cheap credit policy should be continued forever to protect the interests of rural poor, down trodden and other weaker sections of the society.

12. There is a need to de-bureaucratize cooperative institutions with a view to allow them to operate freely, autonomously and be accountable to the members.

13. Modification of the existing policy reforms to allow greater freedom to market forces with due safeguards for the poor in tune with the new economic policy.

14. There is a need to create awareness among the rural people about the type of commodities for export trade along with quality consideration. In this connection restructuring of the agricultural base to take advantage of new opportunities is essential.

15. Steps have to be taken for an effective redistributive system of assets and increasing investment infrastructural development in agriculture.

16. Individual producer's organization particularly small farmers must be strengthened for ensuring benefits of structural adjustment to these group.

17. The commercial and industrial agriculture pollutes the environment hence the susceptibility of ecology should be kept in mind under such circumstances.

18. Development of labour intensive technology must be given top priority.

19. Improve local organization capacity to deal with issues related to off farm activities and rural industry development.

20. Patent rights should not be given to multinationals particularly medicinal herbs, and shrubs used by the rural people.
21. Ensure that farmers especially the small farmers on whom the food security of billions of people rest can save, use, exchange and sell seeds and other propagating material in their customary manner.
22. The transfer of destructive technology to indigenous people should be prevented and support for the development of appropriate and environmentally sensitive technology to be promoted.
23. Recognition and support for indigenous resource management such as forest protection and conservation, sustainable agriculture, hunting and fishing practices etc.
24. Supporting capacity building to allow rural people to be more effective and creative in influencing policies, designing and implanting sustainable development plans.
25. Recognition land rights, water rights and rights of rural people to have control over their culture.

NOTES

1. M.L. Dantwala, "Agricultural Policy : Prices and Public Distribution System : A Review", *Indian Journal of Agricultural Economics,* Vol. XLVIII, No. 2, April-June 1993, p.175.
2. Amit Bhaduri, 'Economic Structure of Backward Agriculture', Macmillan, Delhi, 1983.
3. Ashok Gulati and P.K. Sharma, "Government Intervention in Agricultural Markets; Nature, impact and Implications," *Journal of Indian School of Political Economy,* Vol. 3, No. 2, April-June, 1991.
4. S.L. Bapana, Aggregate Supply Response of Crops in a Developing Region, Sultan Chand and Sons, New Delhi, 1980.
5. Planning Commission, Eighth Five Year Plan (1992-97), Vol. I, Government of India, New Delhi, 1992, p.3.
6. Yoginder K.Alagh, "Macro-policies for Indian Agriculture

Presented at ISID-FAO, Workshop on Agricultural Policies in New Economic Environment", 6-10 September, Institute for Industrial Development, New Delhi, 1993.

7. N.A. Majumdar, "Financial Reforms and Rural Development" *Economic and Political Weekly,* Vol. XXVII, No.14 April 4, 1992.

8. D.K. Desai, "Institutional Credit Requirement for Agricultural Production 2000 A.P." *Indian Journal of Agricultural Economics,* Vol. XLVIII, No. 2, July-September, 1988.

9. Srinivasan, T.M. cited in references Susan Horton and Others, "Labour Markets in an Era of Adjustment", *International Labour Review,* Vol. 30, No. 56, 1991.

10. Sharma and Haque, T., "Impact of Fertilizer Subsidy on Growth and Equity" Highlights of Agricultural Research, *IASRI,* 1987.

26

ECONOMIC REFORMS AND RURAL DEVELOPMENT

S. Michael John Peter & V. Saravanan

Introduction

It was the early nineties, when India fast passing through an unprecedented economic crisis, following political instability that was further aggravated by the impact of Gulf War. Our country was trapped in galloping inflation, stress on balance of payment, frustrated position of foreign exchange reserves, and other micro economic imbalances. To overcome this situation Dr. Manmohan Singh the then Finance Minister introduced the New Economic Policy in 1991-92 Union Budget, several policy measures, popularly known as Economic Reforms. These reforms were directed more or less in a sequential order, first to industrial, then foreign trade and financial sectors.

The new economic policy certainly has direct and indirect impact on agriculture and rural development in the country. Exclusion of agriculture in any serious discussion on structural reforms in the developing countries is indefensible. It is the largest private sector in the developing economies; it produces tradable goods and agricultural products according to economic signals.

Reforms In Indian Agriculture

Reforms in agricultural scenario in India have been slow and cautions for several reasons. Majority of the farmers in our country cultivate in marginal and holdings having a size of less than two hectares. Their dependence on the market for procurement of inputs and for the sale of produce is insubstantial. Markets play a very meager role in this context. Since the strategic objectives related to these section of farming community are the expansion of their marginal production of existing resource base and in all providing them with alternative source of livelihood by protecting them from risks and uncertainties. Secondly for a large and poor country such as India, food security considerations weigh heavily in determining agricultural policies.

Comprehensive reforms, which may jeopardise the prospects of food security for the rural and urban poor, even in the short term will not be accepted with ease. Finally, the complacent attitude of policy makers reinforced with the over emphăsis on the objective of the reform package, led to a continuous decline in the public investment for capital formation in agriculture as well as in the share of the priority sector lending by public sector banks in the 90's. However, the policy changes at the macro level and those instituted at the sectoral level seem to have made some impact on agricultural growth but importantly on the dynamics of production relating. The impact may be discussed at two levels. Firstly, the impact of macro policy reforms, especially the attempts to curtail budgetary deficits and realign the value of domestic currencies on agricultural sector, could be looked into. Secondly, we may examine the impact of sectoral policies, subsidy policies, trade policies, credit, policies, etc., these two sets of impacts are overlapping. Our main attention is on the aspect of economic policies with regard to the sectoral policies fin agriculture, which in turn affects rural development.

Impact of Economic Reforms on India's Agriculture and Rural Development

The Economic reforms focused on reduction of subsidies, reduction of bank lending for priority sector, tariff reduction and trade liberalization do have some impact on agriculture. Agricultural subsidies, which have been provided for agricultural input that includes fertilizers, electricity, and irrigation and for output in the from of Minimum Support Price (MSP) to give favourable and reasonable price to the farmers, have been either or withdrawn completely. Due to total decontrol of potash and phosphate fertilizers, which is the result of partial reduction of subsidy in nitrogenous fertilizers. In India, where more than 70 percent farmers have small and marginal land holding, cannot afford to buy potash and phosphate fertilizer application. It has a deleterious effect on soil structure and composition that ultimately hampers sustainable agricultural production.

Indian agriculture was characterized by low and stagnant growth performance till the mid sixties. However, after green revolution the performance improved till the end of eighties.

Table 1 reveals that, though the other sectors have recorded high growth rates in the eighties there was no significant increase in performance over two decades.

Table 1: Average Compound Growth Rates of GDP and by Sectors During 1980-1990

Year	*GDP*	*Agricul-ture*	*Industry*	*Manu-facturing*	*Services*	*Percapita GNP*
1980-1990	5.4	3.9	6.3	6.1	6.4	3.4
1991-	6.4	3.3	6.5	7.4	8.2	4.9

Source: Economic Survey, Government of India, 2001-2002.

Table 2, reveals that a distinguishing feature in the case of agricultural output is sharp year-to-year fluctuations. These high variations imply unpredictable nature of agriculture in India and the precariousness of our food security position. The share of agriculture to GDP is declining steadily; till it continues to contribute nearly one- fourth of the country's GDP.

Nevertheless, it is interesting to note that agriculture's share in work force particularly in rural areas, is not declining despite

Table 2 : Macro Economic Indicators Relating to Indian Agriculture

Year	*GDP Growth in percentage*	*Agriculture GDP Growth in percentage*	*Share of Agriculture to GDP in percentage*	*Capital Formation in Agri-culture*	*Percentage of Agricul-ture expen-diture to Total Outlay*
1990-91	5.4	4.1	32.7	27.7	5.5
1991-92	0.8	-1.9	32.0	23.4	6.2
1993-94	5.9	4.1	32.8	22.4	4.8
1994-95	7.3	-0.9	30.3	25.8	4.7
1997-98	6.5	-2.4	28.7	24.8	4.5
1999-00	6.1	1.3	27.3	23.6	4.4
2000-01	4.0	-0.2	-	-	4.1

Source : Economic Survey, Government of India Various Issues.

its declining importance in the country's GDP. It indicates that more and more people are depending on agricultural activities; it also suggests low absorption capacity of the secondary and tertiary sectors.

In the banking sector, the lending for priority sector has been suggested to reduce from 40 percent to 10 percent and gradually phased out. The Narasimham Committee has also recommended phasing out of concessional rates of interest on priority sector loan. Moreover, in the name of efficiency and viability, the bank branches in rural areas, which were serving the rural poor peasants and poor sections of the society, are being closed down, similarly number of regional rural bands have also been closed. This would reduce the amount of loans being extended to agriculture and rural development but rapid growth of agriculture and non-agriculture segment of rural economy will seek a larger flow of institutional credit. Banking and co-operative agencies have to gear themselves up to meet this difficult challenge.

The export thrust of new economic policies has also accelerated the cropping pattern shifts which results in declining in the area under food grains in favour of exportable or import substitute crops during the post reform period consequently, the food grains has fallen short for the first time ever since 1975 the benefits from the export oriented policies do not seem to have reached all sections of the farming community while the large farmers are reaping the benefits of policies, small and marginal farmers are languishing for want of resources.

The main macro policy impact on agriculture is the shift in terms of trade in favour of agriculture. It has also resulted in the enhanced market sensitiveness of the producers. However, absence of continuity in policies especially pertaining to agricultural trade has increased the market induced risk and uncertainty. The small and marginal farmers are lured by market signals, but they do not have the strength to deal with the market risks. Their problems are aggravated with declining public investment in agriculture.

Table 3 : Compound Growth Rate of Output of Selected Agricultural Products

Crop	*1980 to 1991*	*1990 to 2001*
Rice	3.6	1.7
Wheat	4.2	3.7
Pluses	1.5	-0.6
Coarse grains	0.4	0.06
Total cereals	3.1	2.1
All food grains	2.9	1.7
Oil seeds	-	4.9
Non-oil food grains	3.7	1.9

Source : Economic Survey, Government of India, Various issues.

The small and marginal farmers, who do not possess the wherewithal that is, the access to capital and hence other resources including water, to face the market, have to defend themselves. The plight of the small and marginal farmers is becoming increasingly serious in the arid and semi-arid regions, which had been even previously neglected by the state.

Agricultural producers in these neglected regions are now faced with degraded environment, poor resource base and unfriendly institutional environment, under this condition, market penetration in recent years has increased the concentration of scarce resources in fewer hands leading not only to inequalities but also pushing the poor farmers to the edge.

Privatisation of rural transportation will naturally cause great inconvenience to people. No private company would like to ply buses in the rural areas, as it would bring them loss. Similarly, privatization of these two may only cater to the need of richer section and a vast majority of people who are poor will be denied to quality education and health.

Challenges to be Faced

1. Will the reform measures have the important repercussions on rural employment, income and welfare of the sections of the society?
2. Will the reform measures protect the farmers' right in production, Marketing and sale of products?
3. What are the measures to be taken exclusively for the backward sections to improve their efficiency?
4. Will the benefits of rapid economic growth reach the large mass of poor people?
5. Can growth in agriculture be achieved with large number of poor farmers with little infrastructure and credit facilities?

Strategies for the Future

(a) A multi-agency approach in agriculture and rural development is crucial for its development. Public, private and NGOs, farmers' organizations must act with better cooperation.

(b) People's participation in decision-marking regarding planning and development process and technology choice is very important to adopt a appropriate technology and to improve the development process.

(c) Capacity building in the poorer section of the society by skill training and up gradation.

(d) Promote private participation in agriculture through contract farming.

(e) Priority should be given to evolve location specific and economically viable technologies, for example, specific region improved varieties of agricultural and horticultural crops, and local knowledge based technologies for rural development.

(f) Initiation of a farming system research which integrates all the factors of production, namely, land, water, labour, capital and all farm activities such as crop production, livestock rising, dairying, sericulture, fisheries, social forestry etc., together to develop a whole farm production system.

(g) In the economic reforms era, when lending to the priority section has been reduced, group approach of credit lending may be increased. Micro financing, supposed to be the better option for credit supply to the peasant and rural artisans, because of in-group lending participants would be more accountable than individual lending. Recent NABARD experiences show a healthy picture regarding repayment capacity of the Self Help Groups particularly women Self Help Groups.

Approaches to Combat Adverse Effect of Economic Reforms on Rural Development

Economic reforms seem to have a negative impact on small and marginal agricultural producers, rural industries, as well as on employment opportunities for the poorer sections of the society. At the moment, when our country has no option other than opening up national economy, the focus should be on adopting the following approaches to mitigate adverse impacts of globalisation and liberalization.

Generation of Appropriate Technologies Rather than High Technologies

Many people consider appropriate technology as traditional or old and thus primitive. This is not true. Appropriate technology means a low cost technology using mainly local or easily available materials and skills to meet a recognised need. We can call it intermediate technology. It refers to such small-scale technologies sustainable for the rural poor. The main requirements of appropriate or intermediate technology are : (a) Need based, (b) Self reliant, (c) Poor oriented, (d) People centred, (e) Employment generating, (f) Eco-friendly cum cultural specific.

Such technologies are more natural, non-polluting and can be locally owned and produced in small units. This would help in avoiding pitfalls of high technologies especially exploitation of natural and human resources.

Participation of Local People in Planning and Developmental Activity

We have experienced from our efforts on rural development that the planning process of any development starts from the top level. The people, fro whom it means have not been consulted in past. Time has come for active participation of the people who are the center of focus of any development process. Agricultural technologies towards involvement of the people in the decision-making process of any development activity of the area. Decentralisation of power to local self-governance would be the next step towards this direction.

Encourage Contract Farming to Boost Agricultural Production

In the present situation, contract farming is viewed as and important tool to increase private corporate involvement in agro-processing and help augment rural employment and income. Presently, companies engage in agro-processing and marketing are entering into contract farming by providing farmers with inputs and then buy the product with a rate specified in advance.

A Company in Contract Normally Provide the Following Inputs

(a) Required seed variety for cultivation, (b) Guidelines to grow the crop, (c) Recommended dose of pesticides and fertilizers with no or less residual toxicity, (d) Free extension services, (e) Other materials if not available locally.

This system would help in eliminating the presence of middlemen and bring the producers and processors in close contact. Farmers can have advantages in terms of assured market access to technology, timely supply of inputs and more accountable extension services.

Participatory Technological Development

Limitation of new agricultural technology brings about the concept of Participatory Technological Development (PTD) that better suited capable to solve the production problems. It is an alternative approach to develop useful technologies. PTD is the process of bringing together the local communities in one platform with the researchers and other professionals. It requires respect for Indigenous Technical Knowledge (ITK) embedded in local society. PTD helps in systematic farm-based research by the local people who face the real problem. This approach sill certainly accelerates the adoption process by local masses.

Farming System Research and Extension

It is farmer oriented, problem solving, comprehensive, interdisciplinary, complementary, interactive and dynamic and responsible to the society. This approach envisages the whole farm activity by integrating all the factors of production namely land, water, family labour, capital and similar other factors. Here the main emphasis is on the collective operation of agricultural, livestock rising, fisheries, sericulture and social forestry, which are complementary but will also improve employment opportunities to the farming families.

Conclusion

As in other developing countries, in fact, more so in developed countries in India also, government intervention in the agricultural sector is quite extensive. The principal agricultural crops are subjected to a variety of administered price regimes (minimum prices, support prices, levy prices, issue prices). There are formal or informal restrictions on the movement of crops and agricultural inputs. Credit delivery is regulated as part of overall financial controls. External trade in agricultural commodities is restricted at the same time; huge subsidies are expended to bring down the real prices of inputs for the agricultural producers.

Even though the policies are formulated at the central level, their countrywide adoption depends on the cooperation of state governments. True, privatization of some of the services in agricultural sector has been carried out in recent years at the state level. The areas of privatization include seed production, veterinary services, de-licensing of retail input supply demonstrations and servers work.

Finally, we need to recognize that the true potential of agriculture can be realized only when we can diversify our agricultural products, both geographically and over time. This would require in accelerating the process of liberalization in domestic market; unfreezing the lease market through revision of agricultural inputs and phasing out input subsidies; working out long term export strategies for commercial crops and other high value crops. Caring procurement operations on commercial lines and involving grass rootinstitutions in the mechanism of public distribution system of food grains. It would also require a reconsideration of the various rules and regulations that govern dovetailing agricultural price and trade policies which frequently act against the interests of the farmers and distort their incentive structure.

REFERENCES

Bhagwati, J., (2001), "Growth, Poverty and Reforms", *Economic and Political Weekly,* March 10.

Government of India, Ministry of Finance, Economic Survey, Various Issues.

Mishra S.K., Puri. V.K., (2002), 'Indian Economy', Himalaya Publishing House, Mumbai-400004.

Nagarajan, R., (1997), "What has Happened Since 1991?, Assessment of India's Economic Reforms". *Economic and Political Weekly,* November 8.

Raju, S.S., & Chowdhry, K.R., (1997), 'New Economic Policy and Its Impact on Rural Development & New Economic Policy and Perspective to Rural Development', Ed. E.P. Singh, NIRD, Hyderabad.

Vyas, V.S., (1996), "Agriculture : Trade Policy for Nineties : Issues and Approaches", *Economic and Political Weekly,* Vol. 29, No. 26, pp. A 54-64.

—— (2001), "Agriculture : Second Round of Economic Reforms", *Economic and Political Weekly,* March, 10.

27

IMPLICATIONS OF ECONOMIC REFORMS: NEED FOR RURAL DEVELOPMENT IN INDIA

V. Rajam & S. Ramalinga Choodambigai

Introduction

There has been a substantial change in the development strategy in our country since 1980–81. The growth strategy of the eighties was mainly based on borrowings, both internal and external, but during the nineties, on investments by Indian and foreign investors. These policy-changes have put the Indian economy on higher growth trajectory. It is, therefore, important to analyse the direction of this growth process. Will it be sustainable? Whether the weaker section and backward states are getting the benefit of higher growth? This paper addresses some of these issues of economic development. The specific objectives of the paper are as follows,

(i) Study the trends of growth of GDP and its main sector since 1980-81;

(ii) Compare the sectoral growth and its fluctuations during the eighties and nineties;

(iii) Study the shift in the sectorial composition of GDP during the period under study and,

(iv) Study the trickle down effect of growth on poverty and unemployment.

Table 1 provides estimated trend-equation for the growth rate of GDP and its main sectors at constant prices for the period of 1980-81 to 1990-2000. It also shows the estimated average annual growth rate for this period.

Table 1: Estimated Trend Equation (y = a + bT)
(1981-82) - (1990-2000)

Sl. No.	*Dependent Variable(a)*	*Constant*	*Coefficient of Trend*	*R^2*	*Growth Rate*
1.	Agriculture	5.5689	-0.1561	0.0188	3.38
2.	Industry	6.1105	0.0238	0.0106	6.66
3.	Transport	5.1937	0.1906**	0.1803	5.27
4.	Finance	5.1595	0.2034**	0.1383	6.54
5.	Public Administration	4.5905	0.1909*	0.1184	5.24
6.	GDP	5.2921	0.0493	0.0165	

Note: (i) **Significant at 5 percent level of significance
(ii) *Significant at 10 percent level of significance
(iii) (a) Annual percent change is taken as dependent variable.

From these estimates, it is clear that the growth rate of agricultural and industrial sectors of the economy, i.e., the commodity producing sector is constant since 1981-82. The growth rate sectors of the economy, i.e., trade and transport, finance and public administrative sectors has improved since 1981-82, as the trend coefficients of these sectors are positive and statistically significant. Thus, the non-commodity producing sectors of the economy alone have improved their growth rates during this period. However, this could not break the overall constancy in the growth rate of GDP during this period. The low value of R^2 indicates high degree of fluctuations around the average value of growth rate.

The sectorial performance of the National Income (NI) has not remained uniform during the period under study. Almost all sectors of the economy have shown improvement in the annual growth rate in the nineties except the financial sector, which has declined. The details of percentage annual average growth rate for the sectors is presented in Table 2.

Table 2: Percentage Annual Average Growth Rate

Sector	*1980-81*	*1992-93 to 1999-2000*
Agriculture	3.84 (139.8)	3.66 (104.13)
Industry	7.16 (25.86)	6.78 (41.20)
Trade and Transport	6.33 (17.07)	9.06 (26.77)
Finance	7.25 (23.24)	7.62 (28.77)
Community Services	6.24 (29.670)	7.47 (42.39)
GDP	5.68 (38.89)	6.247 (14.53)

Note: Figures in brackers are percent coefficient of variance.

The wide fluctuations in the growth of the national income could be curbed in the nineties largely due to the increase in the share of non-agricultural earnings, it is also interesting to note that except the agricultural sector, all other sectors have shown more fluctuations in their annual growth rate after the introduction of economic reforms in 1991. The coefficient of variance in the annual growth rate has significantly increased during this period for all sectors except agriculture This increase is sharper in the case of such sectors as trade, transport and community services. It is difficult to understand why these sectors have been exposed to higher fluctuations in their growth process. It seems that market-oriented economic policies have meant more uncertainties and fluctuations in the growth process of non-agricultural sectors of the economy. This may pose a series problem, for the sustainability of economic growth.

In developed countries, the industrial and service sectors contribute a major share in GDP, with agricultural accounting for a relatively lower share.

However, fall in the share of the agricultural sector and increase in the share of the service sector is evident. But the share of industry has moved marginally and not enough to compensate for the loss in the agricultural sector. Thus, the service sector has, in fact, gained the expanse of both and over performed since 1991.

The service sector has by passed industry in the order of the development process. Economists call it 'leap-frogging' to a higher level of value addition in the service sector. Now the question is, from where did this value addition exactly take place in the sector? It is clear from the table that the share of trade, hotel and transport sector have improved substantially, since 1993-94. higher growth in service incomes is surely an indication of a prosperous economy. But can the growth of income from trade, hotel and transportation be sustained unless industrial income grows proportionately to support their prosperity? Thus, the distortions in the development process are not because the industrial sector has lagged behind, but because the service sector has grown at a higher rate pulling down the share of others. If industry fails to grow at the required rate, not only will the growth of the service sector suffer, but it will also drag down the growth or of GDP. Therefore, industry has to grow faster in order to support the high growth of service sector.

During the period of high growth and significant shift in structural change in the composition of NI, the poverty ratio has not fallen, rather, it has increased in percentage point in India. The details of population of below poverty line is presented in table 3, estimated by planning commission.

1999-2000 figures about the proportion of population below the poverty line reveal that seven states viz., Maharastra, Uttar Pradesh, Madhya Pradesh, Bihar, Orissa, Tamil Nadu and West Bengal account for 199.5 million poor which is 76.7 percent of the total 260 million poor in for 1999-2000. This shows that the rate of poverty reduction in these states has been slower than that in the relatively better-off states. Obviously, these seven states show greater concentration of the poor in 1999-2000 as compared with 1993-94.

Policies of globalization have helped the already industrialized states much more as compared with the less

Table 3: Planning Commission Estimate of Population of Below Poverty Line

		Number of persons in lakhs			*Poverty ratio (%of Population)*			*Poverty reduction*	
		1987-88	*1993-94*	*1999-2000*	*1987-88*	*1993-94*	*1999-2000*	*87-88 to 93-*	*93-94 to 99- 2000*
1.	Delhi	10.3	15.5	11.5	12.4	14.7	8.2	-2.3	6.5
2.	Punjab	25.2	25.1	14.5	13.2	11.8	6.2	1.4	5.6
3.	Chandigarh	0.8	0.8	0.5	14.7	11.4	5.7	3.3	5.7
4.	Himalchal Pardesh	7.5	15.9	5.1	15.5	28.4	7.6	-12.9	20.8
5.	Daman & Diu	-	0.2	0.1	-	15.8	4.4	-	11.4
6.	Haryana	25.4	43.9	17.3	16.6	25.1	8.7	-8.5	16.4
7.	Jammu & Kashmir	17.0	20.9	3.5	23.8	25.2	3.5	-1.4	21.7
8.	Goa	3.0	1.9	0.7	24.5	14.9	4.4	9.6	10.5
9.	Andhra Pradesh	160.4	154.0	119.0	25.9	22.2	15.8	3.7	12.1
10.	Kerala	88.5	76.6	41.0	31.8	25.4	12.7	6.4	6.3
11.	Mizoram	1.7	1.9	1.8	27.5	25.7	19.5	1.8	6.2
12.	Manipur	5.3	6.8	7.2	31.4	33.8	28.5	-2.4	5.3
13.	Gujarat	122.4	105.2	67.9	31.5	24.2	14.1	7.3	6.8
14.	Meghalaya	5.5	7.4	8.2	33.9	37.9	33.9	-4.0	4.0
15.	Nagaland	3.7	5.1	5.5	34.4	37.9	32.7	-3.5	5.2
16.	Lakshwdeep	0.2	0.1	0.1	35.0	25.7	15.6	10.0	9.4
17.	Rajasthan	142.9	128.5	81.8	35.2	27.4	15.3	7.8	7.5
18.	Sikkim	1.4	1.8	2.1	36.1	41.4	36.6	-5.3	4.8
19.	Tripura	8.8	11.8	13.0	35.2	39.1	34.4	-3.9	4.7

Contd....

Table 3: (Contd....)

		Number of persons in lakhs			*Poverty ratio (%of Population)*			*Poverty reduction*	
		1987-88	*1993-94*	*1999-2000*	*1987-88*	*1993-94*	*1999-2000*	*87-88 to 93-*	*93-94 to 99- 2000*
20.	Assam	75.8	96.4	94.6	36.2	40.9	36.1	-4.7	4.8
21.	Arunachal Pradesh	2.8	3.7	4.0	36.2	39.4	33.5	-3.2	3.3
22.	Karnataka	158.6	156.5	104.4	37.5	33.2	20.0	4.2	13.2
	All India	3070.5	3203.7	2602.5	38.9	36.0	26.1	2.9	9.9
23.	Maharashtra	296.3	305.2	228.0	40.4	36.9	25.0	3.5	11.9
24.	Uttar Pradesh	536.5	604.5	529.9	41.5	40.9	31.2	0.6	9.7
25.	Pondicherry	3.1	3.3	2.4	41.5	37.4	21.7	4.1	15.7
26.	Madhya Pradesh	264.3	298.5	298.5	43.1	42.5	37.4	0.6	5.1
27.	Andaman &Nicobar	1.1	1.1	0.8	43.9	34.5	21.0	9.4	13.5
28.	Tamil Nadu	231.1	202.1	130.5	43.4	35.0	21.1	8.4	13.9
29.	West Bengal	283.6	254.6	213.5	44.7	35.7	27.0	9.0	8.7
30.	Bihar	420.9	493.4	425.6	52.1	55.0	42.6	-2.9	12.4
31.	Orissa	165.9	160.6	169.1	55.6	48.6	47.1	7.0	1.5
32.	Dadra & Nagar Haveli	0.8	0.8	0.3	67.1	50.8	17.1	16.3	33.7

Note: States have been arranged in the ascending order on the basis of poverty ratio of 1987-88.

Source: Planning Commission (1998) Ninth Five Year Plan (1997-2000). Vol. I and Press Release of the Planning Commission dt. 22nd Feb. 2001. Regarding Poverty Estimates for 1999-2000 Expert Group (1993), Planning Commissions (1996-97) criteria of poverty line Rs.115.43 for Rural Areas, Rs.165.59 for Urban Areas.

industrialized states and their neglect of agriculture has been responsible for the skewed pattern of distribution in the post-reform period.

Unemployment Rates - Urban and Rural Differences

Data provided in table 4 reveal that unemployment rates are traditionally higher in urban areas than in rural areas, As against an unemployment rate of 10.3 percent in 1977-78 in urban areas, the rural unemployment rate was 7.7 percent (CDS basis). There was a significant fall in the rural unemployment rate in 1987-88 to 5.3 percent, but the urban unemployment rate was of the order of 9.4 percent, significantly higher. After 1993-94, the period of liberalkisation rural unemployment rate again increased to 7.2 percent while urban unemployment also marginally increased to 7.7 percent during 1993-94 to 1999-2000.

Table 4: Unemployment Among Urban and Rural Areas (As Percent of Labour Force)

Survey Period	*Rural areas*			*Urban areas*		
	Male	*Female*	*Persons*	*Male*	*Female*	*Persons*
1977-78	7.1	9.2	7.7	9.4	14.5	10.3
1983	7.5	9.0	7.9	9.2	11.0	9.5
1987-88	4.6	6.7	5.3	8.8	12.0	9.4
1993-94	5.6	5.6	5.6	6.7	10.5	7.4
1990-2000	7.2	7.3	7.2	7.2	9.8	7.7

Unemployment rate on current daily status basis.

Source: National Sample Survey Organization surveys.

Population Manpower and Labour Force

We observe from table 5, that the growth of population has decreased from 2.12 percent in 1983-94 to below 2 percent in 1994-2000. Due to increase in life expectancy, the proportion of population of senior citizens (those belonging to the 60 + age group) has increased, affecting the age structure of the population. As a result, the growth of labour force (i.e., working population minus voluntary unemployed persons like housewives, etc.) has also declined from 2.05 percent in 1983-94 to 1.03 percent in 1994-2000. Hence, the proportion of labour force to total population has also declined from 43 percent in 1983-94 to 40.4 percent in 1994-2000. The rate of increase in total employment, as well as employment in organised sector has declined in 1994-2000 from 1983-94. Also the average annual growth rate of employment in unorganized sector has also declined from 2.23 percent in 1983-94 to 1.05 percent 1994-2000.

Table 5: Population, Labour Force and Employment in Organised Sector in India

Sector	*Employment in Million*			*Growth rates (percent per annum)*	
	1983	1984	1994-2000	1993-94	1994-2000
1. Total population	718.21	895.05	1004.10	2.12	1.93
2. Total labour force	308.64	382.18	406.05	2.05	1.03
3. Total employment*	302.75	374.45	397.00	2.04	0.98
4. Employment in organized sector of which	24.01	27.37	28.11	1.20	0.53
-Public sector	16.46	19.44	19.41	1.52	-0.03
-Private sector	7.55	7.93	8.70	0.45	1.87
5. Employment in unorganized sector	278.74	347.08	368.89	2.23	1.05
6. Employment in organised sector as %of total employment	7.93	7.30	7.08		
7. Total labour force as percentage of population	43.00	42.70	40.40		

*Total employment figures indicate usual status basis i.e., persons employed for most part of the year.

Growth rate of employment in public sector has declined to a negative growth rate of –0.03 percent in 1994-2000 due to government's policy of downsizing public sector labour force and voluntary retirement schemes. But interestingly, the organised sector shows and increase in employment rate from less than half percent per annual to 1.87 percent per annum during 1983-94 to 1994-2000.

Impact on Sector Employment : The table 6 shows that the employment in primary sector has declined by 5.33 percent from 1993-94 to 1999-2000, whereas the secondary and tertiary sectors show improvement. The share of tertiary sector increase in employment is largest (73.2 percent).

Table 6: Sector Wise Employment

	1993-94 (million)	*1999-2000 (million)*	*Change in employment during 1993-94 to 1999-2000 (Annual average)*	*Share in increase / decrease percentage*
Primary	245.16	239.83	-5.33	-23.6
Secondary	55.53	69.91	11.38	50.4
Tertiary	73.76	90.26	16.50	73.2
Total	374.45	397.00	22.55	100.00

Source: For table Economic Liberalization and its Implications for Employment in India: Rudra Datt. 84th Conference Number of IEA Dec.2001.

To conclude the slowing down, rather stagnancy in growth rate reflects on continue distortion in the contours of the economy. It has resulted in mounting unemployment and poverty. The tenth plan seek to create one crore jobs. But the present state of industrial and agricultural trend are not employment oriented. The development of serviced sector is complementary to those two sectors.

Danger of 'Growth with Inflation' is better than Recession with No Growth. An reoriented budgetary and monetary policy along with social sector reforms particularly rural development is the need of the time in India.

Need for Rural Development in India

In the process of liberalization, opening up and competitiveness, the incidence of dis-employment has increased in India resulting in closure of a number of industries in Mumbai, Thane-Belapur, Bhiwandi, Aurangabad, Kanpur, Aligarh, Indore and Several other towns resulting in dis-employment of as many as four lakh people according to and estimate (Chadha G.K., 2000).

The table 7 reveals a highly depressing and in a series dangerous situation for the 1990s compared with the 1980s. For example employment during the 1990s in rural India declined by 1.6 percent every year while in the 1980s, it had registered a highly satisfying rate of expansion of 3.13 percent per annum.

Table 7: Rural and Urban Employment Growth in Pre Reform and Post Reform Period

R/U/Total	*Period*	*Annual growth rate (percentage)*		
		Agriculture and Allied activities	*Non-agricultural activities*	*Total*
Rural	1908-1990	5.62	2.81	3.13
	1990-1998	1.80	-2.15	-1.58
Urban	1980-1990	2.93	2.88	2.88
	1990-1998	3.15	-1.08	-1.01
Total	1980-1990	1.96	2.85	2.99
	1990-1998	3.79	-1.53	-1.27

Source: Govt. of India, Economic Census, 1980, 1990 and 1998, CSO.

(a) School for all children by 2003.
(b) Literacy rate 75 percent from 54 percent.
(c) Infant mortality rate 45 percent from 78 percent.
(d) Forestry 33 percent from 25 percent.
(e) Drinking water to all villages.
(f) Removing pollution from major rivers.

Urban India also tells nearly the same story with a decline in employment during the 1990s by 1.01 percent every year while in the 1980s the growth in employment was nearly 3 percent. There is a decline in employment of nearly 5 percentage points in rural employment and about 4 percentage points in urban employment during the 1990s. This is too harsh reality for the Indian economy to brush aside. Jobless are occurring in areas where the incidence of wage-employment is of higher order, where market forces operate more ruiplessly and where in the future, the economy has to bear the burden of increasing competition from abroad.

Rural India which consists of nearly 6.3 lakhs villages, (about 47 thousand of them are uninhabited ones), accommodates 628.7 million people i.e., about three fourths of India's total ;population according to the 1991 census (Census of India, 1998: 1-2).

India which is one of the largest developing countries in the world, ranks 138th as per the HDR, 1997. Though it has been successful in bringing down the poverty level from 55 percent in 1973–74 to 36 percent in 1993 –94 (Economic survey 1997-98) in absolute numbers, the people below the poverty line remain more or less the same. India's infant mortality rate of 75 per thousand live births (IMR) is still one of the highest in the world. As per 1991 census, nearly 48 percent of population continuous to be illiterate and about two-thirds of females are not literate; access to health care availability of potable water, sanitation, shelters are a far cry, particularly in the rural sector, where over three fourths of the population reside.

It is quite evident from the Human Development Index (HDI) (which combines expectation of life at birth, education attainment and the state domestic product per capita) of the population. Foundation of India, the level of development in India is quite low and the situation of rural India is obviously still lower. (The index is similar to the one prepared by the UNDP).

Herein an effort is made to present and overviews of development in some select areas of rural life such as education, health, development of means of transportation and communication and the supply of power. In other words they are the key- social indicators for India's economic growth, which is presented in table 8. These are the important elements of

Fig. 1: Human Development Index for India and Major States, 1997

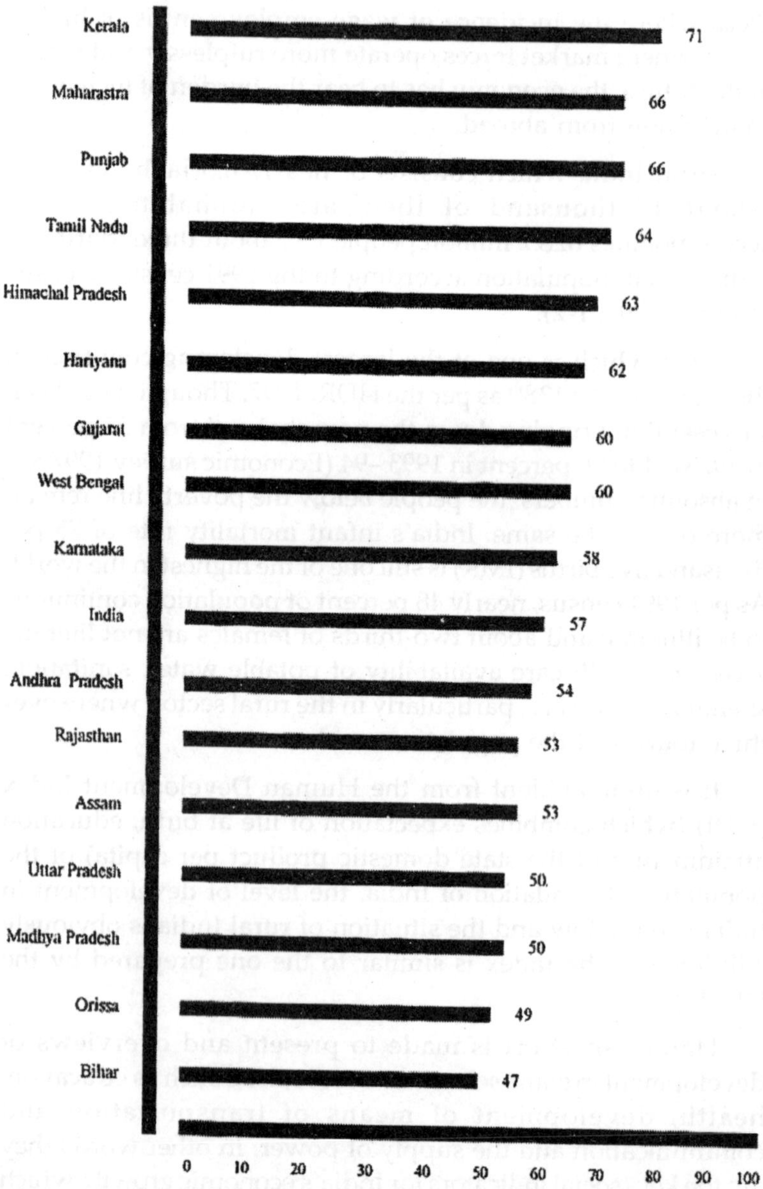

infrastructure for social and economic transformations in the country. Here all these areas are briefly described to throw light on the pitfalls of programmes and policies relating to development in rural areas, which comprise bulk of India's population.

Education

The level of education, compared to most developing countries in the world, is quite low in India, as merely 52 percent of the population were recorded literate at the 1991 census as it is obvious from the latest World Bank report (World Bank, 2000). It is still lower in rural areas, as only 45 percent of the total population is literate as against 73 percent in urban areas (here literacy refers to the number of literates at age 7 and above) according to the 1991 census (the next census is scheduled to be held in February 2001 and the publication of its final results will as usual take fairly long time). This may not be unusual since merely three-fourths of the villages are provided with primary or middle schools in India so far (see table 8). In 1997 there about 28 million children were deprived of school enrolment and most of them were obviously rural children.

There were all together 302 million illiterates in the country at the 1981 census. This number rose 324 million at the 1991 census, marking an addition of about 22 million in a decade. Of 324 million illiterates in the country, 281 million live in rural areas, The population of illiterates in India is larger than the total population of any country in the world except for the people's Republic of China. Every third illiterates in the world is an Indian. This is a very disgraceful distinction. But the real problem is that the number of illiterates is still on increase with the increase in the population.

The level of literacy is much poorer in rural than urban areas, as about 55 percent of the people in rural areas were illiterates, as against 27 percent in urban areas according to the 1991 census. It is true that the current level of education is far below the targets set by the government from time to time, but at the same time the progress made during the post-independent period in the field of education is in a way somewhat satisfying. During 1961-91 the level of rural education climbed from mere 13 percent to 45 percent at the national level in a period of three decades. The enormity of the challenge can be realized from this fact that 10 to 16 million illiterates were added to India's population every year as a consequence of increase of increase in population during 1961-91, making the task of universalization of education increasingly difficult with the lapse of time. In view of this fact the plan for 'Education for All by 2000' quite expectedly ended in a fiasco

Public Health Facilities

For the purpose of initiating and augmenting the pace of development, a good public health system in addition to facilities for education, is also essential. Therefore, there is need to touch briefly upon public health facilities in rural India. As regards the health care facilities in rural areas it is a well known fact that for three-fourths of the total population in rural areas there are less than one-fifth of hospital, less than half of the dispensaries and less than one-fifth of the hospital and dispensary beds in the country. Currently in urban areas 80 percent of the population can avail of facilities for medical treatment within a distance of less than two kilometers, while this advantage is available to merely three percent of the population in rural areas. In fact, more than 20 percent of the people in these areas can get these facilities only at a distance of ten kilometers or more.

Presently about one-third of the villages are covered by the government health services-the only public services available for the rural poor (see table 8).

Rural Electrification

The rural electrification gained momentum with the introduction of minimum needs programme' in the fifth five year plan. In the eighth five year plan, as against the annual target of 3,708 villages for electrification, the achievement till the end of November 1994 was 1.143 villages. Similarly, during

Table 8: Availability of Infrastructure Facilities in Rural India, 1991

Facilities	*Percentage of villages @*	*Facilities*	*Percentage of villages@*
Educational facility		**Drinking water**	
Any education facility	74.8	Well	69.8
Primary school	72.8	Tank	14.3
Middle school	19.3	River	10.0
Secondary school	7.7	Fountain	2.6
Jr. College Hr. Sec. Sr. Sec. Sch	1.3	Canal	3.5
Degree college	0.3	Lake	0.1
Adult literacy center	7.1	Spring	1.7
Industrial training school	0.1	Nala	3.6
Other training schools	0.2	Others	4.5
Any other	3.8		
		Electricity	
Medical facility		Any purpose	69.5
Any medical facility	33.0	Domesticpurpose	63.6
Primary health sub-center	6.7	Agriculture purpose	45.4
Dispensary	3.5	Other purposes	27.2
Primary health center	3.0	Allpurposes	24.8

Contd....

Table 8: (Contd....)

Facilities	*Percentage of villages @*	*Facilities*	*Percentage of villages@*
Health center	1.0		
Hospital	1.7	Post, Telegraph & Telephone	
Nursing home	0.3	Any facility	22.7
Maternity & child welfare center	2.3	Post office	22.5
Maternity hime	0.6	Telegraph office #	2.4
Child welfare center	1.9	Telephone connections	2.6
Family planning center	1.9		
T.B. Clinic	0.1	Communication facility	
Community health worker	17.6	Any comm.. Facility	34.4
Registered medical practitioner	6.4	bus stand	33.8
Subsidised medical practitioner	0.5	Railway station	1.4
Others	1.0	Navigable waterways	0.6
Drinking water		**Transportation**	
Any source	99.7	Pucca road	37.0
Hand pump	55.9	Navigable river	0.8
Tube-well	21.1	navigable canal	.1
Tap	18.2	Other waterways	0.2

Source : Census of India, 1997; V.

the year 1994-95, as against the annual target of 2.80 lakh pump sets energisation the achievement reported till November 1994 was 1.92 lakh pump sets.

Ground water irrigates over 50 percent of the agricultural land in India and this percentage has been increasing over the years (Government of India, 1994-95: 21). Electricity is obviously the main source of power for exploiting ground waters. Despite all plans and efforts only 70 percent of the villages were recorded to have power connection at the time of 1991 census.

Transportation and Communication

It can be seen in table 8 that only a little more than one-third of the villages of India enjoy one or the other type of transportation facility. More than 60 percent of the villages are still deprived of pucca road (metalled road). Most rural roads are without any metal work and are of seasonal nature. These roads are seldom motorable during the rainy season. Anyway, a little more than one-third of the villages are provided with transportation facility in terms of bus stands.

Conclusion

Tasks ahead for rural development with an eye to ameliorating the standard of living of the rural populace are quite gigantic and arduous on the face of the country's resource crunch, slow-growing economy and politics of under development.

The tempo of demographic transition in India has been such that from the 1950s onward India's population has doubled every 33 to 37 years. By the time population stabilizes (most likely by the mid-twenty first century), India will have to be burdened with more than two billion people which is a mind-boggling scenario by all means. Under the given situation planning policies and their implementations together with the measures for exercising greater grips over the phenomenon of rapid rise of population need urgent rethinking both on the part of the government as well as the people as an imperative of India's future.

It is also believed that it was because of the close-door economic policy of India that kept the pace of economic development at a slower pace during the post-independence period. It is viewed that a faster pace of globalization of Indian economy is crucial to effect a change in the moribund society and consequent improvement in the quality of life.

At the same time it is contended that unless the pace of social and economic transformations is augmented, no amount of liberalization or globalization and revolution in information technology can help India develop faster. In order to achieve a faster rate of economic development, rural development should receive a still greater attention. Rapid economic development is not possible without adequate development of social sectors. Furthermore, social and economic development is not possible without efficient and honest bureaucracy,.

This makes our economic model elite- centric. Excessive emphasis on growth may lead to appropriation of gains by elite class leaving the poor high and dry. India needs to increase democratization of political institutions at the grass-roots levels, anti-corruption battles, emancipation of women; bottom up community development-a package of reforms compatible with social justice. The current scenario of rural development has already belied the hope of mahatmas Gandhi who is described as the father of the nation. His dreams, as contained in the following observations, still appear to be quite elusive. " I shall work for an India, in which the poorest shall feel that it is their country in whose making they have an effective voice; an India in which there shall be no highclass and low class of people; an India in which all communities shall live in perfect harmon. This is the India of my dreams. I shall be satisfied with nothing less". (Rao, 1970; 73-74)

REFERENCES

(1993), "Ruddar Datt, "New Economic Policy and its Impact on Industrial Relations and Employment in India", *The Indian Journal of Labour Economics*, January-March.

Census of India, (19770, 'Availability of Infrastructural Facilities in Rural Areas of India, An Analysis of Village Directory Data (Census of India, 1991)', New Delhi, Office of the Registrar General, India, Ministry of Home Affairs.

Chadha, G.K., (2000), "Indian Economy Under the WTO Regime, Happenings Non-happenings and Missing Links", Indian Economic Association Annual, 2000.

Ganes Kawadia, (2002), "Trends and Direction of India's Growth Process", *Man and Development,* Vol. XXIV, No. 1, pp. 26-28.

Government of India (1994-95), Annual Report Ministry of Planning and Programme Implementation, New Delhi : Government of India.

Government of India (1994-95), 'Annual Report, Ministry of Planning & Programme Implementation', New Delhi : Government of India.

Indian Journal of Labour Economics, Vol. 43, No. 1, 2000.

Mahajan, D.J., (2002), "Impact of Liberalisation on Employment in India", *Southern Economist,* Vol. 41, No. 3, June 1, pp. 8-10.

Rao, U.S. Mohan (ed.), (1970), The Message of Mahatma Gandhi, 'New Delhi, Publications Division.

Ruddar Datt, 'Indian Economy', S. Chand & Company, New Delhi, pp. 373, 374, 376 & 417.

Singh, J.P., (2001), "Challenges of Rural Development in India", *Social Change,* Vol. 31, No. 4, December.

World Bank (2000), 'World Development Indicators 2000', Washington: World Bank.

28

THE IMPACT OF IRDP ON CREATION OF ASSETS IN THE UNION TERRITORY OF PONDICHERRY– AN EMPIRICAL EVIDENCE

M. Sangararadje & K.Ramachandran

Introduction

During the last 50 years of planning, India has secured many notable social and economic achievements in eradication of significant levels of poverty in rural areas. Since the majority of population lives in rural India, poverty alleviation programmes have acquired renewed importance in rural areas and for these schemes alone the Government of India spends about Rs. 9,000 crore annually. Among several programmes, the Integrated Rural Development Programme (IRDP) was very significant and it was introduced in 1978-79 on a selected area basis and later extended to the entire country in all the 5,011 blocks from October 2, 1980. The main thrust of IRDP is in the creation of productive asset, which in the process of maintenance and operation would lead to generation of additional employment and income. The present paper attempts to evaluate the impact of IRDP on creation of assets.

Several attempts to evaluate the performance of the IRDP have been made by the Government, private organizations and the researchers. Among those, a few studies showed that the IDP did not much in terms of increase in income, employment and asset creations. Those studies have also revealed that there are significant leakages in disbursements of IRDP benefits.

A few other studies have revealed that a positive and dramatic role played by the IRDP is alleviating rural poverty.. With this backdrop, the purpose of the present study is to analyse the impact of IRDP on creation of assets in the Union Territory of Pondicherry. (with special reference to milch animal scheme).

Methodology

The present study is based on primary and secondary sources of data. The empirical analysis is based on the primary data collected from 300 sample households belonging to different class of target groups in four blocks of the Union Territory of Pondicherry. This is a cross section data analysis pertaining to the year 1998-99. In order to choose the sample units, a proportionate stratified random sampling method is adopted.

Since this study is confined to the milch animal assistance under IRDP, it is necessary to consider and appropriate sample size. As per District Rural Development Agency (DRDA) records, out of total 1,317 IRDP beneficiary families, about 945 families were assisted with milch animals during the reference year 1998-99, of which 300 beneficiary households were randomly selected, as the data set of this study.

Asset Determinants in Milch Animal Scheme Under IRDP

To identify the factors determining the asset gain per unit of investment of the sample households as dependent variable, the following linear multiple regression model is fitted.

$$Y = \alpha + \beta_1 X_1 + \beta_2 X_2 + \ldots\ldots\ldots\ldots + \beta_7 X_7 + e$$

Where,

Y = Asset gain per unit of investment (in rupees per household)

(Dependent or impact variable)

α = Constant or intercept

$\beta_1, \beta_2, \beta_3 \ldots\ldots \beta_7$ = Co-efficient of explanatory or independent variables.

$X_1, X_2, X_3 \ldots\ldots X_7$ = Explanatory or independent Variables.

Independent or Explanatory Variables:

X_1 = Subsidy (SUB) – in rupees per thousand.

X_2 = livestock value (LSV) – in rupees per household.

X_3 = Changes in households expenditure (CHE) – in rupees per household.

X_4 = Expenditure on milch animals (MAE) – in rupees per household.

X_5 = Caste–Dummy variable set (DCA)

0 for scheduled caste and 1 for non-scheduled caste.

X_6 = Sex–Dummy variable set (DSX)

0 for female and 1 for male.

X_7 = Family size-Dummy variable set (DFS)

0 for small family ≤ 4 and 1 for big family ≥ 5

e = Random error term or residual

Results and Discussion

Asset gain is measured in terms of the ratio of change in asset before and after the scheme utilization and the scheme loan investment. The best fitted models are presented in table 1.

In the milch animal scheme, a linear multiple regression analysis has provided a reasonable good fit of the functional relationship between asset gain and its explanatory variables. The final estimated regression equation is

$$AG = 1.484 \quad 0.00034\ SUB^{*} + 0.000231\ SV^{*} - 0.000033\ MAE-$$

(3.15) (6.39) (0.71)

$$0.000017\ CHE - 0.2673\ DSEX - 0.0864\ DFS$$

(0.51) (1.16) (0.42)

$\bar{R}^2 = 0.1304$ $F = 8.25$

(293.7)

Note: Figures in brackets refer to 't' values.
*Indicates 1 percent level of significance.

The model accounts for only 13 per cent of the total variation in the derived asset creation from milch animal investment. The value of F (8.25) also reiterates that the sample taken for fitting the model is a representative of the population. In the model, two variables namely subsidy and livestock value are found to be negative and positive significant at one per cent level respectively. The other explanatory variables, such as expenditure on milch animal, change in household consumption expenditure, sex and family size which are not statistically significant.

Across blocks, asset gain determinants model (table 1) exhibit that Karaikal block sample does not represent population (F=1.03). Hence, only the models for other three blocks are considered for explanation excluding Karaikal block. Ariankuppam block seems to be the best in examining the asset creation of the milch animal scheme (F= 44.79). Of the explanatory variables, subsidy has a negative impact on the asset gain, whereas livestock value has found a positively significant in all the selected four blocks. The high value of asset is attributed to the appreciation in value of milch animals as most of them are in milk or in pregnancy.

Table 1: Determinants of Asset Creation Due to Milch Animal Scheme

Sl. No.	*Variables*	*All Blocks*	*Ariankuppam Block*	*Villianur Block*	*Oulgaret Block*	*Karaikal Block*
1.	Constant	1.4842	0.9432	1.7172	1.8124	1.5153
2.	Subsidy	-0.00034*	-0.00037*	-0.00035*	-.00033**	-
		(3.15)	(8.16)	(4.89)	(2.38)	
3.	Livestock value	0.00023*	0.00029*	0.00019*	0.00023*	0.00024***
		(6.39)	(16.65)	(8.71)	(7.29)	(1.84)
4.	Change In household	-0.000017	0.000013	0.000012	-0.000054	-0.00014
	expenditure	(0.52)	(1.23)	(0.55)	(1.27)	(1.02)
5.	Total milch animal	-0.000033	-0.000064*	-0.000059	-0.00012*	-
	expenditure	(0.71)	(3.07)	(1.44)	(2.57)	
6.	Dummy Sex	-0.2673	-0.2532*	-0.1154	0.2835	-0.4995
	Female = 0 Male = 1	(1.16)	(2.57)	(0.78)	(1.27)	(0.67)
7.	Dummy Caste	-	0.0529	-	-	0.5512
	SC = 0 Non SC= 1		(0.52)			(0.79)
8.	Dummy family size	-0.0864	-	-	0.2053	-0.4982
	Small = 0 Large = 1	(0.42)			(1.01)	(0.74)
9.	Adjusted R square	0.1305	0.7352	0.5563	0.7785	0.0231
10.	F value	8.25	44.79	13.12	12.71	1.04
11.	Degrees of Freedom	299	114	73	20	89

Source: Computed from survey data.

Note: *, **, *** - 1 percent, 5 percent and 10 percent levels of significance respectively.
Figures in parentheses indicate 't' values.

It can be seen from the table 1, that the reason for the low asset creation in the investment scheme is due to decrease in the milk production. Moreover, the beneficiary has misused the funds, for clearing old debts, hence the loan amount turned out to be a low investment. Thus, the milch animal scheme creates an asset and improves the asset base of the beneficiaries. The milch animal scheme investment may also have an inter-alia impact in creating additional assets as a result of reinvestment of surplus derived from the scheme. Hence, an attempt is made to assess the impact of milch animal investment in creating and additional asset base to the beneficiaries.

Assistance to buy milch animals is primarily to add productive assets to the households which have no or insufficient land to sustain their family. Continuous and proper maintenance of animals would ensure not only generation of income but also stability in it. Therefore, the expectation of the scheme in adding this asset is removal of poverty through generation of gainful employment and sufficient income.

Summary and Implications

According to the field survey observation, subsidy variable is one of the dominant factor which is found to be of negative significance with the asset creation of the milch animal beneficiaries under IRDP. Among the livestock variable in the asset creation model of the scheme, it seems to be of positive significance determinant of the beneficiaries. In the context of milch animal scheme under IRDP, milch animal expenditure, sex, family size and caste are not influencing the acquiring of assets. Thus, the milch animal scheme under IRDP creates an asset and improves the asset base of beneficiaries. Taking all blocks together in the Union Territory of Pondicherry, the average asset value has increased by 61.96 percent in post IRDP period. Thus, it reveals that while the loan amount has been increasing, there has been an increase in asset creation among the beneficiaries.

To conclude, the milch animal scheme under IRDP in the Union Territory of Pondicherry is found to be satisfactory. The findings arrived at in this investigation show that the milch animal scheme is the most superior, suitable and easy to practice. Therefore, it should be continued and be treated as the most important component of the anti poverty programme in the Union Territory of Pondicherry.

REFERENCES

Arora, R.C., (1979), "Integrated Rural Development", S. Chand and Company, New Delhi.

Bala Ramulu Ch., (2000), "Technology and Rural Development-Need for Organizational Renewal", Rawat Publications, New Delhi.

Bhanja, S.K. and Venkatadri, S., (1988), "Milch Cattle in Integrated Rural Development Programme", National Institute of Rural Development, Hyderabad.

Bhagyalakshmi, J., (2001), "New Initiatives for Poverty Alleviation", *Yojana,* Vol. 45, No. 11, pp. 12-13.

Desai, Vasanth, (1988), "Rural Development", Himalaya Publishing House, Bombay.

Dhanasekaran, K., (1985), "The Impact of IRDP on Rural Poverty", *Social Science Digest,* Vol III, No.7, pp. 47-48.

Dubhashi, P.R., (1996), "Essays on Rural Development", Kaveri Books, New Delhi.

Hebbar C.K., (1991), "Integrated Rural Development Programme-Retrospect and Prospect", Deep and Deep Publications, New Delhi.

Kannpiran, C., (1992), "Financial impact of IRDP on Rural Poverty in India", *Journal of Rural Development,* Vol. 2, No. 6, pp. 789-801.

Kurien, C.T., (1987), 'Poverty, Planning and Social Transformation', Allied Publishers Private Limited, New Delhi.

Laxmi Devi, (1997), "Policies, Methods and Strategies in Rural Development", Anmol Publications Private Limited, New Delhi.

Ray, C.N., (1992), "Implementation of IRDP-A Comparative Study of West Bengal and Gujarat," *Journal of Rural Development,* Vol. II, No. 1, pp. 69-100.

Ramadass M., (1993), "Economic Development of Pondicherry", Rina Publications, Chennai.

Satapathy, K.M., (1991), "IRDP-Impact of Income Generation", *Yojana,* Vol. XXXV, No. 5, pp. 19-21.

Venkatadri, S., (1998), "Income Generation Process in Dairy Scheme Under IRDP", *Journal of Rural Development,* Vol. 17, pp. 1-13.

29

NEW ECONOMIC POLICY : SOME EMERGING CONCERNS ON RURAL DEVELOPMENT AND HUMAN PROGRESS

P. Arumugam, A. Balasubramanian & G. Senthil Kumar

"The battle of life is, in most cases fought uphill ... if there were no difficulties there would be no success; if there were nothing to struggle for, there would be nothing to be achieved."

—Samuel Smiles in 'Self Help'

Introduction

Economic reforms started in a slow, fragmented and limited way in the eighties and gathered momentum and clear direction in the nineties. Since 1991, Indian economy has been exposed to economic liberalization and globalisation in line with structural adjustment and stabilization policies initiated by IMF and World Bank. Structural adjustment policy advocated privatisation, import liberalization, and export-led growth while stabilization policy emphasizes reduction in fiscal deficit through withdrawal of subsidies given to industry, trade and agriculture. There has been a shift in the Indian economic policy from State-oriented development strategy to market-oriented development, leaving the decisions of production and distribution to the market signals. This policy became controversial as some argued in favour of it while others argued against it (G. Parthasarathy, 2003).

As we entered new millennium, this poses both a challenge and an opportunity. We must accelerate economic growth in the first two decades of the 21st century so as to eliminate poverty and under-employment. We must ensure human development and empowerment of the poor, by ensuring 100 percent literacy and universal primary education. The experience of other countries in Asia shows that it is possible to raise growth to 7 percent, to maintain it for two decades and thus generate full employment, and provide 100 percent literacy. Basic minimum services must be provided to all. To ensure environmental sustainability and quality of life population growth will have to be contained. And all this must be done in a manner that promotes peoples' participation and builds self-reliance and human dignity.

Economic Policy of India: Old and New

India initiated planning for national economic development with the establishment of the Planning Commission in 1950. The aim of the First Five Year Plan (1951-56) was to raise domestic savings for growth and help the economy resurrect itself from the twisted wreckage caused by colonial exploitation and the aftermath of partition. The real break with the past in planning came with the Second Five Year Plan (celebrated as the Nehru-Mahalanobis Plan). The industrialization strategy articulated by Professor Mahalanobis placed emphasis on the development of heavy industries and envisaged a dominant role for the public sector in the economy. The entrepreneurial role of the state was evoked to develop the industrial sector. Commanding heights of economy were entrusted to public sector.

In brief, the emphasis of the first three Five Year Plans was on economic growth with marginal stress on institutional changes like land reforms. The objectives of industrial policy were: a high growth rate, national self-reliance, reduction of foreign dominance, building up of indigenous capacity, encouraging small scale industry, bringing about balanced regional development, prevention of concentration of economic power, reduction of income inequalities and control of economy by the State. During the Second Plan period, the emphasis was to build heavy industries which would lay down the basis of rapid industrialization ("machines to build machines"). The planners and policy makers suggested the need for using a wide variety of instruments like state allocation of investment, licensing and other regulatory controls to steer Indian industrial development on a closed economy basis.

The performance of India's economic plans speaks of both our success and certain setbacks and reveals the extent to which we plugged the gaps in our development. The long term growth rate of Gross Domestic Product (GDP) during the period 1950-51 to 1994-95 was around 3.8 percent per annum while population increased at the rate of 2 percent per annum and per capita GDP remained less than 2 percent.

The turn around in growth rates for macro aggregates started in the 1980s and continues in the 1990s. During the period 1980-95, GDP growth was more than 5 percent per annum. Regarding the period of economic reforms, after showing negative growth in the first year of the reform period (1991-92), GDP growth recovered in 1992-93. The GDP growth has been around 7 percent since 1994-95. Thus, the Eighth Plan is likely to end with an average growth of 6.5 percent per annum. More important for the future is the fact that the average growth during the last three years is 7 percent, probably placing India among the top ten performers in the world during this period. The economy seems to be on a new path of higher growth.

The importance of agriculture in the Indian economy is well known. There appears a general consensus that agricultural policies have and economy-wide impact and that there is a direct correlation between Indian agricultural performance and the standards of living of a majority of our populatio,. In terms of growth, the performance of agriculture has been quite impressive in the post-independence period (a long term growth of 2.7 percent per annum) as compared to the pre-independence period (0.3 percent per annum).

An important feature of the 1980s and the 1990s, however, is that there has been much more equitable spread of agricultural growth. Not having done well during the early years of the Green Revolution, many of the states like Assam, Bihar, Orissa, Madhya Pradesh and West Bengal showed significant growth in the 1980s. Oilseeds have also gained in the dry belt of Rajasthan, Madhya Pradesh, Karnataka and Maharashtra. Thus, there seems to be a reduction in regional disparities in output growth during the 1980s and 90s. (Abid Hussain, 1999).

Finally, it may be noted that the country's current engagement in the process of industrialization and economic development, and its efforts at integration with the global economy, require quality basic education with high enrolment rates and a functioning system of education down to the rural school. It is heartening to note that India has already created an infrastructure to cater to that need. We can take pride in the fact that India has the third largest scientific and technical manpower on the world.

India thus is determined to become the sixth major power in the coming decades. A bright future is bound to usher in. We are not only the children of our time but makers of tomorrow.

Economic Reforms for Rural Development

"India lives in its villages" –Mahatma Gandhi.

Literally and from the social, economic and political perspectives the statement is valid even today. Around 65 percent of the State's population is living in rural areas. People in rural areas should have the same quality of life as is enjoyed by people living in sub-urban and urban areas. Further there are cascading effects of poverty, unemployment, poor and inadequate infrastructure in rural areas on urban centres causing slums and consequential social and economic tensions manifesting in economic deprivation and urban poverty. Hence Rural Development which is concerned with economic growth and social justice, improvement in the living standard of the rural people by providing adequate and quality social services and minimum basic needs becomes essential.

If Rural Development is to be stepped up, there is a need to raise investments in agriculture, especially in power, surface irrigation and rural roads, all of which are generally in the public sector domain and in the States sector. However public sector investments in Indian agriculture have been declining in real terms since 1980-81. Private sector investment in agriculture (mainly groundwater irrigation and agricultural machinery) has been increasing, partly in response to improving terms of trade, but even this has slowed down in recent years. In any case private investment is not a substitute for public investment in all areas. In fact it can be argued that additional public investment in critical areas of agricultural and rural infrastructure is crucial and private investment would go up further once investment in such rural infrastructure picks up.

Investing in rural infrastructure is child up by lack of resources, and to mobilize these resources we must rationalize subsidies in agriculture by carrying out price and institutional reforms in power, canal irrigation and fertilizer sectors. To check the real costs of power and canal irrigation, which are basically natural monopolies, the role of independent Regulatory Commissions would be critical.

Expenditure on R & D for agriculture is not covered under 'investments in agriculture' as defined by CSO but R&D expenditures are critical for the long-term growth of this sector. Public spending on R&D has been only 0.46 percent of agricultural GDP during 1992-97. This is way below the average of about 1.5 percent for developing countries as a group, and about 3 percent in a developed country like the USA.

While there is need to increase public expenditure on R&D for agriculture, there is a much greater need to carry out major institutional hangs in the functioning of our agricultural research organizations. There is reason to believe that our agricultural research organizations have become bureaucratized and are not functioning as research institutions would. They need to chalk out their own agenda of research, work with international and national organizations as well as private sector concerns and exchange personnel and students.

Inadequate seed replacement rates and uncertain quality of seed is a major constraint in raising agricultural productivity. It is necessary to contemplate major reforms in the seeds sector on the following lines:

(i) State seed farms should be converted into joint venture companies with the private sector. The state should be a minority holder. Let the farms be managed by companies on a commercial basis.

(ii) Private seed companies should be exempt from land ceiling laws to develop test and then multiply their seeds for sale on a large scale. We should be aiming, with the help of these companies, and in association with ICAR, to become a major supplier of seeds not only within India but also to the developing world. India has a comparative advantage in seed development and seed companies need to be given similar priority as is being given to software companies.

(iii) To facilitate the entry of seed companies on a large scale, contentious issues related to IPR will have to be resolved in a transparent manner, keeping the interests of farmers in mind.

Agro-processing is a major area for further development of the value addition starting with agricultural production. This sector represents a link between agriculture and industry and holds the prospect for creating good quality jobs in the non-agriculture sector in the rural areas. An urgent review of policies in this area is needed to identify the reasons why this sector is not developing as it has in other countries.

Development Programmes

Within the broad framework of policy, the government has undertaken a wide variety of programmes in agriculture to build up the physical and information infrastructures necessary for sustained development. There are programmes for the betterment of the rural population.

- Research, education and extension programmes;
- Irrigation development schemes,
- Plans to increase the supply of agricultural inputs, such as seeds, fertilizers, and pesticides,
- Plans to change the institutional framework of land ownership; plans to improve agricultural financing;
- Better marketing techniques; and
- Plans to improve technology.

These programmes are administered, financed, and run by the central government and by the state governments, and both levels encourage private-sector development through direct or indirect programs.

Some of the specialized programmes introduced during the Fifth Plan in 1990s. Among them were the Small Farmers Development Agency, Minimum Needs Programme, Hill Area Development Programme, and Drought-Prone Areas Programme. In 1989 two other programmes, the National Rural Employment Programme and the Rural Landless Employment Guarantee Programme, were merged into a single programme called the Jawahar Employment Plan (Jawahar Rozgar Yojana; Jawahar in memory of Jawaharlal Nehru [1889-1964], India's first Prime Minister *rozgar* means daily employment in Hindi; and *yojana* means project or plan).

The Integrated Rural Development Programme, launched in FY 1978 and extended throughout India by FY 1980, is a self-employment programme intended to raise the income-generation capacity of target groups among the poor. The aim is to raise recipients above the poverty line by providing substantial opportunities for self-employment. During the seventh plan, the total expenditure under the programme was Rs. 33.2 million (for value of the rupee-see Glossary), and Rs. 53.7 million of term credit was mobilized. Some 13 million new families participated, bringing total coverage under the program to more than 18 million families. These development programme have played an important role in increased agricultural production by educating farmers and providing them with financial and other inputs to increase yields. They have also alleviated some problems of the rural poor. However, further success has been limited by the lack of efficient administrative mechanisms, the limitation of resources, the magnitude of the task, and the lack of willingness to change the status quo. Many of the programme results appear better on paper than the actual results in the field because of lack of implementation and poor monitoring.

Research, Education and Extension

The central government's Department of Agricultural Research and Education was established in 1973 in the Ministry of Agriculture and Rural Development (later, the Ministry of Agriculture). The department is responsible for coordinating research and educational facilities in agriculture, animal husbandry, and fisheries. The department also provides support services to the Indian Council of Agricultural Research.

Higher education has also seen advances. India has twenty-eight agricultural universities, which include 164 colleges specializing in agriculture, veterinary science, agricultural engineering, home science, fisheries, dairy technology, forestry, horticulture, sericulture, food science, and food-handling technology. They are located through most of the states in India. One of them is a central university that has specialized extension colleges in the seven northeastern sates. The undergraduate student enrollment in the early 1990s was around 9,600 and there was a capacity for some 4,500 graduate students (see Colleges and Universities, ch. 2).

Agricultural, animal husbandry, and forestry research is conducted under the auspices of the Indian Council of Agricultural Research, central research institutes, and various commodity committees. The council had forty-six institutes in operation in 1992. India's largest such institute is the Indian Agricultural Research Institute, established in 1905 at Pusa, Bihar. Because of an earthquake at Pusa, the research institute moved to New Delhi in 1936. The institute was later accorded university status.

In addition to these agricultural research and educational institutions, the Indian Council of Agricultural Research also has a large network of organizations to disseminate agricultural technology information. In the mid–1990s, there were national centers used to demonstrate new crop varieties and production technologies in fourty-eight districts throughout the country. There also were seventy nationwide coordinated research projects operating at 120 centers to test specific production technologies.

Monitorable Targets for Tenth Plan

- Reduction of Poverty to 10 percent by 2006-07 and near elimination by 2012.
- All weather roads to rural habitations having population above 500 by 2004.
- Formation of 1.25 lakh Self Help Groups.
- Integrated Sanitary Complex for women in all Panchayats by 2003.
- Augmentation of water storage capacity of 12,618 village panchayat tanks through renovation.
- Training to 63,044 local bodies elected representatives including SHGs & officials to improve skill and capacity building.
- The goal is reduction of poverty from 21.12 percent in 1999-2000 to 10 percent by 2006-07 and near elimination by 2012. Poverty reduction will be attempted.

- By organizing the rural masses into self-help groups and the establishment of micro-enterprises, training, credit linkages, market support, etc. by substantial flow of investment in physical infrastructure like roads, water supply and social infrastructure like health, education and nutrition.
- Special efforts for generation of adequate employment and creation of durable community assets to improve the rural people especially the small farmers, marginal farmers, rural artisans etc., through programmes like Sampoorna Grameen Rozgar Yojana (SGRY).
- Decentralization of the process of planning by entrusting major role to the Panchayati Raj bodies in the preparation of local level planning.
- Improving the efficiency and capacity of the officials and elected local body representatives.
- Providing all weather roads to all rural habitations having a population above 500 by 2004.
- Strengthening of Grama Sabha the governing body of village assembly as an agency of social audit and to review the implementation of programmes.
- Special efforts will be made to converge various schemes and programmes for accelerating the development process through special schemes like Village Self-sufficiency Scheme etc.
- Emphasis will be given for the maintenance of the assets created under various schemes.

Conclusion

While it is easy to point out the many reforms that could make a difference in India, it is not possible to pinpoint those that would achieve the greatest gains and since policy makers have only limited capacity for implementing reforms at any given time, knowledge of the potential gain could guide the choice of next target for reforms.

Agriculture is, and will remain, the base of our economy. The reform to the economy to make it more efficient and competitive will not be complete, or even successful, without extending it to the agricultural sector so that sector can become a major engine of growth and indeed become a safety net for the reform process as a whole and for its contribution to ecological improvement.

Agriculture has thus to get into the mainstream of reform from the point of view of our national objectives of stimulating growth, generating employment, alleviating poverty, providing essential commodities for domestic consumption and the raw material for industry, a market for the rest of the economy and strong support for our international payments.

India cannot achieve prosperity without agriculture. Prosperity, and agriculture prosperity in turn calls for enhancement of productivity, efficiency and profitability, which is what any programme of structural reform in any sector is all about.

REFERENCES

Anne, O. Krueger , "Economic Policy Reforms and the Indian Economy" Oxford Publication, 2002.

Narasimham, M., "Economic Reforms Development and Finance", UBSPD, 2002.

Patel I.G. Dr., "Economic Reforms a Medium Term Perspective" Recommendations of Prime Minister's Economic Advisory Council, 2002.

Rahul Mudgal, "Economic Dimensions of Rural Development" Sarup and Sons Publication, 1996.

Tenth Plan Proposal (2002-2007).

30

STRATEGIC PLANNING & TECHNIQUES FOR RURAL DEVELOPMENT— FUTURISTICS VIEW

Muaaz Hussein Mohamed &
S.P. Kanaga Anbuselvam

Introduction

For the achievement of the above-mentioned objectives, the ninth plan has put in a growth scenario for the economy. There are two scenarios, one with the growth rate at 6.2 percent called the base line growth scenario, and the second one with the growth rate at 7.0 percent, called the accelerated growth scenarios. We are dealing with the second scenario being more desirable as this is the one that is to be implemented, the other one for substantially reducing unemployment and alleviating poverty. The objective of the ninth plan is thus a growth rate 7 percent. The common minimum programme announced by Government for the attainment of a given growth rate one needs investment. As for the sources, domestic savings, the public sector and public enterprises will contribute 2.8 percent of GDP. The private corporate sector has to contribute 4.5 percent of GDP, and the household sector 18.9 percent of GDP to achieve the above-mentioned target, and development in the related fields where certain achievements have to be ensured. For example, it has been assumed that for a 7 percent growth-rate of the economy, agriculture will grow at 4.5 percent per annum, and industry at 9.3 percent per annum as shown in Table 1.

The rural development is sought with a view to reducing the incidence of poverty in rural areas where it is very acute. For this the various special programmers like Integrated Rural Development, Jawahar Rozgar Yojana, and Development of Women and Children, etc. implying direct intervention of the state, with the other programmers as well the area development programmers within the umbrella of the Panchayti Raj Institutions, as shown in Table 1 have to be implemented.

Table 1: Projection of Nation Poverty Ratios (Percent)

Region	*1996-97*	*2001-02*	*2006-07*
Rural	30.55	18.61	9.64
Urban	25.28	16.46	9.28
Total	29.18	17.98	9.53

Source: Planning commission, Ninth Five Year Plan (1997-2002), Vol. 1, February 1999.

Village and small industries have a great potential for employment, more amenable to widespread regional dispersal and are considerably elastic in responding to changes in the market. They have the great potential for rising the out put and exports. As present they hold an important position in the economy with 40 percent of production in the manufacturing sector, and 35 percent exports as shown in Table 2.

The rate of growth of WTO, India is committed to becoming a more open economy within a stipulated time frame and the preconditions for successfully managing an open trade require need to be created within the ninth plan period. Also, greater flow of external investment resource that has been planned for accelerating the growth rate of the economy necessitates collateral planning for the future stream in payments. The rate of growth of imports can be sustained at 10.8 per annum on an average during the ninth plan, fielding an implicit elasticity of imports to GDP of 1.7 as compared to 1.5 during the Eighth Plan. The growth rate of exports has been targeted to 11.8 percent per annum over the Ninth Plan period.

Table 2: Balance of Payment and its Financing in the Ninth Five Year Plan

(Rs. "000 Crores in 1996-97 prices)

Items	*1996-97*	*2001-02*	*Ninth*	*Plan*
Exports	117.3	205.1	800.9	(10.1)
Imports	132.2	221.0	936.1	(12.2)
Trade Balance	-14.9	-15.9	-135.2	(-1.8)
Net Invisibles	0.5	-2.0	24.6	(-0.3)
Current A/c Balance	14.4	-17.9	-159.8	(-2.1)
Financed By				
Net External Assistance	0.5	1.0	7.7	(0.1)
Net External Debt	15.3	5.9	53.9	(0.7)
Foreign Capital in Flow	8.7	10.7	92.3	(1.2)
Investment	9.3	4.8	23.1	(0.3)
Total Capital in Flow	34.0	22.4	177.0	(2.3)
Charge in Reserves	20.8	4.5	17.2	(0.3)

Source: Planning commission, ninth five year plan (1997-2002), Vol. 1, February 1999.

In the plan allocations of the public sector outlay, reflecting the priorities of the plan, agriculture including irrigation and rural development 19.8 percent, social services 21.2 percent, energy 25.1 percent and transport 14.1 percent, account for about 80 percent of the total outlay. (table 3)

Research and Development

Research and Development is perhaps the most neglected activity in KVI. There are several institutions, agencies and individuals working on KVI problems in isolation. There is therefore a need for technological documentation, transmission of information, co-ordination and supervision over the work

Table 3: Proposed Public Sector out lay by Major Heads of Development

(Rs. Crore as 1996-97 prices)

Sector's	*Total*	*% of total*
Agriculture and Allied Activities	73,546	4.4
Irrigation and Floor Control	55,598	6.5
Rural Development	73,439	8.5
Special Programme	3,649	0.4
Energy	2,15,545	25.1
Industry & Minerials	69,972	8.1
Transport	1,21,324	14.1
Communication	47,616	5.5
Science, Technology & Environment	25,529	3.0
General and Economic Services	26,978	3.1
Social services	1,82,005	21.2
Total	8,59,201	99.9

Source: Planning commission, ninth five year plan (1997-2002), Vol. 1, February 1999.

in progress and dissemination of information. This is a highly specialized work and requires attention form competent experts several committees have stressed that drive, direction and constant supervision should be periodically organized. The committee found lack of interest on the part of national research bodies to discuss KVI issues. KVIC has to shoulder this responsibility. Today, the allocations are not adequate for the task. Without quality testing and quality control, KVI products will not stand competition. ISI standards have to be fixed. There are several unexplored areas where R & D can do miracles and for this leadership has to come from KVIC.

Agro-Industries

Here the common man means the one living in rural India who earns his livelihood by toiling in the fields or one who is engaged in some rural crafts. He is the true representative of India, and until his life becomes liveable, we cannot boast of achieving any development. All our developmental efforts appear to be lopsided, because they are not aimed at improving the life of those people when represent real India. The objective of our development plan appears to be only to increase the Gross Domestic Product (GDP) and not its equitable distribution. Khadi and village industries are the backbone of Indian economy. They are adjunct to agriculture. Without Khadi and village industries, agriculture alone cannot sustain the village economy, because agriculture is a seasonal occupation. Agro-industries are only supplementary to agriculture.

This is the real economic scenario of Rural India. Unless rural India prospers India as a whole cannot prosper. Any plan drawn up for development of India should aim at the development of agriculture and agro-industries like Khadi and village industries.

Environment

Of late the environment is favourable to khadi and village industries sector. During the last tow or three years the production of khadi and village industries has considerably suffered. Many small institutions engaged in this programme have already been closed. The rest are striving for existence. Huge stocks have piled up in the institutions leaving no scope for further production. Lakhs of spinners and weaves are thrown out of employment. The greatest trait of khadi sector is that it is labour intensive. What we need today is employment generation. This is the major task before Indian Government. The government cannot fulfil its task of employment generation by neglecting the khadi and village industries sector.

Employment

Thus the question that faces now in the KVIC sector and other rural industries is how to cope up with the new situation, particularly provide major support to rural population.

The past decade's experience has been grim in so for as khadi and village industries are concerned. We have not been able to provide worthwhile support to a large number of people affected by the new economy. We certainly cannot remain sitting on the fence and have to make a positive move which is in consonance with changed times. The main issue is the need for creating sufficient alternative employment. A venue for the rural population and weaving them away from the no longer sustainable khadi sector as well as other traditional activities which can no longer be artificially supported when they have failed to stand on their own during the last 50 years.

We have Gram Panchayats active in practically every village and this has been a big achievement during the past decade. We have not used this dynamic institution for changing the economic profile of rural areas. It is well known that there is heavy backlog in rural development programme, which in fact constitutes the backbone of national development itself. The reference is obviously to the seniors dearth even of elementary infrastructure without which rural and urban cannot move in unison. Little surprise that most of the development under recent globalization has remained confined mainly to urban areas. How can you expect new economy to make deep impact when two thirds of population is out of its orbit? Thus sooner rural areas are made integral part of urban economy better if it would be the whole nation and this can be done through a network of basic infrastructure facilities rural roads, irrigation channels, drinking water facilities, dispensaries and schools. In fact there is a vast agenda of rural infrastructure to be completed before the nation can make sustainable progress and provide gainful employment to its people here. Panchayats should be brought to a status tone to execute these programme with both technical assistance which would yield long-term results. The modification of this programme should be worked out with care and this programme should be carried out under the leadership of panchayats.

Thus it is no longer khadi industries should have occupied a prominent place. We should have moved away from them much earlier and in its place implemented programmes as outlined above. It has vast growth potential and can generate employment particularly for those who are unskilled and illiterate. It is therefore time that Khadi and village industries commission change to rural infrastructure and technology commission and thus plays a significant role in these areas which are in consonance with the current policy of globalization which hitherto has remained confined to urban areas and made little penetration in the rural areas. It would be effectively accomplished by the new role of khadi and village industries commission.

KVI Part of Rural Development

There is one important issue, which is being faced time and again. It is regarding the place of KVI as a part of rural development or part of development of industry. This question cannot be a screened in either this or that fashion. Since KVI is operating primarily in rural areas many of the industries have closer links with agriculture, either by supplying raw materials or by utilizing rural man power or by marketing or by supplying of inputs like instruments etc. These are part of overall rural development. But at the same time, each individual industry has parental relationship with the industry to which, it forms part first as khadi is also part of textile industry or Ghani oil part of Edible oil industry. Obviously, any development in a particular industry has effect on its traditional partner. So for eveloving a policy this relationship cannot be over looked because ultimately, market forces operate in the commercial world. Thus while undertaking a development effort for any the V.I.S all have to keep in view the requirements of rural development and only a body at the center can perform all work related to the industry and to have a proper control over the industry. In future, such a measure would be required. Similarly, the state KVI Boards have to discharge effectively their dual responsibility towards the respective state governments. However, development resources and support and guidance will be provided by KVIC. If this is not done properly, the successful operation of the industry will not be ensured.

Methodology and Techniques

The study will employ conventional tools of management studies, like cost of production and profitability ratios in order to evaluate the performance of the industries under study. Also the exercise will build models of production planning and inventory control like Q-model, Mini-max model, Just-in-time, TQM and OPT Techniques. Case study method was followed to study the topic supplemented by both participants of non-participant observation techniques during the fieldwork. An interview schedule was formulated to investigate the case under analysis to elucidate from the respondents (staff) engaged in same filled, management and planning and decision making who are having experience. The study has been supported with secondary data taken form management official records and published books and literatures.

Smoothing and decomposition methods of time-series for forecasting are empirically based and are very appealing to practitioners due to their operation simplicity cost of use low computational cost and accuracy of the costs involved. Both the categories lack, of course, the rigour of statistical findings. Smoothing methods attach wrights to past observations in a time series to average the random errors, and provide a smooth forecast. It breaks down the time series into its major components. The seasonality, the trend, the cycling, and the randomness extrapolate the pattern of each of these components and combine them into a final forecast.

Smoothing Methods

There exist two broad categories of smoothing methods namely moving average methods, and exponential smoothing methods. Exponential smoothing methods, are more popular since they require less data storage space and applicable to a very wide range of cases. In this data therefore, more emphasis is laid on these methods than on others.

Exponential Smoothing Methods

Herein the weights attached to the time-series data decrease exponentially and data from the most recent back ward in time. Thus if the weight to the most recent data is "a", the data of one period is given the weight: the weight 'a(1-a)'. The data at 2 periods back are given the weight 'a(1-a)^{2}'. Thus, the sum of the exponentially weighted data must represent and average of the data series and this is called exponential smoothing. The exponentially weighted average is given as:

$X_t = X_{t-1} + a(X_t - X_{t-1})$ whereas $(X_t - X_{t-1})$ is a forecast error. The constant 'a' is called "a smoothing constant".

Single Exponential Smoothing Method

A time-series data may change from one stationary condition to another. A single exponential smoothing method will take along time to track it. The better way to track such changes is to assume a higher value of 'a' once. The forecast error is appreciable, and to revert back to a small value as forecast error is within limit. Continuous adaptation of the smoothing constant is possible by the following equations.

$X_t = \text{At } X_t + (1 + a_t) X_{t-1}$

Where a_{t-1} = (E_t/M_t) E_t = smoothing error, M_t = smoothed absolution error, C_t = forecast error.

Initial values of E_t and M_t are usually taken as zeros often, the maximum value of 'a' is limited to 0.5.

A somewhat different approach is to compute a tracking signal T_t= E_t/M_t with b = 0.1; if the value exceeds 0.51, then the forecast errors are correlated, and a higher value of 'a' is needed.

Normative Forecasting

Normative forecasting is moistly goal oriented forecasting, so that it is primarily need-based forecasting. In normative approach it is emphasized that the future is not fixed, many things may occur, and administrators and managers and policy makers should explore the various possibilities and then set norm or goal to choose and prefer a future and try to realize it (Seth, 1989).

Analytical Hierarchy Process (AHP)

The AHP is a multiple objective, multiple criterion decision-making approach employs multiple comparisons to rank order after native solution to a problem is formulated in hierarchical terms (Saaty and Kearns, 1985). Analytical Hierarchy process was chosen for ranking the various raw materials, working in progress and finished goods etc. That emerged during the interview schedule. The industries were ranked on the basis of cumulative weight age of the attitude criteria.

Scenario

A scenario is a sequence of events; scenarios are narrative and mathematical manifestations of a future state of affairs. It helps to grasp the vision of the future (Seth, 1989). Their scenario included, one role of KVIC as usual scenario, the next to the present thrust on industries and the third of the increased production of KVIC.

Factor Analysis

The factor analysis is a technique by which subjective probability estimates are commonly used to incorporate individual judgment into forecasting. However, this approach handless the forecasting problem somewhat differently. The previously mentioned assessment procedures generally aim at a single point estimate (the expected value of a random variable or, more commonly, the most likely value) as the forecast. In the case of subjective probability estimates, and attempt is made to identify a range of values (the probability distribution) for the uncertain event. It is only a finite number of outcomes of the variables as specified, and the judgment assessment involves determining the probabilities associated with each of these outcomes.

They have developed the techniques of decision analysis in regard to alternative procedures for assessing probability distribution as integral part of forecasting and decision-making. It gives a good comprehensive summary of judgment probability assessment methods, including techniques for situations with discrete outcomes. In addition, the decision maker may be able to improve the accuracy of the subjective probability assessment by relating it to historical frequency by understanding more fully the rules of probability assessment and the implications of various shapes in those probability distributions.

Conclusion

One of the cardinal principles in a democracy is that policy and governance should be so oriented that benefits of progress are passed on to its citizens. This should be irrespective of position, status and religion of the constituents. KVIC has been in fore front in doing yeoman's service in this regard. However in the light of changes in economic scenario all around the world, it is imperative that KVIC should have inbuilt flexibility to modify and match changes in its strategy and organization for encouraging bare foot capitalism. This will help KVIC to fulfil the hopes and aspiration of vast multitude of rural folks who have been deprived of basic necessities of life. This has to be delicately balanced while generating employment opportunities for average persons without compromising on viability and efficiency.

REFERENCES

Alan L. Poter, A. Thomas Roper and Thomas W. Mason Jerru Banks and Bradley J. Wiedfer Holl. Forecasting and Management of Technology, USA, 1991.

Bhabtish Datta, Indian Economy through Twentieth Century Perspectives 1900-1950.

British Standards Institution, Guide to Standards Institution, Guide to Stock control (BS5729) 1981.

Churchman, C.W., R.L. Ack off, and E.L. Arnoff, Introduction to Operations Research, John Wiley & Sons, Inc, New York, 1957.

Thompson, G.C. Forecasting Sales, Studies in Business Policy, No. 25, National Industrial Conference Board, Inc., New York, 1947.

31

EMERGING STRATEGIC TECHNIQUES FOR RURAL DEVELOPMENT

N. Murugan & K. Amutha

Introduction

Rural people constitute the greater part of the population of developing countries and often lack access to basic needs such as water, food, education, health care, sanitation and security, leading to low life expectancy and high infant mortality. Knowledge and information are basic ingredients of food security and are essential for facilitating rural development and bringing about social and economic change. According to Albert Waterson, as quoted by Cohen, the purpose of rural development is "to improve the standard of living of the rural population-is multi-sectoral including agriculture, industry, and social facilities". Rural communities require information inter alia on supply of inputs, new technologies, early warning systems (drought, pests, diseases), credit, market prices and their competitors. The success of the Green Revolution in Asia and the Near East indicates that giving rural energising agriculture.

As the full dimensions of the transformation initiated by Information and Communications Technologies (ICTs) has become more widely understood, the means by which these might be integrated into and enhance the opportunities in such areas as "rural development" have begun to come to the fore. But in a context where there are severe limits to the accessibility and utility of the technology particularly for those outside of urban areas and in developed world contexts, the question arises as to how these opportunities might be realized not just in the abstract as a sense of possibility, but within the real context of specific conditions and limitations in the range of developing world contexts and specifically for those in rural areas.

The speed with which the new Information and Communications Technologies (ICTs) and particularly the Internet have advanced in their dispersal and capabilities is truly astonishing. From what was in effect a standing start, in some five years the overall numbers world-wide to some 250,000,00, with those numbers doubling approximately every 18 months. While these numbers are truly astounding, there is a sad disparity as between the access "haves" and the access "have-nots", with the numbers of those with Internet access and accounts being significantly skewed by income level and by location of residence. Regrettably, those in developing regions and particularly the African continent overall have the least access, and even within those regions, the access is overwhelmingly among the higher income groups and particularly in certain urban areas.

Need for Community Informatics

There is need to connect rural communities, research and extension networks and provide access to the much needed knowledge, technology and services. Studies on information systems serving rural communities have focused on specific sectors such as agriculture or health, instead of covering the rural community needs in a holistic manner. Rural information systems must involve rural communities and local content must be of prime importance. Print, video, television, films, slides, pictures, drama, dance, folklore, group discussions, meetings, exhibitions and demonstrations have also been used to speed up the flow of information. New ICTs, however, have the potential of getting vast amounts of information to rural populations in a more timely, comprehensive and cost-effective manner, and could be used together with traditional media.

Systems by which the disadvantaged gain knowledge underpin livelihoods in developing countries. ICTs offer opportunities for the capture, uptake and use of the global knowledge base by the poor, women and the disenfranchised. However, in order to achieve such change, knowledge management systems and tools are required to enable effective access to relevant and appropriate knowledge, together with the physical infrastructure of ICTs.

Information Technologies and Rural Development

The fact that information and communication technologies are able to eliminate distances in today's increasingly globalised economy means that local and regional development trategies have to be reassessed in rural areas. Information and communication technologies (ICTs) seem somewhat paradoxical. On the one hand, they call to mind the globalisation of the economy, the internationalization of markets, networking on a planetary scale and other heavy tendencies over which it seems difficult to have any influence. On the other hand, their relevance to local development seems evident, since it is the transformation of industries and services that is at stake, as is the future of work and employment. Furthermore, the policies linked to the "Information Society" should be implemented at local level, whether they concern infrastructure, research, and support for businesses, job promotion, and the organization of vocational training or communications policy.

Potential of New ICTs for Rural Development

Some examples of areas where ICTs could play a catalytic role in developing rural areas include:

- *Decision-making Process*: Sound decision making is dependent upon availability of comprehensive, timely and up-to-date information. Food security problems facing developing countries demonstrate the need for informed researchers, planners, policy makers, development workers and farmers. Information is also needed to facilitate the development and implementation of food security policies. E-mail and the Internet could be used to transmit information to and from rural inaccessible areas.

- *Market Outlook* : Farmers could promote their products and handle simple transactions such as orders over the web while payment transactions for the goods can then be handled off-line. It has been shown to be cheaper and faster to trade online than on paper-based medium, telephone or fax. Electronic-commerce could, therefore, enable entrepreneurs to access global market information and open up new regional and global markets that fetch better prices and increase farmers' earnings.
- *Empowering Rural Communities*: ICTs can empower rural communities and give them "a voice" that permits them to contribute to the development process. With new ICTs, rural communities can acquire the capacity to improve their living conditions and become motivated through training and dialogue with others to a level where they make decisions for their own development.
- *Targeting Marginalised Groups* : Most rural poor people lack the power to access information. ICTs could benefit all stakeholders including the civil society, in particular youth and women (UNDP 2000). Other disadvantaged groups that could be targeted include the disabled and subsistence peasants.
- *Creating Employment* : Through the establishment of rural information centres, ICTs can create employment opportunities in rural areas by engaging telecentre managers, subject matter specialists, information managers, translators and information technology technicians. Such centres help bridge the gap between urban and rural communities and reduce the rural-urban

migration problem. The centres can also provide training and those trained may become small-scale entrepreneurs.

Innovative Application of ICTs in Rural Areas

Access

Central to issues of use and usefulness of ICT's for rural development is the question of "access". Without "access", that is the means of making direct use of ICT's and particularly entering into and using the worldwide ocean of information and communications capabilities presented by the Internet, little else is possible. Clement and Shade have developed what they call an "Access Rainbow" which is a systematic rendering of the different "levels" through which access is determined. Their "access" model is freely adapted below.

Defining access

While access is consistently identified as a key principle in policy discussions, it is not an end in itself. Access simply enables further activities that can only partially be specified beforehand.

(a) *Access for what purposes* : In broad terms, enhancing the Information and Communications Infrastructure (ICI) holds the promise of enabling all citizens to participate more fully in all aspects of economic, social, cultural and democratic life. A central notion is the possibility of participative interaction with others. In contrast with existing electronic media, digital networks allow people to be creators as well as recipients.

(b) *Access for whom* : To the extent that network services are valuable, no one should be excluded from the opportunity of participating in their advantages. Furthermore, the benefits for everyone expand, as more people become reachable through the network. However, not all citizens are alike and we need to recognize the diversity of people and their particular access needs. This involves recognizing the obstacles to access characteristic of various 'populations', most notably age, gender, income, education, disability, language, ethnicity, geographic location (urban vs. rural and remote), and nationality (developed vs. developing countries).

(c) *Access to what* : Until recently, models of information/ communications infrastructure emphasized the purely technical aspects, notably physical connectivity. Undoubtedly, digital networks will displace many activities currently conducted via highly evolved conventional media such as the postal service, document publishing and distribution systems, telephone services, TV and radio broadcasting, but are unlikely to render any of them completely redundant. Rather, digital networks will be increasingly interwoven with these other networks in complex and mutually redefining ways.

(d) *Carriage Facilities* : While technical advances in carriage facilities promise greater capacities, wider availability and reduced unit costs, there are well founded concerns that some people, notably those with low incomes or living in rural or remote areas, will actually be worse off. The most prominent access gap results from the expense of providing terrestrial-link carriage services to those living in rural and remote areas. This raises the question of what constitutes the minimum "essential" bandwidth and hence what should be guaranteed in some way.

(e) *Devices* : Current workstations are costly and become rapidly obsolescent. Again it is those with lower incomes who are at greatest risk. Also, many devices are difficult to use and not readily adaptable to individual differences, especially for people with disabilities.

(f) *Software Tools* : Software is the critical new technical ingredient, which expands the capabilities of the ICI. Monopolistic practices in the software industry contribute obstacles to the smooth interoperability of software packages from competing vendors. These factors make software more expensive to buy and learning to use it effectively a major challenge. Furthermore, software is largely written with English speakers in mind, thus disadvantaging other language groups. The general lack of encryption and other privacy protection features (e.g. in web browsers) represents another inhibition to the widespread usefulness of software.

(g) *Content Services* : Many of the essential on-line databases are currently available via the Web without charge to the user. However, commercial influences could undermine some of the diversity and quality of the information. As with software tools, content/service design must accommodate a broad range of users (including people with disabilities), cultures, and languages.

(h) *Service/Access Providers* : Workplaces offer much more than just free access to equipment and connection-they provide a range of supportive services including purchasing, configuring, upgrading, maintaining, troubleshooting, repairing, and documenting systems as well as staffing help desks and training sessions. All of these are skill demanding and expensive but vital to routine, unproblematic ICT use.

(i) *Literacy/Social Facilitation* : New digital media place significant learning burdens on users. Achieving widespread effective use of network technologies must therefore be supported by a variety of formal and informal learning facilities.

(j) *Governance* : Governance is about the ways in which decisions are made concerning the development and operation of the information/communication infrastructure. Current governance and policymaking is centred in the major developed (OECD) countries, with corporate and industry stakeholders playing leading roles. Privatization and the deregulation of global telecommunications markets are seen as the way to foster competition and technological innovation. Important issues, such as public accountability, cultural identity, social inclusiveness and cohesion, and national sovereignty, are being threatened by giving such a priority to market forces.

A 'Community Informatics' Approach

Community Informatics (CI) is and approach that begins with the perspective that access to ICT can provide a set of resources and tools that communities, and individuals living in communities can use to pursue their goals in such areas as local economic development, cultural affairs, civic activism, community based health and environmental initiatives.

CI is an approach to ICT, which includes a concern for the accessibility of the hardware, the software, the connectivity and the information; and for the use and user to which the technology is being applied, particularly within the context of the user's physical community. Incorporating the user and his community into the system design process introduces new elements and new "stakeholders" into an extended approach to ICT design, development, and implementation.

(a) *Access Facilities* : How the user gets access to the technology is of particular interest. For many and particularly in less "connected" regions and countries, this will be through public or community-access facilities, i.e., Telecentres, CAP sites, "cybercafes", etc. These centers, in addition to providing communications and small business support, also may become centres for the delivery of electronically mediated training, and public information including rural extension services.

(b) *The Design of the Service* : For services to be widely useful, information providers must design and provide services of specific interest to the end user, and particularly which takes account of the specific contexts of the various regions and cultural and linguistic groupings. What would be best is if information service providers were widely distributed and close to those using the information so as to localize information from other regions and to develop information of special interest within local contexts.

(c) *Design of the Telecentre* : The telecentre will be central to the capacity of a Rural Development initiative to have a broad impact in local communities. The physical and organizational design of the telecentre should also reflect its possible use as a Rural Development facility and should include among other critical telecentre elements:

1. An institutional linkage and physical base
2. Connectivity
3. Multiple uses—education, extension, small business support, communications
4. A paraprofessional extension worker with online and information management skills
5. Translation facilities for the key languages served in the region
6. Some means to ensure sustainability

(d) *The Design of the Information or Service* : For Rural Development ICT services to be useful it will be necessary to develop the capacity with the information provider to design and provide service of specific interest and relevance to the Developing Country end user and particular information which takes account of the specific contextual circumstances found in particular Developing Countries and regions and their various geo-physical, climatic, cultural and linguistic groupings. It would probably be most advantageous if information service provider facilities were to be developed in the Developing Countries themselves, which could both localize information from other parts of the would and develop information of special interest within the particular Developing Country context.

(e) ***The Community System*** : The design of the community system into which the ICT enabled service or information will be transmitted will be particularly important for Rural Development working through public access telecentres. In the Developing World context, the-on-line information or service will probably for the most part be provided to groups. The group would identify its information needs, the request or search would be undertaken by a paraprofessional trained for such activities and he or she would in turn pass the information back to the group where it would be assimilated/processed/applied. It will, in this context, be necessary to look at the entire service process as a system, including the information or service provider/designer, the para-professional intermediary, the professional, and the group or community information user/recipient. Effective planning and development for all stages of the process will be needed for the service activity to be successful.

(f) ***On-Line Service Delivery*** : Among the rural development related services that are currently being provided or could be provided through the Internet are:

- Information
- Education and training
- Mentoring and consultation
- Diagnosis and monitoring
- Transaction processing

Useful and useable information is at the core of ICT-enabled services. For this information to be retrievable, understandable, and relevant to the consumer there needs to be "mediating structures" linking the electronic "service" with the end user.

(g) ***On-Line Support*** : "On-line support" is the mechanism whereby individuals provide information, comfort and mutual assurance to each other through the medium of the Internet. This can be done either by e-mail, newsgroup or web conference (asynchronous) or by chat

(synchronous), although in most cases it is done asynchronously. Included in this would be a variety of groups of producers working in similar geo-climatic areas, producers working with similar types of crops, supports for a variety of exotic conditions and crop or animal diseases, and individual or cooperative support facilities. These groups provide the opportunity to discuss current conditions, or problems with others that have direct experience of the problem or circumstance. These online support groups are also being used in a variety of ways by researchers including crop and climate researchers and veterinarians.

Features of a CI Rural Development Application

The key characteristic of a CI Rural Development application, of course, is that it is meant to support RD objectives and to be useable by rural actors or agents.

(a) *Training* : The application will necessarily include a significant training: The training should be directed to allow for the non-professional user to manage the system being operated.

(b) *Ease of use* : The application will be designed so as to optimize its ease of use, including installation and on-going maintenance, where possible by the community or end user. While the "backend" of the application may be complex (they often seem to be based on UNIX/LINUX architecture which is famously not user-friendly), the "front-end" should be transparently easy to use and to Implement.

(c) *Mediation* : The application will likely be designed so as to accommodate a "mediator" between the application or service provider and the end user, since the end use of the service is meant to be available to the general locally based producer and not just to specialists.

(d) *Applied Technical System* : The application is for the most part identified by what it does, not how it operates. Its support for community extension, for example, is assessed by its effectiveness in contributing to community extension, not by the elegance of its software design. The particular way in which the contribution is made or its technical features (for example, design elegance) will, from this perspective, be of lesser interest or relevance.

(e) *Governance Structures* : The application is managed or "governed" so as to support processes, which facilitate community consultation and participation in decision-making.

(f) *Sustainability* : Key to the application is the on-going sustainability of the various services. How public access facilities, regional development web sites, or other related applications can be sustained after a transition from volunteer management and / or public sector support is the key to success. Identifying an appropriate "business model" for and ICT-enabled service is thus of crucial importance.

Issue Areas

(a) *The Sustainability of the System* : As yet there is no business or revenue model for rural Development activities through the sale of associated goods or services. The overall business model for the Telecentre itself has not been worked out.

(b) *Literacy, Language and Culture* : A Rural Development programme will need to respond to issues of literacy (or rather, illiteracy), the very large numbers of languages (some without written scripts) and the range of cultures and religions that are found within the Developing World.

(c) *Reliability of Information* : There will be the need for on-going monitoring of the reliability and scientific validity of the information being made available through the program. While it is anticipated that the Information Centre will filter and verify much of the information being made available through the Rural Development services, there will also be considerable scope and likelihood for accessing the broader information base of the Internet.

(d) ***The ICT and the Extension Worker*** : Professionals such as health care or extension workers find themselves to be professionally isolated in their posts, often far from sources of professional support, consultation and continuing education for themselves. The model of ICT use in Developing Countries will for the foreseeable future is one where its most direct application will be in support of existing field. Based professionals and it thus will be necessary to ensure that information sources are designed so as to provide this kind of service. It will be noted that much of the information on the WWW currently is directed toward the individual end user rather than towards professional or paraprofessional intermediaries as the individual end user is the most common mode of practice in Developed Countries.

(e) ***Gender Insensitivity*** : Developing country men and women play different productive and community roles in rural development and have different needs and preferences. Women produce more than half the world's food and face many problems in addressing food security and rural development. When new technologies are introduced, they are seen as a domain for men, and women have often been left out of initiatives associated with new ICTs. Rural women, however, have wisdom and indigenous knowledge that is rooted in culture, traditions, values and experience. Women, youth and the disabled will, therefore, require special treatment (affirmative action), and should be deliberately integrated into all ICT projects and initiatives through gender sensitive project development and implementation (FAO 1999). It is only by so doing that a critical mass of information aware people, and leaders of tomorrow can be developed to ensure that their countries realize food security and rural development goals.

Conclusions

Developing country, governments are increasingly aware that they have a major responsibility for rural development and food security, but lack the capacity and solutions to meet the challenge. Policy and decision-makers thus have to identify possible and appropriate solutions that ensure rural development and food security. There is a window of opportunity at this time when policy decisions are being made in regard to both the creations of a network of Telecentres and the creation of on-line Rural Development support services. Integrating the planning and operation of these endeavours could provide considerable cost savings and increase the effectiveness of programs, particularly if the infrastructure required is coordinated and cost-shared with the extension network that is already in place. A number of useful models and practical experiences are available that might be adapted to the needs of Developing Country communities. In particular, a coordinated network of telecentres acting as Rural Development delivery nodes could be a powerful resource in rural Developing Country contexts for supporting rural sustainability by enabling accurate information about local agricultural matters, and by facilitating cooperation and interaction between organizations, institutions and communities distributed throughout the world.

REFERENCES

Mukta Mital, "Rural Development in India", 1st Edition, (1995), Anmol Publications Pvt. Ltd., New Delhi.

Dr. Tripathy, S.N:, "Rural Development", (2000), Discovery Publishing Home, New Delhi.

Devendra Thakur, "Technology Transfer for Rural Development", Deep & Deep Publications, New Delhi.

Fakhruddin, "Quality of Rural Life", Rawat Publications, Jaipur, 1997.

Kuppusamy. B., "Social Change in India", 5th Revised Enlarged Edition, Konark Publications, New Delhi.

Subramanian S., "Integrated Rural Development", Oxford & IBH Publishing Company Pvt. Ltd., New Delhi.

Bhalla A.S. & Reddy, A.K.N., "The Technological Transformation of Rural India", Oxford University Press, New Delhi.

Thekkamalai S.S., "Rural Development and Social Changes in India", D.K. Publications 1983, New Delhi.

Hartmut-Albrecht, "Rural Development Series", Agricultutal Extension: Volume-1, Basic Concepts and Methods, Wiley Eastern Limited, New Delhi.

32

RURAL UPLIFTMENT THROUGH MICRO-CREDIT

Punithavathy Pandian & R. Eswaran

Introduction

In order to enhance women's access to credit for consumption and production, the establishment of new micro-credit mechanisms and strengthening of existing micro-credit mechanisms, micro-finance institution have to be undertaken so that the outreach of credit is enhanced. Other supportive measures would be taken to ensure adequate flow of credit through extant financial institutions and banks, so that all women below poverty line have easy access to credit.[1]

The definition of micro-credit that was adopted in the First World Micro-Credit Summit held in Washington in February 1997, is that "micro-credit means the programmes that extend small loans to poor people for self-employment projects that generate income and allow them to care for themselves and their families"[2]

Definitions differ, of course, from country to country. Some of the criteria used for the definition include:-

Size	- Loans are micro, or very small in size.
Target users	- Micro-entrepreneurs and low-income households.

Utilization	The use of funds not only for income generation and enterprise Development, but also for community use (health, education and the like).
Terms and conditions -	Many terms and conditions for micro-credit loans are flexible and easy to understand, and suited to the local conditions of the community.

The world micro itself suggests the small size of the loans made, the small size of savings made, the smaller frequency of loans, the shorter repayment periods and the amounts, the micro or local level of activities and the community-based immediacy of micro-credit. In this chapter a brief outline of micro-credit scheme and the results of a field sample survey are presented.

Objectives of Micro-credit Scheme

The main objectives of the micro-credit, focused on poor and disadvantaged women[3] are social, economic and political empowerment. It also aims at capacity building.

(i) Social Empowerment through:

- Increased status, participation and powers of decision-making of women in household;
- Increased status, participation and powers of decision-making of women in community and village;
- Breaking cultural barriers to equal development of women;
- Increased status, participation and powers of decision-making of women in democratic institutions.

(ii) Economic Empowerment through:

- Greater access to financial resources outside household;

- Reduced vulnerability of the poor women to crisis-famine, and the like;
- Increasing access and control over resources at the household level;
- Financial self-reliance of women.

(iii) Capacity Building (is a strategy and an end in itself) through:

- Improvement in functional literacy, numeraqcy;
- Better communication skills;
- Better leadership skills;
- Self-help and Mutual help.

(iv) Political Empowerment through:-

- Participation in Panchayati Raj institutions;
- Negotiating political power;
- Accessing political power;
- Collective identity.

Such empowerment of the poor and disadvantaged women would lead to benefits at two levels-(i) direct benefits to the individual woman and women's groups and (ii) ripple-effect development benefits for other poor families, the community and the village as a whole.

Model of the Micro-credit Scheme

Three broad models of micro-credit scheme through self-help group bank linkage have emerged over the past few years in India. They are as follows:

Model I: Self-Help Groups Formed and Financed by Banks

Under this model, banks themselves act as Self-Help Promoting institutions, for by the ways of forming and nurturing the groups, opening their savings accounts and providing them bank loans. As in March 2001, 13 percent of the total number of Self-Help Groups financed were from this category. After introduction of the 'Low Cost Module" of assistance from NABARD and making it applicable in all States during the ensuing years, it is expected that many more branches of RRBs would be involved in promotion and financing of self-help groups in the coming years.

Model II: Self-Help Groups Formed by Non-Governmental Organisations and Formal Agencies, but Directly Financed by Banks

This appears to be the most popular model amongst bankers. Under this model Non-Governmental Organisations and Formal Agencies in the field of micro finance act as facilitators. They propagate the message, organize groups, train them in thrift and credit management and nurture them over a period. Banks, in due course, link these groups by directly providing loans to them. Major share of self-help groups linked as at March 2001 (76 percent) is under this model as compared to 70 percent as at March 2000.

Model III : Self-Help Groups Financed by Banks Using Non-Governmental Organisations as Financial Intermediaries

In this model, Non-Governmental Organisations take on the dual role of facilitators and financial intermediaries. They help in formation of Self-Help Groups, nurturing them, training them in thrift and credit management. Eventually, the Non-Governmental Organisations approach banks for bulk loan assistance for lending to these Self-Help Groups. The share of cumulative number of Self-Help Groups linked under this model is relatively small that is, 11 percent. However, in the years to come, a need may arise for the Self-Help Groups as also for lending institutions to look for viable sub-structures for financial inter-mediation. This could eventually develop into and effective method to control transaction costs through economics of scale.

Modus Operandi of the Micro-credit Scheme

Micro-credit scheme has been proposed to be implemented through banks. According to this scheme, the beneficiaries need to pay Re.1/- for a loan of Rs.100/- per day. Out of this one

Table 1: Model-wise SHG Linkage- Cumulative Position as at March 2001

(Rs. In Million)

Model	*Self-Help Groups*		*Bank Loan*		*Refinance*	
	Number	*Percentage*	*Amount*	*Percentage*	*Amount*	*Percentage*
I	30,739	13	694.71	15	591.23	15
II	1,78,248	76	3,719.96	77	3,123.30	78
III	25,856	11	394.12	8	292.93	7
Total	2,34,843	100	4,808.79	100	4,007.46	100

Source: Report on NABRD and Micro Finance, 2000-2001, p. 8.

rupee charged on them everyday, fifty to seventy paise would be credited to their savings account. The remaining will be used towards interest and service charges by the banks. After six months, the beneficiaries can withdraw their savings with interest. The rate of interest per annum will differ according to the portion of amount to be credited to savings account.

Role of Self Help Groups

A Self-Help Group is a voluntary association of a homogenous set of people, either working together or living in the neighbourhood, engaged in similar line of activity, working with or without registration, for the common good of the member. The minimum number of members to form a Self-Help Group is 12 while the maximum is 20 without registration. The Self-Help Group will have an animator and two representatives, selected by the group. All the members have to meet regularly every week, every fortnight or every month, in a specified place at an stipulated time, as decided by the group. The members discuss their problems and try to find solutions of their own. During these meetings they collect their small savings and these savings are used to meet the credit requirements of the members. The savings can be either kept in a bank or kept by them. In this approach of Self-Help Group, cash transaction is secondary while participatory approach for solving the problems receives primary importance. Through these meetings the women will be able to understand their problems and they will also be able to plan their future programmes to address the problems that they face. In this process they will be able to estimate their requirements and resources and find out the gap. In fact, the thrift and credit associated with the self-help group dynamics enable them to think of some potential sources of resources from their midst and embark upon the mobilization of local resources as much as possible.

This Self-help group mechanism has been widely accepted as and integral part of micro-credit. Several directives and guidelines from the Reserve Bank of India (RBI) and National Bank for Agricultural and Rural Development (NABARD) to the commercial banks have clearly mentioned the need to recognize the Self-Help Group as a potential tool of micro-credit. The Reserve bank of India has even launched the programme of linking Self-Help Groups with lending institutions like commercial banks so that the credit requirements of the self-help groups can be properly attended by the commercial banks. In this sphere considerable improvements have been made over the past few years.

Performance of Micro-credit Scheme

Micro-credit Scheme at National Level

NABARD has been spearheading the promotion and linkage of Self-help groups to the banking systems through refinance support, capacity building of stakeholders and initiating other practive policies and systems. During 2000-2001, 1,70,680 Self-help groups were financed by banks including 21,630 repeat finance as against the target of 1,00,000 Self-help groups proposed in the Union Budget, 2000-01. The cumulative number of Self-help groups credit-linked to the banks aggregated to 2,63,825, out of which 2,13,213 were refinanced by NABARD, by the end of march 2001.

The significant increase in the number of Self-help groups linked during the year was the collective efforts of 1,030 Non-Governmental Organisations, 314 banks and many other agencies including developmental departments of different State Governments. The credit-linking programme-has covered 412 districts in 27 States and Union Territories. A notable feature of the self-help groups was that more than 90 percent of the groups formed were exclusively of women.

NABARD continued to provide 100 percent refinance assistance to banks at the interest rate of 6.5 percent per annum for financing Self-help groups. During the year, an amount of 287.88 crore was disbursed to Self-help groups by various banking institutions against which refinance support by NABARD was made to the tune of Rs. 250.62 crore. Cumulative till aggregated, bank loans disbursed to the Self-help groups upto March 31, 2001 were Rs. 480.87 crore while NABARD refinance availed by banks aggregated to Rs. 400.74 crore.[4]

Table 2: Cumulative Progress in Micro-credit through SHG Linkage Programme

(Rs. in Crores)

Year	*Cumulative Number of Self-help groups Linked**	*Micro-credit*	*Refinance Assistance*
1992-93	255	0.29	0.27
1993-94	620	0.64	0.46
1994-95	2,122	2.44	2.30
1995-96	4,757	6.06	5.66
1996-97	8,598	11.84	10.65
1997-98	14,317	23.76	21.39
1998-99	32,995	57.07	52.06
1999-2000	94,645	192.98	150.13
2000-2001	2,13,213	480.87	400.74

Source: NABARD Annual Report.

*Excluding those not covered under refinance.

NABARD is also providing grant on a selective basis to Non-Governmental Organisations, primarily for promoting and nurturing Self-help groups. NABARD sanctioned the grant assistance of two crores of rupees to 126 Non-Governmental

Organisations during 2000-2001 for promotion and linkage of 20,033 Self-help groups. With this, the cumulative grant assistance sanctioned till the end of March 2001 for promotion and linkage of Self-help groups aggregated to Rs. 4.6 crore towards 198 Non-Governmental Organisations for promoting 36,944 Self-help groups. NABARD has provided financial and other types of support for training the bank staff, Non-Governmental Organisations and Government agencies engaged in the field of micro-finance. During 2000-2001, more than 1,000 training and awareness programmes were conducted for training 36,370 bank officials, Non-Governmental Organisations and Government agencies. The loan repayment performance of Self-help groups during the year was reported to be more than 95 percent.

SHG-Bank Linkage Programme

The number of new Self-help groups resorting to micro-credit from banks during 2000-01 have increased to 1,49,050 from 81,780 in 1999-00 (82 percent growth during 2000-01). The number of Self-help groups accessing micro-credit from banks reached 2,63,825 at the end of March 2001 when compared to 1,14,775 Self-help groups at the end of March 2000 (130 percent cumulative growth in March 2001). This was made possible by the synergy that developed out of the close co-operation and co-ordination between the different field level partners in micro-finance, namely, banks, Non-Governmental Organisations and Government agencies. The number of Non-Governmental Organisations and other Self-help group promoting Institutions (SHPIs) participating in the programme had increased to 1,030, when compared to 718 institutions during the previous year. More than 15,000 Non-Governmental Organisations and 314 banks were involved in credit-linkage of Self-help groups. The policy support extended by Government of India and Reserve Bank of India and various initiatives taken by NABARD including capacity building of partner agencies contributed to the success of the programme.

Micro-credit Scheme in Tamilnadu

In Tamilnadu, the savings linked micro-credit scheme was commenced on January 1, 1997. It has benefited 95,144 women till May 15, 2000 and a sum of Rs. 9.68 crores have been granted as loan to them and their savings amounted to Rs. 4.85 crores.[5] Micro-credit is generally channelised through the Self-help groups. The micro-credit scheme along with state funding now covers all rural areas of the entire country. In three different phases the scheme has been implemented in various districts.

In phase I Self-help groups were started in the year 1997-98, but the micro-credit was introduced in January 1999. The first phase has covered the following districts: Vilupuram, Dharmapuri, Namakkal, Cuddalore, Ramnad, Thiruvarur, Vellore, Madurai, Thiruvallur, Salem, Karur, Thoothukudi, Theni and Virudhunagar.

In Phase II, Self-help groups were started in the year 1998-99 but the micro-credit was given from January 1999 onwards. The second phase has covered the following districts: Sivagangai, Thirunelveli, Trichy, Thiruvannamalai, Pudukkottai, Nilgiris and Erode.

In Phase III, Self-Help Groups were started in the year 1999-2000. This phase covered Coimbatore, Kanchipuram, Kanyakumari, Perambalur, Thanjavur, Nagapattinam and Dindigul districts.

SECTION — II

The success of any scheme hinges around the awareness of the scheme in the target group. The success of micro credit scheme also depends on the awareness of the scheme among the rural poor. Micro-credit is channeled to the self help groups through the Mahalir Thittam with the support from National Bank for Agricultural and Rural Development (NABARD).

In this part, an attempt has been made to find out the source of awareness and knowledge about the scheme by the sample women beneficiaries. The micro-credit amount provided, its

Table 3: Performance of Micro-credit in Tamilnadu as on 31st March 2001–Cumulative

(Rs. in Lakhs)

Self-help groups Starting Year	*No. of Eligible SHG sent upto the Month*	*No. of women Availing of Bank Credit*	*Loan Sanctioned*		*Loan Disbursed*		*Repayment in Percentage*
			No. of SHGs	*Amount*	*No. of SHGs*	*Amount*	
Phase-I 1997-98	6,236	71,670	4,347	2,184.76	4,205	2,1340.1	100.00
Phase-II 1998-99	1,143	7,611	753	147.27	699	141.56	98.50
Phase-III 1999-2000	717	5,638	425	57.11	371	52.86	100.00
Total	8,096	84,919	5,525	2,389.14	5,275	2,328.43	–

Source: Tamilnadu Corporation for Development of Women Limited, Annual Report 1999-2000, p. 40.

Table 4: SHG- Bank Linkage Programme in Tamilnadu

(Rs. in Lakhs)

Year	*No. of Groups*	*Cumulative No. of Groups*	*Bank Loan*	*NABARD Refinance*
1992-93	22	22	2.239	2.277
1993-94	34	56	4.247	4.08
1994-95	203	259	20.994	20.883
1995-96	205	464	33.468	33.468
1996-97	408	872	59.52	59.453
1997-98	444	1316	217.74	217.74
1998-99	2633	3849	558.935	558.935
1999-2000	7715	11664	1958.237	1958.237
2000-2001	16926	28590	5137.523	5080.448
Total	28590	–	7992.903	7935.521

Source: Tamil Nadu Corporation for Development of Women Limited, Annual Report 2000-2001.

rate of interest and repayment by the sample women beneficiaries are analysed in this part.

Data : To findout the rural upliftment through micro-credit on rural women at Madurai District, Tamilnadu, where 667 Self-help groups are functioning has been selected. 350 women members of Self help groups have been chosen using non-random sampling method from various blocks of Madurai District. With the help of the structured interview schedule information have been gathered.

Analytical Tools: For analyzing the primary data, the following statistical tools have been used.

Garrett's Ranking: The reasons for getting micro-credit and repayment of micro-credit were ranked with help of Garrett's ranking technique[6] using the following formula.

$$\text{Percent position} = \frac{100\,(Rij - 0.5)}{Nj}$$

Rij = Rank given for the item by the jth individual.

Nj = Total rank given by the jth individual.

Chi-square Test : The Chi-square test[7] (χ^2) was applied to test the association between the socio-economic factors of the sample women beneficiaries and the extent of borrowing. The formula for Chi-square is

$$\chi^2 = \Sigma \frac{(O-E)^2}{E} \text{ with (r-1) (c-1) degrees of freedom}$$

where

$$E = \frac{\text{Row Total x Column Total}}{\text{Grand Total}}$$

O = Observed frequency.

E = Expected frequency.

r = Number of rows in a contingency table.

c = Number of columns in a contingency table.

The computed χ^2 value was compared with the table value at 5 percent level of significance to draw inferences. The null hypothesis was rejected when the computed χ^2 value was higher than the table value for a given degree of freedom and vice versa.

Awareness of the Micro-credit Scheme

In the Mahalir Thittam, a district level Project Implementation Unit (PIU) is headed by a Project Officer, assisted by six Assistant Project Officers (APOs) in the various functional areas like training and communication, monitoring and evaluation of schemes, marketing, administration and accounts and credit. Under Mahalir Thittam a monthly magazine named Muttram is published with details regarding the credit, Self-help groups and related matters in Tamil. Advertisements regarding Mahalir Thittam and credit specialties provided under this scheme are given in vernacular language newspapers. But grass root level awareness campaign is carried out through Non-Governmental Organisations and Self-help group members. The animators and representatives of the Self-help group members. The animators and representatives of the Self-help groups meet the women folk of their own area and introduce the scheme to them. Banks also take up a lead role in popularizing the loans provided under micro-credit scheme. When the animators or representatives visit the banks to deposit their SHG savings, the managers and other employees give the details about the schemes. Thus, the awareness of the scheme is created by Mahalir Thittam, Non-Governmental Organisations, Self-help groups and the banks. The human chain of the beneficiaries in popularizing the scheme cannot be ignored. Table 5 gives the sources of awareness of the scheme by the sample women beneficiaries.

Table 5: Sources of Awareness of the Micro-credit Scheme

Awareness Through	*Number of Beneficiaries*	*Percentage to Total*
Mahalir Thittam's Advertisement	12	3.43
Banks	76	21.71
Friends and Relatives	29	8.29
Self-help groups	164	46.86
Non-Governmental Organisations	69	19.71
Total	350	100.00

Source: Primary Data.

Table 5 indicates that 46.86 percent of the sample women beneficiaries got the information through Self-help groups. Self-help groups are the useful medium for promoting the disbursement of loan for productive purposes. Self-Help Groups characterized by ethical and economic homogeneity are able to spread the news among the other women quicker than other medium. Non-Governmental Organisations also play a positive role in popularizing the scheme. Twenty percent of the beneficiaries came to know about the micro-credit scheme through Non-Governmental Organisations. Details about the scheme are also disseminated through banks. This is clear from the study that 22 percent of the beneficiaries got informed through the banks. Advertisement has not reached many. Only 3 percent of the beneficiaries got the information through advertisement. Friends and relatives also play a significant role in making the beneficiaries informed about the possibilities of getting loan. Among the sample women beneficiaries 8 percent came to know about the scheme through friends and relatives.

Amount of Micro-credit Availed by the Women Beneficiaries

The details of Self-help group loan (micro-credit) applications so received by the banks are first recorded in the application-received register. After scrutiny of loan applications bank accords a formal sanction of funds to the group concerned. Non-Governmental Organisations assist in execution of loan documents by the group. The sanctioned amount is divided among the loan applicants of the particular Self-help group. The animator decides the amount to be disbursed to the individual member according to the loan applied for. Table 6 shows the amount availed by the sample women beneficiaries under the micro-credit scheme.

Table 6: Amount of Micro-credit Availed by the Women Beneficiaries

Amount Availed (Rs.)	*Number of Beneficiaries*	*Percentage to Total*
Up to 1000	72	20.57
1000-2000	81	23.15
2000-3000	47	13.42
3000-4000	68	19.43
4000-5000	82	23.43
Total	350	100.00

Source: Primary Data.

Table 6 makes it clear that 43.71 percent has availed of the loan amount up to Rs. 2000, 32.85 percent has obtained the loan amount from Rs. 2000 to Rs. 4000 and 23.43 percent is in the

Rs. 4000- Rs. 5000 loan category. It would also be observed that even though 122 persons have applied for the loan amount between Rs. 4000 and Rs. 5000, only 82 were given a loan amount between Rs. 4000 and Rs. 5000. The opinion about the sufficiency of the loan received by the women beneficiaries is given in Table 7.

Table 7: Sufficiency of Micro-credit Amount Received

Opinion	*Number of Beneficiaries*	*Percentage to Total*
Sufficient	217	62
Not Sufficient	133	38
Total	350	100

Source: Primary Data.

Majority of the women beneficiaries felt that the amount sanctioned was sufficient.

Reasons for Getting Micro-credit

Micro-credit is extensively utilized to promote income generating enterprises among the poor and weaker section, in particular, women. The reasons for obtaining micro-credit and the rank assigned by the women beneficiaries are given in Table 8. Based on the ranks, the Garret's score were calculated.

According to the Garrett ranking, to be employed is the prime reason cited by the women beneficiaries to obtain micro credit. To create more income and additional assets is the second reason given by the women beneficiaries. The availability of marketing facility is the third reason for getting micro-credit. The Non-Governmental Organisations not only provide financial support to start micro-enterprises but also suitable place for marketing the products for entrepreneurs. Marketing centres are available at Madurai East, Kalluppatti, Thirumangalam, Vadippatti and Usilampatti. They also arrange periodical exhibitions to promote the Self-help groups' products. Encouragement and training given by the Non-

Table 8: Reasons for Getting Micro-credit of the Sample Women Beneficiaries

Factors	*Number of Beneficiaries*					*Garret's*	*Garret's*
	I	II	III	IV	V	score	Rank
Encouragement and training received from SHGs/NGOs	72	78	65	63	72	17650	V
Hereditary and experience	126	64	52	44	64	19250	III
Marketing facility	68	80	78	64	60	17860	IV
To be employed	130	74	48	59	39	19925	I
To create more income and Assets	112	84	66	49	39	19675	II

Source : Primary Data.

Governmental Organisation to Self-help group members is the last reason cited by the women beneficiaries.

Extent of Borrowing and Nature of Business

In order to find out the relationship between the nature of business undertaken and extent of borrowing, the sample women beneficiaries are categorized into four groups (units) viz., beneficiaries who have undertaken petty businesses, processing units, production units and service units. The nature of businesses undertaken by the beneficiaries and extent of borrowing are provided in Table 9.

In the petty businesses, 72.92 percent of the sample women beneficiaries have borrowed below Rs. 3000 and only 27.08 percent of the sample women beneficiaries have borrowed above Rs. 3000. In the service units, 62.85 percent of the sample women beneficiaries have borrowed above Rs. 3000 and only 37.15 percent of the sample women beneficiaries have borrowed below Rs. 3000. Majority of the women beneficiaries who are doing petty businesses have borrowed above Rs. 3000. But, those who are engaged in service units have borrowed above Rs. 3000. This might be due to the higher requirements of funds to install service units.

Table 9: Nature of Business and Extent of Borrowing

Nature of Business	*The number of Beneficiaries Borrowed*					*Total*
	Upto 1000	*1000-2000*	*2000-3000*	*3000-4000*	*4000-5000*	
Petty business	58	62	12	29	20	181
	(32.04)	(34.25)	(6.63)	(16.02)	(11.05)	(100.00)
Processing units	7	8	4	13	9	41
	(17.07)	(19.51)	(9.76)	(31.71)	(21.95)	(100.00)
Production units	5	7	11	14	21	58
	(8.62)	(12.07)	(18.97)	(24.14)	(36.21)	(100.00)
Service units	2	4	20	12	32	70
	(2.86)	(5.71)	(28.57)	(17.14)	(45.71)	(100.00)
Total	72	81	47	68	82	350
	(20.57)	(23.14)	(13.43)	(19.43)	(23.43)	(100.00)

Source: Primary Data.

Figures in the parentheses are percentages.

Factors Influencing the Borrowings

The extent of borrowings under micro credit scheme has been influenced by personal, economic and social factors namely age, literacy, social group and nature of the businesses is undertaken. The relationship between these factors and the extent of borrowing has been analysed individually in this section. In order to find out whether there is any relationship between the factor and the extent of borrowing, chi-square test has been applied.

Age Group and the Borrowings

It is commonly held belief that as an individual grows in age he/she tends to mature in wisdom and experience. With maturity and vast experience, beneficiaries at the higher age group can achieve the goals expected of their performance with greater ease and intelligence. At the same time, the young are more enterprising and risk takers. Age of the sample women beneficiaries and the extent of borrowings are given in Table 10.

Table 10: Age of the Sample Women Beneficiaries and Borrowings

Age	*The Number of Beneficiaries Borrowed*		*Total*	*Percentage*	χ^2
	Below Rs. 2500	*Rs. 2500 and above*			
Below 30	29	47	76	21.71	
	(38.16)	(61.84)	(100.00)		
30-50	98	119	217	62.00	
	(45.16)	(54.84)	(100.00)		28.5*
Above 50	46	11	57	16.29	
	(80.70)	(19.30)	(100.00)		
Total	173	177	350	100.00	
	(49.43)	(50.57)	(100.00)		

Source: Primary data.
Figures in the parentheses are percentages.
*Significant at 5 percent level.

The extent of borrowing given in Table 10 shows that out of the 350 sample women beneficiaries, 173 have borrowed below Rs. 2500 and 177 above Rs. 2500. The extent of borrowing in the below 30 age group is that 38.16 percent of the sample women beneficiaries have borrowed below Rs. 2500 whereas 80.70 percent of the sample women beneficiaries have borrowed below Rs. 2500 in the age group of above 50. Here, in this study, other beneficiaries who have age above 50, have borrowed less compared to the beneficiaries below 30 years of age. Majority (61.84 percent) of the borrowers have borrowed above Rs. 2500. In order to find out whether there is any association between age and level of borrowing chi-square test has been applied. The chi-square value is significant 5 percent level, indicating that there is an association between age and level of borrowing. Women beneficiaries below 50 years of age have availed of more loans than the women above fifty years of age.

Literacy Level and the Borrowings

The social aspect of human life is maintained and transmitted by education.[8] Education can be related to all spheres of economic activities such as consumption, investment, employment and human resource development. The educated beneficiaries can wisely plan their family budget and avoid unnecessary expenditures. Education creates better understanding and increases the efficiency. It would also develop beneficiaries' aptitude, initiative and interest in enterprises. To find out whether where is an association between level of education and extent of borrowing, a two way table is prepared. The sample women beneficiaries are divided into literates and illiterates and borrowings by them are furnished in Table 11.

Table 11 : Level of Education and Borrowings

Level of Education	*The Number of Beneficiaries Borrowed*		*Total*	χ^2
	Below Rs. 2500	*Rs. 2500 and above*		
Illiterate	69	27	96	
	(71.87)	(28.13)	(100.00)	
Literate	104	150	254	
	(40.94)	(59.06)	(100.00)	26.33*
Total	173	177	350	
	(49.43)	(50.57)	(100.00)	

Source: Primary Data.
Figures in the parentheses are percentages.
*Significant at 5 percent level.

The extent of borrowing by the level of education shows that 71.87 percent of the illiterates have borrowed less than Rs. 2500 whereas 40.94 percent literates have borrowed less than Rs. 2500. Among the literates 59.06 percent have borrowed above Rs. 2500. The chi-square test is used to find out the relationship between the level of literacy and the level of borrowing.

The calculated value of χ^2 is 26.33. It is greater than the table value of 3.841 at 5 percent level of significance for 1 degree of freedom. Hence, the null hypothesis that literacy level and the level of borrowing are independent is rejected. Therefore, it could be concluded that literacy level influences the level of borrowing.

Social Group and the Borrowings

Caste would also perform certain crucial economic function on the basis of detailed historical evidence from medieval India. The extent of borrowing by the social groups is shown in Table 12. The sample women beneficiaries are classified into two categories. Beneficiaries who belong to Scheduled Caste and Scheduled Tribes, are all grouped into one category and others are grouped into the second category.

Table 12: Social Groups and Borrowings

Social Group	*The Number of Beneficiaries Borrowed*		*Total*	χ^2
	Below Rs. 2500	*Rs. 2500 and above*		
Scheduled Caste/Scheduled Tribes	49 (55.68)	39 (44.32)	88 (100.00)	
Others	124 (47.33)	138 (52.67)	262 (100.00)	1.84
Total	173 (49.43)	177 (50.57)	350 (100.00)	

Source : Primary Data.

Figures in the parentheses are percentages.

Table 12 shows that among the Scheduled Caste/Scheduled Tribes women beneficiaries 55.68 percent has borrowed less than Rs. 2500. In the other communities 52.67 percent has borrowed above Rs. 2500.

Since the calculated value of χ^2 is less than the table value of 3.841 at 5 percent level of significance, the null hypothesis is accepted. The social groups of beneficiaries have not influenced the level of borrowing.

Pre-loan Occupation and the Borrowings

The women beneficiaries were mostly underemployed and unemployed in the pre-loan period and micro-credit schemes have helped to be employed. Table 13 attempts to show the extent of borrowing and the pre-loan occupation of the sample women beneficiaries.

Table 13: Pre-loan Occupation and Borrowings

Pre-loan Occupation	*The Number of Beneficiaries Borrowed*		*Total*	χ^2
	Below Rs. 2500	*Rs. 2500 and above*		
Employed	15 (42.86)	20 (57.14)	35 (100.00)	
Under employed	108 (53.47)	94 (46.53)	202 (100.00)	2.999
Unemployed	50 (44.25)	63 (55.75)	113 (100.00)	
Total	173 (49.43)	177 (50.57)	350 (100.00)	

Source: Primary Data.
Figures in the parentheses are percentages.

In the category of employed, 42.86 percent of the sample women beneficiaries have borrowed below Rs. 2500 whereas 57.14 percent has borrowed above Rs. 2500. In the category of under employed, 53.47 percent of the sample women beneficiaries have borrowed below Rs. 2500 whereas 46.53 percent has borrowed above Rs. 2500. In the case of unemployed category, 55.75 percent of the sample women beneficiaries have borrowed above Rs. 2500 whereas 44.25 percent has borrowed below Rs. 2500.

Since the calculated value of χ^2 is less than the table value of 5.991 at 5 percent level of significance, the null hypothesis is accepted. Therefore, it can concluded that the pre-loan occupations of the beneficiaries have not influenced the level of borrowing.

Present Position of Members in the Self-Help Groups and Borrowings

Present positions of the sample women beneficiaries in the Self-help groups and the extent of borrowings under micro-credit scheme are given in Table 14.

Table 14: Present Positions of Members and Borrowings

Present Position	*The Number of Beneficiaries Borrowed*		*Total*	χ^2
	Below Rs. 2500	*Rs. 2500 and above*		
Animators	15	39	54	
	(27.78)	(72.22)	(100.00)	
Representatives	44	58	102	
	(43.14)	(56.86)	(100.00)	18.76*
Members	114	80	194	
	(58.76)	(41.24)	(100.00)	
Total	173	177	350	
	(49.43)	(50.57)	(100.00)	

Source: Primary Data.
Figures in the parentheses are percentages.
*Significant at 5 percent level.

The extent of borrowings by different positions show that of the 54 beneficiaries who are animators 15 (27.78 percent) have borrowed below Rs. 2500 and 39 (72.22 percent) have borrowed above Rs. 2500. In the case of representatives, 44 (43.14 percent) beneficiaries have borrowed below Rs.2500 and 58 (56.86 percent) have borrowed above Rs.2500. In the category of members, 114 (58.76 percent) have borrowed below Rs.2500 and 80 (41.24 percent) have borrowed above Rs. 2500. The relationship between the present positions and extent of borrowings of the beneficiaries in the Self-help group is analysed with the help of chi-square test.

The calculated value is greater than the table value of 5.991 at 5 percent level of significance. Hence, the null hypothesis is rejected. Therefore, it can be concluded that the present position held by the women beneficiaries in the Self-help group influences the level of borrowing.

Thus, it is concluded from the foregoing analyses that out of six factors, three factors such as age, literacy and present position by the beneficiaries have influenced the extent of borrowings of the sample women beneficiaries.

Repayment of Micro-credit and Number of Instalments

Micro-credit has turned out to be an effective strategy for institutional financing agencies. For the financing institutions, the group lending minimizes the transaction cost and at the same time they can make available small loans through groups. Chances of misutilisation are rare and there is assured repayment because of peer monitoring by the group.

Number of Instalment

There is no holiday for repayment and repayment period is decided by the bank and Self-help group, jointly. The repayment schedule and instalment size take into account the seasonality of earnings of Self-help group members and are reasonable.[9] Data pertaining to the number of instalments allowed to repay the loan by the women beneficiaries are presented in Table 15.

Table 15: Number of Instalments of Repayment of Micro-credit

Number of Instalments of Repayment	*Number of Beneficiaries*	*Percentage to Total*
Upto 5	45	12.86
6-10	84	24.00
11-15	135	38.57
16-20	52	14.86
Above 20	34	9.71
Total	350	100.00

Source: Primary Data.

In more than 38.6 percent of the sample women beneficiaries, the number of instalments range between 11 and 15. Instalments above 20 have been found in 9.7 percent of the sample women beneficiaries.

Regularity of Repayment

The micro-credit experience worldwide has shown that poor borrowers, especially women, make productive use of credit for self-employed micro-enterprises/small firms and are prompt in repayments, with average repayment rating above 95 percent, much better than recoveries under small lending.[10] The regularity in repayment of loan is given in Table 16.

Table 16: Repayment of Micro-credit by the Beneficiaries

Nature of Repayment	*Number of Beneficiaries*	*Percentage to Total*
Irregular repayment	18	5.14
Regular repayment	332	94.86
Total	350	100.00

Source: Primary Data.

It has been observed that only 5.14 percent of the sample women beneficiaries are irregular in repayment of loan, while 94.86 percent are found to be regular in repayment. Sangwan (1996)[11] , Mokbul Morshed Ahmed (2000)[12] , Sundari and Geetha (2000)[13] and Kulshreshta and Archna (2002)[14] have also obtained similar results in their study areas and reported regular repayment.

Wilful default has no place in Self-Help Groups. Members can repay the loan daily from their collection, but this facility is not available with the other financing agencies. Self-help group preaches "self-help through mutual help for common good". It is an ideal combination of one's rights and responsibilities. Realising the significance of Self-help groups in micro-credit delivery mechanism, the micro-credit funding institutions have established Self-help groups for the purpose of lending and getting repayment in time.

Reasons for Repayment of Micro-credit

Banks and financial institutions suffer much due to the non repayment of loan amount by the borrowers. But, generally Self-help groups availing micro-credit, have shown excellent record of loan repayment. Micro-credit has enabled the women beneficiaries to earn income and the poor women consider timely repayment a prestige issue and repay the loan regularly. The pressure from the peer group has discouraged default by individuals. The reasons that have motivated the women beneficiaries and the ranks given by them along with Garret's score and ranks are presented in Table 17.

Table 17: Reasons for Repayment of Micro-credit

Factors	*Number of Beneficiaries*					*Garret's Score*	*Garret's Rank*
	I	*II*	*III*	*IV*	*V*		
Group pressure	106	93	76	43	32	19850	II
Adequate income warning	136	78	54	56	26	20470	I
To avail of further loan	70	134	81	32	33	19445	III
Self ethics	96	99	52	43	60	18960	V
Fear of legal action	88	103	65	62	32	19310	IV

Source: Primary data.

According to Garrett ranking results, the foremost reason cited by the women beneficiaries is the availability of income. The second rank is given to the peer group pressure. Micro-credit based on joint liability of the self-help group and member brings about remarkable improvement in loan recoveries. Close proximity and familiarity of Self-help group members motivate them to pay back the loan without default. Improved loan recoveries lead to improved loan recycling and continue access to borrowing. To avail of further loans, is the third reason cited for regular repayment. Fear of legal action also has motivated the women beneficiaries to repay the loans. Self ethic is the last reason cited by the women beneficiaries.

Summary

Self-help groups and Banks have made the women beneficiaries aware of the micro-credit scheme. Age, literacy and present position held by the women beneficiaries in the Self-help group have influenced the level of borrowings. Most of them have started petty business units and thus, the micro-credit and the Self-help groups have given a new lease of life to the rural women. The expansion of micro-credit to other areas will promise poverty alleviation and prosperity to the rural poor.

FOOTNOTES

1. National Policy for the Empowerment of Women, Department of Women and Child development, *Ministry of Human Resource Development,* Government of India, 2001, p. 9.
2. Micro-credit Summit (2-4 February 1997) Washington, Credit Guide Line for Self Help Groups, *Tamilnadu Corporation for Development of Women Limited,* p. 3.
3. Tamilnadu Corporation for Development of Women Limited, *Working Manual,* 1999-2000 p.10.
4. Report on Trend and Progress of Banking in India 2000-2001, Supplement to *RBI Bulletin,* December 2001, p. 96.
5. M. Karunanidhi, "Implement Micro-credit Scheme or Women in Villages of Tamilnadu", *Tamilnadu Journal of Co-operation,* Vol. 92, No. 4, July 2000, pp. 4-5.
6. Hentry E. Garrett's, *'Statistics in Psychology and Education',* Fetter and Simans Private Limited, 1969, p. 329.
7. Ibid., p. 1094.
8. Gopal Bharagara, *Education for National Integration,* Modern Review, S. Chand and Company Limited, New Delhi, 1962, p. 27.
9. "Credit Guidelines for Self-Help Groups" *Mahalir Thittam,* Tamilnadu Corporation for Development of Women Limited, 2001, p. 29.
10. 'Micro Finance', *Urban Credit,* March 2001, pp. 13-15. (Report on Micro Credit Summit, Washington, February 1997).
11. S.S. Sangwan, "Banking Through Self Help Groups-Experience of Oriental Bank Gramin Project in Dehradun District", *National Bank News Review,* April-June 1996, pp. 43-52.
12. Mokbul Morshed Ahmed, "Distant Voices: Micro Credit Finance and Views of the NGO Field Workers in Bangladesh", *Journal of Rural Development,* Vol. 19, No. 2, April-June 2000, pp. 26-35.
13. S. Sundari and N. Geetha, "Poverty, Credit and Micro Enterprises-A Gender Study", *Kurukshetra,* November 2000, pp. 26-35.
14. Lakshmi R. Kulshreshta and Archna Gupta, "A Study of Micro Finance in India - Delivery System and Impact Analysis with Special Emphasis to Women Upliftment", *Sajosps,* July-December 2002, pp. 104-110.

